World War II

by Keith D. Dickson, Ph.D.

for **dummies®**

A Wiley Brand

World War II For Dummies®

Published by: **John Wiley & Sons, Inc.**, 111 River Street, Hoboken, NJ 07030-5774, www.wiley.com

Copyright © 2020 by John Wiley & Sons, Inc., Hoboken, New Jersey

Published simultaneously in Canada

For general information on our other products and services, please contact our Customer Care Department within the U.S. at 877-762-2974, outside the U.S. at 317-572-3993, or fax 317-572-4002. For technical support, please visit https://hub.wiley.com/community/support/dummies.

Wiley publishes in a variety of print and electronic formats and by print-on-demand. Some material included with standard print versions of this book may not be included in e-books or in print-on-demand. If this book refers to media such as a CD or DVD that is not included in the version you purchased, you may download this material at http://booksupport.wiley.com. For more information about Wiley products, visit www.wiley.com.

Library of Congress Control Number: 2019920278

ISBN 978-1-119-67553-2 (pbk); ISBN 978-1-119-67558-7 (ebk); ISBN 978-1-119-67557-0 (ebk)

Manufactured in the United States of America

SKY10035712_081522

Contents at a Glance

Table of Contents

Introduction

The Most Destructive War

The Second World War (1939–1945) was the most destructive event in history. It was total war covering the entire globe, and the nations that fought it employed every available resource, harnessing both technology and people to one purpose. The farmer and factory worker became just as important to the war effort as the soldier in the field. Aerial attack allowed cities and civilians to become legitimate targets of war. Because of its destructiveness and global scale, the human and material costs of the war were almost immeasurable. The war ended with the development of two new technologies that heavily influenced the course of the postwar world: atomic power and the ballistic missile.

Mass murder of noncombatants and prisoners of war occurred — tens of thousands of defenseless Russians, Poles, and Chinese died at the hands of their enemies. A state-run genocide killed 12 million people, including 6 million Jews. The war also cost millions of lives, resulting from battle as well as non-battle deaths. The Soviet Union lost 28 million people; Germany, nearly 5 million people. Japan lost about 5 million people; China, about 10 million. Great Britain and the Commonwealth lost nearly a half million people. France and Italy both lost over 400,000 combat deaths. The United States, Czechoslovakia, and Yugoslavia each suffered 290,000 combat deaths. Poland, Hungary, Belgium, the Netherlands, Norway, Bulgaria, Romania, and the Philippines suffered significant military and civilian losses as well. The physical destruction of most of the continent of Europe and several Asian nations left an indelible mark.

Undoubtedly, the war has cast a long shadow over recent history. The way that nations form strategy, wage war, make peace, and negotiate treaties is still shaped by the memories and lessons of the Second World War. For better or worse, a new world emerged from the ashes of the old, and we live in the shadow of this most terrible and destructive war. The world has been sensitized to the dangers of ethnic hatred and its accompanying acts of organized killing. The ever changing nature of United States–Chinese relations has its roots in the conditions in China after the war. The creation of Israel by the world community was a direct result of the Jewish Holocaust. The need for collective defense in the form of alliances like the North Atlantic Treaty Organization (NATO) became the primary guarantor of peace in Europe. The United Nations was created to correct the failure of the League of Nations to oversee international norms of behavior. Traditional enemies became partners against a greater threat, and the role of government expanded to meet the burden of greater defense requirements. Nations were willing to take action to guarantee their interests to prevent another catastrophe like World War II.

But the memories of World War II are rapidly fading. Those who lived during this momentous period in twentieth century history will no longer be among us to provide witness to the past. The national World War II monument and local memorials, along with such films as *Saving Private Ryan,* will preserve some understanding of the virtue and sacrifice of the soldiers and civilians who ensured the survival of freedom in the world. The preservation of freedom in World War II became the ultimate weapon in the victory over tyranny in the Cold War. The end of the Cold War itself may be considered the final act in the drama initiated in the Second World War. The people of the Allied nations, through great sacrifice, guaranteed that freedom would be preserved in the face of forces that threatened the existence of civilization. This protection is undoubtedly their greatest bequest to the modern world.

Like all great stories, World War II has its unforgettable villains and heroes. Things are clearly drawn in terms of good and evil. And though often tragic, the story of World War II is nevertheless dynamic, colorful, and exciting. The dedication and courage of the soldier, sailor, marine, or airman in battle and the resilience and sacrifice of those on the home front still stirs the blood. Military professionals all over the world still study the tactics, strategy, and campaigns of the war.

World War II is a universal story, one that may leave you believing that these people were exceptionally heroic because they underwent such a traumatic experience and somehow managed to get on with their lives. For the most part, these people were quite ordinary, but because they were able to rise to extraordinary efforts, they have earned a measure of immortality. If you compare yourself to those who experienced the Second World War, you may find out a bit about who you are.

About This Book

The literature of World War II is large and continues to grow every year. *World War II For Dummies* meets the needs of the reader who wants to be informed without being overwhelmed with details. This book is directed toward several types of readers. First, the person who desires accurate, easily accessible information about the major events and issues of World War II without encountering intimidating historical narrative or ponderous military interpretation. Second, the person who may want a refresher on the major events of the war, but does not want to struggle through the tomes of scholars or the arcane minutiae of military buffs. Third, the person who is looking for a different way to approach history and find out more about the war to enhance his or her appreciation and understanding of an event that has directly or indirectly shaped his or her life. To most people, the past appears remote and inaccessible. The main message of this book is that history is neither remote nor inaccessible! Politics, passions, and conflict (both armed and ideological) have always made up the good stuff of history. Thus, history in the proper context can connect you to the past and allow you to discover similarities to events in your own era.

Conventions Used in This Book

History doesn't have to be boring or intimidating. Everyone who hates history books says that they are nothing more than dry lists of names, places, dates, and jargon. That's true enough, in most cases, if you only look that far. Although this is a different kind of history book, it does follow certain conventions found in most history books. For example, this book is arranged chronologically, and it tells a story. There's a beginning, a middle, and an end. What is *different* about this book is that you can start wherever you want. You don't need to slog through the whole thing from beginning to end to figure out what is going on. You have maximum flexibility to pick and choose what you want to know. You can jump in at any point and still keep up with the story, or you can select a topic to read in a chapter that interests you.

As you move through this book, you encounter key terms. Wherever necessary, I define italicized terms for you, or I reference terms elsewhere with a detailed explanation. I also provide maps that can help you figure out the whys and hows of this global war.

Not surprisingly, World War II has many dimensions and complexities and therefore, many interesting topics and trivia that are part and parcel of discussions about the war. I include some of these facts in gray boxes called sidebars. If you want to dig into the weeds, these boxes are for you. If you are not interested in such detail, these boxes can be easily passed by with no effect on your overall understanding.

How This Book Is Organized

This book covers a span of about 26 years, from 1919 to 1945. This period seems short, but these years defined and shaped the future. To help you break down the years of the war, I've organized this book into seven parts, each dealing with a major period of the war. And the chapters within the parts take you through the major events of World War II, highlighting important facts and points of interest. Each chapter acquaints you with words and ideas that are important to the entire picture.

Every year, someone discovers another cause of the Second World War. Interpretations abound and continue to grow in breadth and imagination. However creative these interpretations may be, almost everyone agrees on several salient points related to the causes of the war. This book focuses on these basic causes.

Part 1: Origins and Causes of the War, 1919–1939

This part takes you from the peace settlement that ended World War I to the opening of the war in Europe — Germany's invasion of Poland. You can examine the time between the wars to get an overview of world events that led to the rise of totalitarian dictators who threatened peace in Europe and in Asia. You also examine the role the United States and the Soviet Union played during this period. This part tells you about the series of tensions, crises, and decisions that eventually led the to the outbreak of the Second World War.

The chapters introduce you to the leaders and the various political systems that existed at this time, as well as the foreign policies of the major states. You get acquainted with the interests and ambitions (and mistakes) that drove the key events that finally led nations to war. You can take a look at the strategies and military preparedness of the nations involved to help understand why and where the war began.

Part 2: Starting the War: The Axis Invades and Conquers, 1939–1942

This part looks at the stunning victories of the Axis powers — Germany, Japan, and Italy — and how they nearly won the war in one rapid blow. You can see how Germany was able to defeat its enemies and dominate the European continent so quickly, leaving a weakened Great Britain as the last remaining opponent. Japan, at war with China since 1937, became the dominant power in Asia. You can also examine Japanese strategy and the reasons for Japan's surprise attacks against

Great Britain and the United States in the Pacific. This part also explains why and how Germany initiated its own surprise attack on the Soviet Union and then declared war on the United States.

These chapters give you details about the most important campaigns in Europe: Poland, Norway, France, and the Battle of Britain. In addition, you find descriptions of Japanese operations in China and the attacks on Pearl Harbor, Singapore, the Philippines, and Wake Island in 1941–1942. You also find out about the first year of the greatest land war in history — the invasion of the Soviet Union.

Part 3: Behind Enemy Lines: Nations at War

This part addresses the contributions of the people who did not carry a weapon on the front lines but played a role that was just as important in waging war. All the resources of the nations were put to task to sustain the war effort. Because their contributions were so critical to victory, they also became targets of bombers seeking to destroy both industrial production capability and the morale of the citizens. Although each nation at war had to accomplish the same goals to conduct total war, each nation approached the total mobilization of its resources quite differently.

The chapters examine government policies and practices that centralized the war effort. You can observe the Allied nations individually to appreciate both the common and unique approaches to war production. On the Axis side, I address the story of German and Japanese slave labor efforts as well as the attempts to overcome shortages and limitations. Even as the war progressed, changes occurred in the societies engaged in war. You can find out how these changes affected the future of women and other people in these societies.

Part 4: Planning and Launching the Allied Counterattack, 1942–1943

This part looks at the strange bedfellows created by the war, especially among the Allies. At first, America and Great Britain formed an uneasy alliance. These democracies had to find common cause with Joseph Stalin's communist dictatorship. Basic and all-important strategic decisions had to be made, and scarce critical military resources had to be properly allocated to fight wars in Asia and in Europe. You also see how the Allies cooperated to strike several blows at the Axis during these critical years. These hits include the all-important Battles of Guadalcanal, the Coral Sea, and Midway in the Pacific; the North African and Italian campaigns and the epic defense of Stalingrad in Europe.

These chapters examine the numerous options the Allies had in conducting the war and how important the survival the Soviet Union was to eventual victory.

You can look at the Allied campaigns and key battles against the Axis in 1942 and why these victories spelled eventual defeat for the enemy. You can also get the lowdown on the Axis leaders' key mistakes, which helped seal their fate. The last chapter again provides you with an overall strategic assessment for 1942.

Part 5: The Long Haul, 1944

This part is an overview of the brutal and bitter campaigns to recapture territory occupied by the Axis. In the Pacific, this meant jungle fighting and amphibious assaults on heavily fortified islands. In Europe, this meant a cross-channel invasion of the continent and a simultaneous struggle against tough German defenses in Italy. The Russo-German War reached a climax, and the Germans were driven out of the Soviet Union. Italy was knocked out of the war and surrendered to the Allies.

Hitler's final offensive in the West began in 1944, even as the Eastern front crumbled. While stationed in the Pacific, the Allies pushed the Japanese even closer to their home defenses. The Allies took other actions against the Japanese in far away places like the Aleutian Islands and Burma. Americans invaded the Philippines while the American navy ended the last Japanese naval threat. Although any hope of victory was fading, Germany and Japan continued to fight on, even as their homelands were subjected to increasingly destructive bombing raids against their cities and industries.

These chapters provide overviews of the strategy that led to the campaigns in the Pacific and in Europe, and they also examine the more famous Battles of the Bulge, Kursk, Leyte, the Philippine Sea, and Leyte Gulf, as well as the terrible Battles of Tarawa, Saipan, and Peleliu. The last chapter looks again at the Allied leaders in conference and at how the strategic picture looked from the point of view of each nation involved in the war.

Part 6: Starting Over: The War's Aftereffects, 1945

This part outlines the last months of fighting that destroyed the Third Reich and the Japanese empire. The giant hammer blows of the Allied armies against the last of the German defenses left Germany devastated and its leader dead in the rubble of Berlin. American and Soviet troops met at the Elbe River, and Americans mourned the loss of their own Commander in Chief. Soviet armies drove deep into Eastern Europe, while American and British forces advanced into Czechoslovakia and Austria. By May, the war was over, and victory in Europe was declared.

The war against Japan appeared to be never ending. Some of the greatest and costliest battles of the war were fought at Okinawa and Iwo Jima. Despite the mounting odds against them, the Japanese refused to surrender. The plans were set for the invasion of the Japanese main islands. This most devastating war ended with the employment of the most devastating weapon ever developed. The atomic bombs that fell on two Japanese cities finally brought the war to an end and opened an uncertain new era in world history.

Part 7: The Part of Tens

This is a standard concluding chapter in the . . . *For Dummies* books that provides the author with a place to put neat things he hadn't already said in the text. These purely arbitrary lists of ten things are intended to stir up a bit of discussion, debate, and appreciation for some different factors involved in World War II.

Icons Used in This Book

Sometimes, you may quickly need some help in finding out what's important. In this book, you find icons — little pictures next to the text that get your attention and point you to the information you want. Look for these icons throughout the book. Here's what each one means:

HISTORICAL TRIVIA

This icon gives you a piece of historic information that can add to your understanding or appreciation of a particular event in World War II.

ARMY ALLIED

This icon highlights information related to the Allies.

ARMY AXIS

This icon highlights information related to the Axis.

REMEMBER

This icon points out especially important information that you need to keep in mind as subsequent events unfold.

MILITARY STRATEGY

This icon points out the technical and strategic aspects in the book, such as how many weapons were used, how they were used, and the nuts and bolts of the offensives.

Where to Go from Here

This book is about war and politics. In most cases, wars are hard to understand unless you look into the political issues that led to conflict. If you have questions about how World War II started, you should start at the beginning of the book. If you are looking for specific campaigns, you can look at background information, move right into the battles, or look for tidbits in The Part of Tens. You can even skip around, switching from one part of the globe to another and come back to other parts of the story later on. Any way you choose to go, you can find what you need to fill in the gaps.

Beyond the Book

In addition to what you're reading right now, this book comes with a free access-anywhere Cheat Sheet. To get this Cheat Sheet, go to www.dummies.com and search for "World War II For Dummies" by using the Search box.

1
Origins and Causes of the War, 1919–1939

Chapter **1**

World War II: Why It Matters and What You Need to Know

World War II is over. It's been over since August 1945. Good guys won. Bad guys lost. What else do you need to know? First you need to know that nothing — and especially not war — is *ever* that simple. World War II — its causes, its battles, its tragedies, and its victories — is almost beyond comprehension.

Want to see what true evil is? Study the German concentration and death camps or think about the 6 million Jewish men, women, and children who were murdered. Want a glimpse of heroism? Look at the stoicism the British displayed when London was bombed for 42 nights straight or remember the ordinary soldiers from any nation who fought against overwhelming odds toward what seemed to be inevitable defeat. Want to understand sacrifice? Consider the 25 million dead from the Soviet Union alone or the resistance fighters who gave up everything to free their countries from Nazism. Want to understand power, fanaticism, devotion to duty, political maneuvering, selflessness, selfishness, and persevering in the face of unimaginable terror? Look at events that led up to and the events that occurred during World War II.

And when you get past all that stuff, think about how World War II has affected the world we live in today: national borders, political loyalties, strategic and military alliances, international trouble spots, the beginning and end of the Cold War, the birth and death of superpowers, the role of peacekeeping forces, and more — in short, our ways of life and how we conduct ourselves as nations — all have been largely shaped by events that happened 80 years ago.

That's why World War II is important.

The War's Beginnings

Officially, World War II began when Nazi Germany invaded Poland in September 1939 and the French and English declared war against Germany as a result of that invasion. But the war's beginnings came long before this invasion. World War II was the product of a lot of things coming together in just the wrong way at just the wrong time.

The World War I peace agreement

When the Great War ended, the winners (Britain, France, the United States, and Italy) wanted the losers (Germany, the Austro-Hungarian Empire, and the Ottoman Empire) to pay. Because the Austro-Hungarian and Ottoman Empires no longer existed, that left Germany to bear the brunt of the victors' vindictive peace agreement. Humiliated and broke, Germany began nursing a big-time grudge. The victors themselves weren't even happy with the outcome. Some (Italy) felt cheated; some (France) felt that Germany hadn't been punished enough, and some (the U.S.) just wanted the heck out of Dodge.

In addition, the peace agreement created new nations (Poland, Czechoslovakia, and Yugoslavia) in Eastern Europe from the wrecked Austro-Hungarian Empire and other pieces of land from here (Germany) and there (the Soviet Union). Think that didn't tick everybody off?

The global economy

All the nations experienced financial troubles following World War I. The European nations (especially Germany, with the war debt hanging over its head) were practically destitute. Slowly, each made an economic recovery — just in time for the world economy to spiral downward. The U.S. stock market crashed in 1929, and the economies in Europe tanked pretty soon after that. Weakened by the war, no European nation was able to stop the economic downturn. And many saw the ruined economy as an indication that capitalism and democracy had failed.

The rise of totalitarianism

With the world in such a mess, folks looked toward their governments to solve their problems, and those countries without a strong tradition of democratic rule were susceptible to promises made by future tyrants who claimed that by consolidating power in one party and one man, they could provide stability and order.

As a result, in Germany specifically (and in Italy earlier), the fledgling democracies gave way to dictatorships and eventual totalitarian rule (that is, all aspects of life are controlled by the dictator). In Italy, this dictator was Benito Mussolini; in Germany, it was Adolf Hitler.

The birth of Fascism and Nazism

Fascism is a political ideology in which the state is exalted above all else. All effort and resources are committed to glorifying the state. Individual freedom doesn't exist; there is only the freedom to serve the state. Fascists believe that people reach their potential only through service to their nation. If the nation is great, the people are great. And the best representation of the nation's greatness is through war. Italy was Fascist, as was Spain after the Spanish Civil War (see Chapter 3).

Nazism is Fascism with a significant difference: the race issue. The Nazis believed that race is the fundamental trait and therefore the *defining* characteristic of a people. Just as dogs are genetically predisposed to certain roles (some hunt and others herd, for example), each race is genetically predisposed to certain roles. Some are leaders; other races (the "inferior" ones) are meant to be mastered. The Aryan race is, according to Nazis, the Master Race. Then, in descending order are non-Aryan Caucasians, Asians, Africans, and finally Jews. The Jewish people occupied a special place at the bottom of the Nazi racial hierarchy for the following reasons:

>> They "corrupted" the other inferior races and the weak minded of the Master Race with what Hitler thought of as Jewish ideas: equality among people and individual freedom.

>> They wanted to take over the world and thus posed a specific threat to the Master Race who, as the Master Race, deserved to rule the world.

>> They were "parasites" who betrayed Germany during World War I.

The rise of Hitler

There have always been tyrants and people who abused power, and in many ways, Hitler was no different than any other dictator. He consolidated power by eliminating anyone who could oppose him. He targeted and abused groups he didn't like. He used propaganda as a tool to lull the German people into believing that what he told them was true.

In other ways, Hitler was different. He had the power of an industrialized nation behind him. He had the capability to export his policies all over Europe through diplomatic trickery and lies and then through war. He had the certainty of his fanatical vision of a Jew-free Europe. And, maybe most frightening of all, he had the ability to make the German people as a whole believe that by following him down the path to hell, they were fulfilling their destiny for greatness.

The British and French fear of another war

The British and French, having just been through one horrific world war (although they didn't call it that at the time) were willing to do just about anything to make sure that they didn't find themselves in another horrific war. For both countries, this determination to avoid conflict resulted in their policy of appeasement. By giving in to the demands of aggressors, such as Hitler, they hoped to avert another crisis that would lead to war. Obviously, this strategy didn't work.

The isolationism of the United States

The United States, separated from Europe by an ocean, wanted to remain separated from Europe. Like the French and British, the Americans had seen enough of war. They learned as much about European politics and intrigue and blood feuds as they wanted to during the Great War, and they had no intention now of allowing themselves to get mixed up in that mess again. So they developed an isolationist policy and naively insisted that what went on in Europe — or anywhere else in the world, for that matter — was not their concern.

The empire building of Japan

Japan, long a key player in Asia, wanted to consolidate its power there. Japan still held the German bases that it had occupied in China during World War I, and as one of the victors, Japan got to keep large sections of Chinese territory that had once been controlled by the Germans, in addition to being given control of islands that had belonged to Germany. Japan also sought to increase its holdings in China, which, in addition to being a problem for the Chinese, was also a problem for the United States, who had interests there, too.

Who's Who of Combatants

Americans may find this hard to believe, but U.S. soldiers weren't the only ones fighting the Nazis and the Japanese. (In fact, they weren't even the first ones to fight the Nazis). A whole lot of other people from a whole lot of other places fought on one side or the other.

The Allies

On the Allied side (the side that fought against Germany and Japan) were the following nations:

>> Great Britain

>> United States

>> France — and after the fall of France to the Germans, Free French, led by Charles de Gaulle)

>> Soviet Union

>> Italy (after 1943)

>> Canada

>> Australia

>> China

>> New Zealand

>> India

>> South Africa

>> Others, including resistance fighters from the German-occupied nations, such as Poland, France, Norway, Denmark, the Netherlands, and Czechoslovakia. Nations from South America also joined in the Allied cause

The Axis

On the Axis side (the side that fought to dominate Europe and Asia) were the following:

>> Germany

>> Italy (before 1943)

» Japan

» Other nations sympathetic to or occupied by Germany or that felt particularly threatened by the Soviet Union, such as Bulgaria, Hungary, Finland, and Romania

The Course of the War

Here is a very brief rundown of the highlights of World War II. For more information about these events, head to the appropriate chapter:

» On September 1, 1939, Germany invaded Poland. On September 3, Britain and France (and other nations) declared war on Germany.

» On September 17, 1939, the Soviet Union invaded Poland, having struck a secret deal with the Nazis regarding Poland's fate.

» On March 18, 1940, Italy joined the war on Germany's side.

» In May through June 1940, Denmark, Norway, Belgium, Luxembourg, and France fell to the Germans, and the Battle of Britain began.

» In March 1941, the U.S., still isolationist, implemented its lend-lease policy, which enabled America to lend supplies, including war supplies, to the Allies.

» In June 1941, Hitler turned on Stalin, and Germany invaded the Soviet Union, at which point Stalin saw the light and joined with the Allies to declare war on Germany.

» On December 7, 1941, the Japanese bombed Pearl Harbor and the United States entered the war. Shortly after that, Germany and Italy declared war on the U.S.

» In 1942, Japanese troops captured numerous Pacific islands and places in Asia, including the Philippines, Singapore, Burma, and Malaya. America struck back with limited success but stemmed the Japanese advance permanently at Guadalcanal and New Guinea. The pivotal naval battle of Midway also took place that year.

» Also in 1942, the fighting in North Africa began in earnest. The Germans were defeated at Stalingrad — the decisive land battle of World War II. British forces defeated German and Italian forces at the decisive Battle of El Alamein. The Allies began their advance against Germany with an invasion of North Africa.

>> In 1943, the tide of the war swung in the Allies' favor. The Soviet troops began to drive Germany from the USSR, the German troops in North Africa surrendered, and the U.S. made progress against the Japanese in the Pacific, capturing key island strongholds and outflanking the Japanese defenses in New Guinea.

>> The Allied invasion of Normandy (D-Day) on June 6, 1944, marked the beginning of the end for Nazi Germany. Germany's last-ditch effort (the Battle of the Bulge in December of 1944) failed to stop the Allied advance into Germany.

>> By early 1945, the U.S. made significant progress in the Pacific. Despite the difficulty of the task, U.S. forces managed to conquer the Philippines.

>> In Europe, by April 1945, Germany had lost the war. Hitler committed suicide on April 30, and on May 7, Germany surrendered unconditionally.

>> By mid-summer of 1945, U.S. soldiers had broken the Japanese Navy and captured Okinawa and Iwo Jima in the Pacific in preparation for an invasion of the Japanese Home Islands.

>> On August 6, the U.S. dropped the first atomic bomb on Hiroshima; on August 8, it dropped the second atomic bomb on Nagasaki.

>> On August 14, 1945, Japan surrendered.

Where in the World Was the World War Fought?

"World War" was not just a grandiose name for what happened between September 1939 and August 1945. It literally was a *world* war. In fact, if you were to stick a pin in a spinning globe, chances are you'd end up stuck in some place that was in some way connected to the war. Maybe it was a supply station or a battleground, or maybe it just had an airfield that pilots could land on en route to or from somewhere else.

The battles in Europe

World War II affected every country in Europe. Most of the nations were directly involved in the war (Germany, France, Italy, Poland, Luxembourg, Czechoslovakia, to name a few). Other places tried like heck to stay out of it — think Switzerland (which was successful in remaining neutral) or Belgium (which wasn't).

The battles in the Soviet Union

Given the state of the Soviet military in 1940 and Hitler's arrogance in thinking that the German army was unbeatable, it's no wonder that he thought Germany could do what no army has yet been able to do: Beat the Russians in their own snowy, cold, forbidding back yard.

When Germany invaded the Soviet Union, Hitler figured five months was all it would take for the superior German army to bring the Soviet bear to its knees. He was wrong, and the Germans ended up in Russia through two Russian winters. It was a different war, one that meant the complete destruction of either Nazism or Communism.

The battles in North Africa

North Africa was another major battleground. It was important for a couple of reasons and saw two of the most respected generals in the war (Montgomery for the British and Rommel for the Germans) battle it out there:

>> The Allies needed to protect access to the Suez Canal, without which they would be unable to supply their troops.

>> Capturing North Africa would enable the Allies to launch an attack across the Mediterranean into Italy.

The battles in the Pacific and in Southeast Asia

The battles in the Pacific and Southeast Asia were brutal. The terrain was a nightmare. Thick jungles, rocky cliffs, deep ravines, and networks of caves posed obvious disadvantages for those who had the unpleasant job of attacking a position. Not only was the terrain difficult to fight on, but the rains, when they came, were unrelenting. Add to this the presence of a determined foe who would rather die than surrender, and you have a miserable and deadly situation. Taking the Pacific islands often meant yard-by-yard advances in hand-to-hand combat. The battles in Southeast Asia were little better.

The battle in the Atlantic

The Battle of the Atlantic centered on protecting the essential movement of men and supplies to Britain and the Soviet Union from German *U-boats* (submarines).

Initially, the terror of the seas, the U-boats used what was called the *wolf-pack tactic:* If a German submarine spotted a convoy, it radioed its location and tracked the ships while waiting for other U-boats to assemble. Usually under the cover of darkness, the U-boats attacked the most vulnerable ships — in the same way that a pack of wolves pursues its prey and kills the weakest.

It wasn't until 1943, when the Allies were able to produce more ships than the U-boats could sink and sink more U-boats than the Germans could build, did the U-boats stop being a threat in the Atlantic.

The Effect of World War II

World War II changed the world. It created and destroyed nations, and it shifted the balance of world power and influence from Europe to the Soviet Union and the United States. It ushered in the atomic age and opened a new war — the Cold War — in which a former partner became a mortal enemy. Although World War II ended the global threat of Nazism, it didn't end hatred or eliminate genocide as a tool for war (think "ethnic cleansing"). The Second World War also brought colonialism to an end, and it created new states with all kinds of problems that are prevalent every day in the Middle East, Africa, and Asia.

World War II was one of those rare instances in history where the threat was obvious. The enemy was well defined and allowed a clear distinction between good and evil. Nations bound together to face a common threat; these nations would not have found common cause otherwise. Think of the democracies joining with Josef Stalin, the Soviet dictator of the same ilk as Hitler. Many thought that in the end, there would be a new world, a more peaceful world, but the result is that we live every day with the aftershocks of World War II.

Chapter **2**

The Great War and the Uneasy Peace: How World War II Happened

W orld War II didn't just happen. Italy didn't start flirting with restoring the Roman Empire in 1935 for no reason at all. Germany didn't wake up in the spring of 1936 and say, "Hey. Master Race. World domination. Sounds good." In fact, by the second half of the 1920s, things looked pretty stable — at least compared to what they looked like just 10 years earlier when the Great War had just ended. What happened to the world that had supposedly been made safe for democracy?

If you want to understand how and why World War II started, you have to look at the how World War I (also called the Great War) ended and the crucial years that followed it. You also need to understand the impact that the Great Depression had on the world economy and how these conditions compelled democratic nations (such as Italy and Germany) to turn to totalitarian principles to solve their problems.

Finally, you have to know what was going on with the other nations — Great Britain, France, and the U.S. — to understand why they didn't act quicker to stop the threat that today, at least, seemed obvious.

The End of One War and the Roots of Another

The Great War (World War I) started in 1914. On one side were Great Britain, France, Imperial Russia (Russia before the revolution that got rid of the Tsar and put the Communists in power), and Italy (which entered later). On the other side were Germany, Austria-Hungary, and the Ottoman Empire (see Figure 2-1).

Although the war supposedly started because of the assassination of Franz Ferdinand (the heir to the Austrian throne), these nations really fought to determine status and power in the world. Each alliance wanted to establish its position as the dominant colonial or military power.

Not long into the war, a stalemate developed along a line of entrenched defensive positions stretching from the North Sea, through Belgium and France, to the Swiss border. Neither side could get the upper hand. After three years of what came to be called *trench warfare* (where one side lobbed highly explosive shells, poison gas, and so on into the trenches of the other side, and then attacked with waves of infantrymen), the result was that hundreds of thousands of soldiers were needlessly slaughtered.

In 1917, Russia, embroiled in a revolution at home, left the war, and the United States entered the war on the side of Britain and France. The U.S. became involved partly in response to Germany's harassment of American ships and the sinking of the *Lusitania* by a German submarine, and partly in an idealistic crusade "to make the world safe for democracy" — the words that President Woodrow Wilson used in his war message to Congress. Shortly after the Americans entered the war, the conflict finally ended. The Allies — America, Britain, France, and Italy — had won.

By the time the war ended (November 11, 1918), it had gone on for four agonizing years. It used poison gas, submarines, and airplanes. It destroyed empires, created new states based on national or ethnic identity, saw a new communist revolutionary state in Russia, and put the United States in a position to control the agenda that would shape the postwar world. Over 10 million soldiers and civilians died in the war. Europe — the dominant economic, political, and cultural force in the world — had exhausted all its material and human resources.

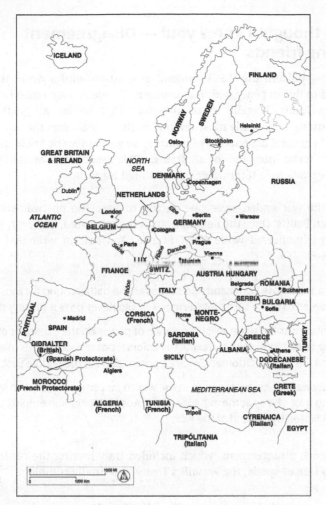

FIGURE 2-1:
Europe, 1914.

The victors and the spoils: The Treaty of Versailles

The peace conference opened in January 1919. The only important attendees were the four nations on the winning side: Italy, France, Great Britain, and the United States. (Russia, which had left the war in 1917, was in the midst of a civil war and was not represented.) The nations that lost were not invited because the winners didn't think their presence was necessary. The terms of the peace would be dictated to them.

But I thought I knew you! — Disagreement among friends

Woodrow Wilson, the U.S. President, wanted to build a world that would allow nations to live in peace with one another. His ideas were embodied in his famous *Fourteen Points*, literally fourteen points that he set as goals for the peace negotiations. One of the most famous of these goals was the creation of what he called "a general association of nations" to guarantee the "political independence and territorial integrity" of all states. (This association would later become the *League of Nations*, a forerunner to the United Nations.)

When the war ended, everyone agreed to base the postwar settlement on the Fourteen Points. Once the negotiations actually started, however, Wilson's agenda was rapidly shelved while Italy, France, and Britain wrangled over their own objectives:

» France, whose homeland had served as the battleground for most of the war, wanted to make sure that Germany would never pose a military threat again.

» Britain wanted to establish a balance of power on the continent and increase the size of its empire by taking the colonial possessions of Germany in Africa and the former Ottoman Empire's possessions in the Middle East.

» Italy wanted its participation in the war to be compensated with land — and a lot of it — at the expense of the Austro-Hungarian empire, which had collapsed by the end of the war.

After much disagreement, which included Italy leaving the conference in a huff over its lack of spoils, the *Versailles Treaty* was finally complete.

Message to the losers: Deal with it

The Versailles Treaty was presented to the German delegation for their signature — without discussion — in June 1919. In this Treaty:

» Germany lost about ten percent of its territory and population, including territories in the east to create the new states of Poland, Czechoslovakia, and Lithuania.

MILITARY STRATEGY

The territories that had made up Austria-Hungary and the Ottoman Empire were redistributed as independent states (such as Poland, Czechoslovakia, and Yugoslavia) or as quasi-colonies (called *mandates*) under the supervision and control of France or Great Britain. Much of the Middle East was divided up this way, too.

- France got Alsace-Lorraine (a territory taken from them in 1870 by Germany); Belgium and Denmark also received German territory.

- The French occupied parts of Germany for fifteen years: the Saar Basin, an important industrial region, and the Rhineland, a strategic territory on the west bank of the Rhine River bordering France.

- Germany lost all its colonial possessions in Africa and Asia.

- Germany was forced to accept full responsibility for the war. This guilt clause made Germany pay the victors for the costs of the war, estimated at 33 billion dollars. Germany was to pay this money in installments over a period of years.

- To add insult to injury, Germany was disarmed, limited to no more than 100,000 ground troops and allowed no tanks or aircraft.

Woodrow Wilson's last card: The League of Nations

As Woodrow Wilson's dream of a new world order faded in compromise at Versailles, he doggedly held to the most important principle from the Fourteen Points. This principle was the *League of Nations*, an international organization dedicated to guaranteeing cooperation among nations and preserving peace and security by settling disputes peacefully. Wilson believed that even if the Versailles Treaty were flawed, the League of Nations could eventually correct the problems and prevent another war.

MILITARY STRATEGY

Beginning operations in Geneva, Switzerland, in 1920, the League of Nations actually had little chance of success:

- The League suffered a severe blow to its prestige when the United States Senate refused to *ratify* (approve) the Versailles Treaty and, therefore, kept the United States out of the international organization. In other words, the country that created the organization refused to join it.

- *Article X* of the treaty, which committed each League member to preserve the independence of every other member, was a big problem for most nations. It implied that if one League nation was threatened, then other member nations had to go to war to defend it, and most nations were not willing to go that far.

- Relations between League members were hardly cordial enough to rule out future military conflict. The last thing some nations wanted to do was have their foreign policy co-opted by the League of Nations. Nations were willing to play along as League members only if membership did not interfere with their own interests.

Thus, the League of Nations, with little power other than moral indignation, could not control the growing threat of war in the 1930s.

The world in the 1920s

The Great War changed the diplomatic and economic face of the world, creating instability and mistrust. The balance of power in Europe had changed completely, and the economies of Europe had been completely disrupted. Europe feared the spread of communism (led by the Russian Bolsheviks). The Treaty of Versailles had created more problems than it solved, leaving many nations and people dissatisfied and leaving the victors holding empty promises of reparations and territory as rewards for all their sacrifices.

You didn't have to be a fortune-teller to know that trouble was brewing.

The U.S. — in denial

Believing that peace was based on revenge, Americans decided that they were no longer interested in the problems of Europe and wanted no part of the quarrels that could lead to involvement in another war. America rejected forming alliances with other nations and spent much of the decade attempting to collect war debts totaling about 7 billion dollars from its former wartime allies.

America also signed a number of disarmament treaties to limit the size of naval fleets among Britain, France, Italy, Japan, and the United States. The idea was to prevent an arms race that could lead to war. In 1928, this spirit of harmony climaxed with the signing of the *Kellog-Briand Treaty*, which outlawed war as an instrument of national policy. The United States and 61 other nations signed the treaty. Comforted by the illusion of security and permanent peace, America enjoyed prosperity at home and maintained a cautious, nationalistic approach to preserve its own interests.

Germany — in flux

The monarchy that led Germany during the war had disappeared, and a democratic republic took its place. But the German Republic was crippled from its very beginning in 1919:

>> Saddled with the Versailles Treaty and its 33-billion-dollar reparations bill, the government had weak support among many Germans.

>> The German economy, disrupted by the war and the occupation of the Saar, Germany's critical industrial region, suffered incredible inflation (in 1923, 4.2 trillion German marks to the American dollar) that drove lower and middle classes into financial ruin.

>> Politically, the nation was deeply divided between Left and Right. The German people, who displayed a general hostility to the new government, were reluctant to trade an authoritarian leader (the monarch, for example) for the ideals of democracy. Only American loans stabilized the economy and allowed a moderate coalition government to be elected.

Despite these problems, Germany was able to regain some economic stability and reclaim its place among the European nations. It signed the *Locarno Treaty*, in which it pledged to respect the borders of France and Belgium. It was admitted into the League of Nations and was given a permanent seat on the Council in 1926. And during the last years of the 1920s, it made a moderate, but steady economic recovery and established a measure of trust among the international community.

Still, Germany tried to avoid or repeal the terms of the Versailles Treaty, especially those terms dealing with the war debt and the restrictions on how much it could rearm.

Great Britain — in a funk

Britain spent the decade of the 1920s dealing with rebellion and civil war in Ireland and unrest in India. It suffered a downturn in its economy as a result of changes in postwar trading and production patterns. Britain's inability to export products profitably from its traditional domestic industries combined with a general fall in the worldwide demand for goods after the war really accentuated this economic nightmare, which included high unemployment and frequent, large-scale labor strikes. The Labour party became the main proponent of social welfare measures to support working-class Britons.

Like the United States, Great Britain looked warily at events in Europe. Ever mistrustful of France, Britain continued to pursue a narrowly defined foreign policy.

France — in trouble

With much of its land and industry destroyed and many of its working-age men dead, France faced a bleak future. Alsace-Lorraine and the Saar (German regions that France regained and occupied, respectively, at the end of the war) served as a slight buffer in stabilizing the economy, but to recover fully, France was dependent on German war payments. As a result, France took a hard-line policy — that included occupying German territory with military forces to ensure compliance — when Germany could not meet its obligations.

France also feared another war with Germany and considered the Versailles Treaty the only guarantee of security. More than any other nation, France tried to gain international support to force Germany to abide by the treaty. Despite Germany's signing of the Locarno Treaty, in which it promised to respect the French border, France made alliances with Poland and Czechoslovakia in an attempt to offset Germany.

Although economically troubled early in the decade, by 1926, France (like Germany) enjoyed a period of economic recovery and stability in the last years of the decade.

Italy — in a snit

At the end of the war, Italy felt cheated. It had wanted to expand into the Balkans in the wake of the collapsed Austro-Hungarian Empire. Instead, it gained little additional territory for its 600,000 casualties. Postwar Italy was also hampered by a series of weak coalition governments that never stayed in power long enough to deal with increasing unemployment, a heavy national debt, and rising costs.

A *constitutional monarchy* (in which the ruler's power is limited by law or by elected representatives), Italy in the early 1920s teetered on the brink of chaos. A new nationalist party, the Fascists, led by war veteran Benito Mussolini, legally took power in 1922 (see Chapter 3 for more information on the dictators in Europe). As Prime Minister, Mussolini gradually consolidated power and established a dictatorship. His goal was to build a state in which every Italian would serve the nation. Intensely patriotic, Mussolini began to revitalize the Italian economy while looking for opportunities to make Italy one of the great powers of Europe.

Russia — in revolt

The Bolshevik Revolution of 1917 ended the Russian monarchy and plunged Russia into a five-year nightmare of civil war. Led by Vladimir Lenin, the Bolsheviks dreamed of spreading communist revolution by force of arms into Europe. Lenin consolidated control over the new *Union of Soviet Socialist Republics* (USSR) by force and terror. Millions of Russians died in a famine from 1921 to 1922 due to the Bolsheviks' failed attempts to create a pure socialist state. The United States alleviated the famine by sending massive food relief. Then Lenin restored limited private ownership of the economy, which allowed the USSR to experience a limited recovery.

After Lenin's death in 1924, Josef Stalin created a totalitarian state and embarked on a program to transform Russia into a modern industrial state. Diplomatically isolated, Russia sought out Germany in the mid-1920s and made a secret treaty that allowed (against the provisions in the Versailles Treaty) the German army to train in Russia with tanks and aircraft in exchange for increased trade.

Japan — in China

Economically and militarily, Japan was a major power in Asia before the Great War. Japan declared war on Germany in August 1914 and immediately occupied German bases on China's coast. Japan also sought to gain concessions from a weak and divided China concerning control of *Manchuria* (a large province in northeastern China rich in natural resources). Much to the anger of Chinese nationalists, the Japanese were allowed to keep major sections of former German-controlled Chinese territory. Japanese troops moved into Russian territory and did not leave until 1925.

The Versailles Treaty gave the Japanese some former German island possessions in the Pacific (the Marianas, the Marshalls, and the Carolines) as mandates. However, they began fortifying the islands in violation of the agreement. Japan also built highly capable modern warships despite treaty limitations to keep its navy proportionally smaller than those of France, the United States, and Great Britain.

Throughout the 1920s, Japan enjoyed a dynamic economic expansion. Although nominally a parliamentary democracy, the civilian government leadership did not control the Japanese military. Thus, a rift continued to grow between the military and the government over expansion into Manchuria. Japan had an army controlling the strategic railway in southern Manchuria, supporting Japan's long-term territorial ambitions in China. The Chinese protests over what amounted to an illegal occupation of their territory by armed force were ignored.

BENITO MUSSOLINI: THE FIRST FASCIST

Benito Mussolini (1883–1945) was the son of a blacksmith. Despite little formal education, he became a schoolteacher. Although he is often associated with intense patriotism, anti-Bolshevism, and militarism, Mussolini had been a pacifist and a socialist early in his life. In 1911, he ended up in jail for opposing Italy's annexation of Libya in its war against Turkey. Freed in 1912, he became editor of the socialist newspaper in Milan, but he was expelled from the party in 1914, when he supported Italy's entrance into World War I. He founded his own newspaper with heavy emphasis on patriotic themes. In 1915, Mussolini entered the army. Promoted to sergeant in 1917, he was later wounded. After the war, Mussolini and other war veterans founded an organization called *Fasci di Combattimento* (a group or association of fighters — see the sidebar "The fighting fiasco . . . uh, fascio," in this chapter) in March of 1919. He was opposed to democracy and the rule of parliament, but he had no definite political attachments. Instead, he associated himself with activities and ideas that would provide him access to political power. Arrogant and pugnacious, but not without certain intellectual gifts, Mussolini had no practical experience with government or diplomacy. Even so, he was able to convince much of the world community for many years that he was a reasonable and responsible leader, a new kind of man who would do great things for Italy.

China — in reform

The Chinese Republic led by Sun Yat-sen had only been in existence since 1911, but it was threatened by warlords who controlled large sections of territory with their private armies. After Sun's death in 1925, Chiang Kai-shek, a professional soldier, took control. By 1928, Chiang unified China under his Nationalist party, the Kuomintang. The government sought to build autonomy from European control through a program of legal reform, education, and economic modernization. These reforms benefited mostly upper-class Chinese, leaving the vast majority of the peasants of China untouched.

In the midst of this reform and modernization effort, the Nationalist party faced internal and external threats. The Chinese Communist party led by Mao Tse-tung, shown in Figure 2-2, who sought to win support among the peasants, represented the greatest internal threat to the Nationalist government.

FIGURE 2-2:
Mao Tse-tung.

Eastern Europe — in place but unhappily

The Treaty of Versailles created several new states from the wreckage of the Austro-Hungarian Empire:

>> The Czechs and Slovaks were consolidated into one nation called *Czechoslovakia*.

>> The south Slavs in the Balkans were consolidated into an artificial state called *Yugoslavia*.

>> The traditional homeland of Poles was consolidated from territory once owned by Germany and Russia to become Poland, with a jury-rigged corridor giving it access to the Baltic Sea (see Figure 2-3).

FIGURE 2-3:
Europe after the Treaty of Versailles, 1919.

Hulton-Deutsch Collection

These nations, with borders largely drawn out on a map in Paris, had little in the way of an economy and no tradition of self-government. Ethnic minorities within these new states were marginalized by the dominant ethnic majority, or the minorities refused to cooperate with the new governments. Many new states looked jealously at the territory of their neighbors, each nursing real or imagined fears that some other nation had gained more than it did.

Collapsing Economies: The Great Depression

The world economy in the postwar period was far more interdependent than many people realized. American commercial loans to Germany (which Germany used to pay war reparations to France and Britain) were essentially supporting the European economies. But the combination of worldwide industrial and agricultural overproduction during the decade eventually drove prices down. Meanwhile, credit granted to Europe became overextended after loans were not being repaid on time. And thus, the prosperity of the last years of the 1920s ended with an economic collapse so severe that the entire world was affected.

The effect on countries' economies

With the collapse of the U.S. stock market in October 1929, prices, wages, employment, trade, and investment all fell in an ever-deepening spiral, and economic distress became worldwide. Economic production dropped by an average of one-third in the U.S., France, and Britain. In Germany, production dropped by half. In Japan, demand for exports dropped by half.

Weakened by the war, no European nation could provide the financial leadership to halt the economic downturn. Only one nation — the Soviet Union — experienced an increase in industrial production at the cost of extraordinary hardships on its citizens. Stalin imposed modernization through terror and force. Millions of people died as a result of famine, deportations, or executions as Stalin single-mindedly pursued his goal. But the suffering of Russia's people was not apparent; what *was* apparent to many people in the West was that the Soviet style of socialism was the cure for the world depression.

In Italy, Mussolini dealt with the economic crisis by extending government control over larger sections of the economy to alleviate unemployment. He also crushed any protests or strikes to prevent the resurgence of pro-socialist activities that could threaten his power. For propaganda purposes, Mussolini often had himself photographed stripped to the waist, pitching hay or digging drainage ditches.

The threat to democracy

Stable democracies were having trouble dealing with mass unemployment and stagnant production, let alone the more fragile and relatively new democratic states. The severe economic distress especially crippled the parliamentary democracies of Germany and Japan.

>> In Japan, unemployment hit the farmers the hardest. As a result, industrialists and the parliamentary government became the targets of attacks by militant nationalists who believed that the military was the only institution that could restore Japan's vitality.

>> In Germany, as the depression drove more and more people from all classes out of work, the *Nazis* (short for National Socialist German Workers' Party) gained more and more support. See the section "Tools for Dictators: Fascism and Nazism" to find out about the beginnings of Nazism.

Fascism and Nazism: Whose Bright Idea Was This?

In the 1920s and into the 1930s, the economic change forced many people out of jobs; the social norms that had defined prewar society had been swept away and replaced with new and alien concepts. Governments lacked the capability or the will to deal with these changes and added to the fear of instability. Democracy and socialism struggled constantly for supremacy.

In the midst of these uncertainties, force seemed to be the answer. Dictators took power in states throughout Europe and eliminated political parties as a means of providing stability and order. In fact, much of Europe turned to these types of regimes between 1922 and 1939. Most notably, these countries include Germany and Italy. But other countries — such as Poland (1926), Yugoslavia (1929), Bulgaria (1938), Portugal (1926), and Spain (1936), as well as Finland, Hungary, Greece and Romania — also succumbed to the allure of an all-powerful leader.

The major reason was the collapse of the world economy. To many, capitalism and democracy appeared to have failed. The logic of giving a strong leader the reins of power to make decisions and carry them out was very powerful. Unfortunately, a totalitarian dictator could also use the nation's power against its own citizens and could pursue aggressive political objectives that would lead the nation into war.

Fascism in a nutshell — if only . . .

Although it had many different forms, the Fascist movement began in Italy in the 1920s under Benito Mussolini. *Fascism* is a political movement in which the nation (and race, according to the Nazis who added this component; see the section "Nazism: Fascism with a twist") is more important than the individual. The nation is represented by a repressive government that is led by a dictator, and any opposition to the government is forcibly suppressed, usually through terror and intimidation. Following are some other characteristics of Fascism:

>> **The ruler as an embodiment of the state:** This is the idea that one supreme leader, who has complete control of the reins of power, will further the interests of the state. In addition, this leader is so closely associated with the nation that he possesses mythic qualities himself — all seeing and all knowing, for example. And any attack on the leader is, therefore, an attack on the nation.

>> **The role of the individual:** Fascists believe that the role of the citizen is to serve the state; individual freedom does not exist. The goal of Fascism is to unite and mobilize society under the direction of the state. A citizen's highest calling, in fact, is to work toward the glory of the nation, as defined by the supreme leader.

>> **The role of the government:** To achieve its goals, the Fascist government, led by the supreme ruler, must have control over not just the political institutions but also *all* institutions: educational, cultural, economic, religious, and so on. In other words, there is no part of the citizens' lives that is not directed by the Fascist leader. In this way, Fascism is openly totalitarian.

>> **The role of aggression:** Fascism openly advocates violence against its opponents, both in and outside the nation's borders. War is seen as a way of validating and celebrating the nation. Fascism justifies this violence as an expression of both the greatness of the people and as the destiny of the nation.

One of the big questions that plagues people to this day is how so many seemingly reasonable and decent people could be led to close their eyes to or openly participate in the horrors to come. Although not enough to really answer the question, following are a few human tendencies that the Fascists played into:

>> **The desire to believe in myths:** Fascism promised order and a return to the ideals and values embodied in the nation in its largely mythic past. It didn't matter whether the myths were true or not; it was only important that the people believed the myths to be true. So, for example, although an Aryan race never really existed (*Aryan* is a largely linguistic designation), the German people, led by Hitler, *believed* that it had existed and that they were the last, best representation of it.

>> **Nationalism:** That is, the loyalty citizens feel toward their country. Nationalism also refers to the existence of a sort of "national consciousness" created by common language and culture, and the idea that some regions, because of these shared experiences, are destined to become a single nation.

Both Mussolini and Hitler tapped into this feeling when they promised to restore their countries — and hence their people — to greatness.

>> **Emotionalism:** Fascism relies on the idea that emotion plays a larger part than reason in spurring people to action. By offering symbols and myths that are compelling enough, the Fascist leader can tap into the primal emotions that overrule judgment and conscience.

Fascism in Italy

In Italy, Fascism attracted young men and others from the middle and lower classes who were dissatisfied with current political and economic conditions. The Fascists also gained support from those that saw Fascism as a bulwark against socialism. The people who supported the Fascists believed that they would bring order to a disorderly parliamentary system and return Italy to greatness.

At first, the Fascists sought to gain power through legitimate means by trying to organize a mass movement of the people. Tapping into the power of symbols, Mussolini's Fascists wore distinctive uniforms, which symbolized a return to old values of discipline and patriotism. They were known as the *blackshirts* because of their distinctive paramilitary clothing. Mussolini became known as *Il Duce* (Italian for "the leader"; see Figure 2-4).

FIGURE 2-4:
Benito Mussolini, known as *Il Duce* (the leader).

CORBIS

The Italian parliament's helplessness in the face of worker unrest allowed the blackshirts to begin a campaign of violence and intimidation against socialist organizations, which the Fascist claimed were to blame for the country's problems. The Fascists' defiance of the government and the rule of law created a power vacuum, which Mussolini sought to exploit as the nation slid toward chaos.

In October 1922, Mussolini threatened to seize Rome by force and take control of the government. King Victor Emanuel III overestimated Mussolini's power. Fearing civil war and unwilling to commit the army against the Fascists, the king invited Mussolini to form a new government. Mussolini thus became Prime Minister of Italy.

Securing power with a parliamentary majority, Mussolini moved to establish a dictatorship. He wanted to create a new state structure by uniting political, social, economic, military, and cultural power under his control:

>> In 1926, Mussolini imposed censorship on the press and suppressed all opposition parties.

>> Also in 1926, he placed the Fascist party under his direct control to prevent any opposition from growing within his own organization.

>> In 1929, Mussolini limited the church's interference in politics with the *Lateran Treaty,* which recognized the Pope's sovereignty over Vatican City and recognized Catholicism as the sole religion of Italy.

>> Mussolini also initiated an aggressive foreign policy aimed at returning Italy to the dominant state in the Mediterranean, gaining an overseas empire, just as the Romans had done.

Nazism: Fascism with a twist

While Fascism is associated primarily with Italy and Mussolini, Nazism is associated with Germany and Adolf Hitler. Nazism shared many concepts and principles with Italian Fascism, but there was one main difference: The overarching concept of blood and race was peculiar to Nazism.

Hitler and the Nazis believed that race was a fundamental characteristic that determined people's role in the world and their destiny. In other words, people are *not* all alike. Certain races are meant to lead and prosper; other races — the "inferior" races — are meant to be mastered. Although based entirely on discredited racial theories from the nineteenth century, Hitler's twisted ideology of race nevertheless became the driving force of Nazi policies and programs.

For Hitler, the German people represented the *Aryan race,* the race that he claimed was responsible for the cultural greatness of the Western world. This race was destined once again for greatness, he said, but obstacles stood in the way of it achieving its destiny. Specifically, those obstacles were the "inferior" races — most notably the Jews in Europe — and liberal and socialist ideas: liberal ideas that promoted the concept of individual freedoms and socialist concepts that promoted the idea of class equality. To achieve German greatness once again, Hitler claimed, the Germans must do the following:

» Control, subjugate, and eliminate "inferior" races: According to Hitler, German people must view the "inferior" races as vermin to be exterminated. They must show neither compassion nor pity.

» Eradicate liberal and socialist ideas (which, according to Hitler, where Jewish ideas): These ideas — like individual freedom and equality among people — were dangerous lies that made even the superior Aryans squeamish and weak. The Nazi book burnings and censorship were a direct result of this mandate.

» Take their rightful place in the world: A great nation needs room in which to grow; thus Germany must expand its borders to accommodate its population. As a result, the Germans felt their invasions into Eastern Europe were justified.

Determined to seek revenge, he developed a belief that his special personality destined him for greatness. Shrewd and arrogant, he spoke with eloquence and showmanship, but hatred molded by frustrations and hostility and political ambition were his prime motivators. Hitler lived largely in a dream world where only his views, opinions, and ideas mattered. To him, these took on the weight of irrefutable historical or scientific fact and could not be challenged. Despite how he used them, he had indisputable political talents, perhaps the greatest of any leader in the twentieth century.

ADOLF HITLER: THE MAN OF DESTINY

The son of a customs official, Adolf Hitler (1889–1945) was born in Austria. He dropped out of school at the age of 16 and moved to Vienna three years later to pursue admission to the Academy of Fine Arts. He failed the entrance exam twice, and he could not apply to the School of Architecture because he had no secondary school diploma. In Vienna, Hitler lived from job to job and sold small drawings of famous city landmarks. He read extensively and voraciously, visited the theater, and spent nights in a men's homeless shelter.

While in Vienna, he absorbed a hatred of Jews, democracy, humanism, and Christianity. He became a fanatical German nationalist with a belief in the use of naked power to effect change. He moved to Munich in 1913. A year later, Hitler volunteered for the Imperial Army when Germany declared war. He spent four years on the Western Front as a messenger; he was wounded twice and awarded the Iron Cross, first and second class for bravery. In late 1918, he was blinded by gas and was recovering in a military hospital when the Armistice ending the war was announced. Hitler was crushed; the war had given him an identity and a purpose. He could not believe that Germany had been defeated on the battlefield. He concluded that cowards and traitors had betrayed Germany.

In essence, under Hitler's leadership, a new Germany would arise, a nation based on a mythic medieval land populated by a pure race of Aryans. This new Germany, led by *Der Führer* ("the leader"), would take its rightful place in Europe. The German people, wanting to believe in their nation's and their own greatness — especially after years of hardship and a humiliating peace — bought these ideas hook, line, and sinker.

The Rise of Hitler

Adolf Hitler — like Mussolini, a war veteran with political ambitions — associated himself with a small nondescript organization called the *German Workers' Party* in 1919. A mesmerizing speaker with a nearly boundless will to power, Hitler soon took control. Under his leadership and direction, the party became the *National Socialists German Workers' Party* (*Nazis* from the German abbreviation) and gained national prominence.

Hitler gave the party its distinctive symbol (the *swastika*), used "*Heil*"(hail) as the party greeting, and copied Mussolini's stiff-arm salute. He also imitated Mussolini by creating a paramilitary force called the *brownshirts* — or the *Sturmabteilung* (SA), which is German for "Storm Troopers." In addition, he created a personal bodyguard called the SS (short for *Schutzstaffel*, meaning "Protection Squad").

The putsch that failed

In November 1923, Hitler led the Nazi party in a *putsch* (revolt) against the state government of Bavaria in Munich. He hoped that control of Bavaria would lead to a national revolt that would put him in power.

When three leaders of the Bavarian government were addressing a crowd in a beer hall, Hitler strode in, stood on a chair, and fired a pistol into the air, declaring that Bavaria was under control of a revolutionary government. Through bluff and bluster, he convinced the three leaders to swear allegiance to the new government. With a crowd of 3,000, Hitler then marched toward the center of Munich to take control of the city. Police fired on the crowd, and the revolt died. Hitler was spirited away, but he was soon arrested and tried for treason. Serving as his own lawyer, Hitler used the trial to promote his views. "A man born to be a dictator has the right to step forward," he declared at one point in the proceedings. He was sentenced to one year in prison.

Mein Kampf

During Hitler's year in prison, from 1924 to 1925, he wrote an autobiographical book that sold over 5 million copies. It was titled *Mein Kampf* (German for "My Struggle). Rambling and poorly written, containing a jumble of half-formed ideas and fractured history, it nevertheless revealed Hitler's aims, motivations, and character. He raged against Jews and communism and spoke about the essence of the state embedded in nationality and race.

By the time he left prison, Hitler was a nationally recognized figure. His putsch had taught him a lesson. He understood that he could not seize power by force. Although he hated democracy, he would use the process to take power legally.

It was Hitler's ability to articulate the common German citizen's miseries and resentment over the Versailles Treaty and frustrations over Germany's impotence under its current government that allowed him to build a broad national base of support. Here is how he did it:

MILITARY STRATEGY

>> He promised to nullify the results of the war and restore Germany to greatness. To do this, he spoke of bonding all Germans together in a single, pure Aryan racial community. Over everything was Hitler's powerful vision of a unified new German *Reich* (empire) that would rise to dominate Europe.

The idea of an Aryan race was Hitler's invention. Actually, *Aryan* is a term that refers to a linguistic group and has nothing to do with race.

>> He focused much of the blame for Germany's condition on the Jewish population, which he identified as a non-Aryan race that had betrayed the nation during the Great War and now lived as parasites. To him, the Jews were the source of all evil and an enemy to the survival of the German nation.

By 1932, the Nazis had become the strongest party in parliament, controlling 230 seats.

Hitler consolidates power

By the end of 1932, Hitler and the Nazis had the support of nearly one-third of German voters, and the Nazis had become the strongest party in the German parliament. As their influence and power grew, the president of the German Republic (Paul von Hindenburg) and the German Chancellor (the equivalent of a prime minister) noted Hitler's rise. Hindenburg was unhappy that the Chancellor couldn't seem to form an effective coalition government without Nazi participation. And the Chancellor, recognizing the threat the Nazis posed to the democratic government, requested the authority to dissolve the government and rule by emergency decree. When Hindenburg refused, the Chancellor resigned, which left

Hindenburg with little choice but to invite Hitler, on January 30, 1933, to become Chancellor and form a new government.

Less than one month after Hitler took office, the *Reichstag* (the German parliament building) burned. (Although a communist was arrested for the arson, many speculate that the Nazis themselves may have set the fire.) Whether planned or not, Hitler used the incident to further his aims:

>> He moved rapidly to suppress opposition parties, limit the authority of the parliament, and impose censorship.

>> He issued the *Presidential Decree for Protection of the People and the State,* in which he suspended the German constitution and all personal liberties, had Nazi party members take over the state governments, and arrested those who opposed the Nazis.

>> With the *Enabling Act,* Hitler assumed full legislative authority for four years. In other words, he could act without fear of restraint.

Because he commanded the ultimate loyalty of the people and the military, President Hindenburg was Hitler's last obstacle to achieving complete power. Hindenburg was an old man — over 85 — when Hitler became chancellor in 1933, and he died one year later, in 1934.

Hitler wasted no time at Hindenburg's death. He combined the offices of President and Chancellor into one office, and he made members of the government and the army all swear a personal loyalty oath to *Der Führer* ("the leader"), the title Hitler assumed (see Figure 2-5). All state and political power became consolidated in one man. Hitler, it seemed, had achieved one of his goals: to eliminate democracy and political parties and replace them with what he called the "untrammeled authority for the leader."

Creating the regime: The alpha wolf takes over

From 1934, Hitler ensured that he would be the unquestioned leader. Even the people who had supported him were not safe: He ordered the murder of a large number of his own storm-trooper leaders who may have represented a threat. At the same time, Jews, communists, and other political opponents were arrested, murdered, or sent to concentration camps. Many people fled the country. Very briefly, here's what was happening in Germany between 1933 and 1938:

>> German Jews became the targets of Hitler's wrath: Jewish businesses were boycotted, civil rights of Jews were curtailed, and the government encouraged physical attacks on Jews and the looting of Jewish businesses and synagogues. Jews could no longer own cars or telephones; they could not wear certain types of jewelry or clothing. They were also forbidden to enter certain public buildings.

>> Seeking to gain control over every aspect of German life, the Nazis purged the culture of any non-Aryan influences — especially modern art and literature. Books of banned authors were burned publicly. Many German artists, composers, writers, and scientists were blacklisted because of their ideas or their ethnic background. The Nazis used fear and terror to intimidate and destroy those who resisted.

>> The Nazis used a massive propaganda program to support their efforts. Radio and newspapers were under the control of the government and constantly trumpeted the glorification of Hitler and the state, promising a Greater Germany. By use of carefully orchestrated mass demonstrations, Germans could witness and experience for themselves the growing power of a resurgent nation.

FIGURE 2-5: Adolf Hitler, known as *Der Führer*.

CORBIS

To the average German, Hitler seemed to have the magic touch. In the midst of a worldwide depression, he eliminated unemployment by 1936 and put the nation back to work, building roads and bridges and government buildings. He also put industry back in full production, making armaments for the new German military.

Nazi top brass: The rest of the pack

Here is a list of men who helped Hitler build the Nazi party and become Chancellor of Germany. An interesting and frightening group, all of these men shared Hitler's vast ambitions for Germany and the Aryan race.

Josef Goebbels (1897–1945)

Josef Goebbels (see Figure 2-6) joined the Nazi party in 1924 and served in the Reichstag in 1928. In 1930, he directed the propaganda effort that turned the national elections in the Nazis' favor between 1930 and 1933. After Hitler became Chancellor of Germany, Josef Goebbels was appointed Hitler's Minister of Propaganda and Public Information.

FIGURE 2-6:
Josef Goebbels.

Bettman/CORBIS.

Goebbels's propaganda was filled with hate, containing lies, character assassinations, and gross exaggerations. For Goebbels, no lie was too big, and no line of misinformation could be repeated often enough. As Minister of Propaganda, Goebbels had complete control of the German media and directed the effort to ensure that Nazi ideology dominated the nation's cultural activities.

Like Hitler, Goebbels hated Jews. He employed a constant barrage of propaganda to build a national hatred for Jews and to unify the country under an all-wise leader — the Führer — who would lead the nation to its destiny. During the war, he continued to produce effective propaganda aimed at sustaining German morale, while simultaneously attacking the Allies and Jews.

In the final days of the Third Reich, Goebbels and his wife killed themselves in their living quarters in the Führer bunker, after first ensuring that their six children were also killed.

Martin Bormann (1900–1945)

Martin Bormann climbed through the Nazi ranks from the *Sturmabteilung* (SA, for "Storm Troopers," the Nazi paramilitary force) to party treasurer to being elected eventually to the Reichstag, where he directed the office of Rudolf Hess, the Nazi party's deputy.

Bormann's administrative skills kept him at the center of activities within the government. During the war, he acted on behalf of Hitler in the administration of party affairs and also with activities related to administration of internal activities in Germany. Like everyone in the Nazi hierarchy, Bormann dealt with Jewish affairs. He supervised the deportation of the Jews to the east and used bureaucratic doublespeak to hide what was really happening. He also monitored forced labor efforts throughout Nazi-occupied Europe.

HITLER'S HENCHMEN

Here are just a few interesting facts about a few of the men in Hitler's powerful inner circle:

- Josef Goebbels, the man who created and used the Nazi propaganda machine to such chilling effect, held a doctorate in literature and philosophy. He also had a clubfoot, which ironically should have made him a member in one of the groups of people the Nazis targeted for elimination.

- Hermann Goering, who had been a commander of a flight squadron during the Great War, failed miserably in his role as commander of the *Luftwaffe*, the German airforce. Despite his promises to the contrary, he failed to bring Britain to its knees, he failed to resupply the German army in Stalingrad, and he failed to protect Germany from Allied air attack. Just before he died, Hitler stripped Goering of his authority and kicked him out of the Nazi party.

- Reinhard Heydrich had been discharged from the German navy in April 1931 for dishonorable conduct. Nothing in his subsequent occupation as head of the Gestapo would indicate that this dismissal had been unjust.

- Heinrich Himmler, the second most powerful man in Germany, had been a chicken farmer.

Of Hitler's henchmen, several (like Hitler) committed suicide: Goebbels, Goering, and Himmler. (Goebbels, family man that he was, made sure that his wife and children were dead first). One (Martin Bormann) disappeared. One (Reinhard Heydrich) was killed by resistance fighters. One (Rudolf Hess) spent the rest of his life in prison. And all of these men, directly or indirectly, had the blood of millions of innocent people on their hands.

In 1944, Bormann became commander of the *Volkssturm* (German for the "People's Army," essentially a militia of old men and boys), and he remained among the few loyalists gathered around Hitler in his last days in Berlin. In the last nightmarish final hours of the Third Reich, he watched Hitler marry Eva Braun and witnessed the Goebbels family suicide. After Hitler's suicide, Bormann (who was in the bunker when it happened) notified Admiral Karl Doenitz that Hitler had appointed him the new head of state. Bormann disappeared from the bunker and was never seen alive again. However, his remains were discovered and identified in West Berlin in 1973.

Hermann Goering (1893–1946)

Hermann Goering, shown in Figure 2-7, commanded a fighter squadron in World War I. In 1922, he joined the Nazi party and became the commander of the *Sturmabteilung* (SA). In November 1923, he was wounded in the confrontation with police that ended the Nazi putsch in Munich. Goering became a member of the Reichstag in 1928, and he was elected speaker in 1932.

FIGURE 2-7:
Hermann
Goering.

Bettman/CORBIS

When Hitler came to power, Goering held several important administrative positions within the government. He was one of the men responsible for the creation of the *Gestapo* (the Nazi secret police) and played a major role in the purge of the SA. In 1935, Goering became commander of the *Luftwaffe* (the German air force), and he was eventually given the rank of *Reichsmarschall*. He was later named as Hitler's successor.

In 1936, Goering directed the Four-Year Plan to restructure the German economy for full war production. This position gave him the authority to eliminate Jews from the German economy. He directed the confiscation of Jewish property and imposed a collective fine of 1 billion *Reich marks* (the basic monetary unit of Nazi Germany) on Jews. Goering also supervised the removal of Polish Jews from western Poland and the confiscation of their property.

On July 31, 1941, Goering ordered Reinhard Heydrich and his *Reich Security Main Office* (RSHA) to "carry out all necessary preparations with regard to the Jewish question in the German sphere of influence in Europe." This was the order that led to the planning and execution of the *Final Solution of the Jewish Question* — the extermination of Jews.

As leader of the *Luftwaffe*, Goering promised far too much and delivered far too little. Just before Hitler died, he stripped Goering of his authority, removed him from the Nazi party, and named Admiral Karl Doenitz as Goering's successor.

Goering was arrested by the Allies and stood trial as a war criminal at Nuremberg. Sentenced to death, he committed suicide in his cell prior to his execution.

Rudolf Hess (1894—1987)

Rudolf Hess served as an infantry officer and a pilot in World War I. In 1920, he was one of the first members of the Nazi party. When Hitler's putsch failed in 1923, Hess served a year in Landsberg prison with Hitler and helped him write *Mein Kampf* ("My Struggle," Hitler's autobiographical book). Hess's loyalty earned him the position of personal aide and private secretary to the Führer, and he rose to become the deputy leader of the party, second to Hitler.

In 1938, Hess played important roles in the *Anschluss* (German for "union"; see Chapter 3) with Austria and the negotiations that led to the occupation of the Sudetenland in Czechoslovakia. At the onset of the war in 1939, Hess became relegated to the background. In May 1941, convinced that he could personally intervene in diplomacy, Hess tried to obtain a peace agreement with Britain before Germany launched its attack on the Soviet Union. He flew to Britain, and he was arrested and detained for the rest of the war. At the Nuremberg trials in 1946, Hess was sentenced to life imprisonment. Hess remained in Spandau prison in West Berlin until his death in August 1987.

Reinhard Heydrich (1904–1942)

Reinhard Heydrich was the director of the intelligence service in the *Schutzstaffel* (SS) — German for "Protection Squad," or Hitler's bodyguards. In this capacity, he carried out the killings of the leaders of the *Sturmabteilung* (SA) in 1934.

In 1936, he was made chief of the *Gestapo* (the Nazi secret police) while also controlling the *Sicherheitsdienst* (SD) — the Nazi intelligence service. The SD's function was to uncover enemies of the Nazi party; the Gestapo was to deal with those enemies. Together, these organizations were the main instrument of terror in Nazi Germany.

After 1933, these two organizations became increasingly involved in activities directed against Jews, including intelligence gathering and arrests. After the invasion of Poland in 1939, Heydrich took control of the *Einsatzgruppen* (special groups) and charged them with assembling Polish Jews. He then unified the Gestapo and SD under an organization called the *Reich Security Main Office* (RSHA). This organization directed the deportation of Jews to ghettos, forced labor, or extermination camps.

Acting on Hitler's orders in 1941, Heydrich developed a plan to use the army to assist in killing Jews and Soviet leaders in the occupied areas of Russia. Heydrich soon took charge of implementing the *Final Solution of the Jewish Question* throughout all the territories under German occupation. This plan called for the extermination of Jews, Slavs, and other "undesirable" groups.

Czech resistance fighters near Prague ambushed Heydrich, and he died in June 1942. In retaliation, thousands of Czechs were arrested, and more than 1,300 were killed. German troops destroyed the Czech village of Lidice, executing every man found and sending the women and children to a concentration camp.

Heinrich Himmler (1900–1945)

Heinrich Himmler (see Figure 2-8) joined the Nazi party in Munich and participated in the 1923 Nazi putsch. In 1926, he became Assistant Propaganda Minister of the Nazi party. He joined the *Schutzstaffel* (SS) and in 1929, became the leader of the two-hundred-man detachment. Himmler was elected to the Reichstag in 1930, and with the rise of Hitler to power in January 1933, he expanded the SS and created the *Sicherheitsdienst* (SD) — the Nazi party intelligence service under Reinhard Heydrich — and separated his organization from Ernst Roehm's SA (short for *Sturmabteilung*, or "Storm Troopers"), which Hitler was already targeting for elimination. Within a few years, Himmler controlled all intelligence collection and police functions in Germany.

Himmler was a true believer in the Nazi racial ideology, and with his skills as an organizer, he was able to turn these evil dreams into reality. The Final Solution would allow the Aryan race to remain pure by eliminating what they considered to be inferior races, the weak, and the infirm.

Using the SS organization, Himmler supervised the deportation of millions of innocent people to their deaths in extermination camps or as slave laborers. He commanded 35 divisions of the best tank and mechanized units of the German army in the *Waffen SS* (elite combat units that fought alongside, but separate from, regular German army units). He also acted as the political governor of German-occupied Europe. With these dictatorial powers, Himmler became the second most powerful man in Germany.

FIGURE 2-8:
Heinrich Himmler.

CORBIS

Himmler read the writing on the wall in 1943, seeking to bargain with the Americans and British by releasing Jewish camp prisoners while at the same time attempting to cover up evidence of mass killings. His bizarre attempt to initiate peace negotiations — proposing that German forces cease fighting in the west in order to continue fighting the Soviets in the east — outraged Hitler. Removed from power, Himmler became a fugitive and was captured by British troops in May 1945. He committed suicide before he could be brought to trial.

Japan and the Militarists: The Army Calls the Shots

Pressed by poor economic conditions in the countryside and declining exports as a result of the depression, many Japanese blamed the government. And so, in Japan, as in Italy and Germany, parliamentary democracy gave way to nationalist and militarist control.

>> Patriotic organizations demanded that if Japan were to be strong and play a dominant role in the Far East, it needed to be militarily powerful and secure, with a people united in loyalty to the state. Western ideas were considered weak and dangerous to Japanese society.

> » The naval treaties that Japan had signed in the 1920s and revalidated in 1930 were criticized by these patriotic organizations, which believed that the government had placed Japan in an inferior position and limited her freedom of action in the Pacific. The navy also turned against the government.

> » The *ultra-nationalists,* with the tacit support of the military, initiated acts of violence against government leaders.

The militarists were also frustrated by government inaction. In Manchuria (a strategically important province in China), the Japanese Kwangtung Army became increasingly impatient with what they saw was their government's unwillingness to settle the Manchurian issue. The army command had engineered the murder of a Manchurian warlord in 1928 as a pretext for an order from the government to conquer the province, but the Japanese leadership in Tokyo made no effort to take advantage of the incident.

The military acts

By 1931, with the government beset by nationalists, the Kwangtung army took action to rally public opinion and unite the nation in the pursuit of a long-held goal: the conquest of China.

In September of that year, Japanese troops responded to a carefully staged incident that appeared to be a Chinese attack on the railway near the Manchurian city of Mukden. Without waiting for orders, the Kwangtung army began combat operations against Chinese forces with the goal of capturing all of Manchuria. Japanese reinforcements arrived, and by the end of the year, Manchuria was in Japanese hands and renamed Manchukuo.

In 1932, Japanese forces were fighting in Shanghai and bombarding Nanking (both cities located in today's Jiangsu province in China).

In Japan, political leaders who opposed the unconstitutional acts of the military were assassinated or intimidated, culminating in an attempted coup against the government by ultra-nationalists in 1936.

The fall of Japanese democracy

The Japanese political parties had little respect among the population, and the concept of popular will reflected in parliamentary elections was never fully instituted in Japanese society. Thus, larger issues of public policy became subject to the group that claimed to speak for Emperor Hirohito.

Unlike in Italy and Germany, in Japan, no single leader emerged to harness and take advantage of this situation. Instead, military officers of all ranks formed conspiracies to forcibly eliminate democracy and restore the connection between the Emperor and his people. The army and navy, with direct access to the Emperor, now determined the makeup of the government, advocating a policy of external expansion and economic preparations for war.

During this time, military spending helped rebuild the slumping economy. Manchuria was integrated into the program, providing raw materials — such as coal, timber, and iron ore — to Japan. And Japanese society became highly regimented, turning back to an older example of duty and subordination to the state that had been the centerpiece of Japanese life for years prior to World War I.

Japan takes control of China

With solid public support for the army's actions in China, and emboldened by the strong nationalist sentiments expressed by the military leadership, the Japanese army between 1933 and 1937 drove into northern China and occupied large areas of the Chinese-Soviet border. In 1937, after a clash between Chinese and Japanese forces at the Marco Polo Bridge near Beijing, China, Japan initiated a full-scale war to conquer China. Over 150,000 Japanese troops were fighting in China by September; Beijing had fallen, and Shanghai was again under attack. Japanese forces began an offensive toward Nanking, the Chinese Nationalist capital.

Chiang Kai-shek had made important improvements in modernizing China between 1928 and 1927, but the war with Japan ended any further reform. Chiang did not have the forces to resist the Japanese effectively, but a truce with the Communist Chinese allowed the Chinese to unite to face a common foe. The truce allowed the Communists to preserve their enclaves and survive as a force to be reckoned with.

By 1939, after three years of open war, Japan had taken control of the most productive and populous areas of China. But contrary to Japan's expectations, Chiang showed no intention of surrendering and continued to fight on.

Chapter **3**

Hoping for Peace: The Rise of the Dictators, 1933–1939

Throughout the 1930s, Germany pursued Hitler's goals — the conquest of the lands east of Germany and the neutralization of Germany's traditional enemy, France. Hitler believed that by achieving these objectives, the German-speaking peoples would be unified into a single empire, which would allow Hitler's perceived Master Race to dominate Europe, as he believed it was destined to do. War was the only means to accomplish such a grandiose scheme. Therefore, Hitler needed to rearm the German nation and select the best approach for war (or series of wars) that would enable Germany to conquer Europe.

Great Britain and France, in the meantime, were attempting to find diplomatic solutions to numerous problems in Europe while dealing with domestic economic, political, and social problems. Because national consensus on foreign policy was hard to achieve, they trusted in the League of Nations (see Chapter 2), avoided rearmament, and embraced appeasement (giving in to demands in the hopes of avoiding war) to maintain peace.

In Europe, the French stood alone on the continent facing Hitler. Great Britain made it clear that it would only support France if Germany attacked directly. Because France's military and industrial capacity was limited in comparison to Germany's, French strategists believed that a full national mobilization would have to take place before they could use any type of military action against Germany. As a result, France was limited to diplomacy in response to Germany's actions. As long as Britain's national interests were not threatened, it maintained a hands-off policy in Europe. After Hitler understood this situation, the path to his objectives was open for him to exploit.

The Steps to War: Taking Advantage of Circumstances

Hitler definitely wanted to wage war. However, he also knew that to pursue his objectives and to create a war, he would need to use diplomacy — or the perception of diplomacy — to get there.

Hitler could not just launch a war against Europe (although he earnestly wanted to). He had to prepare Germany economically and psychologically, and he had to take steps diplomatically to establish the rationale for war. Broadly speaking, here's what he had to do within Germany:

>> Organize the German economy for war

>> Build unity among the German people

>> Build an army, navy, and air force

Here is what he had to do internationally:

>> Nullify the Treaty of Versailles

>> Return lost German territory to Germany

>> Build a super-state of all ethnic Germans

Rebuilding the army

Almost as soon as he became Chancellor of Germany, Hitler began to rebuild German military forces. During a League of Nations disarmament conference, Germany announced that it was going to increase the size of its army to

600,000 men. Claiming that because the French and British were not disarming to Germany's level as laid out in the Versailles Treaty (the Treaty of Versailles had limited the German army to 100,000 men, as explained in Chapter 2), Germany would rearm to levels equal to those of France and Britain.

Buying time

Hitler had secretly established a National Defense Council to oversee Germany's rearmament process. The retooling of German industry for war production took time, so Hitler had to buy time with reassuring actions. Thus, when Italian dictator Benito Mussolini proposed that France, Britain, Italy, and Germany sign a treaty of goodwill, Hitler jumped at the chance. The Four-Power Treaty of April 1933 did nothing more than pledge each power to consult with the others as specified in the League of Nations covenant. But by October, Germany had withdrawn from the League. (Hitler claimed that over 95 percent of voters approved of the action when the issue was put before them. Whether accurate or not, this symbolic finger in the eye of Germany's former enemies signaled a new diplomatic direction for Germany. Moreover, the tepid response of France and Britain to this action only added to Germany's national satisfaction.)

Forging an agreement with Poland

In January 1934, Hitler took everyone by surprise by signing a non-aggression pact with Poland. In this pact, Germany essentially renounced claims to German territory that had been taken to create Poland (as part of the Versailles Treaty). While he had no intention of honoring such a pledge, this treaty accomplished the following for Hitler:

>> **It further isolated France diplomatically.** France had a defensive alliance with Poland that was meant to threaten Germany on two fronts in case of war. (That is, if Germany attacked Poland, it would find itself in a war on its eastern border with Poland and on its western border with France.) But Hitler negated the threat and revealed the Poles to be less than confident of France's guarantees.

>> **It lulled Europe into a sense of false security.** Hitler's often strident rhetoric frightened many in Europe, but his actions made his words sound like so much empty rhetoric. This was all part of Hitler's intent. His words were true; he was seeking political advantage diplomatically. For every threatening act, Hitler would do something non-threatening to offset that action.

Reclaiming the Saar

In the spring of 1935, Hitler took another step that enhanced his prestige in Germany and around the world: He engineered a *plebiscite* (a vote in which the people express their will on an issue put before them) in the Saar Basin. The Saar Basin, a rich coal-mining region located in the valley of the Saar River, had been taken from Germany and placed under France's control as part of the Versailles Treaty.

This plebiscite gave legal weight to Germany's claim that the Saar should once again belong to Germany. The open election was supervised by the League of Nations, and it allowed the people of the Saar to decide whether they wanted to be returned to Germany. Hitler's extraordinary propaganda efforts ensured a victory for the Nazis (*National Socialist German Workers' Party*).

Breaking treaties

Soon after the Saar plebiscite, Hitler announced that Germany would resume *conscription* (drafting civilians into military service). He also revealed that Germany had a new air force called the *Luftwaffe*. These announcements marked the repudiation of the Versailles Treaty that had limited Germany's armed forces to almost nothing. It also ended the *Locarno Treaty* of 1925 in which Germany and France pledged to respect each other's borders as well as those of Belgium. Britain and Italy had also signed this treaty, pledging to come to the aid of any nation attacked by a participant of the treaty. Italy joined with Britain, France, and the rest of the League of Nations in condemning Germany's new actions — but nothing was done.

Advancing into the Rhineland

Hitler had further plans to dismantle the Versailles Treaty. Knowing that France would not resist with anything but protests and requests for League sanctions, Hitler ordered an advance of lightly armed troops into the Rhineland, a German territory that had been given to France in the Versailles settlement.

The Rhineland had been one of the main guarantees of security for France under the Versailles Treaty. The area served as a buffer, keeping German troops away from the French border. Hitler claimed that all he was doing was righting a wrong done to Germany. His reoccupation of the Rhineland appeared to be a reasonable action, and he gained strong support from German citizens, who saw the loss of the Rhineland as a national humiliation.

As expected, Britain did not see any national interests involved in the Rhineland issue, so it stood aside.

Hitler had been willing to fight for the Rhineland, but the empty actions of France and Britain only helped bolster his claim among the international community. In the next two years, Germany promptly began fortifying the new border between Germany and France, creating what came to be known as the *West Wall*.

Getting Aggressive: Italy Makes a War

In the early 1930s, Fascist Italy served as a partner of the French and British to counterbalance Germany, but Mussolini harbored ambitions far different from those of the democracies. Mussolini thirsted for war. To Mussolini, war was a sign of a nation's vitality and a chance to prove Italy's special destiny under Fascist rule. To that end, he consolidated the ministries of the army, navy, and air force under his personal control, and in October 1935, he invaded Ethiopia.

At the time, Ethiopia was a large African nation bordering the Italian possessions of Eritrea and Somalia. Although Italy and Ethiopia had signed a treaty of friendship in 1928, Mussolini saw Ethiopia as a potential colony and an easy target. Possessing Ethiopia would bring prestige to Italy while setting the stage for regional dominance in Africa.

With 650,000 men, in addition to modern airplanes, tanks, and poison gas, Mussolini set out to conquer the primitively armed Ethiopians, who were led by Emperor Haile Selassie. Despite initial success, the Italian conquest bogged down. Selassie addressed the League of Nations in a moving appeal for assistance. The League decided to impose economic sanctions on Italy but refused to impose sanctions on oil — the one product that may have crippled Italy's war effort.

After a year of often frustrating military operations, Mussolini captured the city of Addis Ababa and declared Ethiopia a part of the Italian empire. King Victor Emanuel III was declared Emperor of Ethiopia.

Mussolini had defied the League, ignored ineffectual sanctions, and accomplished his objective, a fact that Fascist propaganda trumpeted incessantly. The people of Ethiopia suffered extensive terror and brutality as the Fascists imposed their authority over the new colony.

THE HITLER-MUSSOLINI PARTNERSHIP

When Hitler first took power in Germany in 1933, he sent a personal message to Mussolini expressing his desire for closer relations with Italy. Hitler admired Mussolini, even keeping a picture of *Il Duce* (see Chapter 2) on his desk for inspiration. The two dictators first met in Venice in 1934. Mussolini, who was seen as the senior statesman, overshadowed Hitler. Mussolini had tried to read *Mein Kampf* (see Chapter 2) but found it too boring and never finished it.

Mussolini treated Hitler with a mixture of caution and condescension, providing advice on consolidating his power while distancing himself from Hitler's obsession on race. Naturally, the Italians were not included as part of the Aryan "Master Race;" nor were they interested in Hitler's focus on Jews as a threat to European life. Hitler's anti-Catholicism was also unnerving to Italians, who were predominately of the Roman Catholic faith. Observing his actions and speeches, Mussolini sometimes suspected that Hitler was a madman. And although Hitler admired the Fascists and believed that they were useful to his goals, he thought that they misunderstood exactly what Germany was seeking to accomplish in Europe. It appeared that Hitler was right. In a few short years, the German-Italian relationship changed dramatically. Mussolini, not Hitler, became the junior partner.

Forging a Pact: The Axis Is Born

ARMY
ALLIED

Shortly after taking the Rhineland in 1936, Mussolini and Hitler signed a pact called the *Rome–Berlin Axis*. The use of the word *axis* implied that the world would center around this new relationship.

This agreement signaled a shift in Italy's allegiance. Until 1936, Italy had followed a foreign policy that sided with France and was generally hostile to Nazi Germany. Mussolini had feared German ambitions regarding Austria, believing that these ambitions conflicted with Italy's own territorial interests in that region.

The Italian assault on Ethiopia, however, brought economic sanctions from the League of Nations, including France, a nation with which Italy had traditionally been friendly. As a result, Mussolini began to rethink his position. Because German supplies helped Italy ignore the sanctions, Mussolini signaled that he was willing to work more closely with Germany.

Hitler indicated that he would go to war with the West in three to four years and that his interests were in Eastern and Northern Europe. In other words, Hitler indicated that Mussolini could have free reign in the Mediterranean. In turn, Mussolini told Hitler that he would recognize Germany's dominant interests in Austria.

The Spanish Civil War: Fascism and Communism Clash

The Spanish Republican government, made up of Socialists, fought a civil war from 1936 to 1939 to retain power against the rebellion of Spanish Nationalist forces led by General Francisco Franco, who refused to accept control by the left-ists. This civil war essentially became a war between Fascism and Socialism, and other nations became involved:

>> The Soviet Union, a communist nation, sent assistance and support to the Republicans (in this case, the Socialists). It helped organize armed volunteer units from Europe and the United States to battle the Fascists.

>> Mussolini sent over 70,000 troops (which he called volunteers) to aid the Fascist side (the Spanish Nationalists and Franco).

>> The Nazis sent advisors as well as the latest tanks and combat aircraft to the Fascists.

>> France and Britain stood by in this conflict, attempting half-heartedly to prevent either the Fascist or the Socialist side from importing weapons. (Italy, Germany, and the Soviet Union all claimed to support the embargo, even though their support to the warring factions was an open secret.)

PLAYING POLITICS AND KEEPING UP APPEARANCES

A year after the Rome-Berlin Axis agreement, Mussolini visited Hitler and was captivated by the carefully staged displays of German prosperity and power, including an address by Mussolini to what was billed as an audience of 1 million Germans. Mussolini was flat-tered to believe that he was the senior partner in the Axis and returned to Rome with his head filled with promises and praise for the excellent combat readiness of the Italian army. In reality, German staff officers had visited the Italian army and assessed its com-bat readiness, and they reported back to Hitler that the Italians would make better ene-mies than allies.

With Italian and German assistance, Franco defeated the Republicans and set up his own fascist-style military dictatorship.

The battle between Fascism and Communism as displayed in the Spanish Civil War led many to believe that it was only a matter of time before such a struggle between these two ideologies broke out in Europe.

HISTORICAL TRIVIA

The bombing of Guernica (a town in the Vizcaya Province in Spain) in April 1937 attracted worldwide attention; it was immortalized by the famous modernist depiction *Guernica* (1937) by artist Pablo Picasso.

Germany: Using Diplomacy and Smoke Screens for War

After 1936, Hitler had every intention of taking Germany to war, which was the only way he could accomplish his goal. Germany needed to acquire *Lebensraum* ("living space") to feed its population and allow it to expand. The land that Germany needed was in Eastern Europe and Russia. Hitler charged that the "inferior" Slavic population was to be driven off the land so that the Aryan Germans could populate it. Hitler believed that this process of expansion and displacement of what he considered racial inferiors was unending and would continue until only the "Master Race" occupied the world. Thus, war with the key nations of Eastern Europe — Poland, Czechoslovakia, and the Soviet Union — was inevitable. However, Hitler needed to eliminate France and Britain to secure his drive to the east. Following are a couple of things that made Hitler's goal easier to achieve:

» France, Britain, and the Soviet Union used diplomacy to ensure peace and stability. Germany, on the other hand, used diplomacy as a screen for initiating a war at the time and place of Hitler's choosing.

» While other nations in Europe focused on the Depression and neglected their defense programs (being heavily pacifist), Hitler initiated a huge military buildup, producing modern tanks, warships, and aircraft in an effort to build the most capable force possible.

By gaining additional time to gear up Germany's industry for war and to equip a modern army, air force, and navy, Hitler believed that he could defeat any opponent before it reached full war production. Thus, he adopted a Four-Year Plan in 1936 to reorganize German industry so that Germany could be self-sufficient during wartime.

Britain: Seeking Mediation and Appeasement

Because of its worldwide interests as an imperial power, Britain had to be concerned with German threats not only in Europe, but in Asia as well. Still Britain made no effort to rebuild its defenses in the face of the trouble brewing in Europe until late 1936. Even then, it wasn't enough:

>> **The British allocated too little money.** Lacking sufficient funding for new equipment or training, the British army and navy continued to deteriorate throughout the 1930s. This meant that in case of war, Britain's navy — once the envy of the world — could not protect its own empire and that its army was insufficient to provide any significant support to France in case of a German attack.

>> **The British made the wrong spending decisions for the money that it did allocate.** Instead of building fighter aircraft to defend the skies over Britain, for example, Britain spent money to build bombers in the mistaken belief that offensive bombers would be a deterrent to Germany.

There was no doubt that any kind of war would bring Britain into the conflict, but France refused to take action on the continent without guarantees of British support in the form of ground forces in France. Because of this and the state of its military, Britain adopted a policy of mediation and appeasement to protect British interests and defuse crises:

>> Britain would act as the mediator between France and Germany to prevent war on the continent and thus keep Britain from having to provide forces if France were attacked.

>> Appeasement was a conscious policy to remove the causes of conflict by giving Hitler what he wanted in return for guarantees that Germany would not threaten the status quo in Europe.

A SIGN OF THINGS TO COME

Hitler decided to use the Spanish Civil War to test out his new equipment and tactics in actual combat. One hundred German aircraft were organized into a unit called the *Condor Legion*. The Condor Legion not only supported Nationalist ground attacks but also bombed villages only to terrorize the population. This new method of warfare shocked the world.

Austria and Czechoslovakia Catch Hitler's Eye

In the spring of 1938, Hitler assumed control of the German armed forces and placed the German General Staff under the direction of his new headquarters, the *Oberkommando der Wehrmacht* (German for the "High Command of the Armed Forces"). At this point, he was ready to begin his move against Eastern Europe: specifically, he had his sights set on Austria and Czechoslovakia. As he had before, Hitler again used propaganda and false diplomacy to achieve his goals.

The Anschluss in Austria

In 1938, Germany began a barrage of intense propaganda in Austria and throughout Europe that did the following:

» Detailed outrageous stories of arrests and horrible murders of pro-Nazi Austrians (whose numbers seemed to grow larger every time that they were mentioned).

» Proclaimed Austria as a German state and part of the larger Germany. The word heard over and over was *Anschluss* (German for "union") But *Anschluss* had larger political overtones. It implied a natural affinity or bond between German-speaking peoples. Hitler intended this bond to be formalized into a union, both ethnically and politically. In other words, he considered Austrians brothers in the Master Race. As such, Austria and Germany must unite — whether Austria wanted to or not.

CHURCHILL'S WARNINGS — 1936 AND 1938

Winston Churchill, a member of British Parliament and a prominent member of the British government for many years, often warned his countrymen of the danger Germany represented to Britain and Europe. In 1936, with the German remilitarization of the Rhineland, Churchill spoke out: "I ask that a state of emergency preparation should be proclaimed, and that the whole spirit and atmosphere of rearmament should be raised to a higher pitch." After the *Anschluss* (German expansion) in 1938, Churchill again sounded the alarm: "Europe is confronted with a program of aggression, nicely calculated and timed, unfolding stage by stage, and there is only one choice — either submit, like Austria, or take effective measures while time remains."

In February 1938, Hitler and Austrian Chancellor Kurt von Schuschnigg met. During this meeting, Hitler went into a tirade. "I have a historic mission, and I am going to fulfill it because Providence has appointed me to do so," he told Schuschnigg. The Nazi strong-arm tactics combined with the thinly veiled threat of an invasion were clearly intended to intimidate the Austrians.

In March, Schuschnigg tried to preserve Austrian independence by holding a national plebiscite to determine whether citizens wanted to be part of a greater Germany or remain independent. This move took Hitler by surprise — the results of a plebiscite would clearly not be in favor of *Anschluss*. So, the day before the vote was to be held, Hitler sent the German army across the border into Austria. The army met no resistance, and Hitler himself was welcomed as a hero when he arrived in Austria.

Hitler justified the intervention by proclaiming that Germany acted in defense of democratic principles and had come as a liberator. The scheduled plebiscite was rigged, he declared, with false ballots and improper counting methods. To make sure there was no chance to contradict Hitler's version of events, the Germans declared the *Anschluss* within 24 hours and held a truly rigged plebiscite in favor of the German invasion.

Behind all the noise of triumph and justification, Nazi secret police units arrested dissidents; Jews were subjected to brutal mistreatment, and Kurt von Schuschnigg, the former Chancellor of an independent Austria, was sent off to a concentration camp.

Onward to Czechoslovakia

Following his triumph in Austria (see the preceding section), Hitler turned his attention eastward to Czechoslovakia. One of the few nations in Europe to have preserved its democratic institutions, Czechoslovakia also had approximately 3 million Germans in the Sudetenland, a mountainous region that bordered Germany. Hitler demanded that the Czech government give the Sudetenland back to Germany. His argument was boringly familiar: The Sudeten Germans belonged to Greater Germany; they were being persecuted; the Czechs were committing atrocities against the German minority; Germany demanded that self-determination of people be respected. With Hitler's demands came the not so-subtle threat of military action.

Czechoslovakia stood firm in the face of Hitler's threat of invasion. It had a security guarantee from France and the Soviet Union. If the Czechs were attacked, both nations were obliged to go to war against the aggressor. And any French military action would almost certainly include Great Britain as well. The political situation appeared to be in Czechoslovakia's favor, but it wasn't.

COULDN'T WE HAVE HAD A CLASS REUNION INSTEAD?

The *Anschluss* was a moment of personal triumph for Hitler. He had been born in Austria (no, he was not a German!). He had never achieved success and in fact had spent the years before World War I as a homeless bum. He moved to Germany and joined the German army when the war broke out. Now he returned to his homeland as the leader of a great and powerful nation.

The French can't help

If the Czechs assumed that Germany would be scared off by the Franco-British alliance, they were in for a shock. Neither the Germans nor the Italians were afraid of either nation. France and Britain had neither the means nor the will to assert their interests. The effective defense of the Czechs depended on France, yet France was trapped in a web that bound it to inactivity for the following reasons:

>> France couldn't assist Czechoslovakia directly; it would have to attack Germany. This meant full mobilization and preparation for total war, something that France wasn't willing to do.

>> France would take no action against Germany without British guarantees of assistance and ground forces on the continent. In other words, if Britain wouldn't commit to help the French, the French wouldn't commit to help Czechoslovakia.

>> The Czech alliance with the Soviets was conditional: If attacked, the Czechs could expect Soviet military assistance *if* — and this was a big *if* — France moved forces first. But the French wouldn't move without the British.

>> The Soviets' guarantee to the Czechs was worthless. Even if France committed forces against Germany, neither Rumania nor Poland would allow Soviet troops to transit their countries to reach Czechoslovakia.

The British won't help

The other major figure in the crisis was the British Prime Minister Neville Chamberlain. He was confident that he understood conditions in Europe and believed that peace would be determined by friendly discussions between France, Britain, Italy, and Germany. These discussions, he thought, would resolve differences and preserve peace.

Chamberlain rejected offers of assistance from the U.S., believing it to be unreliable, and from the Soviet Union, which he considered to be untrustworthy. He believed that any type of broad combination of powers was provocative and would actually help start a war rather than deter it. And to Chamberlain, nothing was worse than war; the experience of the Great War (World War I) was proof that no one won in war. Thus, he was willing to offer Germany anything to preserve peace, which he believed was achieving the greater good, even if certain parts of Europe were lost to Nazi control.

REMEMBER

Interestingly enough, Hitler actually wanted war with Britain and France. Although German propaganda proclaimed that Hitler was willing to negotiate, he never had any intention of doing so. Hitler believed that the time for war was now, and if Britain and France honored their guarantees to the Czechs, so much the better. He was looking for an excuse to eliminate his enemies in the west so he could begin his crusade to cleanse the east of Slavs, Jews, and Bolsheviks and give the German *Volk* their *Lebensraum*. He gave orders to the armed forces to prepare for the invasion of Czechoslovakia no later than October 1938.

Czechoslovakia betrayed

As the crisis deepened, the Czechs refused to surrender the Sudetenland and began to mobilize their armed forces. They resolved to make Hitler fight, and they were confident that France and Britain would fight with them.

But as the pressure on Czechoslovakia mounted, Chamberlain decided to meet personally with Hitler to prevent a war. Hitler assured Chamberlain of the following:

>> He had no other territorial interests in Czechoslovakia except the Sudetenland.

>> He also said that he was willing to risk a world war to settle the issue, but he would not order any military operations until he had a chance to consult with the French and his own government.

"In spite of the hardness and ruthlessness I thought I saw in his face," Chamberlain reported, "I got the impression that here was a man who could be relied upon when he had given his word." Chamberlain came from the meetings confident that he and Hitler had come to an agreement and that Hitler's word could be trusted. So Chamberlain spread the word to the French:

>> Chamberlain informed the French that Hitler only wanted the Sudetenland. The Czechs would have to be convinced to give up the territory in the interests of peace.

>> France could not take unilateral action against Germany — not without British support — and Britain would not fight for Czechoslovakia.

As a result of their discussions, Britain and France informed the Czechs to give in to German demands. If they fought, they would do so alone. Thus, the Czech government gave in, humiliated and angered at the betrayal.

May I have more, please?

The crisis, however, was not over. Hitler presented another series of demands to Chamberlain, including territorial concessions from Czechoslovakia to Poland and Hungary and threatened military action. Confused and angered, Chamberlain ended negotiations and informed the Czechs that France and Britain would stand by them if the Germans attacked. Hitler was informed of this decision, and public sentiment — not only in Germany but also around the world — supported Chamberlain's personal diplomacy efforts. Hitler's own advisors were cautioning against war, and Italy was unwilling to commit itself. Thus, Hitler decided to wait and allow the charade of negotiations to continue.

On September 29, 1938, Mussolini, Hitler, Chamberlain, and Edouard Daladier (the Prime Minister of France) met in Munich, Germany, to decide the fate of Czechoslovakia. Two prominent representatives — the Czechs and the Soviets — were not invited. After more than 12 straight hours of discussions, the four leaders signed an agreement on the future of Czechoslovakia. In the absence of anyone representing Czechoslovakia or the Soviet Union, the terms were as follows:

» German troops would enter and occupy the Sudetenland between October 1 and 10. This effectively would make this piece of Czechoslovakia German territory.

» Polish and Hungarian territorial claims would be considered within 90 days. Poland and Hungary had also lost territory to Czechoslovakia in the Versailles Treaty. This is a case of the buzzards coming to roost on the carcass.

» France and Britain would guarantee the borders of the new Czechoslovakia.

The Czechs were notified to accept the agreement or fight Germany alone. The Czechs responded simply, "We were deserted." Chamberlain held a private meeting with Hitler and produced a pledge that the Führer promptly signed. It stated that Germany and Britain would pledge never to go to war against each other and that they would consult to settle all differences and maintain peace in Europe.

The diplomats — Did they do their job?

Today, we view these negotiations with a mixture of horror and disdain. But how did folks at the time view them? The Czechs, of course, were justifiably bitter. What about the others? Here's a quick rundown.

Mussolini: Returning to a nation of lambs, not lions

Mussolini returned home convinced that Italy was a major power in Europe and that France and Britain were easily intimidated by the threat of force. He received a rapturous welcome, but the enthusiasm of the crowds troubled him. They clearly were expressing relief that there would be no war. It appeared that Mussolini's strenuous efforts to build a warlike mindset in the populace and a love of war failed, and he took this as the sign that a great people had failed.

Hitler: Staying coiled in the grass and hissing

Hitler believed that he had failed. His goal was war and the destruction of Czechoslovakia. What he got was a half measure. He would have to finish off the Czechs later, but he needed to ensure that there would be no more repeats of the Munich negotiations. Hitler also saw that the one roadblock to his ambitions was Britain. Germany would have to defeat the English before it could turn on the Soviet Union in its quest for land to settle the expanding German *Volk*. So Hitler did the following:

>> He subjected German citizens to a barrage of propaganda to prepare them for war, propaganda that was markedly different from earlier messages that depicted the Germans as peace-loving people.

>> He increased armaments production, especially in combat aircraft, in order to prepare for an attack on Britain.

Daladier: A welcome fit for a hero

A morose Daladier returned home to France, fully expecting the vast crowd that was waiting for him at the Paris airport to attack him for betraying the Czechs. Instead, he found himself cheered as a hero.

Chamberlain: Driving on the road to irony

Likewise, when Chamberlain landed outside of London and drove into the city, he found the streets lined with people, cheering his name, climbing on the side of the car, and thrusting their hands through the windows to shake his hand. At 10 Downing Street, the Prime Minister's residence, Chamberlain addressed a huge crowd. Brandishing the paper that Hitler had signed, Chamberlain announced, "I believe it is peace in our time" (see Figure 3-1). The image of Chamberlain saying those words is perhaps the most indelible symbol of irony and futility that exists in the history of the twentieth century.

FIGURE 3-1: British Prime Minister Neville Chamberlain proclaims, "Peace in our time."

Central Press/Getty Images

2

Starting the War: The Axis Invades and Conquers, 1939–1942

See how Germany unleashed what seemed like an unbeatable new type of warfare on Europe.

Examine why Stalin ignored all the warnings of a German attack.

Understand how Hitler's strategic decisions were driven by his pursuit of a greater Germany.

Discover how the Japanese took on their attempted conquest of China.

Get a glimpse of Japan's calculations for dealing with this diplomatic problem.

Find out how this war became a true global conflict and how close the Axis powers came to winning the war.

Chapter **4**

Invading Eastern Europe: Hitler's Power Grows, 1939

At the close of the Munich meeting in 1938, in which Hitler, Neville Chamberlain, Benito Mussolini, and Edouard Daladier met to decide the fate of the Sudetenland (the part of Czechoslovakia that had a large German-speaking population), the French and British participants believed that they had averted war. Many in their countries thought so, too, and welcomed them home as heroes. But the goodwill that had been created during the Munich talks was shattered when Germany overran what remained of Czechoslovakia and then set its sights on Poland.

In the months between March and September 1939, Hitler made no secret of the fact that he *wanted* to bring war to Europe. So despite their attempts to avoid war, Britain and France were forced to accept the truth: In the face of Germany's aggression, they had to take action, even if it meant war. But unlike Germany — whose industry was geared up for war, whose population was mobilized, and whose forces were already well trained, combat-ready, and deployed — Britain and France weren't prepared in any way for war. So, although the cause of the Allies was undoubtedly right, the timing was undoubtedly bad.

Czechoslovakia Disappears: Divvying Land and German Occupation

In March 1939, despite his earlier claim that he only wanted the Sudetenland, Hitler gave the Czechs an ultimatum and then sent troops to occupy Prague. Having been betrayed by Britain and France with the Munich agreement, the Czechs' will to resist was crushed. They gave in, and Czechoslovakia was incorporated into Greater Germany. With Germany's approval, Hungarian troops, backed by the Poles, seized other portions of Czech territory (see Figure 4-1), and Czechoslovakia disappeared as a nation. The people of Czechoslovakia fell under the shadow of Nazi tyranny: Nazi secret police (see Chapter 3) rounded up thousands of suspects who could oppose Hitler, and Jews were subjected to hateful abuse.

Legend:
- March 1936, Rhineland
- March 1938, Austria annexed
- October 1938, Czechoslovak frontier regions (Sudetenland) annexed
- March 1939, Memeland from Lithuania
- March 1939, annexation of Bohemia and Moravia
- September 1939, German occupation of Poland

FIGURE 4-1: German aggression in Europe.

Chamberlain and Daladier wise up

Hitler's plans were clear, and Neville Chamberlain and Eduoard Daladier, despite their hopes that he could be reasoned with and appeased, were forced to confront the truth: War was the only way to stop Hitler. They believed — and rightly — that if they didn't stop Hitler now, he would go on making demands, devouring nations, and growing stronger until, finally, France and Britain would be threatened into submission or a war they couldn't win. So, less than two weeks after the fall of Czechoslovakia, Chamberlain and Daladier issued a guarantee for Poland, promising to come to its aid if Germany invaded.

Why wasn't I informed?! — Mussolini in the dark

The elimination of Czechoslovakia took Mussolini by surprise. Hitler apparently didn't think consulting with his junior partner — the man who ostensibly had brokered the Munich agreement that had allowed Germany to obtain the Sudetenland — was important. Humiliated and angry, Mussolini decided to flex his muscle by making his own territorial demands.

I'll take Albania for a thousand, Alex

Mussolini had been looking for opportunities to raise Italian morale, and his attention turned to Albania, a tiny nation that was virtually an Italian colony. At the end of March, Mussolini ordered a combined ground, naval, and air force attack to invade and occupy Albania.

The operation was a fiasco, marked by incomplete planning, incoordination, and massive confusion. "If only the Albanians had possessed a well-armed fire brigade, they could have driven us back into the Adriatic," observed the assistant to the Italian Foreign Minister. Mussolini covered up his military's ineptitude with propaganda that praised his bold action and declared the invasion to be a masterpiece of planning. Britain responded to the invasion with declarations of security guarantees to Greece and Turkey.

One bad idea follows another

Mussolini completely ignored the dangers to Italy posed by the security guarantees from Britain and France. Instead, buoyed by the good press (which he had orchestrated) and the rise in Italian national pride, he followed up the Albanian invasion with a formal alliance with Germany, called the *Pact of Steel*, in May, 1939. In this pact, Italy agreed to go to war in support of Germany, regardless of whether

Germany started the war or not. Even though Italy had stressed to Germany that it would not be ready for war for three more years, the treaty held no mention of this fact.

The Pact of Steel existed mostly for propaganda purposes and was meant to intimidate potential enemies. But the rest of the world saw the joining of Europe's two fascist states as a clear signal that a war of aggression was looming.

Playing Both Sides of the Fence: Negotiations with the Soviets

After the collapse of the Munich agreement, France and Britain realized that spurning the Soviet Union's offer of assistance to defend Czechoslovakia had been a mistake. Consequently, the French and British opened negotiations to make an alliance with the Soviets. At the same time, the Soviets initiated talks with Germany for a possible broad political agreement aimed against France and Britain. In a display of sincerity to the Nazis, Maxim Litvinov, the Soviet Commissar of Foreign Affairs and a Jew, was replaced with Vyacheslav Molotov.

Talks with Britain and France

In their talks with Britain and France, the Soviets insisted on a two things:

>> That the Baltic states (Lithuania, Latvia, and Estonia) be protected from German attack. The only way to guarantee that the Germans would not attack the Baltic States, however, was for the Soviet Union to occupy these states with military forces.

>> That the Soviet forces be allowed to travel through Poland and Romania in case of war. (Poland and Romania wouldn't allow the Soviet Army — also called the *Red Army* — to cross through their borders because they feared that once there, the Soviet Army wouldn't leave.)

The talks continued through August, but France and Britain, who didn't much cotton to the idea of the Soviet military moving westward into Europe, wouldn't agree to the Soviet terms and didn't think it possible to find common ground on which to build an alliance. In fact, Josef Stalin, the dictator of the Soviet Union (see Figure 4-2), had already made his decision to sign a pact with Germany while he was still holding meetings with French and British representatives.

FIGURE 4-2:
Josef Stalin,
Soviet Union.

Bettmann/Getty Images

Talks with Germany: The Nazi-Soviet pact

While the Soviet Union was holding talks with Britain and France, Soviet ground troops were fighting the Japanese along the Chinese-Soviet border, increasing fears that the Soviet Union could soon find itself involved in a two front-war — fighting Germany in the west and Japan in the east. This fear drove the Soviets to reach some agreement with Hitler. For his part, Hitler didn't like the idea of a two front war, either. He didn't want to have to fight the Soviets in the east while he fought France and Britain in the west. So Nazi Germany and Communist Russia, two countries who had spent years spewing venomous ideological propaganda at each other, now decided that such ideological differences weren't important.

On August 23, the *Nazi-Soviet Non-Aggression pact* was signed in Moscow. Following are the main points of the pact:

>> The Soviets would get to occupy and control Finland and the Baltic States (except Lithuania); the Germans would get a larger share of Poland. (A secret agreement specified how Germany and the Soviet Union would divvy Poland up after Germany invaded it.)

>> Germany would ship finished machinery to the Soviet Union, and the Soviet Union would ship food and raw materials to Germany.

STALIN: THE MAN OF STEEL AND THE SOVIET UNION

Iosif (Josef) Vissarionovich Dzhugashvili (1879–1953) was born in Gori, Georgia. He later changed his last name to Stalin, meaning "man of steel." Although he initially intended to study for the priesthood, he joined the revolutionary Bolshevik party instead. As a Bolshevik, he was arrested and exiled several times for revolutionary activity. When the Bolsheviks, led by Lenin, seized power in 1917, Stalin became the General Secretary of the party. After Lenin's death in 1924, Stalin outmaneuvered other Bolshevik leaders to assume full control of the party in 1929.

Fearful that the West would overwhelm the weak Soviet Union, Stalin decided to replace the Soviet Union's peasant-based agricultural economy with a fully industrialized modern economy. To do this, he launched the first of three Five Year Plans (lasting from 1928 to 1941). In essence, the state took over and directed all economic activity. The peasants lost their land and were forced to join state-run collective farms. Those who resisted were killed or left to starve. About 5 million peasants died in the collectivization, including several million Ukrainian peasants who were purposely starved to death when the government seized their grain for export to pay for foreign machinery needed for industrialization.

The other part of the Five Year Plans involved forcing increases in production in heavy industry. To accomplish this, the state established production goals for every factory. Workers and managers became slaves to the plan, and failure to meet production goals led to severe reprisals. Those who resisted or were believed to be enemies of the state were sent to slave labor camps, called *GULAGs* (a Russian acronym that has become the English term for these camps), located in Siberia and northern Russia, near the Arctic Circle. Millions died from starvation or overwork. Despite the untold suffering of the people and the massive inefficiencies created by this method, Stalin had achieved his goal of building an industrialized economy.

To ensure his hold on power and eliminate any possible internal threats to the Soviet Union, Stalin initiated the Great Terror. Between 1934 and 1938, millions of people were arrested and killed, sent to GULAGs, or deported to the far reaches of eastern Russia. Anyone and everyone were subject to sudden and arbitrary arrest. Many people simply disappeared overnight, their fate unknown to this day. The majority of the Soviet military's senior leadership was arrested and executed.

Stalin became the ultimate totalitarian dictator, using terror and a vast state apparatus to control every aspect of life in the Soviet Union. He became the colossus who strode across the vast nation. Propaganda campaigns portrayed him as the infallible leader, whose vision transformed a backward state into a modern power. Paintings and statues of a smiling, beneficent Stalin dominated every public place in the Soviet Union, and his words were constantly repeated and publicized. Stalin's true personality has never been sufficiently revealed, because he always kept his true self hidden behind the mask of a manipulative politician. But his actions speak of an immense drive for power, motivated by an ideology that viewed human beings as raw material for the survival of the socialist state. At the beginning of World War II, Stalin stood unchallenged and the Soviet Union emerged as a powerful force in European affairs — but only after destroying the lives of tens of millions of Soviet citizens.

The pact was valid for ten years, but neither Hitler nor Stalin expected it to last very long. Hitler's goal for *Lebensraum* (see Chapter 2) in the east could only come at the Soviet Union's expense. After all, part of the plan was for Germany to invade the Soviet Union. Stalin, on the other hand, was the leader of a nation whose very existence was devoted to bringing all of Europe — including Germany — under communism through revolution and subversion.

In making the Nazi–Soviet Non-Aggression pact with Hitler, Stalin committed several serious and nearly fatal errors:

>> Traditionally, Poland had served as a buffer between the two traditional enemies. The secret agreement that partitioned Poland, however, gave Germany a 180-mile common border with the Soviet Union — an inviting invasion route for Hitler into the Soviet homeland.

>> Before the agreement with the Nazis, Stalin had destroyed his military command structure in the *Great Terror* (Stalin's massive program in which millions of Soviet citizens were arrested and executed). During the Great Terror, Stalin ordered thousands of senior and mid-level officers to be killed or sent off to labor camps. Although the remaining officers were thoroughly cowed and compliant to Stalin's will, the Soviet Army had very little combat capability.

>> Despite needing time to refit his units and train a new, politically reliable cadre of leaders, Stalin wrongly assumed that he would not have to prepare for war until 1942 and so failed to take full advantage of this opportunity to advance industrial production for war and improve the combat readiness of the Soviet armed forces.

Talking Peace and Planning War: Hitler Finds an Excuse

For Hitler, the Nazi–Soviet Non-Aggression pact was a sweet deal: Poland would be isolated and unable to get help from Britain or France, and the threat of war with the Soviet Union was neutralized, at least for the time being. Hitler's plan was to first eliminate Poland, then fight Britain and France in the west, and then, after Britain and France were defeated, turn again to the east to deal with the Soviet Union. The first step was the attack on Poland.

Hitler's plans for Poland

Poland had once been a recognized nation before the Germans, Austrians, and Russians divided it amongst themselves in the early 1800s. In 1919, following the end of WWI, the peacemakers at Versailles returned Poland to its status as a national state, but they designed it awkwardly, taking territory from the old empires and assembling it like a patchwork quilt:

>> Poland sat precariously between the Soviet Union and Germany, two nations historically hostile to Polish independence.

>> A corridor was created to give Poland access to the Baltic sea. This corridor stuck out like a sore thumb, splitting German territory apart and leaving a small section of Germany, called East Prussia, sitting awkwardly out alone, surrounded by Lithuania, the Soviet Union, and Poland.

>> The German port city of Danzig became the *free city* of Gidynia (that is, it didn't belong to a nation and was under the protection of the League of Nations).

Seeking a final excuse for war in August 1939, Hitler demanded the return of Danzig to German sovereignty. He also sought rights for free rail and highway access to East Prussia through the Polish corridor.

The Poles insisted that their rights under the treaty be upheld and made it clear that they would fight the Germans.

On the brink — and beyond

The leaders of Britain and France nervously watched events in the east, hoping that the latest crisis was only about Danzig and that war could be avoided through negotiation. In fact, they appeared willing to submit to another Munich if a deal could be made with Germany. Yet, despite their desire to avoid conflict, France and Britain told Hitler that if Germany invaded Poland, they would honor their obligations to Poland and go to war. (The Soviet Union and the United States were neutral, leaving France and Britain alone.)

Hitler had no intention of negotiating. He was prepared and completely willing to fight France and Britain. He believed that Germany's military advantage and head start in war production had given him a narrow window of opportunity over his enemies. Hitler told his generals that the time was now or never — Germany would win total victory or perish — and he told them to prepare the armed forces to attack Poland by August 26.

Given France and Britain's desire to negotiate and knowing that the invasion of Poland would be much easier if he didn't have to worry about France attacking Germany's western border, Hitler purposely delayed his attack orders until the beginning of September to test Britain and France's resolve to fight for Poland. For the next five days, Hitler promised peace, discussed rather moderate demands for access to the Polish corridor and Danzig, and planned for war.

One thing that didn't go as Hitler planned was Italy's participation. At the last minute, he discovered that the Pact of Steel — in which Italy agreed to go to war in support of Germany — was more like a Pact of Paper. Mussolini informed Hitler that Italy would not join Germany in a war against France and Britain; it simply did not have the resources to fight a major war at this time.

Despite this setback, Hitler sent out the final order for the attack. He would have his war.

Chapter **5**

Blitzkrieg in Europe: World War II Begins, 1939–1941

The League of Nations proved powerless to stop aggression in Europe, Africa, and Asia: It couldn't stop Japan's attacks on China, Italy's invasions of Albania and Ethiopia, or Germany's forays into Czechoslovakia. (See Chapters 3 and 4 for more information about these events.)

The security agreements given by the French, British, and Soviets seemed pretty worthless, too. Despite French and Soviet promises to protect the Czechoslovakian borders, Germany reclaimed the Sudetenland. And despite Britain's promise to fight with France in the event of German aggression, Hitler put troops in the Rhineland without suffering any repercussions. In fact, British Prime Minister Neville Chamberlain's policy of appeasement had not averted war; it simply allowed Hitler to turn diplomacy to his own ends. Stalin, seeing the writing on the wall, made his own secret arrangement with Hitler to split Poland and buy time to prepare for the coming war.

And war was inevitable: Adolf Hitler *wanted* war. He saw it as the way in which he could achieve Germany's aims and his own dreadful dream of racial purification and unification. To Hitler, it was all or nothing, and there was no turning back. So the world watched and waited for Germany to strike.

The Invasion of Poland

In the early morning hours of September 1, 1939, German units crossed the Polish border. (The night before, the Germans had engineered several flimsy incidents to justify the attack. In one of these incidents, the German SS dressed political prisoners in Polish military uniforms and then shot them near the Germany-Poland border. The Germans claimed that these men had been Polish military raiders.)

The German onslaught

Fifty-six German divisions, including nine *armored* (tank) and *motorized* (infantry in armored transports) divisions, attacked Poland from three directions (see Figure 5-1):

>> German warships off the coast from Danzig bombarded Polish defenses.

>> Three armies attacked from Slovakia and lower Germany.

>> Two armies cut across the Polish corridor and attacked from East Prussia, driving southeast to Warsaw.

With 600,000 men and nearly 2 million reserves, the Poles believed that they could hold their own against the Germans at least until the spring. They overestimated their capabilities and underestimated the Germans':

>> With 1,600 modern combat aircraft, the *Luftwaffe* (see Chapter 3) eliminated the 900 planes of the Polish air force, destroyed rail lines used for supply and movement of troops to the front, and struck deep at concentrations of reserve forces.

>> The *Luftwaffe* also provided air support for the advancing Germans. The German pilots bombed suppressed Polish defenses by bombing and using low-level machine gun attacks. These air attacks paralyzed the Polish high command and isolated Polish units.

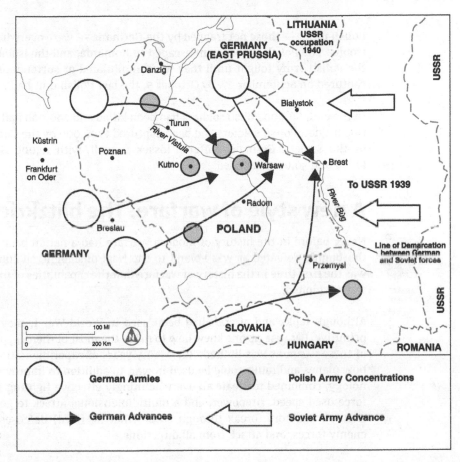

FIGURE 5-1:
The fall of Poland.

>> German infantry units moving on foot opened gaps in the Polish defenses; tanks and infantry riding in armored transport vehicles rapidly encircled the defenders, while other mechanized units drove into the interior to attack reinforcements.

In four days, the German armies had broken through the main defenses, covering nearly 100 miles. Cut off and under constant attack from the air, tens of thousands of Polish troops surrendered. The Poles fought with desperate bravery and even stopped the German drive on Warsaw with several effective counterattacks, but they were outclassed.

The Soviets enter the fray

On September 17, as the German armies from the north and south moved through Poland and met near the Polish–Soviet border, the Soviet Union launched its own an attack on Poland.

Polish units — those not trapped by the Germans — were overwhelmed by Soviet troops. The Polish government escaped to Romania, and the isolated elements of the Polish army fought until they were annihilated or surrendered. Warsaw was captured on September 27. By October 5, the last Polish unit had surrendered.

In the end, 66,000 Polish soldiers had been killed and 200,000 had been wounded. One million Polish soldiers had been captured (700,000 by the Germans; 300,000 by the Soviets. Germany suffered losses as well, with 10,000 German soldiers killed and 30,000 wounded.

A new style of warfare: The blitzkrieg

ARMY ALLIED

Never before in the history of modern warfare had a nation been so quickly and thoroughly defeated as was Poland to the Nazi onslaught. Of course, this battle was the first time in the history of warfare that the capabilities of modern weapons were exploited.

Although tanks and aircraft had been used in World War I, they were new and primitive. Because no one knew how to make the most of their capabilities, the use of these weapons was limited. But twenty years of experimentation and study on how planes and tanks could be used in war, in addition to improvements in technology, combined to create an overwhelmingly effective fighting force. This new force used speed, firepower, and a multidimensional attack to get deep into the enemy's territory, break through static (that is, fixed) defenses and surround enemy forces, and attack from all directions.

This type of new battlefield maneuver also had a psychological effect on the defenders: It broke their will to resist. The Germans had a name for this new kind of slashing, overwhelming offensive. They called it the *blitzkrieg* — lightning war.

Anyone who watched Desert Storm on television saw the most up-to-date incarnation of the blitzkrieg in action.

After Poland's defeat

The Germans and the Soviets each claimed a portion of Poland. What part each country got was scrupulously arranged as part of the Nazi-Soviet Nonaggression pact (see Chapter 4 for more on this secret agreement between Stalin and Hitler). Each dictator then initiated his own reign of terror over the part of Poland that he now controlled.

The Nazis descend

Hitler's quest for *Lebensraum* (see Chapter 3) meant the elimination of every Pole who could possibly serve in future leadership positions:

>> Special action groups (*Einsatzgruppen*) began killing Jews and noncombatants throughout Poland. Other Jews were rounded up and put in ghettos for future elimination.

>> Poles were deported or sent to concentration camps so that their land would eventually be turned over to German settlers.

The savagery inflicted upon the Poles by the Nazis was intended to turn them into cheap slaves, forever subordinate to Hitler's Master Race.

The Soviets take over

In the eastern part of Poland, the Soviets began their own campaign against the 3 million Poles who fell under their control:

>> The Soviet secret police (the NKVD) arrested and deported to Siberian concentration camps (GULAG, from a Russian acronym) anyone suspected of being hostile to Soviet control. More than 15,000 Polish officers who surrendered to the Soviets were moved to camps near Smolensk in the Soviet Union.

>> Because the Polish officers represented the leadership of the Polish nation and potential resistance to future Soviet control, Stalin ordered them all killed in 1940. Each man was shot in the back of the head with a German bullet (to disguise the true criminals) and buried in a mass grave in Katyn Forest.

Among the innumerable tragedies that occurred in Poland in 1939, the murder of the Polish officers was one of the most terrible. These officers joined the many millions of unfortunate victims of Stalin's desire for absolute unchallenged power.

Drawing the Line: Britain and France Declare War on Germany

After the German invasion, Britain and France dutifully declared war on September 3. After that, little else happened. The political leadership of each country simply did not have the will to prosecute a war.

British action — such that it was

Following is the extent of the actions that Britain took:

>> Chamberlain formed a war cabinet, asking Winston Churchill, the most vocal critic of his appeasement policy, to serve as First Lord of the Admiralty (see Figure 5-2).

>> Twenty-five years earlier, Churchill had served in the same position during a portion of World War I. Churchill's appointment served as a tonic for the dispirited British Royal Navy: "Winston is Back" was the signal flashed to all ships of the fleet.

>> The British navy was fully engaged against German submarines (the U-boats that attacked civilian shipping as well as British warships).

>> German torpedoes sank a battleship and an aircraft carrier, but the British tracked down the small raiding battleship and forced it to be scuttled (sunk) by its crew off Montevideo (a Uruguayan port city in South America).

>> In October, the *British Expeditionary Force* (the BEF) went to northern France and took up defensive positions along the Belgian border.

FIGURE 5-2:
Winston
Churchill.

Hulton-Deutsch Collection/CORBIS

French action: Patrolling the border

The French mobilized, but made no effort against German defenses. Instead, they patrolled the border and made air reconnaissance flights. The French claimed that by doing this they were meeting their obligation to Poland. The French also did the following:

>> The French vetoed any British air attacks against German installations, arguing that it would lead to retaliatory German air attacks against French industry.

>> French troops sat comfortably in a chain of formidable, highly sophisticated underground forts extending along the French-German border. This was the *Maginot Line*, a line of defensive fortifications that were intended to protect France from a possible German invasion.

Fighting His Own War: Stalin Goes after Finland

Stalin had been deeply alarmed by Germany's rapid conquest of Poland. Like everyone else, he expected a drawn-out and bloody battle that would last several months. Caught off guard, Stalin had to send unprepared forces hurriedly into Poland just to ensure that he would be able to occupy his portion of the doomed nation.

Stalin also feared for his northern flank, where Finland, once a part of the old Russian Empire, sat overlooking Leningrad (St. Petersburg), the second largest city in the USSR. In November 1939, just a few weeks after eliminating Poland, Stalin decided to secure his open northern flank:

>> He demanded that Finland give up several key military bases to the Soviet navy and air force, including territory on the border near Leningrad.

>> He also demanded that Finland give up the port of Petsamo, the only ice-free port available to Finland in the north.

>> Just as he had done with the Baltic states, Stalin massed troops on the border to intimidate the Finns.

Finland, with a population of only 4 million and 200,000 men under arms, refused to submit and mobilized an auxiliary force of 100,000 women to support the men at the front.

Wave 1: Stalin faces the fighting Finns

Without warning, on November 30, Stalin launched air attacks on Helsinki, Finland's capital. The Soviet navy blockaded Finland's coast, and Soviet units made *amphibious landings* (landing assault troops on a shore from seaborne transports). Stalin then sent four armies into eastern and southeastern Finland, totaling 500,000 men in 30 divisions supported by 1,000 tanks and 800 aircraft. The main attack, with two armies consisting of 13 divisions and five tank brigades, attempted to smash up the isthmus between Lake Ladoga and the Gulf of Finland.

On paper, the Soviet forces appeared to be more than sufficient to overwhelm the small number of Finnish defenders. But the Finns were prepared to resist. Strong points constructed in the pine forests stopped the advancing columns. Then Finnish troops mounted on skis ambushed the columns of Soviet tanks and trucks floundering on narrow, ice-covered roads and disappeared before the Soviets could react.

The weather also worked in the Finns' favor. The November winter weather was cold; the Finns were dressed to fight in extreme cold. The Soviet troops, dressed in lightweight clothing, suffered greatly. By December, the Soviet offensive had stalled completely. For two months, the Soviet leadership reorganized their forces for a second try.

Wave 2: Let's try this again

In February, the Soviets attacked again. Fighting on the *Mannerheim Line* (the defensive positions that straddled the isthmus) was intense. The Soviets kept unrelenting pressure on the Finnish defenders with a combination of air attacks, artillery bombardment, and infantry assaults.

The Soviets took terrible losses, but Stalin was willing to accept them to achieve his goals. It took the Soviets a month to achieve a breakthrough. After the Mannerheim Line had been broken, the Finns were forced to accept the Soviet peace terms, and the war ended on March 13, 1940.

WOULD YOU LIKE CAVIAR WITH YOUR MOLOTOV COCKTAIL?

During the Soviet-Finnish war, the Finns invented a weapon to deal with the large number of Soviet tanks advancing into their country. The Finns mixed ingredients found in their homes with gasoline and then poured the mixture into a wine bottle and stuffed a rag tightly into the opening. Tanks are vulnerable to attack from the sides and rear. As a tank passed, the soldier lit the rag on the bottle and threw it, aiming for the engine exhaust panels on the back of the tank. The material burst into flames, often damaging the engine and making the tank vulnerable to further attacks. The Finns called these fire-bombs Molotov Cocktails, a derisive reference to Stalin's Foreign Minister, Vyacheslav Molotov. The Molotov Cocktail has been one of the weapons of choice for guerrilla fighters ever since.

Although the Finns lost the isthmus, the port of Petsamo (which the Soviets later returned), and bases located in the Gulf of Finland, their defiant courage inspired many throughout the world.

The Finns suffered major losses, with 18,000 soldiers killed and 42,000 wounded. The Soviets, shocked by the fierce Finnish resistance, kept their losses a secret; but estimates of 200,000 killed and 300,000 wounded were common.

Anyone paying attention? The message of the Soviet-Finnish War

In their battle with the Finns, the Soviets were hampered by poor command and control, an inefficient supply system, and a lack of coordination in executing battle plans. The Soviets had attempted a German-style blitzkrieg, but they failed to execute it properly, mostly due to lack of preparation, poor terrain and weather, and an inability to move quickly. Worse, the Soviet Army's incompetence had been revealed to the world. This had two major effects:

» It convinced Hitler that Stalin's army would be an easy target.

» It helped reinforce the French and British belief that Stalin would be an unsuitable partner in their efforts to resist Hitler. (The British would come to regret that decision later in 1940.)

He's B-a-a-ck: Hitler Strikes Norway and Denmark

Even before the conclusion of the Polish campaign, Hitler turned his thoughts to how to defeat Great Britain. Obviously, air and sea power were essential. To attack Britain from the air and sea, German forces needed bases on the perimeter of the North Sea. Norway offered the best bases to accomplish this objective. Controlling Norway gave Hitler other advantages as well:

>> Norway was the transit point for Swedish iron ore, which Germany needed for its war industries. Securing the shipping lanes around Norway would prevent the British from interfering with this all-important source of raw material.

>> Control of Norway would get rid of British efforts to blockade Germany. With German ships and submarines in Norwegian ports, the British navy and Allied merchant ships would be threatened as they sailed across the North Sea.

Hitler also set his sights on Denmark. With Denmark, Hitler could secure German naval access to the North Sea.

The plan

On April 9, Hitler ordered attacks on Norway and Denmark. These operations depended on surprise and speed because all of Hitler's goals had to be achieved before the British navy could react:

>> Five separate German naval task forces had to seize and control five different targeted Norwegian ports: Kristiansand, Bergen, Trondheim, Narvik, and Oslo, the Norwegian capital. All in all, this area covered nearly 1,000 miles of coastline.

>> Once the ports were under Nazi control, the German ships had to protect the landing of troops and supplies.

>> German paratroopers also had to seize airfields in southern Norway to support the *Luftwaffe* air operations needed to protect the invasion.

The attack and the resistance

Danish resistance collapsed immediately as the country was overrun with German soldiers. With control of the strategic straits and the Danish airfields, the *Luftwaffe* was able to control the airspace over southern Norway.

Norwegian resistance fared little better. German troops landed south of Oslo and were supported by German paratroopers who had seized the Oslo airport. By late afternoon, the city was in German hands. The commander of Norwegian forces suffered a nervous breakdown, and no orders were passed to the Norwegian army. The government, paralyzed by the German attack, managed to escape, along with the King of Norway.

Landings elsewhere were unopposed; German paratroopers captured the key airfield at Stravanger. With control of the ports and airfields, the Germans built up forces rapidly within Norway.

Fighting with the hearts of lions: The Allies respond

Despite the years of seeking peace through appeasement and despite being ill prepared to fight a full-scale war, the Allies responded quickly and bravely to the German invasion of Denmark and Norway. Germany had invaded on April 9. The Allied response came on April 10.

The battle in Narvik harbor

REMEMBER

One of the dangers to the German plan was the time involved in keeping warships in the harbors to protect the troops and supply ships. With little room to maneuver, an attacking force could destroy the task force easily. This is what happened at Narvik on April 10.

Five British *destroyers* (warships) entered the harbor and began a fierce battle against the five German destroyers. The British sank two ships, damaged one severely, and crippled the other two. The British also sank several merchant ships carrying precious supplies for the German invasion force.

As additional German destroyers arrived, the battle turned against the British. Two British destroyers were sunk and the captain who so bravely took the battle to the enemy, Captain B. A. W. Warburton-Lee, was killed. His last instructions to his ships: "Continue to engage the enemy." He was awarded Britain's highest award for valor, the Victoria Cross.

The Allies' counter-invasion

The Allies responded with a counter-invasion of their own, landing 30,000 troops with the intent of recapturing Trondheim and Narvik. Although the Allies succeeded in capturing Narvik (primarily because the British naval attack had left the

Germans with limited ammunition), they failed to capture Trondheim and were attacked there by 80,000 German troops.

The poorly trained and poorly led Allied force was ineffective in combat. By June 9, all of Norway's armies had surrendered or escaped to Sweden, and the Allied invasion force, along with the Norwegian government, had been evacuated back to England. The British lost an aircraft carrier and two German warships (*battle cruisers*) suffered heavy damage from torpedo attacks.

Winners and losers

The invasion of Norway again proved the importance of secrecy and surprise as an essential part of the blitzkrieg. Although no tanks were used, the blitzkrieg came in the form of air power, both in providing support to naval and ground combat forces, and in supplying the ground forces. Here's a quick run-down of who lost and gained what:

Norway and Denmark

The Norwegians, who resisted belatedly but with great courage, had no air force to speak of and very few modern weapons. Without adequate supplies or leadership, the Norwegian units were easily overcome, as were the Danish units.

Germany

With the successful invasion of Norway, Germany had gained excellent bases to use for air, submarine, and surface operations against British shipping. Although the later fall of France made these bases less useful, they later became important in attacking convoys to the USSR.

Most importantly, the control of Norway gave Germany an unimpeded flow of iron ore. The Soviets continued to act as a willing partner to Germany, providing important assistance to the German invasion by allowing a German supply ship, headed for Narvik, to be provisioned at a Soviet base.

But the costs of the invasion had also been heavy: The German navy was essentially put out of action. Between the ships that were lost in combat and the ships that were damaged and out of action for lengthy repairs, the entire German surface fleet consisted of exactly one heavy cruiser, two light cruisers, and four destroyers. Thus, at the end of July 1940, when Hitler needed his navy most, at full strength and ready to take on the British navy, he found he had nothing to use.

England

**ARMY
ALLIED**

Perhaps the most interesting result of the Allied disaster at Norway was the fall of Neville Chamberlain's government. Chamberlain faced defections from his Conservative party and decided that someone else should lead the nation. Winston Churchill became Prime Minister of a coalition war government (a political alliance of Liberal and Conservative party members) on May 10, 1940.

With his unquenchable spirit, enormous energy, and brilliant oratory, many believed that Britain had finally found a leader to match Hitler. "I felt as if I were walking with destiny," Churchill recalled afterward, "and that all my past life had been but a preparation for this hour and for this trial." On the very day Churchill became Prime Minister, the news from Holland and Belgium shook the British people.

The Phony War: Using France to Get at Britain

Hitler had been working on his plan to invade France since May of 1938. Hitler had little interest in fighting France. The main goal of the offensive was to defeat Britain. His plan was to do the following:

>> Strike at Holland and Belgium and capture the ports and airfields in the Low Countries, the Belgium area that borders northern France.

>> Defeat enemy forces in northern France. After the French were defeated, Hitler could begin an all-out air attack on Britain.

In anticipation of this eventuality, Hitler had ordered an increase in bomber production just before the attack on Poland began.

The Germans: Making the most of unexpected delays

Hitler wanted to send forces to the west as soon as possible after the invasion of Poland was complete, but poor weather delayed the offensive 29 times. Its original target date had been November 1939. The invasion didn't happen until May 1940. The Germans did not waste this time.

Making repairs and plans

The German army used the delays to fine-tune its procedures from the Poland campaign, train replacements, and repair equipment.

During this period, the focus of the German plan changed as well. Rather than focus on an attack of Belgium and Holland simply to occupy territory and deal with enemy forces almost incidentally, the new plan would focus on destroying the French and British forces themselves.

Hitler's revised plan: Lure the Allies into a trap

Hitler's goal was to destroy the French and British forces decisively and win the war in one swift stroke. Holland and Belgium would still be occupied, but the attack on these countries would actually be a move to draw Allied forces into Belgium. A second German blow, using primarily armored forces, would swing behind the Allied army and drive the army to the coast, where the Germans would surround it and cut it off.

The German plan involved three army groups:

>> **Army Group A:** Consisting of four armies comprised primarily of tanks and mechanized infantry, it would drive through the narrow lanes through the Ardennes Forest, capture Sudan (the site of a great German victory against the French in 1870, a particularly symbolic spot Hitler had focused on), and drive toward the English Channel.

>> **Army Group B:** With two armies supported by paratroops who would seize key river crossing points, it would attack across Holland and Belgium.

>> **Army Group C:** With two armies, it would keep French forces occupied at the Maginot Line.

This was the final plan approved for the offensive on May 10. Hitler had assembled a gigantic force: 102 divisions (including eleven armored divisions and five motorized divisions), 2,439 tanks, 2,779 bombers and fighters, and 7,378 artillery pieces — about 2.5 million men in all.

The Allies: You'd think that they would have been prepared

MILITARY STRATEGY

By September 1939, the Allies had built a strong enough force to conduct defensive or offensive operations, yet the French and British political leaders saw no need to use it. Captured German plans indicated that the main German thrust would come through neutral Holland and Belgium. (Of course, unbeknownst to the Allies, this was the *old* plan. Hitler now had a new plan, as explained in the preceding section.)

WINSTON CHURCHILL: THE GIANT OF THE TWENTIETH CENTURY

Winston Churchill (1874–1965) was a combination of soldier, scholar, artist, and statesman. His father was Lord Randolph Churchill, a brilliant English political leader, and his mother, Jennie Jerome, was an American. His strong affinity for the United States was related to his mother's homeland. Churchill graduated from the Royal Military College at Sandhurst in 1894 and embarked on a unique military career. He saw action in India and the Sudan, and produced a series of books concerning his experiences. After leaving the army, he became world famous as a war correspondent in South Africa. In 1901, Churchill became a Member of Parliament as a Conservative, but he left the party in 1904 to join the Liberals. He took a leading role in laying the foundations of the welfare state. As First Lord of the Admiralty from 1911 to 1915, he responded to German naval advancements by modernizing the Royal Navy and creating a naval air service.

During World War I, Churchill designed the strategy for the Galipoli campaign in 1915. The Galipoli campaign was an indirect attack on the Turks (the Ottoman Empire) to force them out of the war and provide support to Russia. Although the campaign was a failure, it demonstrated Churchill's strategic thinking. He also promoted and helped develop the tank as a weapon to break the stalemate. Leaving politics in 1915, he joined the army in 1916 and commanded a regiment on the Western Front.

From 1919 to 1922, Churchill again served in government. He assisted in defining political boundaries in the Middle East and promoting wide ranging military reforms. During the whole troubled period from 1929 to 1939, Churchill held no major government post. Nevertheless, in speeches and articles, he warned of the danger of German ambitions in Europe. He appealed for rearmament and criticized Chamberlain's appeasement of Hitler. In 1940, when Chamberlain stepped down, Churchill became the nation's choice for Prime Minister.

Churchill was known for his loyalty, wit, and generosity. He combined courage and a willingness to take risks with a powerful intellect; he was undoubtedly a man of genius. He was a master orator who inspired not only the people of his own nation when their very survival was at stake but also free peoples everywhere to resist the enemies of freedom at all costs and win the final victory. Churchill came to personify the spirit of Britain during the war. His gifts of energy and vision would serve the Allied cause well in the difficult years ahead.

Defending against the old German plan

Confident that the Germans planned to fight in Belgium and northern France, the Allies decided to move the bulk of their forces into Belgium to stop them. The idea was to meet the German blitzkrieg with a *defense in depth* — a series of defensive positions that the Germans would have to break through in order to reach France.

The reserve army was moved far westward to back up the British and French forces defending Belgium and Holland. This move left a gap at the Ardennes Forest and the Maginot Line, and it left the troops on the Belgian border covered by some of the weakest units in the French army.

The Allies were making plans based on the original German plan, which had changed by May. The Allies were unwittingly playing into the hands of the Germans and actually making the execution of the revised German plan (the attack through the Ardennes Forest) easier.

Failing to coordinate with the folks they're trying to protect

The Allies also glossed over a key impediment to their planning: Neither the Dutch nor the Belgians would coordinate defense plans with the Allies. Because both countries had maintained their neutrality, they feared that even meeting with the Allies would give Hitler the excuse to attack them. Thus, the Allied move into Belgium would be both unwelcome and out of sync with the Belgian defense plan.

From blitzkrieg to sitzkrieg

The continuous warnings of an impending German attack between November 1939 and May 1940 lulled the Allies into ignoring actual warnings as false alarms. With little to do, the Allied troops whiled away their time, enjoying all the benefits of army life and watching the Germans work on their border defenses on the Siegfried Line.

Unlike the Germans, Allied units had no additional training after being called up. Units would be dispatched to various sectors to build defenses; after they were finished, they were allowed to rest and then they were moved to another sector to do the same thing. As a result, neither soldiers nor commanders ever had a chance to become familiar with the area they were to defend. It was a war, but a war in which no one seemed too eager to initiate any fighting. Some called it the *phony war*, and others mockingly called it *sitzkrieg* — sit-down war.

The first phase: Attacking the Low Countries

Before dawn on May 10, the *Luftwaffe* opened the first phase of the offensive against the West with bombing attacks over Belgium and Holland. Soon afterward, German paratroops seized the key bridges and assaulted the main airfields at the Hague. In three days, German tank units had linked up with the paratroops and passed through the main Dutch defenses. A major air attack on the city of Rotterdam killed nearly 800 civilians and destroyed Dutch morale. The Dutch surrendered on May 15.

On the 10th, German airborne forces also struck Belgium and seized the key bridges across the strategic defense line along the Albert Canal.

MILITARY STRATEGY

The key to the Belgium defense was fort Eban Emael. Built in 1935, it was the most modern defensive fortification of its kind (it was built to withstand any type of ground attack). On the morning of May 10, 80 German paratroopers landed on top of the fort, which had no defenses prepared for such an attack, and blasted their way inside, allowing German armored units and infantry divisions to cross the canal barrier rapidly.

Despite the setbacks for the Dutch and Belgians, French General Maurice Gamelin (the Allied Commander in Chief) and General John Gort (commander of the *British Expeditionary Force* — BEF) remained confident. They had brought their forces into Belgium and positioned them on the Dyle River, just as they had planned. After assembling the retreating Belgian units into their defensive lines, the Allies awaited the German attack. They held their bombers back from attacking German tank formations because of effective antiaircraft fire and kept their fighters in reserve, awaiting German attacks on strategic industrial targets.

The second phase: The attack through the Ardennes Forest

After traveling three nerve-racking days on narrow Ardennes Forest roads, seven German panzer divisions emerged from the woods and crossed the French border on May 12. The following day, German fighter pilots drove Allied planes from the skies, and German infantry divisions, following behind tanks, crossed into France.

The French were taken completely by surprise by the appearance of tanks coming through terrain thought to be impassable for tanks and the speed of the German movement. The French resisted the crossings and fought effectively for a short time, but once several defensive points had been breached, resistance collapsed.

Axis General Erwin Rommel's 7th Panzer Division drove nearly one hundred miles into enemy territory in two days, capturing 10,000 French soldiers — most of whom just dropped their weapons and marched obediently eastward. By May 15, seven panzer divisions were on their way to the English Channel, with nothing to stop them. On May 21, German tanks reached the Channel ports of Abbeville and Boulogne (also the British main supply base), effectively dividing the Allied armies in half.

The Allies: Stuck in Flanders

The BEF, French, and Belgian forces that were trapped in Flanders were in desperate shape. Because they were attacked from the front and rear, they shortened their defenses. Meanwhile, Allied General Gamelin had been replaced by French General Maxime Weygand, an aging hero of World War I. Faced with nearly total disintegration of his command, he ordered counterattacks to link his divided forces together.

The counterattacks, though ineffective for Weygand's purposes, did have an effect on German commanders who began to fear that their narrow corridor to the English Channel could be cut off. This led to an order from the German High Command to halt the tank divisions, consolidate their positions, and bring infantry support forward. It was the wrong order at the wrong time. The German leadership was actually frightened by the brilliant success of its own plan.

War is conducted in the face of great uncertainty; the unknown can drive leaders to become overly cautious and make decisions that, in the end, allow victory to slip away. So it was in Flanders. The Germans had won a great victory, but because of their uncertainties, they let a decisive victory get away. British forces would survive to fight another day.

The Royal Navy to the rescue: Salvation at Dunkirk

Between May 23 and June 2, General Gort, the commander of the BEF, found himself in a desperate situation. The French and Belgian armies were failing, and the British high command had declared France lost. Churchill ordered the BEF to be evacuated from France. The closest port left in Allied hands was Dunkirk. Without German tank attacks along the coast, the British disengaged from the front line and moved to Dunkirk. While the panzers, only ten miles away from Dunkirk, were halted, German infantry units that were located 50 miles away were ordered to march to the port.

Given this breathing space, the Royal Navy assembled every kind of ship or boat that could be found on the southern coast of Britain and sent it across the Channel to Dunkirk. With British and French units defending an ever-shrinking perimeter, 10,000 soldiers were evacuated from the beaches on May 28. The following day, 50,000 soldiers escaped to safety. As the Royal Air Force fought the *Luftwaffe* overhead, more and more men left the area. By June 2, about 340,000 troops had reached Britain. Of these survivors, 123,000 were French. In the battle to save the BEF, the British lost nearly 200 aircraft and 6 destroyers; the French lost 3 destroyers. They left most of the equipment and vehicles behind as well, but the soldiers would return to fight another day.

France falls to Germany

By June 5 — with the BEF abandoning the continent and Belgium already surrendered — the French effort appeared hopeless. Refitted and rested, the German tanks now turned south and headed for Paris and the rear of the Maginot Line (see Figure 5-3).

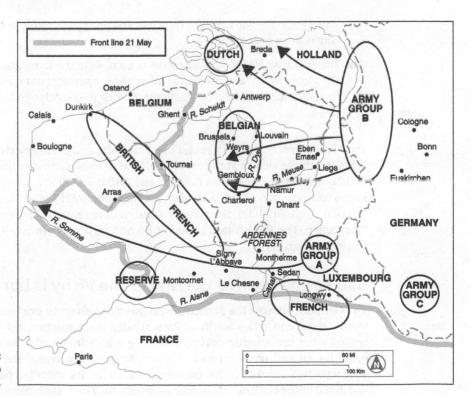

FIGURE 5-3:
France falls to
Germany, 1940.

For several days, the French resisted and held off the German attacks, but they were outnumbered three-to-one in many places and had no significant tank or mechanized forces to fight with once the Germans broke through. The French fell back trying to establish successive defenses behind rivers, but the Germans moved too fast. On June 14, Paris was captured with a fight and then abandoned to prevent it from becoming a battleground. Meanwhile, 136,000 British troops, along with 20,000 Poles, were evacuated to Britain. German forces had trapped 500,000 French defenders in their own forts along the Maginot Line.

The French government was in turmoil. Prime Minister Paul Reynaud resigned, and his deputy, Marshal Philippe Pétain, took control. Pétain was one of the heroes of the Great War, and his presence was intended to inspire France's fight to the death. But Pétain was an old man who was disgusted with the politicians who, in his opinion, had left France to decay. He asked for a cease-fire on June 16.

Hitler, who savored symbolism, treated the French the same way that representatives of the German government had been treated in 1918 when World War I ended. Hitler laid out the following conditions:

>> There was no negotiation; the French would agree to all terms or face a continuation of hostilities.

>> The French would formally surrender at Compiègie, the same place where the victorious French had met the Germans. Hitler even went as far as to bring the exact railroad dining car to the site, making the French sign the armistice there.

Twenty-six years earlier, in 1914, France, Britain, and Germany struggled for four years to achieve victory at the cost of millions of lives. Germany had defeated both France and Britain (as well as Belgium and Holland) in just 42 days. Total German losses were 156,000 killed, wounded, and missing; total French losses were about 330,000 — although the Germans claimed to have captured more than 1.5 million Frenchmen. The British lost a total of 68,000 men and nearly all of their tanks, trucks, and artillery.

Bad karma returns to France: The Vichy is born

The Germans allowed the French government to remain in existence in the city of Vichy, about 200 miles south of Paris. Under the armistice, the Germans controlled all of the Atlantic coast (in keeping with Hitler's plan to use the French coast for air and naval attacks on Great Britain), the remainder of France, the southern two-thirds of the country, and all of its colonial possessions that remained under control of the *Vichy* government. The French army was reduced in strength to 100,000 men, and France was forced to make huge payments to Germany — just as the Germans had been forced to do at the end of World War I.

The French Fleet: Destroyed by the British

The biggest question was the French fleet: Would it come under the control of the Germans? If it did, the French navy (the fourth largest in the world), combined with the German and Italian fleets, would outnumber Britain's navy. Britain, now facing Germany and Italy alone, depended on its navy for survival.

Winston Churchill would take no chances. He had to deny Hitler the means to destroy his nation. He dispatched ships of the British navy to attack and destroy a large portion of the French fleet at Mers-el-Kebir, Algeria (a French colony), killing nearly 1,300 French sailors. Other ships from the French fleet, with the exception of those in port at Toulon, were attacked, disabled, or impounded. The Vichy government, led by Pétain, was cool to Britain from its creation, but now in the wake of the British attack on the French fleet, France broke all relations with its former ally.

Free France: Enter de Gaulle

Charles de Gaulle, a young and unknown general officer who had made one of the only French counterattacks against the Germans in the previous campaign, was appointed Under Secretary for National Defense when Vichy General Pétain formed a new government (see Figure 5-4). De Gaulle refused to accept surrender and escaped to Britain by air. Upon arriving, he suddenly assumed the mantle of the representative of Free France — those Frenchmen who did not surrender or submit to Vichy. Although he was not immediately recognized as the legitimate representative of the French government, he would rise to personify both the honor and symbol of a free people.

Improving their position: The other dictators act

In the midst of the final offensive against France, Mussolini, not anticipating any more wars in Europe after France and hoping to gain some spoils, declared war on France and Britain on June 10. Italy made only a halfhearted effort to attack, however.

Taking advantage of the world's attention on France, Stalin, always suspicious and never secure, sought to improve the Soviet Union's position. Of course, he did this at the expense of independent border states. In June, just after the French capitulation, Stalin occupied two provinces of Romania after threatening war. In August, he incorporated the Baltic states of Lithuania, Estonia, and Latvia into the USSR after declaring that they had formed a conspiracy against the Soviet Union.

FIGURE 5-4:
General Charles
de Gaulle.

CORBIS

A British Epic: The Battle of Britain

MILITARY STRATEGY

Hitler achieved his objective, but he only had a vague idea of what to do next. The hated English lived on an island that had not been successfully invaded since 1066. Britain's enemies hesitated to invade for a couple of reasons: The British Navy and The Royal Air Force with its 59 squadrons of aircraft.

Any attempt to subdue Britain would require neutralizing the British navy and airforce. Even if the Germans could destroy Britain's air and naval power, the next problem was how to actually invade the British Isles. To conquer the British people, German ground forces would have to land, and a peace treaty would have to be dictated in London. The Germans never adequately addressed this very uncomfortable reality. Instead, German planners sought half measures they believed would break British morale and Britain's ability to continue fighting.

Standing alone

ARMY ALLIED

Even though Britain could count on no one — not even her dominions or colonies could provide assistance — the people of Britain had a leader who steeled them for what he called the *Battle of Britain*. "Hitler knows that he will have to break us in this Island or lose the war," he told the people of Britain. "If we can stand up to him, all Europe may be free and the life of the world may move forward into broad, sunlit uplands. But if we fail, then the whole world, including the United States, including all that we have known and cared for, will sink into the abyss of a new Dark Age. . . . Let us therefore brace ourselves to our duties, and so bear ourselves that, if the British Empire and the Commonwealth last for a thousand years, men will say: 'This was their finest hour.'"

Churchill knew full well the consequences of defeat and what it meant not only for Britain, but also for Western civilization itself. Although there had been some discussions of peace talks with Germany, Churchill would accept only one course of action: For the Prime Minister, it was final victory, no matter what the cost. And it would be accomplished alone, if necessary, or with other nations allied in the cause. The Germans would not only have to counter the skills and power of the British navy and air force, they would also have to deal with a leader who possessed the indomitable will to withstand whatever the Nazis could throw against his embattled nation.

Taking to the air: New considerations for aerial warfare

It had always been Hitler's intention to use air power to crush Britain. He turned to *Reichsmarschall* Hermann Goering, the chief of the *Luftwaffe*, to accomplish the task. Goering enthusiastically took on the mission.

The *Luftwaffe* was battle tested, and it had a good balance of *bombers* (planes designed to drop bombs) and *fighters* (planes designed to shoot down other airplanes) that would protect the bombers from British planes. But because air power had never been used in this manner before, no one had yet addressed the following problems:

>> Could a bombing campaign alone bring victory?

>> What targets should be attacked to achieve the goal?

No one could answer these questions in 1940. So the Luftwaffe had to improvise.

First, the *Luftwaffe* took several weeks to recover from the losses it suffered during the campaign against France. Then it had to move its aircraft and support units to airfields in France, Belgium, and Holland along the Atlantic coast.

The not-so-friendly skies

When the first air attacks against Britain began in early August, the Germans had about 2,500 bombers and fighters; the British were depending on 1,200 fighters to stop them.

The German plan was to cripple the *Royal Air Force* (RAF) fighters by eliminating the fuel and ammunition (called *sustainment*) they would need. Without the fighters to threaten them, German bombers could fly over British skies at will. The German attacks focused on ships, ports, air bases, and aircraft factories.

Because German fighters could provide protection to the bombers only over a very limited area of Britain, the German plan relied upon bombers flying over Britain undetected. The British, however, had the advantage of a new technology developed before the war — *radar*. Using radar (combined with German code intercepts), the British were able to spot enemy planes long before they were over Britain and intercept them with fighter aircraft.

Unable to surprise the British, the Germans took heavy losses. The British downed eight German planes for every British plane lost. But both sides lost nearly one quarter of all their experienced pilots.

Descending on London: The Luftwaffe Blitz

By early September, the *Luftwaffe* began attacks on London in the hopes of terrorizing the population and crippling morale. The British called this attack the *Blitz.*

At first, the Germans conducted daylight attacks on London, but British fighters were too effective. So then the Germans began night raids on the city. For 57 nights, Londoners were subjected to bombing raids of over 200 planes a night. In these raids, the Germans used both high-explosive bombs and incendiary bombs to create fires that would cause further damage. Nearly 40,000 civilians were killed during the Blitz.

German attacks eventually shifted from London to industrial targets. On November 14, 500 German aircraft dropped 600 tons of bombs on Coventry (a city in central England), killing 400 people and destroying large sections of the city. Although Britain would continue to suffer bombing attacks throughout 1940, Hitler had abandoned his goal of crushing Britain. Occupied with other goals, Hitler finally tabled his invasion plans (such as they were) of Britain. In the end, the RAF lost 790 fighters, and the *Luftwaffe* lost nearly 1,400 bombers and fighters.

Even though the British only had an average of about 600 aircraft available at any one time during the Battle of Britain, they were able to overcome the German onslaught with a mixture of strategy, technology, and, most importantly, courage. It was courage born of the knowledge that the fate of the nation rested on a young, often inexperienced, fighter pilot's skill and tenacity.

The Balkans: Mussolini's Mess and Hitler's New Target

While the Battle of Britain was raging, Mussolini sought to gain some advantages for Italy. Deeply disappointed that Germany had not awarded France's African colonies to Italy, Mussolini decided to strike at Greece. By occupying Greece, which held a central position in the eastern Mediterranean, the Italians would be able to strike at British bases in Egypt and the Middle East.

Mussolini invades

Mussolini staged the attack from Albania. On October 28, 1940, the Italian army, 162,000 men strong, moved into Greece. The Italian army had some successes initially, but by mid-November, the Greek army — poorly equipped but exceptionally skilled in mountain warfare — had stopped the Italian advance and began to counterattack, actually pushing the Italians back into Albania.

Strengthened by additional reinforcements, the Italians held on. By February 1942, a combination of poor weather and difficult terrain stabilized the Italian defensive lines. See Figure 5-5.

Britain appears on the scene

When Italy invaded Greece, the British sent 60,000 soldiers to Greece for the following reasons:

>> To honor their security guarantee to the Greeks. (Greece was one of the nations that the British, in 1939, had promised to protect in the case of an German invasion.)

>> To offset German gains by occupying the large island of Crete. (Crete was the most important island in the eastern Mediterranean because aircraft located at its air bases could dominate the region.)

>> To protect the Mediterranean.

>> To threaten the Ploesti oil fields in Romania, which were critical to the German war effort.

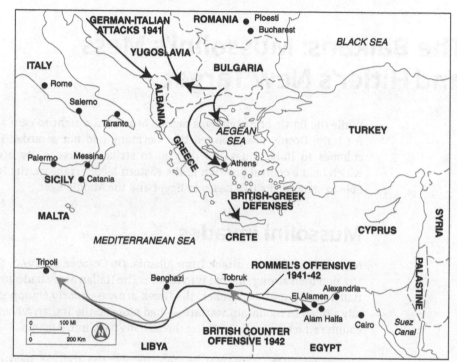

FIGURE 5-5: German-Italian operations in the eastern Mediterranean, 1941.

Hitler jumps on the bandwagon

Hitler wasted no time in putting military planners to work for an attack on Greece. Diplomatically, the Germans were in good shape to accomplish such an attack: Hungary, Romania, and Bulgaria had joined the Axis, allowing German troops access to Greece, but Yugoslavia needed to join the Axis as well to ensure that the attack on Greece would succeed.

Yugoslavian resistance to German persuasion

Facing heavy pressure, the Yugoslavian government agreed to join the Axis in March, but rebels overthrew the government that signed the agreement and refused to accept the treaty as valid.

Although the Yugoslavian government hoped that the Soviet Union would stand by it, Stalin had no interest in angering Hitler. Instead, the Soviet Union signed a meaningless pact of friendship and made no commitments to protect Yugoslavia. Although Yugoslavia had an army of nearly 1 million men, it was deeply divided along ethnic lines, with Serbs and Croats more interested in fighting each other than the Germans.

Yugoslavia falls in line

The German attack began on April 6. It was a depressingly similar routine by 1941: German air power neutralized command and control, disrupted reserves, and turned to attack pockets of resistance.

Nine German tank and infantry divisions moved rapidly into the interior of Yugoslavia, headed for Belgrade. Even the rugged mountains of Yugoslavia seemed to have little effect on the German's movement. Eleven days later, Yugoslavia surrendered. The Germans had lost only 500 men in the campaign; they captured over 300,000 prisoners. Many Yugoslav soldiers deserted to form guerrilla units.

Greece falls to Germany

At the same time that Yugoslavia was attacked (see the preceding section), 12 German divisions swept into Greece from Bulgaria. The Greeks and the British had not been able to agree on a common defensive plan, and no one considered what would happen if the Germans came through Yugoslavia.

Caught by surprise, a large portion of the Greek army was trapped and surrendered on April 9. Outflanked by rapidly moving German tank units, the British army retreated down the Greek peninsula. By April 30, another Greek army had surrendered, the British army had been driven off the peninsula, and Athens was in German hands.

MILITARY STRATEGY

The German campaign to conquer Greece cost Germany 5,000 casualties; the British lost 12,000 men and 26 ships. Most of the British losses came during a Dunkirk-like evacuation, in which the British loaded ships without the protection of British aircraft. Without such protection, the crowded loading areas were prime targets for German planes. German aircraft inflicted heavy damage on the ships sent to ferry the British troops to Crete. Just as they had done at Dunkirk, the British army had to leave most of its equipment on the beach.

Capturing Crete from the air

By holding the island of Crete, the British could minimize German gains in the Mediterranean while protecting their own lifeline to the empire in Asia. Therefore, the Germans needed to take Crete in order to consolidate their hold on Greece and the Balkans. Occupying Crete would also allow the Germans to threaten British land forces in Egypt and naval forces in the Suez Canal.

MILITARY STRATEGY

On May 20, 1941, the Germans introduced another new concept to warfare — the *vertical envelopment*, which employed mass landings of gliders and paratroopers to capture key objectives. Although the Germans had employed these forces since the invasion of Norway, the battle for Crete was the first time they had been used in large units or as the primary force in a campaign. The Germans, without any sort of threat from enemy aircraft, dropped paratroopers in four places simultaneously. An amphibious assault followed.

On the island, the British had about 27,000 troops that were a combination of English, New Zealanders, Australians, and Greeks. Although these troops had limited supplies, they fought the Germans to a standstill (code intercepts gave them the German plans). The Royal Navy destroyed German ships ferrying supplies to Crete but faced fierce attacks from German aircraft and suffered heavy losses. German paratroops succeeded in holding a key airfield, which ensured a regular buildup of forces and supplies. By May 31, the British — outnumbered and exhausted — evacuated the island.

HISTORICAL TRIVIA

For the first time in history, a battle had been won entirely by airborne forces supplied by the air force. However, the costs to the Germans were severe. About 16,000 men were killed or wounded, and nearly 200 transport aircraft out of 500 were lost, along with important naval assets. Although the airborne forces were under the control of the *Luftwaffe*, they were the cream of the German army.

The Italians Take Their Lumps All Over Africa

The Italians had to protect their empire in Africa, but the territory they controlled was widely scattered. It went from Libya to the Horn of Africa (Somalia, Ethiopia, and Eritrea). In between these areas were the colonial possessions of the British Empire (Kenya, Egypt, and Sudan). The key to North Africa was Egypt and the Suez Canal.

ROMMEL: THE DESERT FOX

In the Great War, German Field Marshall Erwin Rommel (1891–1944) fought in France, Romania, and Italy. After the war, he published a book based on his wartime experiences, *Infantry Attacks*. Promoted to Major General just before World War II, Rommel commanded the 7th Panzer Division in the attack into France in 1940. His brilliant performance led to promotion to Lieutenant General in 1941. He took command of German forces fighting alongside the Italians in Libya. His skillful use of maneuver, deception, and combined arms led to the British abandoning Libya completely.

In 1942, Rommel became the youngest Field Marshal in the German army and stood at the threshold of the Suez Canal, the center of British power in the Middle East. But his campaign slowed and eventually stopped from lack of supplies. At El Alamein, Egypt in 1942, he suffered one of the most significant defeats of the war and was forced to retreat nearly 2,000 miles back to Tunisia (in North Africa). He conducted another brilliant offensive against new American troops at Kasserine Pass in Tunisia, but by March 1943, he could no longer stay in the field due to illness and returned to Germany to recover. He commanded an army in Italy, and in January 1944, took command of all German armies defending the western coast against a possible invasion.

Rommel is known as the "Desert Fox" for the way he used the desert to his advantage and employed his forces against the British (and later, the Americans) in North Africa. He is also one of the most famous German generals, a soldier who earned the highest respect of his foes for his courage and skill in war.

The Italians wanted to drive the British out of Egypt. They thought their best chance to do so was while Britain was occupied with the Battle of Britain. In July 1940, in East Africa, Italian forces moved troops into Kenya and Sudan. By August, they occupied British Somaliland. By September, at the height of the Blitz, Italian forces attacked eastward from Libya and occupied a position nearly 60 miles within Egypt.

Running them out on a rail: The Italians surrender

Beginning in February 1941, Indian and South African units, along with a number of other British-African units, captured Mogadishu in Italian Somalia. By April they captured Addis Ababa in Ethiopia. They also drove Italian troops from Kenya and British Somaliland. By February 1942, the British had chased the Italians back 500 miles — all the way back through Libya — and had captured 130,000 prisoners.

The Italians lost nearly 300,000 men, most of whom surrendered. Nearly all the Italian equipment fell into British hands as well.

Helping the Italians: Enter Rommel

In January 1941, the German High Command, concerned about the battle performance of Italians in North Africa, sent Rommel and two divisions — one panzer and one light-motorized — to Libya to deal with the British and stiffen the backbone of the Italians.

In March, Rommel (see Figure 5-6) attacked the British in Libya. Using aircraft and mobile tank units to outmaneuver the British, German units trapped British defenders in Tobruk's port, 100 miles from the Libyan-Egyptian border. German tanks were driving the British back across the Egyptian border, threatening the British hold on the Suez Canal.

But Rommel could go no further; he had outrun his supply bases: His forces were too far away for his supply trucks and fuel tankers. Without gasoline and ammunition, Rommel could do little but hold his position. By June 1941, a bigger show had captured everyone's attention.

FIGURE 5-6:
Field Marshal
Erwin Rommel.

Bettman/CORBIS

Chapter **6**

The Ultimate Battle: Hitler versus Stalin

B y the summer of 1941, Hitler had become the unchallenged visionary of Germany. Again and again, his plans succeeded, even when all of his advisors had cautioned him against taking action. To those who worked under him in these years, Hitler seemed to possess some deep insight into the hearts and intentions of his foes. There was no way to argue with success: Hitler had led Germany to the domination of the continent in just one year.

But between September 1940 and June 1941, Adolf Hitler made a number of decisions that changed the scope of the war in Europe and that ultimately led to the destruction of Nazi Germany. One of those decisions regarded the British. When faced with tenacious British resistance, Hitler turned away from defeating Britain and turned his attention to attacking the Soviet Union.

Once engaged in the Soviet Union, Hitler made other mistakes: He underestimated the will of the Soviet people and how long it would actually take to bring Stalin to his knees. He overestimated the capabilities of the German army as it battled the seemingly endless flood of Soviet soldiers and the brutal cold of the Soviet winter. Perhaps most tellingly, he was overly confident of his own genius, leading him to disregard the advice of men more experienced than he.

If at First You Don't Succeed, Find Another Target

Hitler, never one to underestimate what he believed to be a divinely inspired gift of genius, now began to dream very big.

>> With Britain's defeat, Germany would control nearly all of Africa, sharing the rest with Italy. As an added bonus, the defeat of Britain would give him more than enough naval power to take on the United States.

>> Hitler looked ahead to a future war with the United States. After he defeated Britain, he would have the time and the resources to construct long-range bombers to attack American cities and to build a naval fleet powerful enough to challenge the U.S. Navy.

As you can see, Hitler's dreams seemed to hinge on one factor: the defeat of Britain. Every other nation had fallen to German military force in just weeks. Hitler and Goering believed that it would only take a few weeks to force Britain to surrender. But, unfortunately for the Germans, Britain did not cooperate with their plans. Despite heavy losses in Greece and Africa, despite the brutal bombing of its own cities, Britain refused to give up.

So Hitler, despite the fact that his dreams seemed to require the fall of Britain in order to succeed, simply turned away from that goal and directed his attention toward the Soviet Union.

Why the Soviet Union?

Britain's continued resistance gave Hitler an even greater interest in attacking the Soviet Union. Given that Hitler had never deviated from his original goals, as outlined in *Mein Kampf* (See Chapter 2) this seemingly sudden change in direction becomes a little more understandable. In his quest for world domination, for the eradication of "inferior" races and Bolshevism (Communism), for *Lebensraum* (living space), and for expansion of the German people to the east, the Soviet Union was the obvious target — to Hitler, anyway.

To him, the defeat of France and Britain were only preliminary events to the main event: conquering the Soviet Union. The Soviet Union had always been Hitler's main objective, and the sooner he swept Stalin away, the sooner Germany would triumph. Hitler was certain that defeating the Soviet Union would eliminate Britain and the United States as threats and that the land gained in western Russia would fulfill the German need for *Lebensraum*. (If you want a closer look into Hitler's thinking, take a look at the following section.)

DID FIVE WEEKS MAKE THE DIFFERENCE?

Many have speculated that the March 1941 anti-Nazi coup in Yugoslavia, which led to the invasion of that country, and the British resistance in Greece against the German onslaught tied up German Panzer divisions for five critical weeks, delaying the planned German attack on the USSR from May until late June. Even though they suffered serious defeats, the British, as it turned out, just may have saved the Soviet Union and kept it in the war. Those five weeks may have been just enough time to allow the Russian winter to do its job on the invaders and prevent the capture of Moscow. Others say that bad weather and supply problems delayed the attack. The fact is, the attack was delayed five critical weeks, and that may have made all the difference in the world.

Working the dream: Inside the Führer's mind

MILITARY STRATEGY

But what about Britain? Was it really a good idea to turn away from defeating the English and instead attack the Soviets? This was a sound strategic question — one that was asked several times by German generals and planning staffs that reported to Hitler. Hitler was so wrapped up in his determination to reach his goals that he developed an elaborate rationale for why his idea would work. Here's how Hitler's logic went:

>> Britain was still fighting because it was hoping for help from the Soviet Union and the United States. If the Soviet Union were knocked out, then Britain would see that its struggle was hopeless.

>> Likewise, the defeat of the Soviet Union would free the Japanese to pursue their goals in Asia, putting them on a collision course with the United States.

>> Facing a threat from Japan, the U.S. would have no interest in supporting Britain in Europe.

On top of that, the defeat of the Soviet Union was necessary for Germany to gain *Lebensraum* in western Russia. Therefore, Hitler concluded, a war with the USSR was the best choice for Germany.

Faced with this kind of logic, German military leaders were, not surprisingly, a bit skeptical that everything would work out in the way Hitler had outlined it. But, like always, the Führer waved aside all doubts.

Laying the groundwork: Operation BARBAROSSA

Hitler estimated that the conquest of the USSR would take five months, so he wanted to attack in the late spring of 1941. By attacking then, German forces wouldn't have to fight in the bitter Russian winter.

In December 1940, Hitler gave the directive for the attack on the USSR, naming it *Operation BARBAROSSA*. The plan was completed in January 1941. Three separate groups of armies would attack simultaneously across a front of nearly 1,200 miles. Here was the plan:

>> One group (Army Group North) would attack from East Prussia with the objective of taking Leningrad.

>> A second group (Army Group South) would start from Poland and Romania and attack toward Kiev.

>> The third and most powerful group (Army Group Center) would attack with most of the tank forces available and drive toward Smolensk. Its ultimate objective would be Moscow, nearly 650 miles away from the group's starting point.

Originally scheduled to start in May, the USSR operation was postponed, by the Yugoslavia invasion, until June. The Germans also brought the Finns, the Romanians, the Slovaks, and the Hungarians into the plan.

Appeasing Germany: Stalin Is Clueless

Soviet foreign policy after the fall of France can only be described as appeasement. Stalin didn't want to do anything that would antagonize Hitler.

>> He stood by and watched as the German overran the Balkans, often considered the Russians' backyard, and he offered nothing more than a meaningless treaty of friendship to Yugoslavia when that country looked to the USSR for help in the crisis that preceded the German invasion.

>> He scrupulously followed the terms of his treaty obligations to Germany. From the initiation of the Nazi-Soviet Non-Aggression Pact in 1939 until the day after German armies invaded the Soviet Union in 1941, Stalin dutifully supplied Germany with critical raw materials, including 1 million tons of petroleum, 2 million tons of grain, and 100,000 tons of cotton, according to a strict schedule of delivery. In fact, on the morning of the invasion, German troops watched as a Soviet train, headed for Germany loaded with material required by the treaty, passed them.

Information Stalin ignored

Stalin turned a blind eye toward any information contrary to his policy of friendship with Germany. Not only were Soviet intelligence agents reporting that Germany was planning an attack, but the United States and Britain were also relaying intelligence information to Stalin, warning him that Germany would invade soon. Not only did Stalin ignore these warnings; he publicly announced that any rumors of a German attack on the USSR were not true.

By ignoring clear intelligence information that indicated that he should be preparing for a German attack and by clinging to the hope that Hitler would not attack, Stalin set his military and the Soviet people up for disaster.

The signs of an impending attack were so strong that Stalin finally sent an alert message to the Soviet armed forces. But the wording of the message, which went out about four hours before the actual German attack, said nothing about the attack and reflected Stalin's indecision. The message simply said, "The task of our troops is to resist any provocation which could lead to major complications." Those major complications were on their way.

Mistakes Stalin made

Stalin should have learned a couple things from the experiences of other armies that had faced the Germans: First, placing troops in a linear defense was an invitation to disaster. After Germany's armored forces broke through such a line, nothing could stop them. Second, the *blitzkrieg* (German for "lightning war") showed that the German army's objectives were focused on both political and military objectives. Beginning in 1939, the German campaigns sought not only to quickly defeat the army of the enemy but also to bring down political leadership of the country. For every German attack, a nation's capital had been a prime target. Disregarding these things, Stalin made the following strategic mistakes:

MILITARY STRATEGY

>> He believed that Soviet troops needed to be placed as far forward as possible to defend the USSR's borders.

>> Assuming that the Germans would head for the strategic oil fields, he deployed the Soviet forces in the south where he believed the main attack would come.

The Germans hit hard and fast

The Germans struck the USSR at 4:15 a.m. on June 22. The German force contained over 3.7 million men organized into 148 divisions. It included 19 panzer (tank) divisions — 3,350 tanks in all and 13 motorized divisions — supported by 7,000 artillery pieces and 2,500 aircraft. Germany's allies added another 1.3 million men.

On the Soviet side were over 2 million men of the Soviet Army organized into 130 divisions — 40 in the center, 30 in the north, and 60 in the south. The Soviet High Command had given no warning of war, and the Soviet military had no time to prepare. In fact, the Soviet Army was in the midst of reorganization and in no way prepared for combat.

Before dawn on June 22, the *Luftwaffe* attacked Soviet aircraft bases, destroying 1,200 aircraft in the first eight hours of the war. Inexperienced Soviet pilots were no match for the German fighters. Combat losses averaged over 300 a day in the first week.

Easily breaking through the Soviet defenses, German armored and mechanized infantry units were miles behind the front lines before the Soviets realized what had happened. Hours after the initial attack, the Soviet High Command was issuing orders for counterattacks to units that either no longer existed or had been completely bypassed by fast moving German formations. Hitler's plan (Operation BARBAROSSA) seemed to be working (see Figure 6-1):

>> Army Group North advanced 200 miles in four days; by late July they had captured Riga and were only 200 miles from Leningrad, its main target.

>> Army Group Center, whose ultimate target was Moscow, was encircling entire Soviet armies near Minsk in late June, capturing 340,000 prisoners. By August 5, they had surrounded more Soviet units at Smolensk, capturing another 300,000 prisoners and advancing 500 miles.

>> Initially delayed and partially prepared Soviet defenders, Army Group South held up before Kiev. But by August 20, this group encircled Soviet divisions and captured 103,000 men.

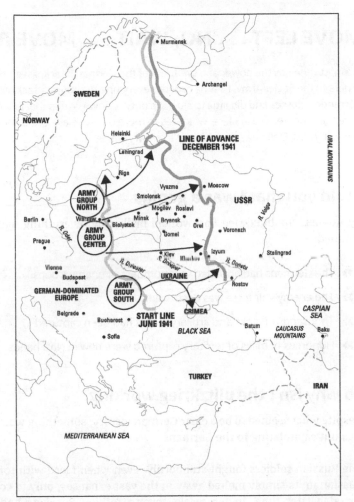

FIGURE 6-1:
Germany attacks
the USSR, 1941.

CHURCHILL PLEDGES SUPPORT TO THE SOVIETS

On the day of the German invasion, Churchill addressed the people of Britain. "We are resolved to destroy Hitler and every vestige of the Nazi regime . . . Any man or state who fights on against Nazidom will have our aid. Any man or state who marches with Hitler is our foe . . . we shall give whatever help we can to Russia and the Russian people." Churchill had despised Bolshevism from its first appearance; in fact, he believed Stalin's regime to be nearly indistinguishable from Hitler's. Yet, as he put it, "If Hitler invaded Hell, I would at least make favorable reference to the Devil in the House of Commons."

I told you that I was a genius

By August, the blitzkrieg had worked brilliantly. Everything had gone as Hitler planned:

>> The Germans had encircled vast numbers of enemy troops.

>> The enemy's air force was destroyed.

>> Thousands of tanks and artillery pieces had been captured.

>> Hundreds of miles of territory captured were now in Nazi hands.

So why isn't the blitzkrieg working?

Despite what seemed to be a clear German victory, something was wrong — Stalin was not capitulating to the Germans.

The Russian soldiers fought stubbornly, even when faced with total defeat. Other Russian units simply melted away in the vast expanses, only to come back stronger at a later time. In ten weeks, over 1 million Russians had been killed or wounded, but the Germans had lost 450,000 men. And the Russians kept coming.

Forgetting What's Important: Hitler's Fatal Decision

By August, the German generals had to make a decision about their strategy in the Soviet Union: Where should they focus their military might? The Ukraine or Moscow? They awaited Hitler's decision.

Vast distances were yet to be covered, and although most of the Soviet units had been destroyed, the Soviets were mobilizing what appeared to the Germans to be an unlimited supply of men — over 5 million.

A COUPLE FORMIDABLE ENEMIES

Despite meeting their initial military objectives in the Soviet Union, Germans faced obstacles as well. One obstacle was the Russian terrain:

- Despite having millions of men and thousands of machines, the German army seemed to get swallowed up in the vast expanses of the interior of Russia. The Germans couldn't effectively cover the immense amount of space with the troops, cannons, or tanks they had — and they had a lot.

- The roads were hardly worthy of a name — most were dirt tracks that were dry and dusty — and they appeared limitless, and the rivers broad and fast.

For all their effective modern equipment, the German army still heavily depended on a supply system that had not changed much since the late nineteenth century. The German army was supplied largely by horse drawn wagons. In fact, most of the German army walked through Russia, just like Napoleon's army did in 1812.

The Soviet T-34 tank was another nasty surprise for the Germans. Superior in nearly every category to German tanks, it was a fearsome weapon when properly applied in combat, and it racked up large numbers of kills.

The Soviets were organizing and moving the new troops against the Germans. Although these troops were poorly trained, equipped, and led — and hardly a match for the combat hardened Germans — the sheer weight of their numbers was wearing the German units out. In fighting this seemingly endless flow of Soviet troops, the German army consumed ammunition, fuel, and men in alarming numbers.

German military commanders at the front and at the main headquarters in Berlin agreed that Moscow had to be taken to end the war. Hitler, however, had other ideas. Focused on his objective of *Lebensraum*, he decided that Ukraine and its major city of Kiev had to be conquered first for the following reasons:

- ›› Ukraine was the vital food producing area.

- ›› Its vast plains, or steppes, represented Hitler's dream *Lebensraum*.

- ›› Ukraine also possessed large mineral resources that Germany could eventually exploit.

As he always had done before, Hitler overruled his generals, relying on his instinct for guidance. His generals redirected their panzer units away from Moscow and began a vast encirclement of Ukraine from the north and south.

By mid-September, the two German forces had linked up 100 miles east of Kiev. In two weeks, the pocket of over 1 million Soviet soldiers who defended Ukraine had been crushed. By all measurements, it was an impressive victory for the Germans: Four Soviet armies had been destroyed and 665,000 prisoners had been taken. But 100,000 more Germans had been lost, tanks and tank crews had been pushed to their limits, and it was October.

Stalin rallies the Soviet people

In the first few days after the German attack, Stalin seemed to be in a stupor. Almost a week had gone by before any directives for national defense were sent out. Stalin himself did not address the Soviet citizens by radio until early July. Then, the man who had murdered tens of thousands of innocent people and imprisoned tens of thousands more, who had taken property away from citizens and wiped out the leadership of the Soviet army, and who had left the nation unprepared for war, appealed to the Soviet citizens. They were, he said, his brothers and sisters.

Conveniently forgetting Soviet propaganda, Stalin called on the spirit of Mother Russia and appealed to a historic sense of national duty and patriotism that not even Stalin at his worst had been able to eradicate entirely. Fortunately, the spirit of patriotism was still alive; otherwise, the USSR couldn't have survived the German attack. In many areas, the population rose en masse to resist the invaders. Men went to the army, and women, children, and the elderly went to work in factories. (In other places such as Ukraine, where Stalin's repressions had cost millions of lives, the Germans were welcomed as liberators.)

The *State Committee for Defense* was established to direct the war effort. Factories and their workers, threatened by the German advance, were dismantled and relocated far into the interior of the USSR. Nationalities (mostly Moslems, as well as Chechens) suspected of possibly collaborating with the Germans were deported to Siberia.

The road to Moscow

By the end of September, the Soviet weather had already started to turn bad; the fall rains were turning the dry, dusty roads of the summer into bogs of impenetrable mud. Given the conditions, the Soviets felt certain that the Germans would not attempt another offensive until spring 1942.

On October 1, the Germans launched the attack on Moscow. Called *Operation TYPHOON*, the attack caught the Soviets unaware. They had spread their defenses too thin across the center before Moscow and had made no defensive preparations.

TAKING NO PRISONERS: MARSHAL ZHUKOV

Georgi Zhukov became Russian Chief of Staff in January 1941. Born to a peasant family, he joined the Russian army during the Great War and, as a noncommissioned officer (sergeant), was awarded the highest decoration for bravery. After the Bolshevik revolution, Zhukov joined the Soviet Army in 1918 and fought in the cavalry during the civil war. He made his mark in the cavalry, rising to command a squadron. In the 1930s, Zhukov had the opportunity to study the new German military thinking. He also went to Spain to observe how tanks and aircraft were employed in combat. Shortly thereafter, he was in China to observe the Japanese Kwangtung Army's war against Chiang Kai-shek. Because he was a relative unknown and did not serve on the general staff, Zhukov survived Stalin's purges, in which half of the 75,000 serving officers of the Soviet Army were executed or sent to the GULAGs (Soviet work camps in Siberia for political prisoners and other undesirables).

Zhukov rose to prominence in the little known, intense fighting that took place in 1939 between Japanese and Soviet forces in Mongolia, a Soviet protectorate. Taking command, he carefully prepared his forces for offensive action while maintaining a strong defensive posture. In August, his attack, which used an overwhelming number of tanks in combination with infantry and cavalry, drove the Japanese out of Mongolia. The victory showed his willingness to take enormous casualties to achieve his objective. Zhukov participated as a staff officer during the second campaign against Finland in 1940. He then served as Chief of Staff for Marshal Timoshenko, the Commissar of Defense.

When the German invasion began, Zhukov became indispensable, rushing from one danger point to another. Ruthless, he gave his subordinates two choices: Obey orders or face a firing squad. In the crisis of 1941, Zhukov was one of the few officers who could speak his mind to Stalin without fear of being arrested and killed. His recall to Moscow in October 1941, after he had organized the defenses around Leningrad, gave him the opportunity to use his combat talents. His December counterattack saved Moscow and marked a pattern that would continue throughout the rest of the war: careful preparation, followed by aggressive tank and armor attacks intended to cripple the enemy without concern for friendly casualties. The only objective was victory, and those commanders who failed would not live long enough to make other mistakes. Zhukov was Stalin's kind of general.

Again German tanks and aircraft pummeled the enemy units. Six Soviet armies were surrounded at Vyazma and Bryansk, with the Germans capturing 600,000 prisoners. Bad weather arrived, however, preventing the *Luftwaffe* from flying, slowing advances to a crawl, and preventing supplies from reaching combat units. Tanks began breaking down, and the Germans were without spare parts.

REMEMBER

The weather turned cold, and the Germans had no winter clothing (the war was supposed to be over before winter started). As temperatures dropped, the mud went from glop to concrete. The mud froze on tracks and wheels and had to be chipped off with axes, picks, and shovels. The German units approached Moscow under the poor weather conditions; by December 5, they were within 15 miles of the city. But this time, though, the Germans were fighting both the Russians and "General Winter." High winds and snow made every activity difficult. The temperature was 25 degrees below zero. Weapons no longer fired, radios didn't work, engines wouldn't start, and the wounded and sick quickly froze to death.

New fire for the Soviets: Zhukov takes command

Marshal Georgi Zhukov had taken command of Moscow's defenses in October. He had just returned from Leningrad where he had organized that city's defenses. In Moscow, Zhukov found that Stalin had committed the last reserves. Zhukov gathered together anyone capable of holding a rifle and anxiously awaited the arrival of first-rate combat units from Siberia. When he believed that the Germans had reached their limit, Zhukov ordered a counterattack. Threatened with encirclement, the Germans retreated towards Vyzama and safety.

Corporal Hitler Takes Charge of the Eastern Front

The first week of December 1941 marked the first time, since World War II had begun, that the German army had been forced to retreat. For Hitler, the retreat was too much to handle: He gave impossible orders — the first of many — to army commanders and demanded that no German units retreat. When they did invariably retreat, he began relieving generals left and right. In one fell swoop, Hitler took over personal direction of the war against the Soviet Union.

Of course, Hitler's only experience in war was as a corporal in the trenches during World War I — hardly preparation for overseeing perhaps the greatest land battle in the history of the world. Now the corporal was in charge, and his generals could only stand by and watch. Soon Hitler became so absorbed in his crusade, which he described as a war of annihilation, that he wasn't keeping an eye on the overall strategic direction of the war.

Hitler had come to his final confrontation with Bolshevism. He would pour the entire might of Germany into the struggle that would end only when one side or the other was completely destroyed. In the process, he diverted vast resources of the state to his program for eradicating Jews and Slavs.

IN THIS CHAPTER

» **Talking the isolation talk**

» **Ignoring the signs of trouble**

» **Twisting the law**

» **Waking up to reality**

Chapter 7

America on the Sidelines: 1933–1941

mericans are interesting people. In some ways, they are the most forward-looking people on Earth, eager to push the past behind them and run as fast as possible to a better future. But at the same time, Americans like to think that they understand the past and can easily draw all the right lessons from previous experiences.

So it was with Americans in the 1920s and 1930s. They believed they had learned and applied all the right lessons from the experience of the Great War: They joined the war in Europe in 1917 in a burst of patriotism and idealism, anxious to right wrongs and make the world a better place. But when victory didn't make those things happen, they became deeply disenchanted with international politics and alliance systems. Many Americans came to believe that the war had been a ghastly mistake; they had poured blood and treasure into a snake pit of ancient rivalries and ethnic hatreds.

From these experiences, Americans learned two things:

» Avoid any involvement in European or Asian affairs and remain strictly neutral if war came to any part of the world.

>> Secure between two vast oceans, America didn't need any allies; it needn't rely on any other nation, and it could pursue its interests regardless of what happened anywhere else.

This approach to foreign policy was called *isolationism*. It was also naïve.

Looking Inward: A New President and a Neutral Stance

The worldwide economic depression hit the United States very hard. In 1933, America inaugurated a new president, Franklin D. Roosevelt (see Figure 7-1), who promised to beat the economic bad times by harnessing the power of the national government to secure prosperity. The day after Roosevelt took office, Adolf Hitler became Chancellor of Germany. Ironically, the destinies of the two men and their nations became entwined in quite unexpected ways.

FIGURE 7-1:
Franklin
D. Roosevelt.

Bettmann/Getty Images

Upon his election, Roosevelt worked to stabilize the sinking U.S. economy and so took little action in international affairs. As a result, Congress took the initiative to form foreign policy. At the time, isolationists dominated Congress, and the U.S. Senate created a committee to study how America ended up in the Great War.

The committee discovered that (surprise!) American bankers and arms manufacturers had made huge profits from loans and from selling war materials to the Europeans, especially the French and British. The Senators stretched the point further: Starry-eyed idealists (such as President Woodrow Wilson) had been duped by American big business into committing the nation to war on the side of the Allies. The reason? So that big business could reap even bigger profits and ensure that the French and British could repay their debts.

The publicity that these "discoveries" generated led Congress to pass legislation to prevent America from ever making such a mistake again. Between 1935 and 1937, Congress passed the first of a series of *Neutrality Acts*.

FDR: LEADERSHIP FOR VICTORY

Franklin Delano Roosevelt (1882–1945) first dealt with military issues as Assistant Secretary of the United States Navy during World War I. He advocated a large, two-ocean navy and believed in being prepared for war. As the Democratic vice-presidential nominee in 1920, he supported a strong presidency and an active foreign policy, including United States participation in the League of Nations. Left paralyzed from a bout with polio in 1921, Roosevelt remained active in public affairs. He was elected Governor of New York in 1928.

By 1932, Roosevelt was the only Democrat with enough political clout to challenge Herbert Hoover for the presidency. Roosevelt became the thirty-second President of the United States in March 1933, in the midst of one of the nation's greatest crises — the Great Depression. Between 13 and 15 million Americans were out of work. Roosevelt attempted to solve what he thought were the root causes of the Depression by creating the welfare state and making the federal government the agent of social and economic reform. Although his policies were very controversial, his greatest gift to the nation was his optimism and ability to reach Americans directly through press conferences, speeches, and his famous fireside chats on the radio. He inspired people's confidence in the government and in themselves. As a result, he served an unprecedented three terms, carrying America through economic depression and war.

As a director of the nation's foreign policy prior to the war, Roosevelt showed himself to be the master at accommodating the dominant point of view. Yet he maneuvered and stretched in every way to slip the bonds of the Neutrality Acts when he realized that Britain was in danger. He also pressured Japan through an economic embargo, an act that unintentionally pushed Japan to attack Pearl Harbor. Heavily influenced by Winston Churchill early on, FDR understood the importance of British and American unity and capably balanced domestic unity with Allied interests throughout the war.

The Neutrality Act of 1935 and its extension

The first Neutrality Act was a temporary one. Passed in August of 1935, the act was intended to expire after six months, in February 1936. This act authorized the President to prohibit arms shipments to nations at war (called *belligerents*) and to declare no responsibility for American citizens traveling on the ships of those nations.

In 1936, Congress extended the Neutrality Act for another 14 months and banned any loans or credits to nations at war.

The Neutrality Act of 1937

Congress passed another Neutrality Act in 1937, just as Japan initiated full-scale war against China and began bombing Chinese cities. Unlike the Neutrality Act of 1935, the Act of 1937 was permanent. This act contained many of the same restrictions as the earlier act — banning loans to belligerent nations and mandating an embargo of belligerent nations, for example, but it contained a few changes:

» Whereas the travel ban on belligerent ships had been discretionary before, in the Neutrality Act of 1937, the ban was now mandatory.

» The 1937 Act included a mandatory ban on arming American merchant ships that traded with belligerents.

» The Act established a discretionary two-year cash-and-carry policy: This meant that warring nations could get products, including war material, from the United States, but they had to pay for it in the United States and only their ships could carry the cargo.

The effect of the Neutrality Acts

Although America had enacted these laws with the best intentions, the Neutrality Acts actually appeared to help aggressor nations:

» When Italy invaded Ethiopia in 1935, Roosevelt ordered an arms embargo on both nations, even though Ethiopia was clearly a victim of aggression.

» When Germany declared in 1936 that it was no longer bound by the Versailles Treaty and reoccupied the Rhineland, the administration was silent.

» America's strict neutrality contributed to the French and British position of neutrality during the Spanish Civil War, which allowed Hitler and Mussolini to interfere freely in the conflict. As a result, Spanish dictator Francisco Franco's Nationalist forces won the war.

WANTING THEIR SAY: THE LUDLOW AMENDMENT

Louis Ludlow, a Congressman from Indiana, introduced a proposed amendment to the United States Constitution in January 1938. It stated, "Except in the event of an invasion of the United States or its Territorial possessions . . . the authority of Congress to declare war shall not become effective until confirmed by a majority of all votes cast thereon in a Nation-wide referendum." Public opinion polls showed that 75 percent of Americans thought that the Ludlow Amendment was a good idea. Only after a monumental effort by the Roosevelt administration and its supporters in Congress did the vote to present the amendment to the states for ratification fail, 209 to 188. (A majority of the House voted for the amendment, but sending an amendment to the states for ratification requires a two-thirds vote in both the House and Senate.)

In light of future events, the complications this amendment would have caused are almost unimaginable. Yet Americans were so adamant about staying out of war that they were willing to change the basic law of the land.

In 1936, Germany, Italy, and Japan signed a pact soon designated as the *Rome–Berlin–Tokyo Axis*. Although it appeared that the militarists were uniting in a common cause, American public opinion was solidly in favor of any and all measures to stay out of any conflict.

Message from Japan

Faced with what appeared to be a disintegrating international situation, Roosevelt spoke in Chicago in 1937 comparing the current trend of international lawlessness to a disease. Just as a disease must be quarantined to protect the community's health, so he implied must the world community quarantine an aggressor. These innocuous remarks led to calls for his impeachment and solid public approval of neutrality and noninvolvement.

Just a few months after Roosevelt made this speech, Japanese aircraft attacked the American warship USS *Panay*, sinking the ship, killing three Americans, and then machine gunning unarmed sailors in lifeboats. Although the Japanese denied that the attack was deliberate, they had clearly sent a message to the United States to stay out of China. America asked for an apology, a monetary settlement (2.2 million dollars), and a promise not to do it again. In isolationist America, this was as far as U.S. indignation went.

Bad Signs in Europe

ARMY ALLIED

As events in Europe moved swiftly to crisis from the *Anschluss* (or "union") with Austria in 1938 to the invasion of Poland on September 1, 1939, America watched impassively as Hitler hoodwinked everyone, claiming that Germany's foreign policy simply involved reincorporating German territory that had been taken from it unfairly by the Versailles Treaty. After these innocent adjustments were made, Hitler claimed, Germany had no other ambitions in Europe.

But the March 1939 occupation of the rest of Czechoslovakia and Hitler's threats to Poland revealed that his true objectives were the conquest and subjugation of Eastern Europe — not the restoration of German people to Germany, as he had claimed. Americans also noted Hitler's persecution of German Jews, mostly because so many began arriving on American shores. Among those escaping Nazi Germany were Albert Einstein and other artists and scientists who represented the cream of Germany's intellectual community.

ARMY ALLIED

In 1938, Roosevelt was able to get Congress to allocate 1 billion dollars for a military buildup. He used the money to build battleships, cruisers, and aircraft carriers as well as to expand air and ground forces. The *isolationists,* who opposed any involvement with other nations and were a national force to be reckoned with, strongly opposed this plan. But Roosevelt was able to sell his buildup as a simple preparedness measure. He argued that these additional forces would help America make sure that Europe's problems stayed in Europe.

Roosevelt Plays the Neutrality Game

The day after France and Britain declared war on Germany (in September 1939 after the German invasion of Poland in March), President Roosevelt addressed the nation. While declaring the United States legally neutral, he said that Americans could not remain neutral in thought: "Even a neutral cannot be asked to close his mind and conscience."

After the war began, neutrality legislation placed an embargo on all American arms shipped to warring nations. Because the embargo was hurting the unprepared democracies, Roosevelt asked Congress to extend the cash-and-carry policy to nations currently at war (specifically Britain). Roosevelt also declared a combat zone, which excluded American ships or citizens from traveling to the west coast of Europe.

REMEMBER

The cash-and-carry policy allowed Americans to sell products, including war supplies, to warring nations as long as the buyers came to the U.S. to get and pay for the items and took the stuff back on their own ships. See the section "Looking Inward: A New President and a Neutral Stance" for more on the Neutrality Acts.

Roosevelt unwittingly assisted Hitler's naval war against Britain by making submarine attacks on British shipping more effective. With the combat zone, which kept American ships out of the waters off of Western Europe, the Germans no longer had to worry about figuring out whether a ship was a neutral ship or an enemy ship before torpedoing it.

France's Fall: America's Wake-up Call

No one was prepared for the kind of attack that Hitler unleashed on Britain and France in the summer of 1940. Denmark, Belgium, Holland, Luxembourg, and then France collapsed in the face of the Nazi onslaught. The British army, cut off by fast moving German tank forces, just barely escaped from the port of Dunkirk. Just a few weeks later, Americans listened to radio reports from American newsmen in London describing the German bombing raids. (See Chapter 5 for more info on these events.)

Suddenly, Americans were scared. What would happen if Britain surrendered? What would become of the British fleet? Couldn't it be used against America? What if Greenland (a possession of Denmark) and Iceland were occupied by the Nazis? Wouldn't that put German ships and planes in range of the North American coast? What, they asked, would happen if the Germans controlled all of Europe?!

The answer? America would be alone and vulnerable. And everyone knew that Hitler's guarantees to respect neutrals were worthless.

Wheeling and dealing with Britain: Talkin' belligerent

With the fall of France and the prospect that Britain might be the next to topple, the U.S. Congress got religion, and the money began to flow for American defensive measures. "Preparedness" was the word on everyone's lips. The President got 10.5 billion dollars for national defense in 1940. (For seven years, Roosevelt's domestic policies had failed to end the Depression; the vast increases in military production ended it in a year.)

In May, British Prime Minister Winston Churchill made an urgent request for 50 reconditioned American destroyers to replace combat losses and fight German *U-boats* (submarines). The U-boats were crippling Britain's economic lifeline — its merchant fleet, which provided the nation with raw materials, food, and military supplies.

The deal

Roosevelt looked for a way to sidestep the U.S. neutrality laws. Working carefully, he built Congressional support for a deal with Britain: The U.S. would give Britain 50 old destroyers; Britain, in turn, would have to give the U.S. its naval bases in Bermuda and the British West Indies. It was a hard bargain. Churchill nearly choked on the deal but accepted it in the interest of future American-British cooperation.

The effect

The deal between Britain and the United States (see the preceding section) marked the movement of the United States from a neutral to a belligerent.

>> In September 1940, the nation's first peacetime draft went into effect; 16.5 million American men registered for military call-up.

>> The President asked for and received an extension of the draftees' service period, which had initially been one year.

REMEMBER

The extension was bitterly debated in Congress as isolationists fought to prevent America from making any preparations that would lead the nation to war. The measure passed, but by only one vote in the House of Representatives. Isolationist sentiment clearly remained strong in the nation, even as the threat of war with Germany and Japan loomed.

Help thy neighbor: The Lend-Lease Act

Churchill informed Roosevelt that Britain would soon be bankrupt if the current cash-and-carry policy for arms and ammunition continued.

Searching for a way to skirt the neutrality laws, Roosevelt came upon an obscure 1892 law that authorized the Secretary of War to lease property not required by the military. Roosevelt knew that if the U.S. could lease war material to Britain, Britain could stay in the fight. But he had to sell the idea to the American public first.

"If your neighbor's house caught fire and he had no garden hose," he posed to Americans, "the prudent thing to do in order to prevent the fire from spreading is to lend him your hose." This little homily helped convince Americans that

Britain's survival was essential to American security. To clinch the argument, Roosevelt used a brilliant metaphor: America would become "the great arsenal of democracy."

The legislation that passed Congress, numbered interestingly enough *H.R. 1776* (House of Representatives Bill number 1776), would do the following:

>> Give the President the authority to exchange, lease, lend, or dispose of any defense material to any nation that was vital to United States security.

>> Allocate 7 billion dollars for what became known as lend-lease material.

>> One restriction of Lend-Lease was that American ships couldn't move lend-lease material into combat zones, nor could American warships escort American merchant ships.

The *Lend-Lease Act* passed in March 1941. Winston Churchill, in one of his classic rotund phrases, called this legislation "the most unsordid act in the history of any nation."

Lend-lease material began to flow to Britain and China, which was threatened by the Japanese. When Hitler's armies invaded the Soviet Union in 1941, Roosevelt extended lend-lease to the Soviets as well. Over the course of the war, more than 50 billion dollars of lend-lease aid went to nations fighting the Axis.

American ships go out

Britain was losing 500,000 tons of shipping a month to German U-boats and air-craft prowling around the British Isles. This meant that the Germans were sinking ships at about twice the rate at which American and British shipyards could replace them.

FDR'S PROMISE: NO AMERICANS IN FOREIGN WARS

Roosevelt faced reelection in 1940, seeking an unprecedented third term. The election was tough, with both candidates having to pledge to keep America out of war while advocating support to Britain. When accused of plotting to bring the nation into the war in Europe, Roosevelt responded with a pledge that became famous — "I have said this before, but I shall say it again and again and again: Your boys are not going to be sent into any foreign wars." By the way, Roosevelt kept his promise. By the time American troops entered the war, it was an American war.

ARMY ALLIED

Roosevelt helped Britain in the following ways:

>> He sent American destroyers on what he described as *"neutrality patrols."* The Americans would not attack German U-boats, but they would report their location to the British.

>> He placed an American base in Iceland. Now American warships were escorting American ships and stopping at Iceland, where the lend-lease material could be transferred (Iceland was not a combat zone) and British warships would continue the convoy to Britain. Very often, British, Canadian, or other ships would join the convoys of American ships crossing the Atlantic.

Enough is enough: A neutral starts shooting

The Germans could not allow this masquerade of neutrality to continue for long. By the summer of 1941, the American effort was having an effect on German U–boat operations. Here are some important events that transpired:

>> In September 1941, the USS *Greer* shadowed a U-boat off the coast of Iceland, and the German sub fired a torpedo at the American ship. In response, Roosevelt issued a shoot-on-sight order for any German U-boat encountered between the coast of America and Iceland.

>> At the end of October, the USS *Reuben James* was sunk; over 100 men were lost. By now, Roosevelt was dismantling the Neutrality Acts with a vengeance.

>> In November 1941, Congress allowed modifications of neutrality legislation to arm merchant ships and permit them to travel into belligerent ports.

For all intents and purposes, the war with Germany had begun.

THE WOLF PACK

The reason for the German's success against the British ships was its use of *wolf-pack tactics,* in which several submarines worked together to attack the British convoys from different directions. These convoys, often containing up to 50 British merchant ships, traveled at night to avoid detection. When a convoy was detected, the U-boats slipped into the midst of the convoy and attacked on the surface, actually a more effective attack than from underwater. Only the newest destroyers could chase the U-boats effectively. Until new ships for escort duty were built and new tactics to counter the wolf packs developed, Britain would continue to suffer.

IN THIS CHAPTER

» Japanese plans for the domination of Asia

» Negotiations and war preparations

» The attack on Pearl Harbor

» The beginning of the war in the Pacific

» MacArthur's stand in the Philippines

Chapter **8**

Collision in Asia: Japan and America, 1937–1941

Since the beginning of the twentieth century, Japan's goal had been to become economically self-sufficient by gaining direct access to raw materials. As China underwent political and economic revival under the leadership of Chiang Kai-shek in the 1920s, Japan began to worry about China's potential as a rival in Asia. Between 1931 and 1933, Japan occupied Manchuria, a valuable region rich in raw materials, and expanded into Jehol province. In 1936, Japan signed a pact with Germany and Italy, and by 1937, it had entered into a war with China.

This aggression brought Japan onto a collision course with the United States. Japan had not only violated a number of treaties with the U.S., but it was currently trying to subdue a nation that the U.S. had long stood by as protector and sponsor. For the Unites States government, Japan's only option was to withdraw completely from China.

A Brief History of Politics in Japan

Japan had transformed itself from a medieval society of knights and warlords to a fully industrialized modern nation in less than 60 years. It built both a Western-style parliamentary government and a first-class army and navy. But within

Japan, the historical traditions of centuries past couldn't be left behind in such a short time.

Although moderate and liberal parties existed in Japan, the ministers of the army and navy were always high-ranking officers in the military, and they had enormous power. A civilian prime minister had to select an admiral or general who would agree to serve with him. If the officer refused, the prime minister had to resign. As a result, the army and navy had veto power over any government.

By 1936, the army gained the dominant voice in the Japanese government and advocated expansion as the only means to ensure the nation's survival.

Building the Perfect Machine: Japan Thinks War

Between 1936 and 1941, Japan's army grew by 30 combat divisions and 100 aircraft squadrons. By 1940, Japan's navy was stronger than the combined fleets of the United States and Britain in the Pacific. By 1941, Japan had 300,000 regular troops and 2 million trained reserves. Its industries were at full-scale war production. Japan was not simply building up its military and war machines; it was also flexing its muscle:

>> The Japanese attacked the American gunboat the USS *Panay* in December 1937. They escaped retribution by claiming that the attack was an accident.

>> Between August and December 1937, Japanese forces captured the major Chinese cities of Shanghai and Nanking and forced Chiang Kai-shek to move his government deeper into the interior of China at Hankow. Chinese forces had succeeded in halting the Japanese with a series of desperate counterattacks and by causing the Yangtze River to flood. Nevertheless, Hankow and Canton fell to the Japanese in October 1938.

Although Japan controlled most of eastern China and its major road and rail networks, the vast interior of the country remained unconquered.

Choking China into surrender

The Japanese were surprised by the Chinese resistance, and the costs of the war had already been far more than expected. The prospect of fighting for years in the interior of China was not something that anyone wanted. So in 1939, Japan decided to isolate China from outside support.

Cutting off China's supply lines

China's only means of sustaining its war against Japan was through military aid from other nations, primarily the United States. By the end of 1939, the Japanese had succeeded in cutting off the seaports in China, and only two supply routes were left: a rail line from Haiphong harbor in French Indochina (now Vietnam) and a dangerous, twisting road from British-controlled Burma (now Myanmar).

Conquering Southeast Asia

Nearly all of Southeast Asia was under the control of three colonial powers — the British, French, and Dutch — and the area was rich in natural resources. Germany's defeat of Holland and France in June 1940 and what appeared to be the impending defeat of Great Britain (covered in Chapter 5) opened up new opportunities for the Japanese. They decided to take advantage of this opportunity by expanding into Southeast Asia and creating a protectorate over the entire region:

>> The Japanese occupied airbases in French Indochina, with the agreement of the Vichy government (helped along by the intimidating hand of Germany threatening terrible things if the Vichy did not agree).

>> Japan cut China's access to supplies from Haiphong.

>> Japan threatened Britain with war if the Burma supply line remained open. British Prime Minister Winston Churchill, not wanting to fight two foes at the height of his nation's greatest crisis, closed the road.

China was now alone.

Diplomatic chess: Japan's big plans

By the end of 1940, Japan had an ambitious plan: wage an all-out attack on East Asia. Called *The Greater East Asia Co-Prosperity Sphere*, the plan sought to achieve the following:

>> Japanese control over all the raw materials in the Pacific

>> Japanese domination of the people of Asia

Japan saw the fulfillment of this plan as a way to secure its future. By July 1941, the Japanese occupied all of French Indochina and obtained a number of air and naval bases to launch attacks on Singapore, the Dutch East Indies, and the Philippines.

Oops! Miscalculations in diplomacy: Japan joins the Axis

While preparing for a military strike on East Asia, the Japanese sought to neutralize the United States through diplomatic moves. Here's what they did:

ARMY
ALLIED

>> Signed the *Berlin-Rome-Tokyo Axis* with Germany and Italy. This pact obligated Japan to enter the war on the side of the Axis if the United States joined Great Britain in the war.

>> Signed a five-year nonaggression pact with the Soviet Union. By eliminating the Soviet Union as a threat in Asia, Japan indicated that it had only one enemy in Asia — the United States. The idea was to make Americans think twice about opposing Japanese moves in Asia.

ARMY
ALLIED

Japan's plan to cow the U.S. by signing these pacts backfired. President Roosevelt made very clear that the United States would take "any and all steps necessary" to oppose Japanese aggression. To that end, Roosevelt did the following:

>> Froze all Japanese assets in the United States. Now Japan didn't have the money it needed to buy war material.

>> Banned all trade with Japan. Japan could no longer buy American steel or oil — two strategic materials Japan depended on to continue military operations. (Back in those days, the U.S. was the world's largest exporter of oil.)

Roosevelt's intent with these steps was to jerk the leash tightly and make the Japanese think twice. The Japanese did think twice, but not in the way the Americans anticipated.

A new guy takes over

In October 1941, the Japanese army forced its moderate prime minister to resign and replaced him with General Hideki Tojo, who consolidated the positions of War Minister and Home Minister under the office of the Prime Minister.

With the oil embargo already cutting into Japan's reserves and only about 14 months of supplies left, Japan's choice was simple: give in to U.S. demands and withdraw from China or go to war. So, as the new Prime Minister, Tojo decided to prepare for war with the United States.

>> Japanese ground forces trained for jungle warfare.

>> Japanese planes flew scouting missions of Malaya and the Dutch East Indies.

>> Admiral Isoroku Yamamoto (see Figure 8-1) and his staff worked on a plan to attack the United States Pacific Fleet at Pearl Harbor, Hawaii.

FIGURE 8-1:
Admiral Isoroku Yamamoto.

Historical/Getty Images

Japan's gamble: How the war would go

Between October and December 1941, the Japanese agreed on a plan of attack to achieve their strategy. With limited resources available to continue military operations, the Japanese decided on the following:

>> To make a simultaneous attack against the centers of power in Asia, the British naval base at Singapore, the important American air and naval base in the Philippines, the smaller American bases at Wake Island and Guam.

>> To destroy or cripple the United States Pacific Fleet at Pearl Harbor by using aircraft launched from carriers. This attack would prevent any immediate response from the Americans.

MILITARY STRATEGY

By striking simultaneously, the Japanese intended to seize a broad band of territory, gain control of the raw materials, and then build strong defenses to wear down the enemy (the United States and Great Britain) and protect the Japanese homeland.

>> After they had captured these areas, the Japanese would combine their forces and attack the Dutch East Indies.

By accomplishing these goals, the Japanese believed that when the British and Americans were able to launch a counter-attack, costs of recovering the lost territory would be too great to pursue. And the war would end with the Western nations negotiating and accepting Japanese control of Asia.

Dancing diplomats: Japan and America do the two-step

The Japanese plan (see the preceding section) became more attractive given the gains the Germans made against the Soviet Union since the summer of 1941 (covered in Chapter 6). In fact, it appeared that Hitler's armies would be in Moscow before December. The Japanese thought that with the Soviet Union out of the war neither Britain nor the United States would concentrate on a fight with Japan. Instead, these countries would direct all resources toward saving Britain. By the time the U.S. and Britain could turn to deal with Japan, the Japanese would have already built up a solid defensive perimeter.

Even despite the growing attraction of the plan, the war between the Japanese and Britain and America was not inevitable. Negations with the United States continued even as Japanese planners prepared for war:

>> The Japanese wanted the United States to accept current conditions in Asia, leaving Japan to determine China's future. The Japanese also had special interests in Indochina.

>> The Americans wanted the Japanese to withdraw all forces from China and Indochina and recognize the government of the Republic of China.

Despite the diplomatic dance, there was little hope that the negotiations would be successful, so both sides continued to prepare for war: The Japanese prepared by dispatching the strike force for Pearl Harbor; the Americans prepared by passing alerts to forces in the Pacific to be ready for *something*.

The United States had broken the Japanese secret diplomatic-military code. All indications pointed to an attack, but when and where the attack would take place were not clear.

War Comes to America: Pearl Harbor

Japan's ambassadors delivered the first part of a final Japanese diplomatic note to U.S. Secretary of State Cordell Hull on December 6, 1941. On the morning of December 7, the final portion of the note arrived from Tokyo to the Japanese ambassadors. The note broke diplomatic relations with the U.S. and provided instructions to destroy the code machines in the Japanese embassy. The ambassadors were to deliver the note in the early afternoon. While the Japanese ambassadors received this information, so too did American intelligence. Everyone understood the note's meaning: War was to be declared that afternoon.

Soon after receiving the note, warnings were sent to American commanders in Hawaii, the Philippines, Panama, and San Francisco with the information that the ultimatum would be delivered at 1 p.m. Eastern Standard Time. Separate messages were sent to the United States army and navy. Somehow, the alert messages bound for Hawaii ended up being transmitted by commercial telegraph and radio. A bicycle messenger, on his way from Honolulu to deliver the coded messages, found himself in the middle of a war.

A MATTER OF (MIS-)TIMING

The Japanese ambassadors were to deliver the ultimatum message breaking relations with the United States at 1:00 p.m. Washington D.C. time, which was 7:30 a.m. Hawaii time. The attack on Pearl Harbor was to begin about 7:55 a.m. Legally speaking (according to the accepted laws of warfare), the United States would be notified that a state of war existed *before* the Japanese bombs would begin to fall on the Pacific Fleet. But the ambassadors were late, arriving at 2:20 p.m. Washington time, which was 8:30 a.m. Hawaii time. The attack on Pearl Harbor had been underway for nearly a half-hour before the ultimatum had been delivered.

Secretary of State Cordell Hull had the intercepted instructions, and in fact, had just received a call from the President informing him of the attack. To the Americans, it appeared that the Japanese had deliberately delayed the delivery of the message. Hull, deeply angry, told the Japanese diplomats, "In all my fifty years of public service, I have never seen a document that was more crowded with infamous falsehoods and distortions . . . on a scale so huge that I never imagined until today that any government on this planet was capable of uttering them." Without a word, the Japanese left the office.

For Americans, the shock of a surprise attack was compounded by outrage that the Japanese had intentionally ignored the rules of civilized nations. Ironically, neither of the diplomats knew that their nation had attacked Pearl Harbor when they delivered the message just a little bit late.

JAPAN'S SUCCESS

The ships and planes of the Japanese fleet had conducted one of the most successful military operations in history. From Japan's perspective, the attack was a complete success. A combination of U.S. unreadiness and surprise, and superb execution by the Japanese combined to make Pearl harbor a significant victory for the Japanese.

The attack

War came to America at 7:55 a.m. on a quiet Sunday morning at Pearl Harbor, Hawaii. The base on Oahu Island was the home of the United States Pacific Fleet and about 50,000 American troops. At Pearl Harbor was the largest concentration of U.S. forces in the Pacific.

A fleet of six Japanese aircraft carriers and escort ships stationed itself 230 miles off Oahu and launched its first wave of 183 fighters, bombers, and torpedo planes. They were to inflict as much damage on the fleet as they could. They were to especially target the eight U.S. battleships and two U.S. carriers. They also sought to destroy aircraft parked on the ground.

MILITARY STRATEGY

The first wave of Japanese bombers found plenty to attack. About 200 American ships and smaller craft were anchored in the harbor, and hundreds of warplanes were parked wingtip to wingtip at the airfields (planes arranged this way are easier to protect from sabotage).

A second wave of 170 Japanese aircraft followed up and found the harbor obscured by giant columns of black smoke and antiaircraft fire. During this wave, the Japanese lost 19 aircraft from ground fire and American fighters that had managed to get into the air.

The entire attack lasted only about an hour and fifty minutes.

The aftermath

ARMY ALLIED

The attack on Pearl Harbor killed 2,400 Americans and wounded another 1,200. Of those dead, 1,103 sailors and marines were killed when a Japanese bomb penetrated the forward *magazine* (the compartment where a ship's ammunition is stored) of the battleship USS *Arizona*, sinking the ship and the men aboard it. The USS *Oklahoma*, another battleship, was also sunk with heavy loss of life. The other six battleships were damaged, and so were a number of cruisers and destroyers. Over 340 of the 400 aircraft on Oahu were destroyed or damaged as well.

Japanese gains

In the short run, the Japanese accomplished their objective. They had knocked the United States Pacific Fleet out of action temporarily. But how temporarily was the most important issue. In the long run, the United States was able to overcome the damage at Pearl Harbor for the following reasons:

>> The aircraft carriers weren't touched. The carrier would prove to be the decisive weapon of the naval war in the Pacific, not the battleship, which every naval strategist before 1941 thought would be the primary naval weapon.

>> The submarines were not attacked. Submarines became one of America's most potent weapons in crippling Japan's vital supply lines.

>> The repair dockyards and fuel-oil storage tanks were undamaged. Thus, Pearl Harbor was able to serve its important role in wartime as a repair and refitting base for the Pacific Fleet. In fact, most of the American ships damaged in the attack were repaired and entered action against the Japanese later in 1942 and 1943.

Nevertheless, Pearl Harbor was a bitter defeat for the United States. American territory had been attacked, and American lives had been lost. Pearl Harbor unified the divided and uncertain American population as no earlier action could.

The U.S. declares war on Japan

Japan had underestimated the Americans, who they believed would prefer to negotiate rather than fight. To the contrary, America wanted revenge.

Although deeply divided over war issues and neutrality before Pearl Harbor, the U.S. Congress was now united in seeking a declaration of war. As outlined in the United States Constitution, the president must ask Congress for such a declaration, which Roosevelt willingly did. In his message to Congress, Roosevelt captured the emotions of the day:

"Yesterday, December 7, 1941 — a date which will live in infamy — the United States was suddenly and deliberately attacked by naval and air forces of the Empire of Japan. . . . Always will our whole nation remember the character of the onslaught against us. No matter how long it may take us to overcome this premeditated invasion, the American people in their righteous might will win through to absolute victory."

British Prime Minister Winston Churchill had no doubt what Roosevelt's words meant for the British. "So we had won after all!" he wrote. "After seventeen months of lonely fighting and nineteen months of my responsibility in dire stress. We had won the war. England would live; Britain would live; the Commonwealth of Nations and the Empire would live."

The Japanese Wage War

In the Pacific, the Japanese were employing their own style of lightning warfare (blitzkrieg) by striking hard simultaneously at key outposts. The Americans were not the only victims of surprise attacks in the days after Pearl Harbor. The British and Dutch would also suffer astounding military defeats at the hands of Japanese forces. While the Japanese fleet hit Pearl Harbor, Japanese aircraft and ground forces attacked Hong Kong, the British controlled city in China. The 12,000-man garrison was trapped and forced to surrender on Christmas day. (See Chapter 5 for an explanation of how the Germans used the blitzkrieg.)

Malaya: The worst defeat in British history

Malaya, a British colony, provided nearly half the world's rubber and nearly one-third of its tin. Both of these strategic materials were essential to the Japanese strategy for controlling Asia.

At the end of the Malay Peninsula, at Singapore, was the British naval base. By controlling Singapore, the Japanese would control access to the Pacific from the west through the straits of Sumatra. But the British were a tough target; they had a large army and excellent harbor defenses that were protected by two powerful naval vessels, the HMS *Prince of Wales* and the HMS *Repulse*.

MILITARY STRATEGY

Nonetheless, the Japanese displayed a nearly perfect blend of air and land power against the surprised defenders. A series of amphibious landings on the Malay peninsula followed by infantry infiltrating through what was assumed to be impenetrable jungle quickly broke the British defenses. When the HMS *Prince of Wales* and the HMS *Repulse* sallied out to attack the amphibious support ships, they were attacked by Japanese aircraft from bases in Indochina.

HISTORICAL TRIVIA

For the first time in history, ships fought against air attack alone. Up to this time, few believed that air attack alone could sufficiently damage warships. In two hours, the British ships and their crews were lost.

By January 1942, the Japanese had thoroughly whipped the British and trapped them in Singapore. The siege went on for another month before 130,000 British troops finally surrendered in February. The British military had never suffered a greater defeat.

The Dutch East Indies

MILITARY STRATEGY

Following the example that the Germans had set in Norway, Holland, and Belgium (see Chapter 5 for details), Japanese paratroopers landed on Borneo, Indonesia, in December and January to seize key installations and airfields. A naval escort then brought troopships protected by a dense umbrella of combat aircraft.

A scraped-together collection of American, British, Dutch, and Australian forces tried to stop the invasion. Four American destroyers surprised and sank a Japanese convoy in January. But by February, superior Japanese naval and air power had taken its toll on the Allied ships trying to defend the maze of channels and straits that divided the islands.

By chance, the Allies encountered a major amphibious force off the island of Java, Indonesia. Although outgunned and outnumbered, the Allies attacked and sank several troop ships before being wiped out by the Japanese task force. About 93,000 men of the Allied land forces defending Java surrendered on March 9, 1942, completing the first phase of the Japanese offensive. The Japanese now had control of the oil they needed to continue the war (see Figure 8-2).

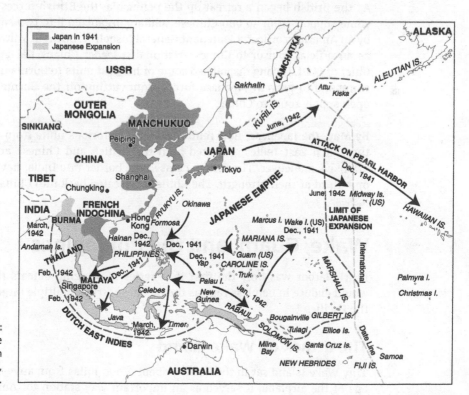

FIGURE 8-2: Japanese conquests in the Far East, 1941–1942.

THE "FLYING TIGERS"

In 1937, a retired American army fighter pilot, Captain Claire Chennault, became an advisor to the Chinese government. The craggy faced Louisianan organized the American Volunteer Group to fight the Japanese for the Chinese. The men were paid $600 a month and received $500 for every kill. Flying the American-built P-40 fighters with a distinctive sharp-toothed snarling mouth painted on the nose, they became known as the "Flying Tigers."

"A hell of a beating" in Burma

In January, a Japanese army, supported by a large number of fighters and bombers, landed on the southern tip of the British colony of Burma and captured the capital and strategic port of Rangoon by March. The British defenders — a collection of British, Indian, and Burmese units — were hard pressed by the Japanese infiltration tactics that continually slipped around their defensive lines.

As the British began a retreat up the peninsula, the British forces received welcome support from 30,000 Chinese soldiers organized into two small armies led by an American officer, Lieutenant General Joseph W. Stilwell. Stilwell served both as an official advisor to Chinese Nationalist leader Chiang Kai-shek and as his Chief of Staff. Chiang dispatched some of his best units to Burma under Stilwell's command to prevent Japanese forces from cutting off the Burma road, the last open supply route to China.

By May, the Japanese, now reinforced with victorious units from Singapore and the Dutch East Indies, defeated both the British and Chinese armies by rapid offensive maneuver. The British crossed the border into India, having lost nearly one-third of their strength. The Chinese retreated back into China with minimal losses.

Wake, Guam, and the Philippines

Pearl Harbor was only the first in a series of stinging defeats that Americans would endure in helpless rage as the Japanese struck multiple targets throughout the Pacific.

The attack on Wake Island

Tiny Wake Island sat in the Pacific, about 2,000 miles from anywhere. Yet in the age of the airplane, it served as an important way station for American aircraft moving from Pearl Harbor to the Philippines.

The day after Pearl Harbor, Japanese aircraft attacked Wake Island, which was defended by 450 U.S. Marines and 12 marine fighters. By capturing Wake Island, the Japanese could isolate the Philippines and gain an important outpost for their own aircraft and navy.

As a Japanese landing force approached the island, marine gunners sank two destroyers, forcing the surprised attackers to retreat. A few days later, the invasion force returned, supported by the two carriers that led the Pearl Harbor attack. Just before Christmas, after a fierce resistance, the marines were overwhelmed.

The battle on Guam

Like Wake Island, the large island of Guam served as a stopover for ships and aircraft travelling across the Pacific between the Philippines and Hawaii. The Japanese attacked Guam on the same day that they attacked Wake Island.

Because of a 1922 treaty with Japan that forbade the fortification of Guam in return for a smaller Japanese fleet, the 500 United States marines stationed there had no defenses. Although they fought the overwhelming Japanese naval force and 5,000 Japanese troops, the U.S. Marines had no chance of victory. In a few hours, the island was in Japanese hands.

The fight in the Philippines

By 1941, President Roosevelt recalled American General Douglas MacArthur, shown in Figure 8-3, out of retirement and placed him in command of all American and Philippine forces in the Philippines. (MacArthur was an obvious choice for this assignment because he had been spending his retirement working for the Philippine government, which had hired him to organize and train its military in preparation for its promised independence from the U.S.)

The forces that MacArthur would now command included 13,000 American soldiers and about 12,000 highly trained Philippine scouts. (The rest of the Philippine army numbered about 100,000 men, but they were only partially trained and poorly armed.) MacArthur also had 140 American combat aircraft at his disposal.

Later in 1941, as war with Japan seemed certain, MacArthur received additional ground reinforcements from the U.S. National Guard and modern heavy bomber aircraft, the B-17 (see Chapter 25 for a list of formidable weapons of World War II). These troops and weapons were of little value to MacArthur, who needed additional ground forces and naval support. But by December, there was no American fleet and there were no Regular Army troops available in any sufficient numbers to do any good. MacArthur was stuck in an unwinnable situation.

FIGURE 8-3:
Allied General
Douglas
MacArthur.

Historical/Getty Images

Ignoring the Writing on the Wall: MacArthur Fights

Japanese forces struck the Philippines at nearly the same time they attacked Pearl Harbor. The American air force in the Philippines was eliminated early and Japanese amphibious landings began a few days later. Ignoring landings that were intended to divert his forces, MacArthur prepared to defend against the main attack. Major General Jonathan Wainwright attempted to contain the initial landings, but the Philippine forces were no match for the veterans of the Japanese Imperial Army.

The Philippine forces began the retreat to the Bataan peninsula (in the Philippines), while MacArthur abandoned the capital city of Manila and moved to the fortress island of Corregidor, Philippines, in Manila Bay. MacArthur's plan was to hold out at Bataan and Corregidor until reinforcements arrived from the United States. But with the destruction of the fleet at Pearl Harbor, no help would be coming. MacArthur's troops were alone. By February, the battle for the Philippines had become a brutal battle of attrition on the Bataan peninsula. Filipino and American troops were running out of food and ammunition, while the Japanese forces were reinforced and resupplied.

DOUGLAS MacArthur

The son of a Civil War veteran who won the Medal of Honor for bravery, Douglas MacArthur (1880–1964) attended West Point and began his initial service as an engineer in the Philippines. Just before America entered World War I, MacArthur participated in the expedition to seize Vera Cruz as a warning to the Mexicans. In 1917, MacArthur helped organize and train the 42nd Rainbow Division for combat in France. In the trenches, MacArthur won a reputation as a fearless combat leader. He commanded a brigade in the division, and by the end of the war, was its commander. MacArthur returned to the United States as the most highly decorated American soldier of the Great War. He followed his success with appointments as West Point Superintendent and Chief of Staff of the Army. In between, he commanded United States forces in the Philippines. Finding the peacetime army stifling, he retired and returned to the Philippines to mold its army.

MacArthur was by all measures a brilliant man and an exceptional combat leader. His experience and skill as a peacetime administrator was unmatched in the army. But he tended to be high-strung and overly dramatic. He thirsted for military glory in a way that seemed out of touch with modern war. He could be controversial, but he was an adept political maneuverer. After the attack of Pearl Harbor — and despite some hesitation — Roosevelt knew that MacArthur was indispensable to the American defense of the Philippines. Beginning in 1941, MacArthur would have his chance at wartime glory in a way that he had often dared to hope but never believed could happen. In a short time, he would become one of the most recognized figures in the world.

Giving the Allies hope: "I shall return"

The harsh truth was that the Philippines were lost. America had taken a beating at the hands of the Japanese for three solid months. MacArthur had become more than a commander at this point: He became a symbol of determination for the American people. His loss would only increase the magnitude of the coming disaster by crippling the nation's morale.

In March, President Roosevelt decided to act, sending MacArthur a personal order to slip through the blockade of the Philippines and escape to Australia. (Australia, part of the British Commonwealth of Nations, had been actively fighting the Germans since 1941. Now with the war in the Pacific underway, Australia was the last Allied bastion in the Pacific that the Japanese did not control.)

MacArthur left General Wainwright in command and reluctantly departed. Narrowly escaping capture, he arrived in Port Darwin, Australia, where he made a short statement to the press: "The President of the United States ordered me to break through the Japanese lines . . . for the purpose, as I understand it, of organizing the American offensive against Japan, a primary objective of which is the relief of the Philippines. I came through, and I shall return." Overnight, MacArthur became a national hero, and the last three words of his statement became both his trademark and an article of faith.

Defeat and the Death March

When General MacArthur arrived in Australia, he fully expected to take charge of a growing army that would relieve the hard-pressed Filipino-American forces. He found 25,000 support troops, but no combat forces. (None were available due to the low preparedness of the United States army prior to 1941.) MacArthur, like most Americans in the first months of the U.S. entry into World War II, stood on the sidelines in impotent rage as the final drama in the Philippines played out.

On May 7, 1942, after a determined defense first of Bataan and then of Corregidor, General Wainwright surrendered 11,000 sick and starving defenders. Some defenders, however, did not surrender. A large number of Americans and Filipinos melted into the jungle to carry on a guerrilla war against the Japanese. The surrender at Corregidor was the greatest defeat of American arms in history.

**ARMY
ALLIED**

About 75,000 prisoners (including 12,000 Americans) were marched to prisoner of war camps, but only 54,000 reached their destination. About 600 Americans and nearly 10,000 Filipinos died along the way, resulting from extreme cruelty, disease, and exhaustion. This event came to be known as the *Bataan Death March*. Coming on the heels of the surprise attack on Pearl Harbor, the stories of the mistreatment of American soldiers served to strengthen American resolve against the Japanese.

Hitler Declares War on the Mongrel Race

**ARMY
ALLIED**

In all the confusion and bad news that rolled out of the Pacific in the last days of 1941, it is often forgotten that Germany declared war on the United States. Guaranteeing the destruction of Hitler and Nazism, Hitler's decision was suicidal — why add yet another enemy to your list? Hitler's decisions, as always, originated in his ideology.

In his eyes, Americans were a *mongrel race,* incapable of meeting the Master Race on an equal basis. He also discounted America's capability to wage war or threaten German actions. The United States was, like Britain, only a naval power and would not be able to affect German ground operations. Besides, the German *U-boats* (submarines) would take care of the American fleet. No doubt, Hitler ignored the fact that American manpower had turned the tide of the First World War against Germany.

Hitler believed fervently in the myth that the German army had never been defeated on the battlefield during World War I but had been betrayed by weak-willed politicians and traitorous Jews. This fantasy played into both his hatred of the Jews and his rage over Germany's military defeat in World War I. Thus, he declared war almost as an afterthought. Hitler would learn the full effect of his colossal mistake soon enough.

Now It's a World War

The United States responded to Germany's declaration of war with one of its own, thus ensuring that America would not fight only Japan in the Pacific but also assist Britain in defeating Hitler in Europe.

To top it all off, Italy, Romania, Bulgaria, and Hungary also declared war on the United States. Roosevelt made diplomatic approaches to the three Eastern European nations to have them withdraw their declarations. When that failed, the United States responded in kind, almost as if to say, "All right, you asked for it." Now everybody was in the soup.

3

Behind Enemy Lines: Nations at War

See how nations' citizens participate in the war effort.

Understand how nations mobilize entire populations to fill the factories, grow the food, and fill the bureaucracies necessary to carry on the war effort.

Discover how the tyrants in the Soviet Union and Nazi Germany used different methods than the democracies.

Find out how the Nazi state was fulfilling Hitler's mad dreams of racial extermination to prepare the way for a new Germany.

IN THIS CHAPTER

» **Organizing a nation in arms**

» **Keeping up morale**

» **Fighting a war within a war**

» **Staying alive**

Chapter **9**

Maintaining Resources: The Axis

T he Axis powers of Nazi Germany, Imperial Japan, and Fascist Italy faced unique problems in fighting World War II. Unlike the Allies, the Axis powers didn't cooperate in the war effort. Each largely fought its own war against the Allies. Because of their lack of important raw materials, Axis strategy often focused on getting or protecting access to the raw materials they needed. For the Axis nations, the war became a constant struggle to acquire the resources necessary to sustain the armed forces. As the power of the Allied forces wore the Axis nations down, the war for civilians on the home front became a struggle for survival.

Like the Allies, the Axis powers had to mobilize their populations to support war production and supply as well as sustain morale. Japan and Germany used a variety of methods — some ruthless and brutal — to meet the demands of total war. Italy was never prepared for such demands and fell quickly by the wayside.

Nazi Germany

Adolf Hitler rearmed and militarized Germany before the beginning of the war in Europe in 1939. In the process, he unified the German people under his leadership, giving them a sense of nationhood and pride. National Socialism (Nazism), with its focus on German territorial expansion at the expense of "racially inferior" Jews and Slavs, became the creed of Hitler's new state and the driving force behind all of the strategic decisions that he made.

Unlike the other warring nations, however, Germany did little to mobilize its economy and resources until 1942. Until that point, Hitler tried to fight a major war without overtaxing the nation or the German people (at least the Germans who were also members of his Master Race). But because of the heavy losses in men and material in the Soviet Union, the Nazis were forced to take measures to replace the losses. Nevertheless, at the beginning of the war, 6 million German men were in uniform in either the armed forces or the security apparatus (like the SS).

A well-fed German is a happy German

So why didn't Hitler — who wanted to control everything else — not insist on a full mobilization of the economy? The answer has its roots in 1918, the last time Germany fought a war. The Nazis believed that the collapse of the German government and society in 1918 was not the result of the German army's defeat; it was the result of food and fuel shortages that placed the civilian population near the point of starvation. The revolt that toppled the *Kaiser* (emperor) and formed a revolutionary government ready to negotiate to end the war was a direct result of this suffering.

The Nazis, therefore, decided to keep the burden on the population as light as possible. During most of the war, the rationing was mild. The Nazis didn't impose severe wartime government controls on food, wages, and prices until 1944. Furthermore, food was rationed in such a way that civilians would have access to food first. Anything left over was given to the slave labor force. Thus, Germans ate reasonably well only because millions of others were purposely starved to death.

Spearheading the production process

Facing a new war in 1942, Hitler organized a war production office to mobilize the German economy under Albert Speer. Speer accomplished prodigious feats in the last two years of the war, organizing production to meet the demands of total war. In many ways, Speer succeeded, but the jump in production came a little too late.

>> In the first four years of the war, Germany produced an average of about 10,000 aircraft a year. Between 1943 and 1944, that average shot up to about 32,000.

>> For tanks, production averaged a little over 5,000 a year between 1940 and 1942; in 1943 and 1944, the average was 23,000 a year.

Using slave labor (outside of skilled workers, virtually everyone working in a German war factory was a slave laborer), Speer achieved this increase in production in the face of other things that were going on:

>> The Allies were bombing Germany night and day.

>> Hitler's meddling interfered with the efficient operation of the production process. He decided what was to be made and when, and he often changed priorities, depending on what new weapon struck his fancy.

Slave labor and other workers

Germany, unlike the Soviet Union or Great Britain, didn't have many women in its workforce — nor were women encouraged to participate. In the Third Reich, women were considered childbearers whose responsibilities were in the home. For a nation at war, this type of exemption seems a luxury. If the men were fighting, and the women weren't working in the factories, who was?

In Nazi Germany, the answer was slave laborers. By forcing the nearly 7 million people from conquered territories to work as slaves in their factories, the Nazis didn't need to mobilize the German labor force. The use of slave labor also allowed more German men to be drafted into the army.

Most of the slave laborers were prisoners of war from Poland, France, and the Soviet Union. After Italy's surrender in 1943, captured Italian soldiers also became slave laborers. The Russians made up the largest group of prisoners of war — 5 million, of which 3 million died; they were killed or worked to death.

Nazi racial policies dictated how well or how badly prisoners and slave laborers were treated. The less "inferior" races were treated slightly better than the more "inferior" races. So, according to the Nazi racial hierarchy, Russians and Slavs were treated the worst, followed by Poles, and then Western Europeans.

Under the illusion: Morale

The Nazis used propaganda, film, music, and radio to keep up morale. Because, after all, keeping people happy was part of the overall Nazi war strategy. Hitler was popular with the German people: He gave them sweet revenge over their old enemies. And putting smiles on German faces was easy enough to do in 1939 and 1941 with the victories in Poland, Norway, Denmark, Holland, Belgium, the Netherlands, and France. But the good times couldn't go on forever:

>> The disasters that came one after another after Hitler invaded the Soviet Union made it pretty darn hard to convince the people that Germany was winning the war.

>> Stalingrad and the surrender of German forces in North Africa had an especially negative impact on morale.

>> The bombing campaigns led by the Allies affected morale as well, but not in the way the Allies hoped: German citizens endured and continued about their daily lives just as Londoners did during the Battle of Britain in 1940 and the V-1 and V-2 attacks in 1944.

>> Himmler's system of terror helped sustain (at least in public) a hatred of the Allies and support for the war.

Himmler and the *Schutzstaffel* (SS) — the German state security organization — controlled internal security and could arrest anyone for subversion. An arrest led to internment in a concentration camp or execution. (See Chapter 2 for more on Heinrich Himmler and other important men in the Nazi party.)

After 1944, Germans faced the awful possibility of Soviet troops invading Germany. It was at this time that Hitler became a very remote figure, giving few speeches and rarely appearing in public. As confidence in victory waned, so did confidence in *Der Führer*. Hitler had been relegated to the background as people focused on survival and how to deal with what a vengeful peace might bring. Despite what was actually going on in the war, the propaganda of Joseph Goebbels, the German Propaganda Minister, continued to the very end, proclaiming the victory of the German people in enduring hardships and suffering.

Resisting Hitler inside Germany

It may seem hard to believe, but Hitler had many enemies in Germany. Many Germans, especially professional soldiers and those from well-educated families, hated Hitler and his Nazi regime. Open resistance to Hitler and the Nazis disappeared early though, with arrests of key leaders and the intimidation of others. The growth of the Nazi secret police and the Nazis' internal security apparatus made any secret or underground resistance movement very hard to develop. However, as the war went on, small groups of conspirators voiced their desire as patriots, hoping to save Germany from disaster. The Allied demand for unconditional surrender led these groups to take desperate measures to prevent Hitler and the Nazis from allowing Germany to be completely destroyed.

Hitler must die!

To stop the Nazis required the death of Adolf Hitler. With *Der Führer* out of the picture, a coup could take power, and a new government could be established to negotiate with the Allies on different terms to end the war. In March 1943, military conspirators planted a bomb in Hitler's aircraft, but a faulty timer saved Hitler's life. Hitler never knew how close he came to death that day.

Another, more elaborate plot was developed in 1944. A bomb planted in his wartime headquarters in East Prussia would kill Hitler. Hitler always attended a daily briefing from his military staff in a concrete bunker. A bomb placed there would be sure to kill nearly everyone in the tightly enclosed space. Once Hitler was dead, the conspirators planned to seize key buildings in Berlin, declare a new government, and rally the nation behind them. Unfortunately, this plan also failed.

On July 20, 1944, Colonel Claus von Stauffenberg attended the daily briefing. He was surprised to discover that the meeting was held in a rickety wooden structure. Stauffenberg planted the bomb under the map table near Hitler. It exploded, but by a perverse miracle Hitler was not killed, only slightly injured. Believing that Hitler was dead, Stauffenberg returned to Berlin, where other conspirators were in the process of announcing the death of Hitler and ordering the army to arrest Nazi officials. Before long, Hitler came on the national radio and announced that he was alive and well. Although there was confusion and uncertainty for a few short hours, only a handful of Germans came out in support of the coup. The conspirators were undone. After they revealed themselves, they were rapidly rounded up. Stauffenberg and other patriots were shot as soon as they were captured. Other patriots were arrested later and met agonizing deaths.

Hitler cracks down

As a result of this failed assassination attempt (see the preceding section), the Nazis took more and more control of the war away from the professional soldiers, committing the nation to total destruction rather than surrender.

Hitler also cracked down on his enemies — real and imagined. Among the accused conspirators was Field Marshal Irwin Rommel, Germany's most famous soldier. Although aware of the plot, Rommel did not participate. Still recovering from wounds suffered in an attack by an Allied plane, Rommel was home when he was given an ultimatum: Commit suicide and receive full military honors at your burial or stand trial and jeopardize the safety of your wife and son. Rommel chose suicide. The Nazi propaganda machine announced that Rommel had died of his wounds. Rommel's family was left alone, and Rommel was given a state funeral.

Unready and Unwilling: Fascist Italy

With the possible exception of the United States, no nation was less prepared for war than Italy — despite the fact that Italy had been fighting in Spain, Albania, and in Ethiopia since the mid-1930s. But the battles in these countries were sideshows, meant to enhance the prestige of Italy and Mussolini's dreams of empire. When the real war began with the declaration of war on France and Great

Britain in 1940, Mussolini made little effort to prepare the population for the sacrifices that would come. Mussolini believed that he embodied the will of the nation, but in reality, the people's support for Mussolini lasted only as long as things went smoothly. In fact, many Italians had no interest in the war, and although dissent was rapidly quashed, the mood of the people was one of fearful concern. When things started to go sour, Mussolini lost control of the war effort.

Wartime production

Italy had little in the way of the strategic raw materials necessary to maintain a war production effort. In the three years that Italy was in the war, the Italians produced 10,500 aircraft, 64 ships (including a battleship but no aircraft carriers), 3,000 tanks, 7,000 artillery pieces, and about 60,000 other vehicles. Much of the equipment the Italians produced during the war was out-dated and obsolete, even as it left the factory or the shipyard.

One of the problems was the independent nature of the Italian arms industries. The Fascists never assumed control over production; as a result, individual industries made the decisions regarding what to produce. Large government deficits limited any economic leverage. The Italians found themselves outmatched on the battlefield; the collapse of the Italian army can be directly correlated to the inefficiencies of wartime production.

Struggling for labor

Italy never recovered from the dual problems of low wages and high unemployment that were left over from the Great Depression. Much of the Italian population engaged in small-scale agriculture, not heavy industry. Inflation was high, cutting into wages, which had been frozen during the latter years of the war. These factors, combined with shortages of imports due to the Allied blockade, limited the capacity of Italy to develop a fully mobilized war economy.

Wondering what to do: Morale

Italian morale during the war was never strong. Many questioned the need for war, doubted Germany's aims in the alliance, and saw little advantage to the territory the Italian army captured. Rationing (which became more and more restrictive), combined with the Americans entering the war in 1941, made the population uneasy about the war's direction.

When the defeat at El Alamein became known (see Chapter 5), Italians immediately took all their money from the banks, creating a financial crisis that caused the Bank of Italy to print 40 billion lire to cover it.

The disaster at Stalingrad in late 1942, where Soviet forces encircling the city overwhelmed the Italian front line troops, was the final blow. Confidence in Mussolini evaporated, which was reflected in a number of strikes that further crippled his prestige and the war effort. After the Allied landing at Anzio in 1944 — and with the Allied bombing raids taking place — Italians were looking for a way out of the war.

Believing in Victory: Imperial Japan

For Japan, the war began in 1937, and the nation had been almost completely mobilized several years prior. The rapid advance in the Pacific against the British and Americans built public morale and led to overconfidence among leaders who believed that the war was already won. But the war in China stretched Japan's war-making capability, as did the need to defend the vast expanse of the Pacific that had come under Japanese control. Heavily dependent on foreign imports of raw materials, Japan's Achilles' heel was its limited war production capacity, which would force Japan to surrender the initiative to the Allies after 1943.

Taking control: Production

Japan possessed advanced modern technology and a disciplined cohesive labor force. Prior to the war with China, the Japanese government took control of all strategic industries, such as electricity and petroleum. In agriculture, the production of the nation's staple food, rice, also came under government control and rationing. Industrial output increased rapidly, and by 1938, 75 percent of Japan's national budget was spent on war production. This spending led to heavy government debt and borrowing, which in turn led to inflation.

Despite the stockpiling of raw materials (especially oil) before the war, Japan ran short rather quickly. Even with a full-scale agricultural effort, Japan needed to import food. The rationing of food prevented any hardships for the population until late in the war, when the destruction of Japan's merchant fleet and strategic bombing caused food shortages.

Between 1941 and 1945, Japan produced 18 aircraft carriers, 6 cruisers, 64 destroyers, and 130 submarines. With the exception of a few submarines and destroyers, Japan didn't produce naval warships after 1944. Japan's production of tanks was modest, averaging less than 1,000 a year. Aircraft production rose from 5,000 in 1941 to its peak of over 28,000 in 1944. These production numbers fell off after 1944, primarily because Japan exhausted its supplies of raw materials. Even at full capacity, the Japanese factories, as modern and efficient as they were, could not match the output of the American war industry. The Americans commonly produced more in a month than Japan did in a year.

The Japanese labor force

A nation at war commonly has many workers move from farms to factories. But unlike other countries, much of the total workforce in Japan stayed on the farms. After 1943, to deal with the labor shortages, the Japanese government took the unprecedented step of drafting women into the workforce. By 1944, 33 million Japanese — men and women — were working in factories 11 hours a day.

The government promoted productivity in the following ways:

>> Organizations stressed the solidarity of members within the factory.

>> A Welfare Ministry looked for ways to improve the general health and fitness of the population, believing that healthy workers would be more efficient and make better soldiers when called into service.

The problem was that men were drafted into the armed forces regardless of their skills. Thus, many workers whose skills were needed in the factories were sent into the army. As a result, women, Korean laborers, and often children were left in the factories.

One of the unknown stories of the war was Japan's use of prisoners of war as slave laborers. Many American prisoners were brought to Japan from the Philippines to perform hazardous work (in dangerous mines, for example) under brutal conditions. Likewise, the Japanese used British prisoners as slave labor to build roads and railroads through Burma. Hundreds of thousands of men died from overwork, disease, and starvation at the hands of their captors.

The Emperor's new clothes: Morale

The Japanese government's generally undefined war aims created some morale problems initially, but an aggressive program of patriotic displays and support for the troops helped push doubts about the war effort into the background. Leftist groups were closely monitored. Western culture and ideas, such as individualism and liberalism, were attacked as unpatriotic. After 1943, the increasing number of bombing raids in the major cities of Japan weakened civilian morale, causing a large number of refugees to flee to the countryside and creating absentee problems in the war factories. But loyalty to the Emperor encouraged the population to prepare for invasion and called upon every man, woman, and child to repel the invaders.

Chapter **10**

Working Together: The Allies

A modern war is total war, meaning that the nations involved direct all their resources to producing the material for waging war. Civilians must contribute as much as the soldier, sailor, or airman. In other words, civilians also bear the brunt of war. The strategy of World War II involved not only the destruction of enemy military forces but also the creation and maintenance of factories and population centers to produce the vehicles, food, fuel, uniforms, and weapons those military forces needed.

In general, Great Britain, the Soviet Union, and the United States used similar methods to mobilize their populations and sustain morale to meet the demands of total war. In essence, they had to accomplish three major tasks:

» Provide enough food for the military and labor forces

» Retool their factories from peace-time production (building things like refrigerators) to wartime production (building things like tanks)

» Maintain national will and morale

As democracies, the United States and Great Britain instituted measures with the support and consent of the people. The Soviet Union, under the control of one man and one party, could coerce and compel citizens to meet whatever necessity the state required.

Staying United: The United Kingdom

Great Britain endured the demands of war longer than any other nation. The British government gained extraordinary power to direct the activity of British citizens and take charge of property necessary for the war effort. Heavy taxes were imposed to finance the war and stop certain businesses from making excessive profits from production of war material. Still, the British had to ration:

>> By 1939, Britain was already instituting measures to ration fuel.

>> Unable to independently feed its population in peacetime, let alone wartime, Britain rationed food in 1940 as it struggled through the dark days of the war when Britain stood alone against Germany and German *U-boats* attacked British ships.

   British farmers started farming additional resources, but such basic items as meat, sugar, eggs, and milk were often not available to the civilian population. Tea was rationed, but bread, potatoes, and fish were readily available.

>> By 1942, the government had also started rationing clothing as well as food.

The Yanks are comin' again

American soldiers began to arrive in Britain in large numbers in 1942 and continued to do so until the June 1944 invasion of Normandy, when over 1.5 million men were living and training in Britain. Although some Britons resented the presence of the Americans, the British people in general accepted the U.S. soldier as the price to pay for victory.

In addition to their different habits and mannerisms, the American also brought food. Americans fed the famished Britons, at first as a matter of kindness and later as a matter of policy:

>> The well-supplied American troops often had more food than they could eat, so they frequently shared their rations with the British population.

>> After 1943, with the decline of the German U-boat menace, American ships began to provide food to the British people as well.

Mobilizing manpower: Labor and the war effort

Britain mobilized its manpower like no other nation. Of the 15 million men who made up the labor pool of the nation in 1944, 4.5 million were in military service.

Unemployment was nonexistent, and some people were doing more than one job. A total of nearly 7 million women were mobilized for war work. Over 400,000 women were employed in the military as well. The greatest success in British war production was combat aircraft. Between 1940 and 1943, Great Britain produced more aircraft annually than Germany did.

Keeping a stiff upper lip: British morale

The people of Great Britain were unprepared for modern war and were lulled by the inactivity of the first months of the war. But between 1940 and 1941, civilians became legitimate targets of war. During that period, 43,000 civilians died from German bombing raids. Later, another 17,000 were killed from bombs and V-1 and V-2 rocket attacks. Despite these losses, British morale never wavered.

Children and the elderly were moved into the countryside, and the citizens of London slept in the subway tunnels. People from other cities often left London before night, when most of the bombing raids took place. Then these people would return to work or go home in the day.

The British people remained united in their commitment to total victory. Prime Minister Winston Churchill deserves credit for directing the war effort and heartening the British people as they faced the greatest test in their nation's history.

Working Hard: The United States

Although deeply uncertain about what to do as the world fell into war in 1939, America went to war in 1941 with a grim determination to right several wrongs. The attack at Pearl Harbor, the humiliating defeat in the Philippines, and the German attack on U.S. merchant and warships led Americans to accept sacrifices as they prepared for war.

America remained dreadfully unprepared for war, despite all the money allocated to the war fund (at least in 1940), price controls, and the initiation of a peacetime draft of men for military service. The economy still felt the effects of the Great Depression. Unemployment was high, and industrial production was low. These circumstances meant that Americans would have to work hard to build up the strength of their military if they wanted to defeat Germany and Japan.

THE ARSENAL OF DEMOCRACY

By the end of the war, the United States had produced 181 billion dollars in war material, representing nearly half the nation's yearly total production. The power of the American industrial economy was truly staggering. In 1944, at the height of production, Americans produced 96,000 aircraft (one-third more aircraft than Germany and Japan produced together). They built 61,000 tanks between 1942 and 1944, compared to 48,000 German tanks during the same period. The U.S. also built 147 aircraft carriers and nearly 1,000 other warships during the war, dwarfing Japan's production during the same period. For all the amphibious landings needed in the Pacific and in Europe, more than 60,000 landing craft were built. To carry cargo and oil worldwide, American shipyards built 5,600 merchant ships and tankers. More than 10 million rifles were produced to supply not only American forces but other Allied forces as well. In 1940, President Roosevelt had called the United States "the Arsenal of Democracy." At that time, his words were meant largely to inspire Americans. By 1945, there was no doubt that they had come true.

Building the arsenal: The America triumph

You could argue that World War II was not won on the battlefield as much as it was won in America's factories and farms. Nearly everyone got involved and did what they could to see America succeed.

>> Farmers, buoyed by high prices for their products and by exemption from the draft, produced enough food to feed not only the American troops and citizens but also Great Britain and the Soviet Union. Although meat, butter, sugar, coffee, gasoline, tires, and shoes were rationed, Americans did without very little. They actually ate better and had more variety of foods to eat than they had before the war.

>> Factories employed millions in war work, both men and women. Lured by high wages and steady work, millions of Americans moved to where the work was in the West (California's population increased by 2 million people during the war years), the big cities of the Midwest, and the South. Factories operated day and night, and workers built ships, planes, and tanks in record times.

Building armaments: Women and African Americans at work

As more and more men entered the army (by the end of the war, nearly 12 million men and 250,000 women were in the armed forces), the demand for workers in armaments factories brought women into the work force as never before. In 1943, with war production at its highest level, 36 percent of all women were working, representing one-third of the entire labor force. The bombers and fighters that ruled the skies over the Pacific and Europe were almost entirely built by women. One factory in Michigan in 1944 could produce one aircraft per hour. With more than 12.5 million people employed in war work, unemployment nearly disappeared.

REMEMBER

Women weren't relegated to the factories or the home. They also served in the armed forces. During the war, 86,000 members of the *Women Accepted for Voluntary Emergency Service* (WAVES) supported the war effort at home for the Navy, and nearly 100,000 members of the *Women's Army Corps* (WAC) served in every part of the globe where U.S. army forces were located.

African Americans and new immigrants also benefited dramatically during the war years. The number of African Americans employed in industry increased from 500,000 to 1.2 million. Although discrimination remained a fact of life, the federal government banned discrimination in defense industries.

The good life: A glimpse of things to come

For all Americans, weekly wages rose by 70 percent during the war, and opportunities grew as the industry accommodated both skilled and unskilled workers to meet production schedules.

During the war, American workers enjoyed benefits that they had not known in more than a decade. The general change in the standard of living set the stage for future economic growth and prosperity that would be unmatched in world history.

RIVETER'S ARM

Working in a factory during the war was not all that easy. An average of 200 women per day were injured on the job. The famous image of "Rosie the Riveter," with her overalls, big clunky safety boots, welding helmet, and work shirt, became a standard stereotype during the war. Today, of course (with the exception of the welding helmet), Rosie's work outfit is the standard worn by women on most college campuses. However, during the war, women riveting day after day over long hours complained of arm pain, which was then diagnosed as "riveter's arm."

Back home on the range: Morale

Unlike the rest of the Allied nations, the continental United States never suffered bombing raids, invasions, or occupation. Also unlike the other Allied nations, the bulk of the U.S. male population didn't go to war. For most Americans, World War II was a good war, giving the nation far more benefits than losses.

Americans enjoyed a spirit of unity in the face a common enemy. To a large extent, this unity — at least regarding America's role and purpose in the war — transcended regional boundaries and social class. To aid in the war effort, Americans did things like the following:

>> Bought war bonds. (Americans bought *lots* of war bonds, essentially lending the U.S. government 135 billion dollars).

>> Held drives to collect scrap metal, aluminum, waste paper and, yes, even cooking grease.

>> Planted "victory" gardens, small gardens that grew enough produce to support the family.

Hollywood also helped in the effort to keep up morale:

>> It loaned out its actors and actresses (those not already in the service) to support bond drives and to entertain servicemen.

>> The movies made during the war years often had patriotic themes and portrayed Americans as they have always wished to be seen: honest, strong, courageous, and generous.

The dark side of American zeal: The internment camps

After the Japanese attack on Pearl Harbor, Americans were afraid that Japan would attack the western coast of the U.S. Two months after Pearl Harbor, President

Roosevelt signed Executive Order 9066, which allowed him to define military areas and then remove whoever he wanted to from those areas. The target? Japanese Americans. Rumors were rife that Japanese Americans were more loyal to the Emperor of Japan than to America, and they would assist Japanese landing forces. The public reaction to the Pearl Harbor attack made every Japanese an enemy. Unfortunately, the government blindly followed public opinion.

Using information from the U.S. Census to discover where large concentrations of Japanese Americans were, Roosevelt declared much of the West Coast a military area. From these areas, the U.S. began the forced evacuation of thousands of Japanese Americans. Roosevelt claimed that the internment was necessary to prevent spying and to protect Japanese Americans from other Americans with strong feeling against the Japanese.

In March 1942, the round up began. Some people had as little as 48 hours to leave their homes. Many were taken to *assembly centers*, where they stayed until they could be moved to permanent camps, called *internment camps* or *detention centers*. Barbed-wire fences surrounded these camps, and armed soldiers guarded them. Japanese Americans had to submit not only to forced detention far from their homes and livelihoods but also travel restrictions and curfews. In all, over 120,000 Japanese Americans, most of them American citizens and more than half of them children, were relocated to internment camps. The government continued the internment policy long after the threat of a direct Japanese attack on the mainland had faded.

Head of the Western Defense Command, John DeWitt, most succinctly expressed the government's misguided and wrongheaded belief that by curtailing the freedom of some, it was protecting the safety of many. Instead, this thinking allowed the government to ignore the United States Constitution and the principles on which it had been founded: "A Jap's a Jap," DeWitt said in defense of the policy, "and that's all there is to it."

Interestingly, during all the years of the war, only 10 people were convicted of spying for Japan. All were caucasian.

The Soviet Union

In one form or another, the Soviet Union played many roles in World War II. It fought a near full-scale war with Japan in Mongolia in the summer of 1939; it opened the war in Europe as Hitler's ally in 1939; it waged war against Finland; it occupied the Baltic states; and it became the victim of German aggression in June of 1941. Then the USSR became a partner of the Allies and was the primary combat force that defeated Nazi Germany, capturing Berlin to end the war.

The Soviet Union also invaded large parts of China in 1945, helping to force the surrender of Japan. All in all, quite a bit of flip-flopping. Few people other than Soviet dictator Joseph Stalin could have pulled it off. As the leader of the Communist Party — and helped by an efficient secret police organization — Stalin held absolute power over the state and its people.

Despite engaging in all this military activity, however, Stalin and the Soviet Union were not prepared for total war. Largely caught by surprise, the Soviet people fought for their very existence. The Germans were waging a war of annihilation against the Soviets. The choices for the Soviets were rather stark: slavery and death at the hands of the Nazis or repression and minimal comfort under Stalin.

Staying alive: Production

The Soviet Union had developed heavy industry during the 1930s, and in 1940, it began stockpiling the raw materials it needed. Despite these efforts, however, the USSR was still plagued by its inadequate food production and its poor transportation networks. It suffered additional setbacks when the Germans invaded in 1941. By 1942, the Germans had conquered nearly half the Soviet people, more than half of its industrial production, and most of the fertile land in the country. The Soviets took what steps they could to keep the people and their hope of surviving the war alive:

>> As the Nazis advanced, millions of people fled or were evacuated by the Soviet government.

>> The government physically relocated nearly 3,000 factories (and most of their workers as well) to prevent their capture. These factories were torn down brick by brick and rebuilt hundreds of miles behind the lines.

>> The government requested lend-lease support from the U.S. and war material from Britain. Nevertheless, war production stalled as the Soviets waited for these things to arrive. (See Chapter 7 for information about the lend-lease program).

When the support from the U.S. and Great Britain finally did arrive, it — along with domestic production — was just barely enough to cover the battlefield losses.

Despite these setbacks and problems, by 1942, Soviet industrial might began to be felt:

MILITARY STRATEGY

>> No other nation produced as many tanks as the Soviet Union. Production of the high-quality T-34 tank shot up from 6,500 in 1941 to an average of 26,000 per year in 1943 and 1944.

>> Aircraft production was second only to the United States, growing from 25,000 in 1942 to 40,000 in 1944.

Soviet weapons were crude, moderately durable, and easy to make. The Soviet approach to war production was simple: quantity over quality. If it broke or was destroyed, they made a new one and sent it into battle.

Although the industrial production effort was closely monitored, Soviet agriculture had no supervision. The work force declined as men were drafted into the army or left for factories. The few people who were left on the land labored without sufficient tools or equipment to grow crops on a large scale. Food production declined drastically as a result. In the cities, there was rationing. Factory workers and those engaged in heavy industry or mining received the most food; all the rest were considered nonproductive and received far less. This was intentionally done to force people into factory work by threat of starvation. Most people kept themselves fed from small private plots.

Worked to death: Soviet labor

Soviet citizens, already accustomed to deprivation and terror, labored long hours under often primitive and dangerous conditions. Housing was crowded and inadequate, and food supplies were always limited. No consumer goods were manufactured or available. Anyone who complained could be arrested as a subversive and sent to a GULAG (See Chapter 6).

In fact, Stalin sent 2 million people to the camps, where they became slave laborers, producing ammunition, clothing, and gas masks. They also labored in mines and built roads and rail lines. Manpower shortages were so acute during the war that of the 30 million people who served in the Soviet Army, 800,000 of them were women. Women served in every position, combat and noncombat. Women also became the main primary farmers as the men left for military service.

The Nazis were partly to blame for the Soviet labor shortage. They deported 2.4 million Soviet citizens to Germany as slave laborers. But Stalin ordered deportations of his own people as well. When many people in the Baltic states and Ukraine welcomed the Germans as liberators from Stalinist tyranny in 1941, Stalin turned the power of the Soviet state against his people once more. He ordered the deportation of 950,000 ethnic Germans to Siberia to prevent them from helping the enemy. When the German army struck south into the Caucasus Mountains in 1942, Stalin deported another 1.5 million people to prevent them from giving the Nazis aid. Of those shipped off, a quarter died.

Becoming a world power: Morale

Discussing the morale of the Soviet people is difficult. At one end of the nation, the Germans were exterminating people by the thousands and sending millions back to Germany as slave laborers. On the other end, Stalin was deporting over 1 million people to Siberia, and another 1.5 million people were in the GULAG (concentration) camps. Over the course of the war, the Soviet Army lost over 84 percent of their soldiers due to wounds, disease, frostbite, and capture. Civilians died by the millions from disease, malnutrition, overwork, and combat actions. Yet despite all these terrible events, for those who survived, the war was a unifying experience.

The Communist Party took a backseat to Holy Mother Russia (the age old patriotic concept held dear by many Russians), and the Orthodox Church was given more freedom to build old-fashioned patriotism among the people. Stalin was the leader, the father of the nation, who guided the Soviet people through the most terrible test — the privations, the dangers, and the costs of war. Nonetheless, the Soviet people triumphed and conquered the Nazis and became a world power in the process. For them, World War II was just as much a good war as it was for the United States. Even today, the Russians call it "The Great Patriotic War" and consider it one of the shining moments in Russian history.

Chapter **11**

The War against the Jews

What makes Nazi Germany so reprehensible is this simple fact: Hitler's government carefully planned and organized itself to accomplish the eradication of an entire group of people. Mass murder on an industrial scale had never been accomplished before in history. But the power of the modern state, combined with technology, enabled Hitler's perverse dreams to become a horrible reality.

Hitler's persecution of the Jews is known as the *Holocaust*, the *War Against the Jews*, and the *Final Solution*. Each name represents a single event that was both part of the Second World War and separate from it, an event that changed Europe and the world forever and that forces us, as it forced the world 50 years ago, to confront the face of evil.

The Rationale: Nazi Thinking

The war against the Jews was a direct outgrowth of Hitler's twisted ideas, which he outlined in *Mein Kampf* (My Struggle) in 1923. What had once been nothing more than the ranting of a frustrated philosopher became national policy.

To grasp Hitler's hatred of the Jews, you need to understand the following Nazi ideas about race:

>> Race is the most important characteristic. It outweighs experiences, education, nationality — everything — in determining the place that a people hold in the world.

>> Given that different races have different roles, some races are more valuable than others. In the Nazi racial hierarchy, the order was this: Aryan (the Master Race), other non-Aryan Caucasians, Asian, and African American.

>> For people to deny the truth of this, regardless of what group they fit into, is to deny their destiny.

(See Chapter 2 for a more detailed discussion of Nazi thinking.) To fulfill their destiny as the Master Race, the Nazis had to control and subjugate "inferior" races in order to get the living space that their great empire (the Third Reich) needed. To this end, the Germans waged war as a means of imposing their will on outsiders. They targeted the Slavs and the Russians, for example, who could be forcibly removed from their lands so that the true inheritors of the future, the German Master Race, could take control.

The Jews, however, were another issue entirely. Hitler's hatred of them went beyond the vitriol he spewed at the "inferior" races. To Hitler, Jews were the source of evil in the world. They were parasites that betrayed and fed off the German people. Hitler's mission, as he saw it, was to become the instrument of their destruction.

The Persecution Begins: Jews in Germany

Hitler had made clear in *Mein Kampf* (see Chapter 2) what his plans were, but it wasn't until he had the full control of the German government that his attention turned toward implementing the plan. In their quest for *Lebensraum* (see Chapter 2), the Nazis needed to remove Jews from Germany (which belonged to the Master Race) and relocate them elsewhere. To this end, Hitler made the German Jews targets of hate and suspicion and began a systematic persecution that would eventually strip them of everything. During these years, some Jews left Germany. But many, despite Hitler's rhetoric and the first early actions against them, didn't see the full extent of the danger until it was too late.

>> By the end of 1933, Hitler had forced the retirement of almost all non-Aryan government workers (except for in the military). The Nazis had also started arresting Jews and sending them to concentration camps.

>> By the end of 1935, the Nazis had passed the Nuremburg Laws, which stripped Jews of their German citizenship, banned them from political participation, and outlawed marriages between Jews and German citizens. (Jews and Germans who were not married but who continued their relationships were considered "race defilers" and sent to concentration camps.)

>> By the end of 1937, Jews could no longer get passports or travel out of Germany, except under certain conditions.

>> By the end of 1938, Jews had to carry identification cards; Jewish children were kicked out of German schools; and Jewish students were banned from German universities. In addition, Jews had to register all property above a certain value. Jewish doctors and then lawyers lost their licenses.

>> By the end of 1939, Jews had to surrender all their gold and silver to the government.

>> By the end of 1941, Jews over six years old couldn't leave home without police permission and, when out, had to wear the yellow Star of David.

At the beginning of this period, a half million Jews lived in Germany; by 1941, this number had fallen to just over 100,000. As Germany invaded other nations (Austria, Poland, Belgium, France, and so on), it brought along its policies against Jews.

Mobile Killing Units: The Einsatzgruppen

When the war in Europe began with the invasion of Poland in 1939, Hitler fully intended to pursue his program of extermination in the wake of his military victories. After the German front line forces had moved through an area, another element followed behind. These were the Action Groups, or *Einsatzgruppen*, also known as "Mobile Killing Units." In the wake of the Nazi invasion of the Soviet Union in the summer of 1941, the Action Groups came with orders to kill all Soviet government administrators and Communist Party officials. They were also to target Jews as the bearers of Bolshevik (Communist) ideology — as if the Jews were the source of this ideology and carried it like a contagious disease. (The Jews, in fact, were completely dehumanized by Nazi propaganda and equated with rats carrying a plague.)

In every village, the Action Groups rounded up Jewish men, women, and children. They took them to a relatively secluded area (such as a woods or a ravine) and then shot and buried them. In the first year of Nazi occupation in the Soviet Union, nearly 500,000 men, women, and children were executed in this way. By 1944, nearly all the Jews (approximately 1 million) who had lived in Ukraine before the war had been killed.

KRISTALLNACHT

Known as the "Night of Broken Glass," *Kristallnacht* was the Nazi response to the death of Ernst von Rath, the Third Secretary of the German Embassy, who was killed by a Polish teenager (and Jew) seeking revenge for his family. After Rath's death, Goebbels (Hitler's Minister of Propaganda) encouraged violence against the Jews in Berlin. Nearly 100 people died, Jewish stores windows were broken, and synagogues were burned. To add insult to injury, the Germans claimed that the damage, and therefore the cost of it, was the responsibility of the Jews.

Those who survived the Mobile Killing Units, both Jews and non-Jews, took up arms against the Germans and formed partisan bands to wreak a heavy vengeance on the conquerors. Knowing what was in store for them if captured, Soviet soldiers and partisans fought with a fanatical desperation.

Deportation to Ghettos, Concentration Camps, and Death Camps

As early as 1933, the Nazis had been sending folks to concentration camps. Initially, these camps were located in Germany (like Dachau and Bergen-Belsen) and were used for "undesirable" people: To the Nazis, these undesirable people included Communists, Democrats, Socialists, political prisoners, homosexuals, and Jews. During the war, these camps also held Soviet prisoners of war and slave laborers. Executions were commonplace, and most inmates of the camps were simply worked to death. It wasn't until later, however, that the camps came to be associated with Jews. The death camps, on the other hand, were intended only for the Jews from the beginning; these were the camps the Nazis created in order to exterminate them.

As the Nazi control spread through Europe, the deportation of Jews to concentration camps and death camps grew: Between 1939 and 1941, Austria, Hungary, and even France (led by the Vichy government; see Chapter 5) deported Jews. Although Germany had been removing Jews from Germany for some time, it wasn't until 1941 that the Nazis began a massive deportation of Jews.

The ghettos of Poland were another Nazi creation. To get the *Lebensraum* he wanted from Poland, Hitler needed to clear the Jews from the Polish countryside. To do this, the Nazis forced the Jewish population to sections of cities, which they were then forbidden to leave. Often, walls surrounded these areas, which were patrolled by heavily armed guards, trapping the people within.

THE "RIGHTEOUS AMONG THE NATIONS"

The "Righteous Among the Nations" are non-Jews who risked arrest, torture, and death to help Jews during the Holocaust. Approximately 10,000 men and women have been so honored. They hid Jews from the Nazis, helped them escape deportation, adopted Jewish children whose parents had been deported or killed, provided food and supplies and medical care, and more. The "Righteous Among the Nations" includes people from all walks of life: farmers, industrialists, factory workers, housewives, salesmen, nurses, government officials, nuns and priests, and resistance fighters, just to name a few.

By 1942, as the Nazis implemented the last phases of the Final Solution, Jews were being sent from ghettos, concentration camps, and *transit camps* (essentially way stations) to their deaths.

Life in the ghetto

Each ghetto had a Jewish council (the *Judenrat*), which was responsible for ensuring that people followed Nazi policies. The council, made up of rabbis and other leaders in the Jewish community, was also responsible for distributing food, policing the ghetto, and taking care of the health and welfare (such that it was) of the people.

The living conditions in the ghettos were horrible. Deprived of food (the people in the ghetto were to receive the leftovers from the general population, but not more than was needed for bare sustenance), medical care, many of the basic necessities of life, and used extensively as slave labor, many Jews died of malnutrition, disease, and starvation. Several Jews were also executed for alleged crimes.

Like the concentration camps, the ghettos were simply a temporary solution to the Jewish problem for the Nazis. Eventually, these ghettos would be emptied and the inhabitants murdered.

Life in the concentration camps

During the years that Hitler ruled Germany, over 100 concentration camps appeared all over Europe. Although not used strictly for extermination purposes, the living conditions at the concentration camps were brutal and the death rates high.

The function of the prisoners in the concentration camps was to work, but their lives were worthless to the guards, the camp commanders, and the ever-present SS. Anyone who couldn't work was killed, and those who could work were usually worked to death.

MORE COULD HAVE BEEN DONE TO HELP

Although they may not have wanted to believe it, many of the Allied nations knew of the atrocities against the Jews fairly early in the war. After all, prior to the war, the Nazis' actions had been public, and consequently, reported in the press. Information was harder to get after the war started, but intelligence reports and reports from informants and members of the underground in various occupied countries began to filter to the West. The Allies, in essence, did little in response to the information.

Working long hours at hard labor in all kinds of weather and under constant beatings by the guards, many prisoners died from exhaustion and exposure. With only a little food a day (usually a piece of bread and weak soup), many others died from malnutrition and starvation. Even those prisoners who managed to avoid starvation or death by exposure were still vulnerable to death at the hands of the guards.

Medical care did not exist. The ill and the weak were abandoned to die. Others, many of them children, died at the hands of doctors who conducted barbaric medical experiments on them.

Because so many prisoners died — in fact, the goal in many concentration camps was "extermination by work" — most camps had crematoriums so that the guards could dispose of the bodies. Near the end of the war, these camps were used as holding areas for Jews from death camps who were moved westward to avoid detection.

The "death factories"

The death camps, like Auschwitz, Birkenau, Chelmno, Treblinka, and Sobibor, were unique in that they were simply temporary holding areas for the mass murder of people. Jews were unloaded from train cars and in many cases herded directly to gas chambers or firing squads. Those that escaped immediate death were often used as slave laborers at the camp itself. They were placed in work details that supported the execution process (working the crematoriums, for example) until they, too, were killed. In Auschwitz, some able-bodied prisoners were kept alive as slave labor to assist in war production until they succumbed to overwork and starvation.

The death camps used gas chambers as their means of murder, and these were chillingly efficient (see the section "The Final Solution and Why It Failed" to understand what the Final Solution was). Some, such as the twin chambers in

Auschwitz–Birkenau (the largest death camp), could accommodate over 4,000 people at a single time. Victims destined for the gas chambers were forced to remove their clothing; then they were shoved into the death chamber itself. About 20 minutes after the gas (usually Zyklon-B) was released in the room, everyone inside was dead.

The bodies of the victims were stripped of any remaining valuables, such as gold from their teeth and rings, and then burned in ovens built especially for this purpose. When the ovens gave out, as they did in some death camps because of the sheer number of people killed, the Germans burned the bodies out in the open.

The Final Solution and Its Ultimate Failure

By 1942, trainloads of Jews were being sent east, where the execution squads (see the preceding section) killed them immediately. From the Nazi standpoint, however, the process was slow, inefficient, and problematic. The executions took place out in the open. As such, they were hard to conceal from the general population and German soldiers and officers, who, with some exceptions, found the executions destructive to morale and to the fighting spirit. (Even some of the men doing the actual killing, it seems, were having some difficulty shooting the women and children.)

So the Nazis changed the way that they carried out the executions. German Field Marshall Hermann Goering ordered Nazi administrator Reinhard Heydrich to organize a program to solve what he called "the Jewish question." Heydrich initiated a program that used poison gas (trade name "Zyklon B") to kill large numbers of people at one time. The program, which was termed *the Final Solution*, represented the Nazis' plan to move all Jews in occupied Europe to killing centers in isolated areas. Their goal was to eliminate every Jew in Europe.

In 1942, Nazi bureaucrats met to organize their effort of identifying, collecting, transporting, and killing Jews throughout Europe. From the farthest corners of Europe, Jews were collected by police and moved either to ghettos for later transit to the death camps, or they were sent directly to death camps in eastern Poland. (See the earlier sections "Life in the ghetto" and "The death factories.")

The Nazis acted with terrible efficiency: Before they were finally stopped, they had murdered 6 million Jews. About 300,000 European Jews survived the horror.

ANNE FRANK: ONE VOICE AMONG MILLIONS

In 1933, Otto Frank took his family from Germany to Amsterdam. When the Nazis began deporting Dutch Jews in 1942, the Frank family went into hiding in the secret annex of a townhouse in Amsterdam. For two years, the family lived in isolation. In August 1944, they were betrayed by unknown informers and sent to Bergen-Belsen concentration camp. There, everyone in the Frank family — except Otto — died from disease.

After the war, Otto returned to Amsterdam and met Miep Gies, one of the people who had protected the family. She gave him a diary that she found in the annex after the family had been captured. The diarist was Otto Frank's 14-yearold daughter, Anne. Otto published Anne's diary, which has become one of the most famous books of the twentieth century and a testament to the resilience of the human spirit. More than 25 illion copies have been published worldwide.

Just one month before the Frank family's hiding place was discovered, Anne wrote: "I simply can't build up my hopes on a foundation consisting of confusion, misery, and death. I see the world gradually being turned into a wilderness. I hear the ever-approaching thunder, which will destroy us too. I can feel the suffering of millions." She ended this entry with these words: "I think it will all come right, that this cruelty too will end, and that the peace and tranquillity will return again." In her sad yet ultimately hopeful words, Anne Frank became a symbol of the millions of Jews who perished, and she became the voice that reminded the world of their humanity.

Hiding their crime

When it became clear to everyone that Germany was going to lose the war, Heinrich Himmler, the chief of the SS and the director of the Final Solution activities, decided that the Nazis needed to keep their crimes against the Jews a secret. He ordered the transfer of prisoners from Auschwitz and Birkenau to Germany, where they were to be used as slave laborers in underground factories or sent to the prewar concentration camps — such as Dachau, Bergen-Belsen, and Buchenwald — intended for political prisoners.

Tens of thousands died or were killed as they were marched westward ahead of the advancing Soviet armies, and many thousands more died of starvation and overwork in the months before the arrival of the Allies.

The arrival of the Americans, British, and Soviets

But by September 1944, the Soviet armies had pushed into Poland, and the American and British armies were nearing the borders of Germany. The Fifteenth Air Force, stationed in Italy, was flying bombing missions deep within Germany and Eastern Europe. As Soviet forces approached from the east the Nazis tried to hide their crimes. But the monstrosity of their evil acts could not be hidden. They began clearing out the death camps, destroying the evidence, and moving the thousands of remaining Jews to concentration camps in Germany. This is where American and British troops discovered the living skeletons of people meant for execution. The Soviets discovered the abandoned camps and found prisoners left behind; those who had been too weak to travel and who had not been killed because the Nazis, fearing retribution from the Soviets, had simply run away. Nazi concentration-camp guards sometimes were often shot on sight by enraged American soldiers who liberated the camps in Germany. This sight horrified them. It has horrified the world since.

If the Nazis had been given the time needed to fulfill their plans, the Final Solution probably would have succeeded. Hitler had every intention of eliminating the Jews, regardless of what else was happening with the war. "We shall regain our health only by eliminating the Jews," he said in 1942. As it was, the Nazis could not simply carry on a war against an entire people and fight the Soviet Union, the United States, and Great Britain at the same time. Military defeat prevented the Final Solution from being final.

4

Planning and Launching the Allied Counterattack, 1942–1943

Discover what America, as a latecomer, had a lot to learn about this war.

Find out how the most important decisions directing the course of the war were made and why American forces ended up fighting.

Uncover how important the Soviet contribution was to the overall conduct of the war.

See how the British-American offensives were aimed at knocking Italy out of the war.

Understand how American and Australian forces took on the Japanese in New Guinea.

Chapter **12**

The Politics of Compromise, 1942

Throughout history, war has often meant cooperation, alliances, and deal making. Like politics, it can make strange bedfellows. World War II was no different. The Germans, for example, entered into agreements with the Japanese, who according to Nazi philosophy were members of an "inferior" race; the Italians, whom they considered little more than incompetents; and the Soviets, whom they intended to conquer. Likewise, the democracies of Great Britain and the United States joined with Josef Stalin, a Soviet dictator not unlike Hitler, to defeat Germany, Japan, and the nations that fought with them.

Alliances and coalitions can last a long time (such as the alliance between the United States and Great Britain), or they can quickly fall apart (for example, the alliance between Germany and the Soviet Union before World War II, and the alliance between the Soviet Union and the United States after World War II). How long an alliance lasts depends a great deal on how long the common cause exists. When the source of the common cause disappears, the alliance is in danger.

The Axis Powers: Deals among Desperados

The partnership between Germany, Italy, and Japan (called the *Axis powers*) was really nothing more than a loose association of outlaw states. Even though Germany and Japan seemed to have a strategic coordination, in reality these nations cooperated little during the war. Italy, of course, followed Germany's lead, providing support and troops throughout Europe and the Mediterranean. These nations signed the following agreements:

ARMY AXIS

>> **The Anti-Comintern Pact:** In 1936, Germany and Italy made a pact with Japan called the *Anti-Comintern Pact.* (Comintern was derived from *Communist International,* an organization promoting world revolution sponsored by Stalin and the Soviet Union.). This treaty was an attempt to link three very different nations together in a common cause: to fight the spread of Communism.

REMEMBER

Other nations that fought with the Axis powers included Czechoslovakia (under German control and occupation), Romania, Hungary, Bulgaria, and Finland. Even Spain provided troops for Germany. Many of these nations fought with Germany not because they shared Hitler's ideology but because they hated Stalin and the Soviet Union more.

MILITARY STRATEGY

ALLIANCES AND COALITIONS: WHAT'S THE DIFFERENCE?

A *coalition* is an agreement in which two or more nations agree to cooperate to achieve a common goal. An *alliance* is a formal agreement between two or more nations to achieve broad, usually long-term, objectives. Simply put, coalitions are friendships of necessity, and alliances are friendships of choice.

Militarily speaking, alliances and coalitions require that the armed forces of the involved nations work together. The various nations' combat units, ships, and aircraft have to be able to fight together. The folks in charge have to be able to work together to develop battle plans. Everyone has to agree on critical issues, such as what to do first, who is in charge, and who has responsibility for what has to be hashed out. The challenges are compounded by differences in training, equipment, language, supplies, and capabilities among the participating nations. Getting the disparate units organized into a cohesive fighting force and hammering out agreements between the leaders is a monumental task, and the process isn't pretty.

>> **The Tripartite Pact:** In September 1940, the Axis countries signed the *Tripartite Pact*, which bound the three nations together in a cooperative agreement. In this pact, Japan agreed to accept the leadership of Germany and Italy in Nazi-Fascist controlled Europe, and Germany and Italy agreed to respect the leadership of Japan in a Japanese controlled Asia. In addition, the three countries agreed to help one another in case of attack.

REMEMBER

In August 1939, just before Germany invaded Poland, the USSR and Germany made an alliance (of sorts) called the Nazi-Soviet Non-Aggression Pact. The alliance lasted until June 1941, when the Nazis invaded the Soviet Union. It was not much of an alliance, but it served its purpose. Head to Chapter 4 to find out more about this alliance, which gave the two bloodthirsty dictators what they wanted in the short-term: additional territory and the elimination of the threat of war.

American-British Cooperation: Not a Bed of Roses

The British and the Americans had a rough road to travel to achieve their common objective of defeating Germany and Japan. The initial contacts between the two countries began in August 1941, when the United States began openly supporting British convoys in the North Atlantic.

British Prime Minister Winston Churchill and American President Franklin Roosevelt met on board a British warship off the Newfoundland coast. They discussed common defense issues and the coordination of policy against Japan. Because the United States was neutral and the Japanese had not yet initiated a war against either nation, the meeting between the two leaders was held in secret.

The Atlantic Charter

The result of the 1941 secret meeting between Roosevelt and Churchill off the coast of Newfoundland was the *Atlantic Charter*, the document that became the basis for the American-British alliance. More importantly, the Atlantic Charter affirmed principles that the two countries shared and outlined the principles that countries should abide by. The principles in the Atlantic Charter were clearly in opposition to the programs of the Italian Fascists, the Nazis, and the Japanese militarists. When other nations entered the war on the side of the Allies, all were invited to affirm that they were fighting for the principles outlined in the Atlantic Charter (see the following section).

An Allied picnic: The Arcadia Conference

**ARMY
ALLIED**

From the end of December 1941 through mid-January 1942 — only a few weeks after the Japanese offensive in Asia and the U.S. and British declarations of war against Japan — Roosevelt and Churchill and their advisors met in Washington, D.C., to organize war plans. This meeting was called the *Arcadia Conference*. The participants in this meeting accomplished two important things:

>> They created a Combined Chiefs of Staff to cooperate on strategic planning.

>> They issued the *Declaration of the United Nations*, which bound signing nations to the principles of the *Atlantic Charter*, along with a pledge to combine their resources. (See the sidebar "The eight points of the Atlantic Charter" if you want to know what the Charter's eight points are.) Twenty-six nations signed the treaty. Eventually, 51 nations, including the Soviet Union, signed.

THE EIGHT POINTS OF THE ATLANTIC CHARTER

The eight points of the Atlantic Charter, which follow, mirror many of American President Woodrow Wilson's Fourteen Points, issued in 1918 to end World War I:

- No interests in territorial expansion and no territorial changes without the consent of the people concerned (from Wilson's concept of the self-determination of peoples)

- The right of people to choose their own form of government and have their governments restored to them (Wilson's Fourteen Points)

- Free access by all nations to raw materials and markets (from Wilson's concept of free trade)

- Security of peace and freedom from fear and want (from Wilson's concept of four basic freedoms, speech and worship being the other two)

- No limitations on nations traveling freely on the world's seas and oceans (from Wilson's concept of freedom of the seas)

- A permanent system of security among nations and of easing the burden of armaments (a clear reference to Wilson's League of Nations and disarmament proposals)

For more information about Wilson's Fourteen Points and the League of Nations, see Chapter 2.

These 51 nations became an informal military coalition collectively called the *United Nations*. It was not a formal alliance and no treaty or formal agreement was signed. Nevertheless, the partnership had the feel and trappings of a formal alliance to such an extent that the three major powers — Great Britain, the United States, and the Soviet Union — became known as the *Allies* or *Allied powers*, which later included France and China.

REMEMBER

America and Britain did not fight alone against Hitler. Others who participated on the British-American side included the Soviet Union (after Hitler's invasion of the USSR), Free France, Poland, and the *Commonwealth nations* (Canada, Australia, New Zealand, and South Africa), as well as Algerian, Moroccan, and Brazilian units. Even Italy, after its surrender to the Allies in 1943, joined in the fight against Hitler.

Clashing Strategies: A Debate among Friends

While British and American interests would seem to be easy to coordinate, that was not the case in 1942. Although each country obviously wanted to defeat the Germans and the Japanese, the sticking point was how to do it. The U.S. wanted to go after Japan first; the British wanted to go after Hitler. And the Soviet Union just wanted a little help.

Japan first?

The Americans wanted to fight the Japanese first. The surprise attack on the U.S. and subsequent humiliating losses the U.S. suffered in the Pacific had many strategists pushing for a full American effort in the Pacific (see Chapter 8 for more details on the Japanese attack in the Pacific). Although revenge was a prime motivator, the argument to focus on Japan first also made good strategic sense: If Japan were not defeated first, it would have time to build up its defenses in Asia. China was already cut off from Allied support by Japanese forces; the Allies couldn't afford to give Japan the time to solidify control over the huge populations and vast raw materials of Asia.

Or Germany first?

For the British, the problems were more immediate — their survival was at stake. Just a few months prior to the Allied conference, Hitler had nearly destroyed Britain. In early 1942, with German forces on the outskirts of Moscow, the Soviet Union didn't seem to be far from collapse either. If the Soviet Union fell, what would prevent Hitler from turning against Britain again? In addition, the idea of an untouched Germany dominating Europe for years while the Allies fought in Asia was unthinkable. For the British, the Allies had to defeat Germany first, which meant that American resources had to be devoted to Europe, not Asia.

What about North Africa?

While the debate about which enemy to fight went on, Winston Churchill added something else to the mix. At the Arcadia Conference, Churchill proposed to Roosevelt a joint attack to occupy French North Africa. At this point, the British were fighting German General Erwin Rommel's forces near Tobruk in Libya (see Chapter 13 for more information on Rommel's forces in North Africa). Churchill pointed out the very real danger that by early summer, the Germans could take Cairo and seal off the Suez Canal, Britain's lifeline to India and its empire in Asia. For the British, a North African attack had several strategic advantages.

>> It provided an opportunity to close a ring around Germany and Italy from the Mediterranean, which Churchill called the "soft underbelly" of the Axis. British planners believed that an attack should be launched from the south through the Balkans, Greece, or Italy.

>> The British already had forces in the Mediterranean (Gibraltar, Malta, Egypt, and the Middle East). The British also had historic interests in the region dating back at least two hundred years.

>> Although a southern attack was an indirect approach to getting at the Axis, it could put Britain in a position to control events in the region for years to come.

The Americans, however, had no interest in the Mediterranean or the Middle East. The French and British colonies in North Africa didn't make the slightest impression on the American planners. Being a former colony itself, the U.S. wasn't interested in helping either nation maintain its colonies. What the Americans wanted was a direct approach, one that would enable them to hit the enemy right where it hurt and get the war over quickly. Thus, the Americans advocated a strategy of invading Europe from across the English Channel. Forget about fighting on the fringes, they said. Let's fight the Germans on their own territory.

Heating up the debate: Stalin's call for help

While the arguments went back and forth, the Soviets were screaming for help. Without a British–American attack in 1942 to draw off German forces from the east, the Soviet Union was in grave danger. Always mistrustful of the capitalists, Stalin believed that the Americans and British were purposely stalling so that Germany and the Soviet Union would drain all their strength fighting each other.

REMEMBER

The Americans and the British needed to do something to keep the Soviet Union in the war. Without Soviet manpower, defeating the Nazis would be extremely hard, maybe even impossible. But neither the British nor the Americans seemed willing to give up its plan.

Making the First Decision: Germany First

By July 1942, British and American military planners had made no progress. Finally, President Roosevelt broke the deadlock. As Commander in Chief, he decided that a combined British and American force would land on the

North African coast. Roosevelt's military advisers were stunned: He had rejected their advice completely and taken the British side. With this decision, Roosevelt accomplished two things:

MILITARY STRATEGY

>> He ended once and for all the question of priorities. Hitler was to be defeated first, followed by Japan.

>> He committed the Allies to an indirect approach. This decision delayed a cross-channel invasion and decisive defeat of Germany for at least a year.

Most importantly, Roosevelt's decision in support of the attack on North Africa fulfilled two important political objectives:

MILITARY STRATEGY

>> **It got American combat troops into the war as quickly as possible.** Roosevelt did not believe that the nation's morale could withstand doing nothing for the year it would take to organize a cross-channel invasion.

>> **It kept the Soviets in the game and eliminated the risk of another Hitler-Stalin deal.** (See the section "Creating the Axis Powers, the Desperados," earlier in this chapter, for more information about the alliance between the Soviets and Germans before World War II.) The last thing the Allies wanted was another Hitler-Stalin deal, which would allow Germany to turn her entire might against Britain before the United States could build its industrial base and armed forces. By committing American troops quickly, Stalin could see that the British and Americans were sincere in helping take some of the pressure off the Soviets.

Chapter **13**

Taking North Africa, Sicily, and the Boot

I f Germany and Italy were going to win the war in Europe, 1942 was the year of opportunity. Although German forces were stopped short of taking Moscow in December 1941 (see Chapter 6), signs were good that they could defeat the USSR in the summer. Bolstered in North Africa by German tanks, Italy out-maneuvered the British on land, air, and sea. Britain held on, but just barely. German U-boats took a terrible toll on merchant ships. And the United States at that time was too weak to have an impact in Europe.

In the beginning of 1942, the Allies had their backs to the wall. But by the end of the year, they had defeated Germany and Italy on all fronts. The tide of the war had finally turned.

Rommel's Desert Defeat: El Alamein

By July 1941, the British were unable to free the trapped British forces at Tobruk, Libya, and in a running tank battle with Rommel's German and Italian forces, the reinforcements sent to General Wavell were defeated. Retreating to Egypt, the British discovered that they had a new commander, General Sir Claude Auchinleck.

THE FIRST DESERT STORM: IRAQ AND SYRIA, 1941

Nothing was easy for British Field Marshal Archibald Wavell, who had the unenviable job as Commander in Chief of British forces in the Middle East. With 100,000 men (including Free French units), he faced 500,000 Italian soldiers in Ethiopia and Libya. In late 1940 and the middle of 1941, his victories in Libya against the Italians were negated by Churchill's orders to dispatch troops to stem the German invasion of Greece and by the arrival of German General Rommel's desert force. On top of all this, Wavell had to deal with German and Italian activities in Iraq and Syria. Iraq, a former British possession, had been granted independence in 1932, but Britain still maintained two military bases in the country. Syria, a French possession, was under control of the Vichy, with 35,000 men guarding the country. The Axis provided aircraft, advisors, and supplies to the pro-Nazi Iraqi leader Rashid Ali, convincing him to attack the British bases in Iraq.

Using a collection of air and land forces in Palestine (roughly modern Israel), Wavell defeated the Iraqis and captured Baghdad, ending Ali's control of the country. The Germans had also been busy in Syria, preparing the French to threaten Palestine. With his units fighting simultaneously in Iraq, the Greek island of Crete, and Libya, Wavell assembled yet another force and struck from Palestine and Iraq, capturing Damascus and defeating the Vichy French in just over 30 days and turning the country over to General Charles de Gaulle and the Free French. Wavell's maneuver was one of the most brilliant but least known achievements of World War II. General Norman Schwartzkopf, the American commander of the Persian Gulf War, would be envious.

HISTORICAL TRIVIA

In Egypt, Auchinleck received additional troops and aircraft, as well as large numbers of American tanks from the *lend-lease program* (which allowed the United States to help supply the nations that fought Hitler; see Chapter 7 for more information). Auchinleck designated his new command the *British Eighth Army*, which became one of the most famous Allied units of the war.

The Eighth Army takes on Rommel

The British offensive in North Africa began in mid-November 1941. By January 1942, the British had driven German General Erwin Rommel back nearly 400 miles. Despite the superiority of British combat power, Rommel (nicknamed "Desert Fox" because of his elusive tactics and ability to hide and reappear in unexpected places) gave up ground and outfought the dispersed British units, making raids deep behind British lines and disrupting the momentum of the attack and causing heavy casualties.

Although British General Auchinleck could claim success, he had not beaten Rommel's forces completely, and Rommel would return to fight another day. Nonetheless, pushing Rommel back was a victory, and any success was good news for the British. Unfortunately, Auchinleck had little time to enjoy his victory. Elsewhere in the world, things were going very badly, especially in the light of Japan's attacks on British possessions in Asia and the bad news from Russia as Hitler's armies moved forward.

Rommel returns and Montgomery enters

By January, Auchinleck was still trying to regroup; Rommel, on the other hand, had been resupplied and reinforced more quickly. That month, Rommel quickly launched his own offensive, catching the British defenders poorly prepared and without supplies. Rommel moved so quickly that the retreating British often found their supply depots in German hands. By June, Rommel moved nearly 300 miles and recaptured Tobruk, Libya and 25,000 British prisoners. By July, after driving his troops and tanks relentlessly in pursuit of his defeated enemy, Rommel reached his limit of food, fuel, and ammunition. He was also under constant attack from the *Royal Air Force* (RAF) and was stopped by strong British defenses at El Alamein, Egypt. Only 60 miles from Alexandria, Egypt and 100 miles short of the Suez Canal, Rommel dug in at El Alamein and awaited resupply.

The situation in Egypt was critical enough that Churchill flew to Cairo, Egypt to discuss strategy and make changes. Striding up and down the room during the meeting, Churchill cried "Rommel, Rommel, Rommel, Rommel! What else matters but beating him?" Churchill replaced Auchinleck with General Harold Alexander, and the new Eighth Army commander became General Bernard Law Montgomery. Spurred on by the Prime Minister, these men went to work to reorganize the army and prepare it for an attack.

Between a rock and a hard place: Rommel's position

German General Rommel was still waiting near El Alamein to be resupplied. He needed fuel, ammunition, and additional tanks. None came, however, because Hitler had placed all his eggs into one basket. Unfortunately, that basket was in Russia for the summer offensive. Essentially, Rommel was stuck.

He couldn't attack because he didn't have the necessary supplies, and the British defensive position at El Alamein, Egypt was 35 miles long. The Mediterranean seacoast anchored the position in the north; an impassable depression anchored it in the south. In addition, the British forces were well prepared: They stood behind barbed wire and minefields, and Montgomery carefully placed tanks and artillery behind the main defensive line to stop any German breakthroughs.

FIELD MARSHAL MONTGOMERY

Bernard Law Montgomery (1887–1976) served in France and Belgium during World War I. At the outbreak of World War II, Montgomery was a Major General commanding a division. His division was sent to France in 1940, and in the debacle that followed, was evacuated from Dunkirk. In 1941, Montgomery oversaw preparations for the defense of Britain against a German invasion. In August 1942, Montgomery took command of the Eighth Army in Egypt. On October 23, leaving nothing to chance, Montgomery initiated a carefully planned attack against General Erwin Rommel's Axis forces at El Alamein in northern Egypt and won the first Allied victory against the German army. While still in pursuit of Rommel's defeated columns across Libya, he became Sir Bernard Montgomery and was promoted to full General. In 1943, Montgomery (or "Monty" as his troops called him) led the Eighth Army in Sicily and the initial campaign in Italy. In preparation for the invasion of France, he was ordered back to Britain in 1944 to serve as commander of all land forces under General Dwight Eisenhower, the Supreme Allied Commander. He became a Field Marshal, the highest rank in the British Army.

Montgomery had no doubt that he was the finest general in the Allied armies. He never shook his initial impression that American soldiers and leaders were hopeless amateurs, an opinion he usually did not hesitate to express. These two characteristics often made him hard to get along with. He was a superb motivator and organizer with a colorful personality that inspired his men. He loved his soldiers and looked after their welfare, never needlessly exposing them to danger. But he lacked the spark of brilliance on the battlefield that other Allied officers possessed. The battles he fought were usually successful because he took no chances, and he was content to wait until everything went in his favor. At his best, Montgomery could usually force an enemy from a position, but he could not find the means to prevent the enemy from reforming and defending another position. Yet this approach suited his style of war — to move head-on but limited in scope and goals. Montgomery had a supreme, sometimes misplaced, confidence in his plans and preparations. This fault led to several major setbacks for the Allies in the later stages of the war.

And although Rommel believed that he should retreat back into Libya, Hitler ordered him not to. So, unable to attack and ordered not to retreat, Rommel prepared his defenses as best he could.

Rommel's defeat: Montgomery gives chase

British General Montgomery attacked Rommel on October 23, 1942. The battle lasted for ten days. The British had nearly twice as many troops as Rommel did, and British aircraft controlled the skies over the battlefield. Still Rommel and his troops fought skillfully and inflicted great damage on the Eighth Army. In the process, however, Rommel lost most of his tanks. After fierce fighting by the Australian and New Zealand divisions, the British finally broke through the German lines. Rommel had no choice but to retreat, despite Hitler's order not to fall back.

**HISTORICAL
TRIVIA**

In El Alamein, Egypt, Montgomery won one of the decisive battles of World War II. Never again would Axis forces threaten the Suez Canal or the Middle East. This battle made Montgomery, shown in Figure 13-1, one of the greatest military figures in British history.

FIGURE 13-1:
Field Marshal
General Bernard
Montgomery.

Bettmann/Getty Images

After El Alamein, the British army would never experience another retreat or humiliating defeat at the hands of the Germans again. El Alamein, Egypt pointed the way to victory. Montgomery accomplished this victory by careful preparation, rehearsal, and detailed coordination and planning. Nothing would move until everything had been set. This careful, set-piece approach to combat would continue to be the pattern Montgomery displayed in all the battles that he fought for the rest of the war — even though his tactics often infuriated and frustrated his American allies.

Throwing the Torch: The Allies Strike in North Africa

While the British Eighth Army fought its decisive battle against German General Rommel's army at El Alamein, Egypt, a British-American invasion force was converging on North Africa. Planning for the campaign began in July 1942, after President Roosevelt determined that American forces would invade North Africa.

The leader of the invasion was Lieutenant General Dwight D. Eisenhower (see Figure 13-2), who commanded an infantry battalion as a Lieutenant Colonel in 1939. In less than four years, Eisenhower advanced to lead the largest amphibious invasion in history — Operation TORCH — even though he had been given only about 12 weeks to put the operation together. Eisenhower faced a nearly unimaginable burden: The entire Allied war plan for 1942 depended on the success of Operation TORCH. If his plan failed, the Allies would face the following problems:

>> The Spanish and Vichy French (the new French government formed after the German defeat of France in 1940) could join the Axis, adding enormous naval and ground forces to Hitler's powerful war machine.

>> Any hopes of an invasion across the English Channel would be delayed for years.

FIGURE 13-2:
General Dwight Eisenhower.

Library of Congress/Getty Images

GENERAL DWIGHT D. EISENHOWER

Dwight D. Eisenhower (1890–1969) was a Captain in World War I, but instead of going to France to fight in World War II, he remained in the United States to train American soldiers. From 1933 to 1939, Eisenhower worked for General Douglas MacArthur. Between 1940 and 1941, Eisenhower served in key staff roles as the Army prepared for war. One of his responsibilities included planning the army-level maneuvers in 1941, a milestone in the development of the modern U.S. Army. Within a year, Eisenhower had risen from Lieutenant Colonel to a Brigadier General.

Just after America's entry into the war, Eisenhower was put in the War Plans Division. His skills earned him another promotion, this one to Major General. He was then promoted to Lieutenant General and sent to London to take charge of the joint British-American planning effort for Operation TORCH (see the section "Throwing the Torch: The Allies Strike" in this chapter). Eisenhower commanded the Allied armada that invaded North Africa in 1942 and Italy in 1943. Later in the year, he returned to London to take command of the *Supreme Headquarters Allied Expeditionary Force* (SHAEF) to plan the invasion of France.

Eisenhower was a brilliant choice for these difficult roles. He had the uncanny ability to get officers who could never cooperate before to finally work together — a critical skill for the success of a coalition. Although Eisenhower always wanted to lead troops in combat, his skills as a strategist made him more valuable at headquarters. He was thorough, incisive, and analytical, cutting through complexities to see into the heart of a military problem. He was also able to share his insights and build consensus among the Allies. His open and friendly personality reflected an honesty and sincerity that made it hard not to like him. In many ways, the secret of the Allies' success was their ability to see beyond narrow concerns and focus on their ultimate common objective — the defeat of Nazi Germany. The man who made this happen was Dwight Eisenhower.

Getting organized: The invasion force takes shape

The first goal in creating the plan was to get the American and British to agree on the strategy:

>> The British wanted a landing on the African coast deep inside the Mediterranean, closer to where British forces were fighting and closer to Egypt and the critical lifeline of the Suez Canal.

» The Americans wanted to land on the Atlantic coast of Africa, outside the choke point of Gibraltar. They were leery of running a huge invasion force into the Mediterranean, and noted with some concern that only a year earlier, German U-boats sank two British ships and seriously damaged two others.

American and British forces finally determined a blueprint for the invasion of North Africa. It was a compromise that involved three task forces:

» **The Western Task Force:** With 35,000 men and led by General George S. Patton (see Figure 13-3) — a mercurial and brilliant tank officer and World War I veteran — this group would land near Casablanca, Morocco's main city. Patton's task force would make the perilous journey across the Atlantic, dodging German U-boats. His landing would be supported by 47 warships of the United States Navy.

FIGURE 13-3: General George Patton.

» **The Central Task Force:** With 39,000 men and led by untested American officer Major General Lloyd Fredendall, this force would leave from Britain and land near Oran, the second largest city in Algeria. Twenty-one British warships would support it.

>> **The Eastern Task Force:** Led by a highly decorated World War I veteran and friend of Eisenhower, Major General Charles W. Ryder, this force would also leave from Britain. With 33,000 British and American troops and supported by 22 British warships, Ryder was to capture Algiers, the capital city of Algeria.

The operation begins

On November 8, 1942, the three task forces made their landings:

>> At Algiers, all went well: The French forces declared their support for General De Gaulle after Admiral Jean Darlan, the commander of all Vichy armed forces, was captured in Algiers by the Allies.

>> In Oran, the Vichy troops put up a fight until November 10, when Darlan ordered them to cease resistance.

>> At Casablanca, the French land and naval forces fought particularly hard, delaying the American advance for more than a day. After receiving orders from Darlan, however, they surrendered on November 11.

POLITICS MAKES STRANGE BEDFELLOWS, BUT DO WE REALLY HAVE TO SLEEP WITH THIS GUY?

In Algiers, the Allies found a surprising visitor: Admiral Jean Darlan, the commander of all Vichy armed forces, was in the city visiting his son. Caught completely by surprise by the invasion, Darlan became a prisoner of the Allies. Darlan was an opportunist, and his capture was an extraordinary stroke of luck for the Allies. Realizing that he might be able to cut a better deal with the Allies than with the Germans, he agreed to order his troops to stop fighting. The Vichy forces obeyed Darlan's cease-fire order, which brought the Algiers invasion to a quick end. He later gave the cease-fire order to the Vichy French fighting the Allies in Casablanca, ending that city's resistance.

Darlan was pro-Nazi and had a well-known dislike of Jews. Nevertheless, the Allies placed him in charge of French North Africa as an expedient to keep the population under control and to influence French forces in Tunisia to surrender to the Allies. Politically, the situation was tricky, and one Roosevelt and Churchill had trouble explaining. If the Allies were fighting the Axis, why was a pro-Nazi Frenchman put in charge of a recently captured country? Truth was, nobody liked Darlan, but for the moment his presence was essential in keeping the French colony quiet. Politcs, as they say, makes strange bedfellows.

The end of Vichy France

Infuriated by Vichy Admiral Darlan's cooperation with the Allies (see the section "The operation begins" this chapter) and in reaction to the Allied occupation of French North Africa, Hitler eliminated Vichy government control of France and placed Nazis in charge. In a vain attempt to mollify Hitler, Vichy General Henri Pétain tried to cancel Darlan's orders to Vichy's armed forces. But Hitler ordered the occupation of France in November 1942 anyway.

German troops also tried to capture the French Fleet at Toulon, thinking to combine the French ships with the German ships in order to attack the Allies. But the Nazis were stopped by the courageous actions of a few French patriots who *scuttled* (purposefully sank) the French Fleet in the harbor, making it useless to the Germans. The Vichy government became little more than a figurehead for the remainder of the war.

Winning ugly: The Americans' steep learning curve

The Allied invasion of North Africa was successful. The Americans started out with the most complex of military operations — the amphibious landing — and had done well. But they also showed poor planning skills. For example:

>> Paratroopers that were to seize Oran's airfields were dropped 20 miles away from their target.

>> Green American infantrymen, entering combat with only limited training, used up all their ammunition early and drank all their water (it was the desert, after all), and they couldn't be resupplied because the ships had been loaded incorrectly.

>> Landing craft, which were limited in numbers and could not be spared, were left on the beach. The high tide damaged or destroyed them.

>> Command and control were lost early on in the landings. General Patton, for example, was preparing to go ashore when his flagship became engaged in a shootout with a French battleship. For many hours into the battle, Patton had no communications with Eisenhower or his troops on the ground.

In the face of the mistakes the Americans made, it was fortunate that the enemy resistance had been light. Nevertheless, Americans gained valuable experience that they put to use in the days ahead.

Turning toward Tunisia

The next significant battle ground between the Allies and the Axis was Tunisia. Characterized by arid desert and rugged mountains, Tunisia was a nondescript place, but the country, which had excellent port facilities and was only a short distance by air and sea to Sicily and the Italian peninsula, turned out to be important to both the sides:

>> For the Germans, Tunisia was a critical place to collect Rommel's army for refitting and resupply, and it was a convenient place to protect Italy and the central Mediterranean.

>> For the Allies, Tunisia was the logical place to end the North African invasion. They also wanted to set up a base of operations there for future offensive action against Axis forces.

Hitler sends reinforcements

Hitler reacted to the Allies' invasion of North African by pouring air and ground reinforcements, as well as tons of supplies, into Tunisia. The first wave of reinforcements brought in 50,000 Germans and 18,000 Italian troops; Hitler eventually sent an additional 100,000 German and 10,000 Italian soldiers as reinforcements. He also placed General Juergen von Arnim in charge of the new organization called the *5th Panzer Army*.

General von Arnim counterattacked Allied forces that were trying to capture two key Tunisian port cities — Tunis and Bizerte. By December 1942, Arnim achieved a stalemate. For Arnim, it was probably the best situation that he could hope for. Hitler somehow envisioned that Arnim's forces could destroy the Allied invaders and retake all of Northern Africa. Hitler ignored the growing Allied supply base in North Africa and the continuous flow of reinforcements arriving daily from the United States, which quickly outpaced the German capability to reinforce Tunisia and thus made his plan impossible to accomplish.

Rommel returns . . . again

Rommel's army arrived in southern Tunisia after retreating over 1,500 miles from Egypt (see the section "Rommel's defeat: Montgomery gives chase" earlier in this chapter). Even after such a disastrous defeat by the British, Rommel was able to reorganize his remaining forces into a credible combat unit again. They dug in to await the attack of the British Eighth Army. But Rommel preferred not to wait and give the enemy the initiative. Rommel's plans were to do the following:

>> Attack the inexperienced American II Corps, which included soldiers from Operation TORCH and soldiers that had just arrived from basic training in the U.S. These soldiers occupied the key mountain passes in south central Tunisia.

>> Follow up the attack on the American II Corps with an attack into the Allied rear. Rommel's goal was to disrupt communications and supply and perhaps deal a severe blow to the tenuous Allied coalition of British, French, and American forces.

Kasserine Pass: The first battle

MILITARY STRATEGY

In February 1943, Rommel struck at the key mountain pass at Kasserine, Tunisia against elements of the American II Corps. This attack was a disaster for the Americans. Rommel's tested combat veterans made quick work of the untried troops. His breakthrough threatened the rear of the Allied armies and its key supply depot, which, if captured, could have forced the Allies to abandon Tunisia and retreat into Algeria. The attack failed, however, because German General von Arnim didn't launch supporting attacks to pin British forces while Rommel swept northwest.

As a result, an American armored division and Allied aircraft concentrated solely on Rommel's force. Short on fuel and realizing that he had done as much as he could, Rommel withdrew, but he left the Americans shaken and demoralized. The Kasserine operation threw the Allies off their timetable by at least a month and gave the Germans a better hold on Tunisia.

The Americans regroup and attack

For the Americans, Kasserine was a hard lesson in war. It exposed their weaknesses in training, tactics, and command. Thus, Eisenhower took immediate action to make the American II Corps a decent fighting force. He put General George Patton in charge and ordered him to get the force organized. By March, Patton had whipped the troops into shape enough for Eisenhower to launch a coordinated attack to capture the port cities of Tunisia that kept the Germans supplied and to trap the German army against the coast. Supported by British General Montgomery's British Eighth Army attacking from the South, Eisenhower sent Patton's Corps in a slashing attack toward the African coast. The Montgomery-Patton attack forced Rommel to retreat northward along the Tunisian coast. General Eisenhower also had valuable assistance from British General Alexander, Montgomery's commander, who became Eisenhower's deputy and integrated the British Eighth Army into the attack on Tunisia.

MILITARY STRATEGY

Because of his success, Patton was promoted to Commander of an army making preparations for an attack on Italy, and General Omar Bradley became the new Commander of the II Corps.

In early May, Eisenhower ordered a general attack against the German defenses. The Germans fought well, but with the sea at their back, they could give up little ground. Trapped by the Allies, 248,000 Axis soldiers surrendered to Allied forces on May 13. Most of these 248,000 captured Axis soldiers were some of the best combat troops in the German army; German General Arnim was also one of those captured. The Germans lost irreplaceable tanks, artillery, aircraft, and transport ships.

A Day and Night in Casablanca: The Allies Go-Forward Plan

After the battle in Tunisia, decisions had to be made to determine the strategic direction of the war. In January 1943 in Casablanca, President Roosevelt and Prime Minister Churchill met with the Combined Chiefs of Staff to plot the next move. (Casablanca, Morocco was one of the first cities captured by American forces in the North African invasion in November 1942; see the earlier section "Throwing the Torch: The Allies Strike in North Africa.") The two leaders made the following decisions:

>> Follow up the destruction of Axis forces in Tunisia with an invasion of Sicily in June or July 1943 to try to knock Italy out of the war and maintain the second front in support of the Soviet Union.

>> Sustain the British bombing offensive aimed at destroying Germany's war industry and crippling German morale.

>> Increase assistance to China and build up forces for offensive operations in the central and southwest Pacific and in Burma (called Myanmar today) in Southeast Asia.

>> Ensure a declaration of unconditional surrender of the enemy.

Operation HUSKY: Invading Sicily

While the offensive against Tunisia was underway (see the earlier section "Throwing the Torch: The Allies Strike in Northern Africa"), Eisenhower had begun forming the nucleus of another army to prepare for the invasion of Sicily, a large island at the toe of the boot-shaped Italian peninsula. Only 90 miles from Tunisia, the island served as a choke point for sea traffic, as well as an excellent air and naval base for attacks against Allied shipping in the Mediterranean. Capturing the island would give the Allies air and sea control over this critical passage. It was also a perfect stepping stone for an attack against the Italian peninsula, which would eventually lead north to Germany.

For this operation, code named HUSKY, the Allies formed the Fifteenth Army. Commanded by British General Alexander, this group consisted of the 7th Army, commanded by American General Patton, and the Eighth Army, commanded by British General Montgomery.

MILITARY
STRATEGY

The Fifteenth Army totaled 160,000 men, 600 tanks, and 1,800 artillery pieces, whereas the Axis forces defending Sicily consisted of 350,000 German and Italian soldiers, 260 tanks, and 1,400 aircraft.

Although the Axis forces outnumbered the Allied forces and would seem to give the Axis the advantage, these high numbers didn't reflect the morale of the Italians: The Italian army had had a bellyful of war, and it was clear to all of them — from general to private — that they were out of their league. The main fighting was therefore left to 75,000 superb German infantry and *panzer* (tank) troops, who would be badly outnumbered.

An Allied victory, an Italian surrender, and a few snafus

Operation HUSKY was an amphibious invasion: 3,000 British and American ships and nearly 4,000 aircraft supported the ground forces.

MILITARY
STRATEGY

At dawn on July 10, 1943, Montgomery's British Eighth Army landed on the southeastern coast of Sicily near Syracuse, and Patton's American 7th Army landed a few miles to the west (see Figure 13-4). After a stiff initial defense, the Germans decided that a timely retreat was better than ending up in prisoner-of-war camps with their Italian allies. Falling back to the mountains, the Germans held Montgomery's advance, while Patton advanced slowly along the northern coast, trying to get behind the German defenses. Patton finally forced the Germans out of their positions by making several amphibious landings on the coastline directly behind the Germans. Enough was enough as far as the Germans were concerned. By August 17, they escaped across the Strait of Messina to the Italian mainland, leaving the demoralized Italians to surrender to the victorious Allies.

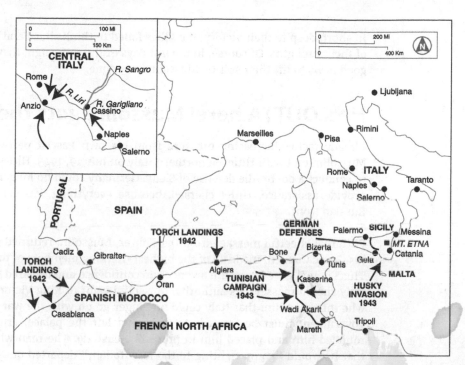

FIGURE 13-4:
The Allied invasion of Italy, 1943.

The Allied victory in Sicily was less than satisfactory. Despite the Allies' superiority in numbers and their eventual victory over the Germans and Italians, the operation proved that the British and Americans were still having a little difficulty figuring everything out:

» Imitating an earlier German assault on the Greek Island of Crete in 1941 (see Chapter 5), American and British airborne troops were dropped on the island to disrupt the defenders. But due to bad weather, incompetence, and pilot error, the Allies dropped the paratroopers far off their targets, neutralizing their effect.

» The Allied naval forces mistook the second wave of gliders and aircraft as the enemy and shot many of them down.

» Although most of the Italians surrendered, the Allies let high-quality veteran German combat troops escape, even though the Allies had complete control of the sea and air and could have trapped the German forces whenever they chose — the enemy was on an island, after all.

In short, despite their victory, the Allies failed to think ahead and take advantage of their strengths. Of course, in the last days of the campaign, they did get a little good news to lift their spirits: Mussolini was gone.

He's OUTTA here! Mussolini gets the hook

Already facing increasing pressure from his own Fascist party to step down, Mussolini met with Hitler in northern Italy on July 19, 1943. Hitler told Mussolini to conduct a do-or-die defense of Sicily. Germany could no longer be expected to provide assistance, Hitler claimed, because everything was committed on the Russian front.

With that cheerful message from Der Führer, Mussolini returned to Rome to face his Grand Council, made up of the highest-ranking members of the Fascist party. This Council gave Mussolini a vote of no confidence and declared that the King of Italy should reassert his authority. Mussolini went to King Victor Emmanuel III, who informed him that Italy could no longer go on with the war and that a new government must be formed. As Mussolini left the palace, armed police surrounded him and placed him in protective custody. The man who had declared that he would "go on fighting to the last Italian," departed quietly. Mussolini's careless presumptions about Italy's capabilities and the weaknesses of his enemies led directly to his downfall.

Who needs a friend like you? Italy declares war on Germany

The new Premier, Marshal Pietro Badoglio, immediately began secret peace negotiations with the Allies to get Italy out of the war. On September 3, 1943, an agreement was signed. This agreement was announced to the world on September 8. In response, Hitler moved troops into Italy and sent German aircraft to attack the Italian fleet. Italy's new government declared war on Germany on October 13, 1943.

What followed was essentially the fall of Italy to Germany. While the new Italian government dithered over terms with the Allies, German ground forces seized Rome. German aircraft sank Italian ships headed for Malta to surrender. The German army replaced Italian troops on the front lines.

In the meantime, the Allies arrived on the Italian mainland.

Up the Boot: Invading the Italian Mainland

As he had in Sicily, General Alexander remained in command of the Allied Fifteenth Army invasion force. British General Montgomery's Eighth Army also remained part of the invasion force. The American 7th Army did not; it was sent to England to train for the cross-channel invasion scheduled for 1944. The 5th Army, commanded by American General Mark Clark, took the 7th Army's place.

On September 3, 1943, the Eighth Army crossed the Strait of Messina and, in true Montgomery fashion, stayed in place until supplies had built up sufficiently to allow a measured forward movement. After several days, Montgomery finally began to move north.

Meanwhile, Clark's army landed at Salerno on September 9, the day after Italy's surrender was announced. The British-American force didn't find eagerly surrendering Italians standing on the beaches, however. A German division waited for them instead.

German Field Marshal Albert Kesselring was in charge of the waiting troops and had orders to make the Allied advance as costly as possible. Kesselring, the one-time commander of Axis forces in the Mediterranean and North Africa, was an exceptional combat commander and an astute soldier. The Allies faced a formidable opponent.

Salerno to the Winter Line

The first few days at Salerno were touch and go. The Germans nearly succeeded in driving the Allies right off the beach. Only the combined effort of Allied air support and naval gunfire, plus the determined, almost desperate resistance of Allied troops, kept the Germans from succeeding. As Montgomery's army began approaching Salerno, Kesselring, whose resources were limited, withdrew. He had, for the most part, done his job: inflict as much damage on the Allied forces as possible, delaying their advance while preserving the combat power of his own forces.

The 5th and Eighth Armies linked up on September 16, and the two armies began moving north side by side. On October 1, 1943, the 5th Army captured the port of Naples, Italy.

In the wake of the victory

After the capture of Naples, several divisions from the Eighth and 5th armies were dispatched to England for invasion training. The replacement divisions were a mixture of American, British, Canadian, Indian, New Zealand, Polish, and French units. This jumble of soldiers was not only difficult to command and control, but most of the units also lacked combat experience. Reorganizing and preparing for combat took time. In the meantime, the Germans strengthened their defensive positions.

The Allied attacks on the *Winter Line* (the name given the German defensive line in Italy) began in late November and lasted nearly a month, but with no success. The bitterly cold weather, the skillfully built German defenses, and the inexperience of the Allied units all combined to bring an end to the uninterrupted advance of British and American land, air, and naval forces that began on the beaches of North Africa one year earlier.

Chapter **14**

Germany a Three-Time Loser: In Russia, At Home, and in the Atlantic

You may be surprised to find out that Hitler had the chance to win the war against the Soviet Union in 1942 with a breathtakingly ambitious plan to destroy the Soviet Army and seize critical geographical objectives. Hitler's plan raised two big questions: Could the German army accomplish all its objectives before the resources to sustain the offensives ran out? Would the events in North Africa and the Mediterranean prove to be fatal distractions? At the same time, Hitler was employing his submarines to destroy the seagoing flow of supplies headed from the United States to Great Britain and the Soviet Union to keep them in the war. This, too, was a matter of time and cruel logic. Could the U-boats sink supply ships faster than the Allies could produce new ships?

Faced with very few options to take the war directly to German territory, the Allies began day and nighttime air raids on German cities and industries. The Allies pinned many hopes on this campaign, and many strategists believed it would shorten the war by crippling critical defense industries and German civilian morale. In this chapter, you can evaluate Hitler's chances for victory in 1942 for yourself and look into the origins of the concept of victory through air power.

Hitler's 1942 Offensive in Russia

Hitler had targeted the Soviet Union from the beginning. Despite the pact that he and Stalin signed — The Nazi-Soviet Non-Aggression Pact (see Chapter 4) — he had always intended to invade the USSR. Eastern Europe and the USSR would provide the *Lebensraum* (see Chapter 3) that Hitler's Master Race and great empire would need.

Hitler's original plan had been to invade the Soviet Union and conquer it in five months (see Chapter 6 for more information about Germany's invasion of Russia). This plan didn't go as Hitler expected, however, and the German troops found themselves stuck in Russia for the winter. So they suffered through the harsh Russian winter and waited for summer, when the German offensive would begin again.

Hitler's plan: Bold but flawed

Hitler viewed south and central Russia as the home of future generations of Germans. Hitler's strategy for renewing the offensive against the Soviet Army was aimed at occupying the south-central part of the USSR — Ukraine and the Caucasus Mountains. Ukraine had rich, fertile soil that could feed the population, and the Caucasus had natural resources (primarily oil) that could fuel Hitler's mechanized armies. The added immediate benefit for the Germans, of course, was that these valuable areas would be denied to the Soviets for their use in the war.

On paper, Hitler's plan looked sound (see Figure 14-1), but it required that he stretch his front lines more than 600 miles farther south and put the bulk of his most capable forces there. This plan left the less capable units defending the northern half.

Hitler's Generals advised that the main attack continue toward Moscow, according to the original plan. Moscow was the heart and brain of the Soviet resistance, they argued. To win, they said, Moscow must fall.

But Hitler was blinded by his own strange vision, and he no longer had faith in his generals. Thus, Germany's best armies headed south, toward the industrial city of Stalingrad on the Volga River and the Caucasus oil fields. (Hitler believed that the capture of Stalingrad would cut off the flow of oil to the rest of the USSR.)

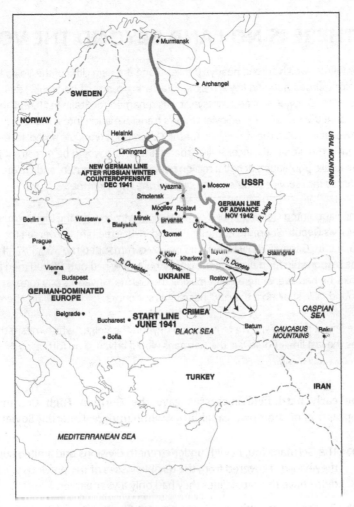

FIGURE 14-1:
German summer offensive, 1942.

Soviet response

As good strategists, the Soviets knew that Moscow was the key to German victory. They placed the bulk of their forces in their capital, fully expecting the Germans to attack. But they were taken by surprise when the German *panzers* (tanks) headed south. The first few weeks seemed like a replay of the summer of 1941 — German tank divisions made huge gaps in the front lines, Soviet units were trapped and surrounded, and tens of thousands of Soviets became prisoners. (See Chapter 6 for more on Hitler's invasion of Russia in 1941.)

Just as had happened since 1939, Hitler seemed to have been right and his Generals wrong. It appeared that the German armies really could advance at will against the Soviets and that the Soviet Army might actually be on its last leg.

"THERE IS NO LAND BEYOND THE VOLGA"

Stalingrad, which spread nearly 20 miles along the high cliffs of the Volga River, was a major railroad hub and key arms manufacturing center. It had tank, steel, and chemical factories. Originally called Tsaritsyn, it was renamed for Stalin in 1928. The city had become the model for the Soviet Union's transformation into a modern industrial power; it was also the showplace for the Communist worker's paradise. Because of its great symbolic significance, Stalin ordered that there would be no retreat from the city. The entire population of half a million people — men, women, and children — were pressed into service to defend the city. No one was exempt.

Stalin appointed General Zhukov, the savior of Moscow during the German invasion of 1941, as Deputy Supreme Commander and instructed him to oversee the defense of Stalingrad. General Vasily Ivanovich Chuikov commanded the Soviet 62nd Army and was responsible for defending the city. Although he had only 55,000 men and a few tanks, he had every intention of making the German invaders pay for every foot of ground. "We shall hold the city," he told his superiors, "or we shall die there!"

The Soviet slogan was "There is no land beyond the Volga," which meant that Stalingrad was the last line of defense; the Germans would advance no further.

The early battlefield successes gave the German High Command the wrong impression of their own capabilities while underestimating Soviet resilience:

>> The Germans fought with under-strength divisions and limited supplies — they hadn't recovered from the terrible losses of the previous winter and didn't have the capabilities they had only a year earlier.

>> For the Soviets, the Lend-Lease Act (see Chapter 7) and the factories in the Ural Mountains had replaced most of their material losses. The USSR's vast pool of manpower allowed it to replace combat losses quickly.

>> As Germany advanced across the endless plains of southern Ukraine, their supply lines grew longer and more exposed to attack, especially from partisans, who preyed on road and rail systems.

Hitler dooms his troops

In such large-scale operations as the German offensive in the USSR, the supply experts play the most important role in achieving success. (Although this tends to insult the commander who is always focused on moving and shooting, nevertheless it's still true.) With his armies advancing south 300 miles in the first month of the offensive, Hitler wouldn't listen to recommendations from his generals to slow down. Then, when supplies ran low, Hitler couldn't decide which army to give priority to for the fuel, food, and ammunition that kept the units in battle. So he pushed everybody ahead equally. That decision had two effects:

>> It sent an under-strength army half starved for supplies against the well-fortified city of Stalingrad.

>> It sent a strong army crashing into the Caucasus Mountains looking for oil fields, which the Soviets had conveniently destroyed before the Germans arrived.

In short, Hitler gained empty real estate and lengthened his supply lines more than 600 miles. His great offensive resulted not in the final collapse of the Soviet Union, but in a stalemate in the Caucasus Mountains and an impending disaster for the Germans at Stalingrad.

The agony of Stalingrad

HISTORICAL TRIVIA

As the German 6th Army approached Stalingrad in September of 1942, the German *Luftwaffe* bombed and devastated the city in the hopes of crushing the defenders' morale. Although the attack turned the city to rubble and killed 40,000 civilians, the destruction actually gave the defenders more places to hide, making the German ground attack harder to conduct.

The Germans attacked with infantry and tank forces totaling nearly 200,000 men. Their goal was to capture the city and seize the ferry crossings on the Volga. (The Soviets used these crossings to bring reinforcements and supplies to the city's battered defenders.) Throughout September, the battle for the city raged. The Germans captured the main ferry crossings and had 90 percent of the city under their control. The Soviets suffered 80,000 casualties. Yet they fought on, reinforced and supplied by boats and rafts from the opposite bank of the river.

DID THEY GET TIME-AND-A-HALF FOR THIS?

The Stalingrad tractor factory, which had been converted to assembling tanks a year before, remained in operation even while the fighting went on outside and, in many cases, inside the factory. As soon as factory workers completed a tank, it literally drove out of the factory to fight down the street. The workers themselves, mostly women and teenagers, often stopped work on the tanks to join the infantry defending the plant. As a result of this heroic effort, the Germans couldn't capture the Stalingrad tractor factory.

Constant air bombardment and artillery fire darkened the sky and created a sense of permanent night within the city. The battle deteriorated from army fighting army to wild, ruthless battles between groups of 15 to 25 men. They fought with grenades, flamethrowers, machine guns, and shovels over rooms in ruined houses or piles of rubble on street corners. For 80 days and nights without rest, these small but terrifying battles continued. The Germans fought all day to clear a street of the enemy, only to find Russian soldiers back in the same places the next day.

Setting the trap for the Germans

By late October, the Germans controlled all but a nine-mile strip of terrain along the Volga riverbank. Victory seemed to be in their grasp. However, the German troops were exhausted and badly battered. They had concentrated all their power into a narrow, knife-like thrust into Stalingrad. To the north and south of the city, Romanian and Italian divisions (fighting with the Nazis) spread themselves thin to defend against any Soviet counterattack. The Germans were so focused on the Battle of Stalingrad that they failed to notice other activity along the front.

General Zhukov was gathering Soviet reinforcements, most of them transferred from Moscow (where little activity was going on). He soon had more than 1 million troops in 9 armies, 13,000 pieces of artillery, 1,000 aircraft, and 900 tanks poised on each flank north and south of Stalingrad. Zhukov intended to change the course of the war in one massive attack by sending his forces around and behind Stalingrad, trapping an entire German army and opening a giant gap in the German front line.

REMEMBER

By the time Hitler made his second push in the Soviet Union, the German armies were not all German. Heavy casualties made replacements sometimes difficult to find. To cover the massive front line, essentially stretching across the continent of Europe, Hitler needed troops. He got them from Italian and Romanian units. Italy, of course, had been a long-time ally, and Mussolini provided Italian troops to support the war against Stalin. Romania, occupied by German forces since early 1941, provided troops in Russia as well. These units were far less combat-ready than German units, but they enabled the German units to go where the fighting was heaviest. During the Stalingrad offensive, more and more German troops had been pulled into the battle in the city, leaving the front lines above and below the city occupied by less capable Italian and Romanian units. This was where the Soviets aimed their attack.

The bear trap snaps shut: The Soviets attack

By mid-November, the weather turned cold and snowy. In the early morning hours of November 19, Romanian troops were shattered by heavy artillery attacks followed by masses of Soviet infantrymen clad in white winter camouflage and supported by T–34 tanks. The Romanians, with only obsolete equipment, were no match for the Soviets. The Romanians who weren't killed or captured ran away. The Italians weren't much better off. In less than a day, the Soviet armies had closed in 40 miles behind the Nazi army.

When Paulus, the General in charge of the troops battling for Stalingrad, requested that Hitler order a retreat, Hitler refused. He and Hermann Goering, the Nazi *Luftwaffe* Chief, fooled themselves into believing that Paulus's army didn't need to retreat. They ordered that the army keep fighting in Stalingrad and be resupplied entirely by air. This was a bad decision for a couple of reasons:

REMEMBER

>> **The Nazis weren't able to provide the needed supplies.** Hitler had been an infantry corporal in World War I, and Goering had been a fighter pilot. Neither of them had the slightest appreciation for planning *sorties* (quick raids on the invaders by the people being invaded), including how many planes or how many airfields were needed every day to supply several hundred thousand men with sufficient food, fuel, and ammunition to conduct offensive operations. As a result, Hitler and Goering grossly underestimated the needs of the units fighting in Stalingrad, failed to provide the promised supplies, and doomed their men.

>> **Resupplying the troops in Stalingrad was a waste of effort and resources.** Stalingrad no longer had any military significance to the Germans. A 1 million-man Soviet army was 40 miles behind the German lines, and the Romanians and Italians were gone, leaving a huge hole in the German lines.

More prudent strategists would have cut their losses and regrouped in order to pursue other priorities. But Hitler had been lured into expecting spectacular success from his armies. Not accustomed to defeat, he failed to appreciate the magnitude of the disaster that had just happened on the Volga.

Stalingrad: A decisive Soviet victory

In December 1942, German panzers attempted to break through the Soviet lines to relieve the troops from Stalingrad. They actually came within 30 miles of Paulus's troops. Paulus, however, refused to leave the city and link up with the relief column without an order from Hitler. The Führer had no intention of giving such an order. As the tanks retreated under a Soviet counterattack, the men of the German 6th Army were left to their fate. Starved, frozen, and blasted, 108,000 Germans surrendered on February 2, 1943. Of this number, no more than 5,000 ever returned to Germany.

MILITARY STRATEGY

NAZI MATH

In case you're wondering, here are the facts: Every day, the German 6th Army needed 120 tons of fuel and 250 tons of ammunition, plus at least 150 tons of food. Delivering that much required 235 planeloads daily.

Before telling General Paulus that the German army couldn't retreat from Stalingrad, Hitler and Goering should have asked themselves the following questions: How many planes could Stalingrad's existing airfields accommodate? Where could the *Luftwaffe* put 520 tons of supplies every day? Who was going to move the stuff to the front-line troops? How long could the *Luftwaffe* sustain such an effort? What happened if the weather turned bad or they lost planes?

Well, no one asked these questions, and the results were tragic. The Germans could send only 30 to 40 aircraft to support the troops in Stalingrad (which had only two airfields). Many planes were shot down by Soviet fighters, or they got lost in bad weather and never delivered the supplies. From November to January, the *Luftwaffe* lost 500 transport aircraft and 300 fighters and bombers in its attempt to resupply the city. At best, the 6th Army received 140 tons of supplies in any given day. This short lesson in logistics is one that Hitler never learned.

By March 1943, the Germans in the south had been pushed back more than 200 miles, driven out of the Caucasus Mountains, and were battling for the city of Kharkov. In the north, the Soviets pushed back German forces occupying advanced positions near Moscow and opened a narrow corridor to Leningrad, which had been under siege by German and Finnish forces since 1941. Without a strategic reserve to counter these attacks and faced with another harsh winter, the German armies were forced to give ground to slow the Soviet attacks.

ARMY ALLIED

All in all, the Battle of Stalingrad cost each side 750,000 casualties. But this battle was the turning point in the war in Europe. Hitler would never be able to overcome Soviet land power again. He had wasted much of his irreplaceable air and ground forces, and six-month's worth of the total war production of Germany had been funneled into the futile struggle.

Stalingrad became the epic defense of the Soviet people against the Fascist invaders. The victory showed that Germany could be defeated. Bolstered by mountains of weapons, ammunition, and equipment provided by sea from the United States and Great Britain, the Soviet armies were growing stronger.

Amassing Ammo and Men at Kursk

By the spring of 1943, the Germans were standing roughly in the same place they had been in the spring of 1942. Now Hitler was faced with another strategic dilemma: Because the great southern offensive in Russia had been a disaster, could anything be done to win the war? Or more importantly, what could he do to avoid losing the war? The Allies were heading for Italy, the Allied strategic bomber offensive was crippling German war industries, and the possibility of an attack from across the English Channel was always a possibility.

Once again, Hitler ignored the advice of his generals, who wanted to go on the defensive. Instead, he decided to attack in the center in an attempt to break the Soviet lines and drive deep into Russia. (Ironically, this is what his generals had advised him to do the year *before*.)

Hitler focused on the Soviet 360-mile bulge in their defensive line at Kursk. (In military terms, this bulge is called a *salient*.) Here, the Soviets were vulnerable to a *pincers movement*, in which flanks move simultaneously to close in on an enemy. The Soviet troops defending the area would be cut off from supplies and destroyed (in the same way the German 6th Army had been at Stalingrad), leaving a 50-mile-wide gap in the Soviet lines for German armies to move through.

MILITARY STRATEGY

Hitler sought a decisive victory. But Germany could no longer conduct such an operation without carefully marshaling forces and resources. To do so took time, enough time for the Soviets to figure out Hitler's plan and make their own preparations to defend Kursk. By July, the Germans had massed nearly 1.5 million men and 3,000 tanks (most of them the newest models). These were backed by nearly 10,000 artillery pieces and 1,800 aircraft. The Soviets, however, were waiting with 1 million men, 3,000 tanks, and 13,000 artillery pieces that were arrayed for 18 miles and protected by a series of trenches, obstacles, and mines. More importantly, the Soviets had 400,000 reserve troops. The Germans had no reserves to speak of.

ARMY ALLIED

THE SOVIET TANK: T-34

The *T-34 tank* proved its capability as the best all-purpose fighting vehicle of the war. With its 76-millimeter main gun and two machine guns, the tank was low and wide, designed for the mud and snow of the Russian plains. Mechanically reliable and well armored, the tank had a top speed of 30 miles per hour and could travel 180 miles before refueling. This tank, along with the well-trained crew, won the Battle of Kursk and changed the entire balance of the war. From then on, the Germans were on the run.

The plum of Stalin's eye: Operation Zitadelle

The plan for the attack on Kursk was called *Zitadelle* (Citadel). The Germans began their attack on July 5, 1943. But the Soviets weren't surprised. For years, Soviet intelligence agents in Switzerland had recruited spies with access to German army military plans. *Zitadelle* was one of the plums that fell into Stalin's hands. Thus, 30 minutes before the German attack began, the Soviets opened the battle with a monstrous barrage of artillery fire, catching German troops in the open as they moved to their attack positions. The battle only got worse.

As German and Soviet airmen fought for control of the skies, German and Soviet tanks fought at close range back and forth across the rolling hills. Although the Germans managed to slug their way into open terrain, the Soviets launched effective counterattacks. The 4th Panzer Army lost 350 tanks and 10,000 men in one of these counterattacks.

Kursk: Another big win for the Soviets

By July 12, it became obvious that the Soviets were too strong, too well prepared, and too skilled for the Germans. The last *blitzkrieg* in the East had failed. (For information about the battle strategy of the blitzkrieg, see Chapter 5.) For the first time, the Soviet air force held its own against the *Luftwaffe*, and the Soviet tank proved its worth. The Battle of Kursk was a decisive Soviet victory, and from that point on Germans were on the defensive in the East.

**MILITARY
STRATEGY**

The Battle of Kursk was the largest tank battle in history and one of the largest battles ever fought in world history. In addition, the Germans fired more artillery shells during the Battle of Kursk than they did in their attacks against Poland (1939) and France (1940) combined.

Taking It to the Streets: Bombing Germany

The Allies' bombing campaign was the second strike for Germany, already reeling from two major defeats in the war against Russia (see the preceding sections "Hitler's 1942 Offensive in Russia" and "Amassing Ammo and Men at Kursk"). As German combat forces were hammered by the Soviet war machine, Hitler had another distraction, this time from the air.

When the Germans unleashed the blitzkrieg on Holland, Belgium, and France in May 1940, Winston Churchill ordered British bombers to attack industrial targets in Germany. During the Battle of Britain (explained in Chapter 5), Churchill ordered retaliatory air raids on Berlin after German bombers attacked London in August 1940. Mostly to sustain British morale and as a way to strike back at Germany directly, the raids continued against German industrial targets. German defenses were sophisticated and tough, equipped with radar, searchlights, night fighters, and antiaircraft guns.

In 1942, the *Royal Air Force* (RAF) was given instructions to begin regular strikes against German transportation networks and other targets that would weaken civilian morale, especially industrial workers. The strikes began in February. The British organized mass nighttime bombing raids against German cities in the industrial Ruhr Basin. Soon, the RAF was sending over 1,000 planes at a time to drop incendiary and highly explosive bombs on major German cities such as Cologne, Essen, and Bremen.

Striking in daylight: The Americans join in

After the declaration of war on Germany in December 1941, the Americans wanted to strike a direct and quick blow against Germany. Bomber planes were the quickest means to do so. General Henry Arnold (nicknamed "Hap") believed, as did the British, that the heavy bombing raids would help end the war more quickly by destroying Germany's war industries and attacking civilian morale. Arnold believed that daylight raids were preferable to the British nighttime raids because they were more accurate. The Americans also brought with them two aircraft that, equipped with the most accurate bombsight in the world, could bomb targets during the day:

>> **The B-17:** Called the Flying Fortress because of its armament to protect itself against German fighters (see Figure 14-2).

>> **The B-24 Liberator:** A smaller, fast and heavily armed bomber.

American B-17s and B-24s began arriving in Britain in July 1942. Organized as the U.S. 8th Air Force and commanded by Lieutenant General Carl Spaatz, these bombers began daylight raids while the British continued to attack at night. Because most of the planes being produced were sent to support Operation Torch (see Chapter 13) in North Africa, the 8th Air Force had few aircraft at first and made only limited attacks against targets in France. The first major attack was against German U-boat docks in June 1943.

FIGURE 14-2:
The B-17 Flying
Fortress.

By late 1943, Americans were building enough planes to supply the 8th Air Force with enough bombers to join Britain in a concentrated attack on Germany. The British had conducted heavy raids on Hamburg; now American bombers pounded the city by day after the British attacked at night. Over 44,000 German civilians died in the firestorm that engulfed the city. The Germans called it "terror bombing." Propaganda Minister Joseph Goebbels for once was not lying when he called the attacks "a catastrophe."

"BOMBER" HARRIS

The Germans had opened the genie in the bottle when they bombed London, making civilians a target of war. Until that time, air attacks had never been directed against civilians before (another one of the unfortunate firsts of World War II). In their air strikes on German cities, the British returned the favor.

Blunt and single-minded British General Arthur "Bomber" Harris took charge of Bomber Command (the British strategic bomber force) in February of 1942. Although the British apparently accepted the uncomfortable fact that civilians were legitimate targets during war, Harris remained a controversial figure during and after the war, and after 1945, was passed up for honors by successive British governments.

Changing Allied strategy

Although British and American bombers caused damage, they took heavy losses in the process. These losses only increased as the Germans adapted to the Allied tactics. For nearly every raid conducted, almost half of the bombers were lost or badly damaged. The attack on Hamburg alone cost the 8th Air Force 100 aircraft. Initially the Americans believed that heavily armed bombers flying in close formations would be able to defend themselves from enemy fighter attacks, but they were wrong. Enemy fighters found a number of ways to shoot down bombers with little threat to themselves. The results were very costly in crews and aircraft.

The problem was that the Allies didn't have fighter aircraft capable of escorting the bombers after they crossed over the English Channel into Germany. Although the U.S. had fighters that were able to serve as watch dogs for the U.S. bombers — their maneuverability and firepower were equal to the German fighters — they didn't have enough fuel to fly into Germany with the bombers they were escorting. As a result, the bombers were left to across into Germany alone. The German fighters, unchallenged by Allied fighters, attacked the formations and kept after them all the way to the target and then all the way back until Allied fighters picked up the formation again.

By June, the Allies shifted the focus of their air attacks from bombing German cities to attacking and destroying German air power. Here's why:

>> As long as German fighters were in the air, the bombers would continue to suffer enormous casualties (the most obvious reason).

>> The Allies had to achieve air superiority before they could invade Germany from across the English Channel.

In short, the Allies had to put German fighters out of action. Thus, American bombers concentrated on aircraft production facilities, while the RAF continued bombing attacks on other German industries.

Raiding Ploesti and Schweinfurt

As part of the campaign to cripple German aircraft production, the Americans launched two spectacular raids:

>> One was against the oil refineries at Ploesti, Romania, where much of the German fuel supplies were produced.

>> The other was against a ball-bearing factory at Schweinfurt, Germany.

Ploesti

On August 1, 1943, 178 B-24 Liberators flew from North Africa heading for Romania, nearly 1,000 miles flying distance. Never before had an air attack been launched at such a distance. The planes came in low at treetop level, hoping to avoid radar and antiaircraft fire. The Germans were ready, however, and the Americans took a terrible beating. Forty-six of the 178 planes were shot down, and 58 were badly damaged; 310 Americans were killed, and 110 were captured. Worst of all, the damage to the refinery was minor.

Schweinfurt

In October 1943, hundreds of American B-17s attacked Schweinfurt in hopes of destroying a key war production facility. The results were depressingly similar to the August attack on Ploesti: The Germans shot down or heavily damaged nearly half the Allied bombers. The Germans lost only a few fighters, and production was not seriously interrupted.

REMEMBER

The Allied bomber crews suffered higher casualty rates than any other combat force and had little to show for all their courage and sacrifice. During the winter of 1943–1944, the Americans slowed the bombing campaign until they could find a long-range escort fighter to protect the bombers from enemy fighter attacks.

Rating the raids: Were they worth it?

In the bombing campaign of 1941 through 1943, the RAF dropped about 21,000 tons of bombs. The Americans, starting in 1943, dropped closer to 38,000 tons of bombs. That's a lot of bombs. Was it worth it? The answer is not really.

REMEMBER

THE IMPORTANCE OF THE BATTLE OF THE ATLANTIC

All too often, narrators of World War II get fixated on the land battles to the extent that they forget that for all the battles fought between 1942 and 1943, none was perhaps more important to Allied victory than the Battle of the Atlantic. This struggle was fought above, below, and on the sea. The economic survival of Britain and the ability of the Soviet Union to stay in the war were at stake. The Germans may not have been able to defeat the British directly in combat, but they could eliminate it as an effective enemy by cutting off Great Britain's economic lifeline: the merchant fleet that brought food, raw materials, and other essentials to keep the island nation functioning. Cutting the Soviet supply line would limit the Soviet Union's ability to sustain armies currently fighting against German troops. Whoever won this battle in the Atlantic would eventually win the war.

>> Although tens of thousands of Germans were likely killed and injured, the raids had little overall effect on German industry or morale.

>> Losses among Allied crews and planes were extremely heavy. Only 30 percent of bomber crews survived a full tour of 25 (later 30) missions.

High Tide of the U-Boat: The Battle of the Atlantic

The third strike against the German war effort was the success of the Allied naval and air forces against Germany's U-boats (see Figure 14-3). Germany relied on the U-boats to cripple the British war effort by sinking merchant ships headed to Britain with much-needed supplies. While the U-boats' success rate remained high, sinking lots of merchant ships, the Allies couldn't build up forces for a cross-channel invasion. But the Allied effort in the Atlantic began to pay off, and the U-boats' power began to wane.

The fearsome U-boats

The German U-boats were a fearsome adversary of the Allies. Hunting in wolf packs, these subs stalked Allied convoys, picking off the most vulnerable targets and pursing the ships until they made port. This tactic was very successful, and although U-boat losses averaged fewer than 20 a year, new subs being produced quickly replaced the lost subs. (See Chapter 7 for more info on the wolf-pack technique, developed by German Admiral Karl Doenitz.)

Making Britain make do with less

With the entry of America officially into the war, the unrecognized shooting war with Germany in the Atlantic became official. To get convoys of supplies to Britain and the Soviet Union safely and in sufficient numbers so both nations could continue fighting, the Americans had to cooperate with Britain and Canada. Although a large part of the U-boat fleet was diverted to the Mediterranean and Norway for other combat operations and even though the British and Americans knew the whereabouts of most German subs in the Atlantic from decoded radio transmissions, the Germans scored many kills. One reason was that the German U-boats parked off the eastern coast of the United States had torpedoed the ships when they left ports to assemble convoys.

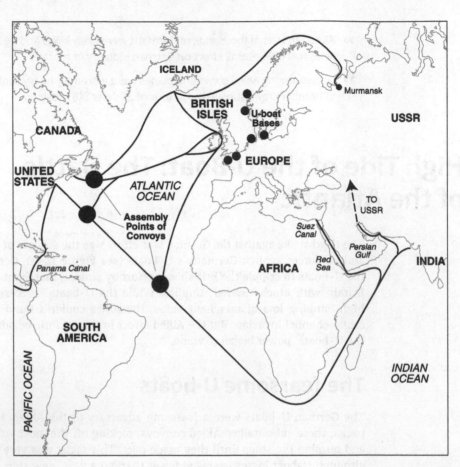

FIGURE 14-3:
The Battle of the Atlantic.

Because of the U-boats, British merchant ships could provide only 23 million tons of supplies in 1942. The problem was that they were losing more merchant ships than they could build.

Sitting ducks on the East Coast: The Americans

For most of 1942, the Germans had a field day — they sank hundreds of American ships until the British and Americans could build and assemble enough ships and aircraft to patrol the U.S. East Coast and drive the subs off.

Into the Atlantic

As the U-boats moved away from the coast in September 1942, they concentrated in the mid-Atlantic. This area was the best place for the subs to attack because air cover was almost nonexistent, and nearly all the convoys to Britain had to cross over an area that the U-boats could patrol easily day and night. The Germans also began to concentrate their subs into packs again.

The result was terrible for the Allies, who lost 1,700 merchant ships, equivalent to about 8 million tons of supplies. The losses were compounded because the Allies couldn't replace all that they lost.

Keeping the USSR strong: The Murmansk run

In 1941, it quickly became clear that without help from the British and Americans, the Soviet Union would be defeated. Without the supplies they needed (the Soviets had dismantled and moved most of their industrial base hundreds of miles to the Ural Mountains to avoid German capture; see Chapter 6), Allied aid was critical. The Soviets needed everything from boots to tanks, and getting the supplies to them was a difficult and dangerous undertaking:

>> In the Arctic Ocean, the USSR had only one port that remained ice-free and open all year long: Murmansk, located on the northern coast of the USSR. This port became the USSR's lifeline.

>> Convoys to the USSR had to travel past German-occupied Norway, a major surface and submarine base.

The wolf packs took a terrible toll on Allied (especially British) shipping between 1941 and 1942. But when the devastated convoys arrived in Murmansk, the Soviets refused to believe that the Germans destroyed so many merchant ships. The Soviets accused the Allies of purposely withholding supplies and making up stories of losses so the USSR would lose the war. Nevertheless, what the Allies were able to provide kept the Soviet Army in the field and bought some time until the Soviets could get their own war production back on line.

Sinking the U-boats: The turning point, 1943

ARMY ALLIED

The elimination of the U-boat threat to Allied convoys is equal to the land battle victory at Stalingrad in terms of having a decisive effect on the course of the war. Several factors combined to turn the tide decisively in favor of the Allies:

>> Ship construction outpaced German sinkings nearly five to one: American shipyards produced one ship per week.

>> Technological advances in radar, sonar, and weapons — such as depth charges and the long-range bomber (especially the B-24 Liberator) — led to sinking U-boats at a rate faster than German naval yards could replace. That meant the loss of skilled and nearly irreplaceable crews as well.

>> Intercepts of German U-boat instructions came regularly to the Allied ships, allowing convoys to be rerouted away from subs.

>> Convoy techniques of the ships became better coordinated and more efficient.

>> Escort aircraft carriers accompanied ship convoys to provide air cover.

MILITARY STRATEGY

The airplane became the U-boat's greatest enemy. The Allies built aircraft capable of flying longer distances and with better technology, such as radar, to help them protect the ships. As soon as a sub raised its periscope or fired a torpedo, it could almost always expect an air attack. By May 1943, German Admiral Doenitz had to admit defeat and leave the Atlantic to the Allies.

By 1944, despite some dramatic improvements in U-boat design and capabilities, the loss of France and the Mediterranean for secure harbors doomed the U-boats to dangerous but limited operations. After 1943, the U-boats ceased to be a great threat to the war effort. (Consider that although U-boats sank 2 million tons of shipping in 1944, Allied ship production that year equaled 14 million tons.) The defeat of Doenitz's U-boats opened the way for the liberation of Europe.

The Germans lost nearly 700 U-boats — just over 80 percent of their fleet. That translates to a three-quarter chance of being killed or captured by the Allies. No other force in the war had such a high casualty rate. Yet, the small but determined band of 41,000 men nearly came close to ending the war between 1941 and 1942. There could be no cross-channel invasion and no victory in Europe without a victory first in the Atlantic.

WHAT THE SOVIETS GOT

Between 1941 and 1945, the USSR received the following supplies from the United States and Great Britain:

- 25,000 aircraft

- 12,000 tanks

- 3 million tons of fuel

- 375,000 trucks

- 114,000 tons of rubber

- 15,000,000 pairs of boots

After the war, the Soviet government refused to recognize the support given to them.

Chapter 15

Guadalcanal, New Guinea, and Midway: Japan's Three Strikes

For the Japanese, 1942 promised total victory. Japan was poised to fulfill its objectives in the Far East. Australia and the American fleet appeared to need only one more blow to finish the war. Yet in a few short months, Japanese land and naval forces were reeling from devastating losses at Guadalcanal, Midway, and New Guinea. These three strikes put the Japanese out, placing them on the strategic defensive and on the road to inevitable defeat.

The Rope-a-Dope: Japan Fights for Time

The heavyweight champion Muhammad Ali used a tactic that he called the *rope-a-dope.* In the first rounds of a fight, Ali would purposely cover up and back up against the ring ropes, inviting his opponent to punch himself into exhaustion. Although he absorbed some punishment, Ali preserved his strength and would suddenly strike back with lightning quickness when he sensed that his opponent had tired himself out. This was essentially Japan's strategy in late 1942. By grabbing so much territory, the Japanese had thrown the Allies into disarray. As the Allies reorganized, the Japanese sought to capture the last remaining outposts and then hunker down and wait in their defenses for the Allies to attack and batter themselves into exhaustion, allowing the Japanese fleet and Japanese aircraft to strike back at the attackers (see Figure 15-1).

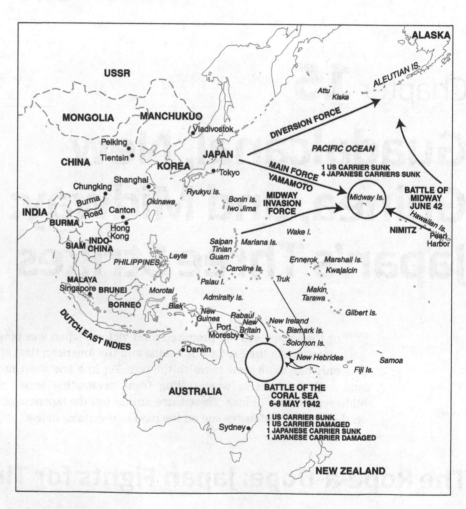

FIGURE 15-1: Operations in the Pacific, 1942.

This strategy depended on the Allies taking several months or even a year to respond to the multiple shocks they absorbed between December 1941 and May 1942. Based on what they had seen so far from the Allies, the Japanese were confident that they would have the time.

Raising American morale: The Allied counterpunch

Although taking a severe blow at Pearl Harbor (see Chapter 8), the United States Navy still had plenty of fight left. The three U.S. aircraft carriers (USS *Lexington*, USS *Saratoga*, and the USS *Enterprise*) had escaped any attacks on the day Japan attacked Pearl Harbor. The carrier USS *Yorktown* was transferred from the Atlantic fleet, giving American Admiral Chester Nimitz (see Figure 15-2) significant mobile combat power.

FIGURE 15-2: Admiral Chester Nimitz.

Historical/Getty Images

In the first three months of 1942, Nimitz used his carriers to raid Japanese bases throughout the Pacific. Although the raids had negligible effects, they nevertheless raised American morale and kept the Japanese off balance. The Japanese were never certain where American warplanes would suddenly swoop from the skies to attack.

Unsatisfied with attacks on peripheral Japanese bases on scattered Pacific islands, the Americans decided to attack the Japanese mainland, specifically Tokyo, the country's capital city and the home of Japan's emperor, Hirohito. The problem was getting U.S. bombers over to Japan and back safely. The Japanese had certainly shown how effective carrier-based aircraft were against unprepared targets, but only the United States Army (not the Navy) had bombers capable of carrying heavy bomb loads. The planners had to solve two basic problems: where to launch the bombers from (no Pacific island was close enough) and where to land them.

The solution? A daring plan to launch 16 U.S. Army Air Force bombers from an aircraft carrier that would move the bombers within range of Japan. After dropping the *incendiary bombs* (bombs that cause fire rather than explode) on targeted Japanese cities, the bombers would continue to fly westward, crossing into friendly territory in China.

MILITARY STRATEGY

The bombers couldn't return to the carriers for two reasons:

» The bombers were too big and heavy to land back on the carriers.

» The carrier had to leave as soon as the planes set off on their attack; otherwise it would be a sitting duck for the Japanese.

Setting Tokyo on fire: Doolittle's raid

The commander of the mission was Lieutenant Colonel James H. Doolittle. Known as "Jimmy," he had a reputation as a daredevil and seemed to be the natural choice for the job.

As the carrier *Hornet* sailed toward Japan carrying Doolittle's bombers, it ran into Japanese patrol boats about 700 miles from Japan. This encounter forced the raiders to launch early in daylight (the raid had been planned as a nighttime raid) at the limit of the B-25's range.

On April 18, Doolittle led his bombers toward Japan. The bombers appeared over Tokyo just as a practice air-raid drill was going on. The Japanese fighters ignored the American bombers, thinking that they were part of the exercise. The American planes flew low over their targets and dropped their bombs.

Heading for China and low on fuel, the crews had to parachute out before reaching any airfields. Although the bombers caused little physical damage on the Japanese mainland, they reaped great psychological damage on the Japanese leadership, who now knew that the Japanese homeland was not secure. The Americans, it seemed, planned to bring the war directly to the Japanese.

ARMY ALLIED

Doolittle's raid was a portent of things to come. Badly bruised American morale soared with the news of the raid. President Roosevelt, conducting a triumphant press conference, was asked where the Army bombers had come from. Smiling slyly, he told the reporters that they had come from Shangri-La, a mythic, ideal place made popular in a film currently playing in the United States. Doolittle won the Medal of Honor for his feat of courage.

A Military First: The Battle of the Coral Sea

In the early months of the war in the Pacific, the Japanese had the advantages. Possessing the dominant air and naval power in the region, the Japanese sought to expand their conquests and build their defenses for the Allied counterattack that was sure to come. Here's a list of areas that Japan wanted to control:

>> **The Solomon Islands:** A chain of islands stretching about 1,000 miles off the northeastern tip of Australia. Control of these islands would effectively cut off American support to Australia, isolating it and putting the Japanese in a position to force the Australians to submit to Japanese control.

>> **Midway Island:** An island in the Central Pacific and the last American base outside of Hawaii. By seizing this base, the Japanese would complete the ring of islands blocking American naval offensive action.

Without Midway, the Americans would have to use Pearl Harbor as the base of all operations against Japan, because Hawaii was too far away to mount any large-scale attack without the Japanese knowing about it and attacking it far away from the main defensive perimeter.

>> **Papua:** An Australian possession on southeastern New Guinea. The goal was the capture of Port Moresby, a town that could be used as a Japanese naval and air base. With Port Moresby, the Japanese could effectively control the Coral Sea and virtually all of Australia's north coast. Combined with Japanese bases in Java and Borneo, Australia would be effectively neutralized, leaving the Americans with no choice but to mount offensives from Hawaii.

Intercepting helpful info: A critical tip-off

In April 1942, the Allies appeared completely unable to stop the Japanese from achieving these goals. The problem for the Americans was that the Japanese were playing a giant game of hide and seek in the vast Pacific. The American carriers and their support ships couldn't inflict damage on the enemy until they could find the enemy. Every area was vulnerable to attack: Australia was defenseless and could be invaded easily; the Japanese could pounce on Midway at any time. The question for Admiral Nimitz was to figure out what the Japanese were going to do next.

Again, fortune smiled on the Americans. Intercepted Japanese naval codes clearly indicated that the Japanese intended to take Port Moresby in New Guinea and the island of Tulagi in the Solomons. A formidable striking force of two carriers with 123 aircraft, 4 cruisers, and 6 destroyers would cover the amphibious assault forces (soldiers delivered by water craft to a beach for an attack). Nimitz sent the only two carriers available — the *Yorktown* and the *Lexington*, with 141 aircraft supported by 5 cruisers and 11 destroyers — to meet the Japanese force.

CHESTER W. NIMITZ

Admiral Chester W. Nimitz (1885–1966) wanted to be an Army artilleryman, but he couldn't get into West Point. Instead, he was nominated to enter the United States Naval Academy. After an initial tour with the Asiatic Fleet, Nimitz transferred to a new arm of the navy — the submarine. He commanded several submarines and became an expert on undersea warfare. Between the world wars, he built the submarine base at Pearl Harbor, founded one of the first Naval Reserve Officers Training Corps units, and moved up to command the flagship of the Asiatic Fleet and a battleship division.

After the disastrous attack on the Pacific Fleet at Pearl Harbor, President Franklin Roosevelt sent a message to the Secretary of the Navy: "Tell Nimitz to get the hell to Pearl and stay there until the war is won." Nimitz became Commander of the United States Pacific Fleet on December 31, 1941. In 1942, he became Commander in Chief of the Pacific Fleet. Immediately, Nimitz used his strengths against enemy weaknesses, relying on the striking power of the aircraft carrier to achieve victories at the Battles of the Coral Sea, Midway, and Guadalcanal. He conducted an advance through the Gilberts, the Marshalls, the Marianas, and the Palaus, using amphibious and naval power to overpower Japanese defenses.

Nimitz supported General MacArthur's reconquest of the Philippines in 1944, and he directed the fleet in the Battle of the Philippine Sea and Leyte Gulf that ended Japanese naval power in the Pacific. By 1945, Nimitz had directed the capture of the key islands of Iwo Jima and Okinawa to support bomber raids against the islands of Japan. Nimitz was famous for allowing his subordinate officers wide latitude in carrying out his plans and orders. Nimitz was a superb judge of men and selected subordinates who would guide the U.S. Navy for nearly a generation. Never hurried or excited, Nimitz was the calm in the storm of war, inspiring confidence even in the gravest crisis.

Engaging in pea soup on the way to Port Moresby

Aircraft from the American carriers began to attack the Japanese invasion force at Tulagi on May 4, but they had little effect. What the Americans were looking for were the Japanese carriers of the strike force, which they knew were in the vicinity of Port Moresby.

In fact, the Japanese carriers were closer than anyone thought. Bad weather had masked their presence from the American spotter planes looking for them. The American and Japanese naval forces were steaming directly toward each other in the Coral Sea. Everyone — Japanese and American alike — had a hard time recognizing which ships belonged to whom and exactly what type of ship they were looking at:

>> On May 7, Japanese launched an attack on what they thought were two American carriers. They were actually an American oiler and a destroyer.

>> The Americans launched an attack against two Japanese cruisers and two destroyers. They thought they were aiming at two Japanese carriers.

>> American bomber planes from Australia mistook American ships for Japanese and bombed them. Luckily, none of the bombs hit.

>> As it grew dark, 21 Japanese planes actually tried to land on the USS *Yorktown*, thinking that it was a friendly carrier. Ten planes were shot down, and the others beat a hasty retreat.

While dive-bombers from the USS *Lexington* were on their way to attack what they thought were two Japanese carriers, they strayed off course and accidentally found a *real* Japanese carrier, the *Soho*, covering the Port Moresby invasion force. Although built for speed, the *Soho* was no match for the dive-bombers. It capsized and sank ten minutes after the attack began.

Going after the carriers instead

The following day (May 8), the Japanese decided to postpone the attack on Port Moresby and take out a far more important target — the American carriers. Although the Japanese were not sure how many carriers were in the vicinity (they estimated as many as five), they knew the general location of at least two. The Americans also had designs on the Japanese carrier force. Both forces launched aircraft, seeking the other carrier out. The Americans spotted the Japanese carriers at about the same time that the Japanese spotted the American carriers. Each side inflicted damage. One Japanese carrier was badly damaged and withdrew from the battle. The USS *Lexington* was hit by bombs and torpedoes but continued to launch and receive aircraft until internal explosions destroyed it.

A Japanese victory, an American triumph

The loss of the two Japanese carriers ended Japan's attack on Port Moresby. The Americans also withdrew, crippled by the loss of the USS *Lexington*, which had to be torpedoed by an American destroyer after her crew was rescued.

ARMY AXIS

The Japanese could look upon the Battle of the Coral Sea as a *tactical victory*. After all, they sank an irreplaceable aircraft carrier (in fact, they believed that they had sunk both carriers) and shot down 66 aircraft. But the Japanese suffered a loss of 77 aircraft and lost a light carrier.

ARMY ALLIED

In reality, Coral Sea was a *strategic victory* for the Americans, who had momentarily stopped the invasion threat to Port Moresby and put two heavy Japanese carriers out of action for several months.

HISTORICAL TRIVIA

Most importantly, the Battle of the Coral Sea marked a new chapter in warfare. For the first time in history, a naval battle had been fought without either force ever seeing the other. All combat had been accomplished by aircraft launched by carriers.

Midway: Naval Aviation's Finest Moment

The admirals in both the American and Japanese navies had grown up believing that the decisive naval action in the Pacific would be one straight out of the age of sail — two big battle fleets fighting within sight of each other, with the heavily armored and armed battleship providing the decisive edge. For nearly a generation, the war plans of both nations had envisaged such an engagement — that's why both Japan and the United States built big battleships and why the disarmament efforts of the 1920s focused on reducing the size and number of battleships in the world's fleets.

But the sinking of the British battleship *Prince of Wales* by Japanese aircraft and the Battle of the Coral Sea had proven that the future of naval warfare lay in the hands of *the naval aviator,* not the battleship captain. If the Battle of the Coral Sea (covered in the preceding section) taught anyone anything, it was that the age of the battleship was over. Whichever side figured this out first would win the war in the Pacific.

Setting a trap: The Japanese three-pronged approach

Japanese Admiral Yamamoto sought to take Midway, the last American base in the Pacific outside of Hawaii. Not only would possession of Midway expand the Japanese defensive zone, but it would also force the Americans, who couldn't afford to lose the island, to react. Yamamoto expected the Americans to respond by bringing out their carriers to stop the Japanese or by trying to retake the island. As a result, Yamamoto assembled the largest battle fleet ever used in the Pacific Ocean — 160 ships (eight of them aircraft carriers) and 400 aircraft. This massive fleet would wait until the Americans approached Midway, and then the Japanese carrier aircraft and giant battleships would finish off the Americans once and for all.

A RISKY BUSINESS

Flying a plane off the pitching deck of a carrier is dangerous. Landing a plane on a frighteningly small space in all kinds of weather is even more dangerous. Today, modern navies have sophisticated electronics, fancy navigation, and highly capable multimillion-dollar aircraft — and it's still dangerous! In 1942, all these pilots had were their eyes and a lot of hope. They were given general headings to their targets and had to carefully watch the ocean for signs of a ship. Once they spotted their targets, they would make the attack (if they survived the enemy planes and antiaircraft fire) and then turn back to find their own carriers before the fuel ran out.

Attacking a ship from the air with a torpedo or a bomb was a skill all its own. The torpedo pilot had to approach the ship as close to the water as possible and then drop the torpedo just hundreds of yards away. Meanwhile, the targeted ship fired every gun it could directly against him, and enemy fighter planes tried to shoot him down.

A dive-bomber pilot started several thousand feet directly over his target and began a vertical dive, falling at 300 miles an hour until just a few hundred feet over the target. Then he would release the bomb — precisely at the correct moment if he wanted the bomb to hit the target and explode — while jerking the plane back up into the air. If he was lucky, fighters wouldn't shoot him down, antiaircraft fire wouldn't take him out, and his bombs would hit what they were supposed to so that he wouldn't have to perform this insane maneuver all over again.

If the carrier pilot returned from the attack and was lucky, the carrier was roughly in the same spot it was when the pilot left. If not, he had to search until he either a) landed safely on the carrier's wood-planked deck in a bone-jarring controlled crash, or b) ran out of fuel and ditched his plane in the ocean. This was a tough way to fight a war, and such pilots — both American and Japanese — were not a dime a dozen.

In his plan, Yamamoto divided the fleet up into four forces:

» One force would conduct an attack on the Aleutian Islands to divert American attention from the Midway attack.

» Yamamoto himself would command the main Japanese battle fleet in the climactic battle against the American fleet.

» A third fleet would bring in the amphibious landing force to capture Midway.

» A screen of submarines would search the waters between Pearl Harbor and Midway to scout for signs of the American fleet.

Having two aces in the hole: The Nimitz shuffle

Japanese Admiral Yamamoto's plan was good, but American Admiral Nimitz had the upper hand, at least initially:

>> **He knew the Japanese plan.** Again, intercepted Japanese codes had given him a detailed understanding of the Japanese plan and plenty of time to prepare a counterplan for Midway. Nimitz also learned that the Japanese had spread out their fleet into widely scattered small groups to avoid detection.

Nimitz decided that no giant naval engagement off Midway would occur, as Yamamoto expected (see the preceding section). He also realized that his battleships would be no help to him. The advantage was the aircraft carriers, which could strike targets from long distances. Nimitz would rely on surprise and the skill of his naval aviators to offset the Japanese strength in numbers.

>> **He had more carriers than the Japanese realized.** In addition to two U.S. carriers that the Japanese knew about, Nimitz also had one — the USS *Yorktown* — the Japanese thought they sank in the Coral Sea battle. Despite the extensive damage to the ship, which would take three months to repair, crews at Pearl Harbor accomplished nothing short of a miracle by making it battle worthy again in only 72 hours.

But even with these advantages, the Americans still didn't have the upper hand. Yamamoto had superior numbers and lots of ocean to hide in. Nimitz would commit all the American carriers, 12 cruisers, 14 destroyers, and 19 submarines to this battle — a laughably small force to match the Japanese fleet headed for Midway. For the United States Navy, Midway was a gamble with enormous stakes.

Opening moves: Bombs over Midway

The Battle of Midway would be the decisive battle of the Pacific in World War II, and in the end, it would change both the course of the war and the future of naval warfare.

First phase: June 3

On June 3, 1942, the Japanese began the first phase of the battle with air attacks on American bases in the Aleutians. Japanese forces landed on the Aleutian Islands of Kiska on June 6 and the following day, on Attu. Japanese aircraft conducted raids throughout the islands.

Although Nimitz had dispatched a naval force to deal with the invasion, land-based aircraft kept the Japanese fleet at bay. To Yamamoto, it appeared that his Aleutian Island diversion had worked. But in reality, the American carrier fleet was heading for Midway — a fact that Yamamoto didn't know. Tipped off by the intercepts, Nimitz had dispatched his fleet days before the Japanese submarines were to arrive to search for the Americans. The Japanese were in the dark. To them, it appeared that all was going according to plan.

Second phase: June 4

Yamamoto began the next phase of the battle with an attack on Midway on June 4. He sent half of his carrier aircraft against Midway, while he held the other half back in case the American fleet showed up. As the Japanese aircraft returned from the Midway strike, it became clear that another attack was necessary.

As the Japanese armed the planes for another attack, Japanese Admiral Nagumo received disturbing news: One of Japan's spotter planes reported sighting enemy ships, possibly a carrier. By the time Nagumo became aware of the American ships, aircraft from the USS *Hornet*, *Enterprise*, and *Yorktown* were already on their way to attack the Japanese carriers.

Nagumo took bombs off his planes and rearmed them with torpedoes to attack the most dangerous threat. Thus, at the moment American planes appeared, the Japanese carriers had more than 100 planes on the decks, fully fueled, with stacks of bombs and torpedoes sitting above and below the flight deck.

American torpedo planes began their attack. The U.S. pilots of the slow moving torpedo planes kept on course and were rapidly shot down one after another by the Japanese fighters protecting the carriers. Those few that were able to launch torpedoes missed their target. The annihilation of the American torpedo planes meant that American carriers were in range of Nagumo's torpedo planes. In just a few more minutes, Nagumo would be able to launch his own attack against the Americans — these were a few minutes that he didn't have.

Off the beaten path: McClusky's miracle

American Lieutenant Commander Wade McClusky led 33 dive-bombers from the USS *Enterprise* in search of the Japanese carriers. McClusky's planes, getting low on fuel, would have to turn back soon. On a whim, McClusky flew off the prescribed track to look elsewhere. Minutes later, he found them. In fact, he found them just as the last of the torpedo planes had finished their fatal runs (see the preceding section, "Second phase: June 4"). All the Japanese fighters were close to the water, enabling McClusky's dive-bombers to come in without any interference. Dive-bombers from the USS *Yorktown* then appeared, and McClusky signaled for the attack. The result was devastating.

Caught completely by surprise, without protection from their own aircraft, and with decks fully loaded with fuel and weapons, the Japanese carriers were sitting ducks. Within minutes, two carriers were completely engulfed in flames. Another carrier quickly followed. The last Japanese carrier was lucky: It avoided the air attack and launched its planes against the *Yorktown*, damaging it with bombs and torpedoes until the carrier was dead in the water, the Americans abandoned the ship. However, the rearmed and refueled American planes found the last Japanese carrier and destroyed it.

Yamamoto tried to continue the fight with his battleships, but the Americans weren't interested in slugging it out. The American force withdrew, leaving the Japanese with no choice but to abandon the attack on Midway.

One Japanese cruiser was lost in the air attack, and a Japanese submarine sunk an American destroyer and the abandoned hulk of the USS *Yorktown*. There were no further losses in the battle. The Americans lost 137 aircraft and 300 men, and the Japanese lost over 330 aircraft and 3,500 men, many of them highly skilled, experienced combat pilots.

Midway: A Strategic Analysis

The story of the Battle of Midway is essentially the clash between old and new methods of waging naval war. Japanese Admiral Yamamoto represented the old method of fighting naval battles. He wanted to engage the American fleet in a surface battle, using battleships. American Admiral Nimitz left his battleships behind and relied on a new style of naval warfare, in which ships didn't fight within sight of each other. Instead, aircraft, launched from the ships, would be the decisive factor.

In the Battle of Midway, the new concept of warfare won out. The Americans had demonstrated their faith in the aircraft carrier, and Yamamoto, for all his belief in carriers, had packed most of his punch in battleships, which were essentially useless. The loss of four carriers and the fact that the U.S. was building more carriers than the Japanese (13 to 6, respectively) ended the Japanese hold on the Pacific.

New Guinea: Green Hell

The large island of New Guinea is probably the last place on Earth that anyone would want to fight a war. In 1942, it was a fever-ridden, mountainous jungle swept constantly by rain from heavy clouds. Running down the center of the peninsula of eastern New Guinea, like a spine, is the Owen Stanley mountain range, reaching a height of over 7,000 feet. On the east side of the spine is the small town called Buna, and on the other side is Port Moresby, a strategically important position: Whoever controlled Port Moresby controlled the approach to northern Australia.

The Japanese had tried to take Port Moresby once (as explained in the section "A Military First: The Battle of the Coral Sea"), but the Allies had turned them back in the Battle of the Coral Sea. In July 1942, the Japanese tried again. This time, they landed about 4,400 troops at Buna, intending to travel on the Kokoda Trail that led over the Owen Stanley Range and then attack Port Moresby from behind. Such an approach would prevent the U.S. Navy or the Australian Navy from interfering.

REMEMBER

Early in the war, Australia faced the Japanese alone. Although American forces were sent to support the Australians, they were not trained or ready for combat in the forbidding jungles of New Guinea. In addition, since 1940, Australian soldiers had been fighting with Great Britain, primarily in North Africa and Greece. With their country threatened, these combat experienced troops were sent back to Australia to face the Japanese threat moving into New Guinea.

Jungle fighting: The Aussies hold the Japanese

MILITARY STRATEGY

In their military campaigns since 1941, the Japanese took advantage of their skill in jungle fighting. Untrained Allied soldiers avoided the jungle, and commanders mistakenly believed that the jungle was impassible to the Japanese. They were often surprised when the Japanese soldiers moved easily through mountainous jungle areas and emerged ready to fight in unexpected places, forcing Allied units to retreat or be destroyed. This had happened in Malaya, in Burma, and in the Philippines (see Chapter 8 for Japanese blitzkrieg in Asia).

The Japanese force landing at Buna had every intention of using the mountains and the jungle to their advantage. But what they discovered as they made the dangerous and exhausting climb on the muddy Kokoda Trail was that the Australian soldiers were also trained in jungle warfare. The jungle had become neutral territory. The odds were now even.

ARMY ALLIED

Between August and September, the Australians held the Japanese on the Kokoda Trail, keeping them from Port Moresby and eventually pushing them back over the Owen Stanley Range. Small units fought brutal battles in murky jungles, often in the midst of torrential rain. Disease and hunger stalked the men constantly. The only supplies that could be brought up to the upper mountain ridges were what mules or men could carry on their backs. By November, the Japanese gave up and began to retreat toward Buna.

Bringing the Americans: MacArthur and his troops

As the Allied commander responsible for the defense of Australia and the Southwest Pacific, American General Douglas MacArthur had little available to hold off the Japanese. While the Australian 7th Division was fighting on the Kokoda Trail, MacArthur assembled whatever forces he could beg, borrow, or steal from America. What he got were two poorly trained National Guard infantry divisions and a limited number of aircraft. MacArthur was determined to get Americans into the fight, and he committed troops into battle without proper training or support.

The Japanese retreated back to Buna and another small town called Gona and awaited the enemy. These experienced soldiers established one of the most formidable defensive positions in all of the war. Carefully camouflaged defensive positions protected by logs formed an interlocking net dominated by machine guns. For infantry to attack these positions without artillery or tanks was sheer folly, yet the Australians and Americans spent six weeks doing just that. The ground was low and swampy, and the weather was wet and hot. The Japanese were so well hidden that casualties mounted at an alarming rate.

ARMY ALLIED

MacArthur sent General Robert L. Eichelberger to take command of the Allied attack. The Japanese defenders fought for every foot of ground. Gona fell in early December, and Buna fell a month later. These wins had been terribly costly:

>> From MacArthur on down, every American leader made dreadful errors in fighting a resourceful and determined foe.

>> Casualties from disease and wounds reduced units by more than 90 percent.

>> Supply was haphazard and inadequate, as was air support, and improvisations became the norm.

But the Americans learned during their experiences, and they became very adept at jungle warfare. The Allies had their first victory over the Japanese in New Guinea (see Figure 15-3). From January 1943 on, they never looked back.

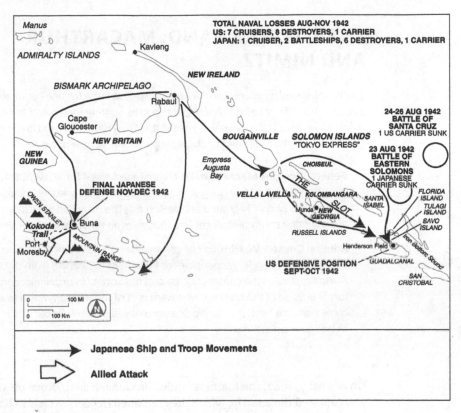

Manus

ADMIRALTY ISLANDS

Kavieng

TOTAL NAVAL LOSSES AUG-NOV 1942
US: 7 CRUISERS, 8 DESTROYERS, 1 CARRIER
JAPAN: 1 CRUISER, 2 BATTLESHIPS, 6 DESTROYERS, 1 CARRIER

NEW IRELAND

BISMARK ARCHIPELAGO

Rabaul

Cape
Gloucester

NEW BRITAIN

**NEW
GUINEA**

**24-26 AUG 1942
BATTLE OF
SANTA CRUZ**
1 US CARRIER SUNK

BOUGAINVILLE

SOLOMON ISLANDS
"TOKYO EXPRESS"

**23 AUG 1942
BATTLE OF
EASTERN
SOLOMONS**
1 JAPANESE
CARRIER SUNK

Empress
Augusta
Bay

CHOISEUL

**FINAL JAPANESE
DEFENSE NOV-DEC 1942**

VELLA LAVELLA

KOLOMBANGARA

SANTA
ISABEL

FLORIDA
ISLAND

OWEN STANLEY

Munda NEW
GEORGIA

TULAGI
ISLAND

**Kokoda
Trail**

Buna

MOUNTAIN RANGE

RUSSELL ISLANDS

SAVO
ISLAND

Port
Moresby

Henderson Field

Iron Bottom Sound

**US DEFENSIVE POSITION
SEPT-OCT 1942**

GUADALCANAL

SAN
CRISTOBAL

0   100 Mi
0   100 Km

Japanese Ship and Troop Movements

Allied Attack

FIGURE 15-3:
New Guinea and
Guadalcanal
offensives, 1942.

Protecting Australia: Allied Pacific Strategy

After Midway, the overall strategy for 1942 was to protect Australia by pushing the Japanese back from their naval and air base at Rabaul, on New Britain Island, just northeast of New Guinea in the East Indies. While General Douglas MacArthur forced the Japanese from New Guinea, Admiral Chester W. Nimitz was to drive the Japanese out of the Solomon Islands, where a large Japanese airfield was being built on the island of Guadalcanal.

The Americans take the offensive

Admiral Nimitz was in charge of driving the Japanese out of Guadalcanal. The infantry force to accomplish this mission was the First Marine Division commanded by Major General Alexander A. Vandegrift. Vandegrift's marines were only partly trained, most of them new volunteers. Nevertheless, these were the only troops available in the early months of 1942.

SHARED COMMAND: MACARTHUR AND NIMITZ

The Pacific posed problems for the Allies: It was too large for one commander to oversee, and the different Allied services were having spitting matches: If the navy had command of the Pacific, the Army was mad; if the Army had command, the navy was mad. The Allies, therefore, decided to divide responsibility between two American army and:

- **General Douglas MacArthur:** He commanded Allied forces within an area that included Australia, New Guinea, the Dutch East Indies, and the Philippines. He was in charge of primarily ground and air forces. (The navy had a hard time letting an army general command a fleet — although even that eventually happened.)

- **Admiral Chester W. Nimitz:** The commander of the Pacific Fleet, Nimitz was also the Allied commander responsible for the rest of the Pacific, from the west coast of North America to the coasts of China and the Soviet Union. Nimitz had no ground forces outside of the Marines, who were part of the navy anyway. His air forces came from the fleet. (Nimitz would eventually have army forces under his command as well later on in the war.)

On August 7, 1942, the Marines landed on Guadalcanal, drove off the labor troops, and captured the airstrip, which they renamed *Henderson Field* in honor of a Marine aviator who had died at Midway.

A Japanese naval task force arrived undetected and badly damaged the American ships that were supporting the operation, which included three carriers (the *Saratoga*, the *Wasp*, and the *Enterprise*); the Japanese then escaped unharmed. In addition, Japanese aircraft also threatened the carriers, forcing the U.S. fleet to withdraw, leaving the 10,000 American Marines isolated on Guadalcanal without supplies and drawn in a tight defensive line around Henderson Field (the renamed airstrip).

The Japanese poured reinforcements into Guadalcanal. Japanese ships moved down the sea corridor formed by the many small islands of the Solomons (called "The Slot" by the Americans) to bombard the Marines and land troops on the island. Japanese aircraft also fought the Allies for control of the skies above Guadalcanal.

Reinforcements and supplies came for the Americans also. The Marines, dug in on a ridge only one mile from Henderson Field and supported by 30 aircraft and several tanks, fought off several Japanese assaults. By October, the stage was set for the decisive battle for the island.

"The Fork in the Road": Battles on land and sea for Guadalcanal

The capture and control of Guadalcanal held great strategic significance for the Japanese. They seemed to sense that this head-to-head battle between naval and ground forces would determine the future of the war in the Pacific. Thus, the Japanese called this battle "The Fork in the Road." The side that prevailed would win the war.

The Japanese signaled their resolve with their infantry assaults against the Marine positions on the island. They also sent a large fleet to challenge the Americans for control of the sea. (This fleet contained 3 carriers, 8 battleships, and 27 cruisers and destroyers.)

This engagement, the Battle of the Eastern Solomons, much like the Battles of Coral Sea and Midway before it, was decided by carrier-based aircraft. The two fleets never saw one another. The Japanese lost one carrier, while the American carrier *Enterprise* suffered heavy damage. The Japanese also lost 90 nearly irreplaceable planes and pilots in the Solomons.

Admiral Nimitz compared the American victory to the one at Midway. Indeed, the victory at Midway had resulted in such a catastrophic loss of carrier planes and pilots that the Japanese had very few left.

Bloody Ridge: The Americans hold Guadalcanal

Although the Marines, now reinforced by Army troops, had held the perimeter around Henderson Field on Guadalcanal since August 1942, the worst was yet to come. From October 25 to October 28, assisted by torrential rains that grounded American fighters and aided by a heavy artillery bombardment, the Japanese launched a series of determined attacks. Day and night, the Japanese bravely assaulted the ridge occupied by the Marines. Although the Japanese came close to breaking the line, the Marines and Army defenders held. The Japanese were forced to retreat. The Marines named their defensive position *Bloody Ridge*. And for good reason: The Japanese lost nearly 3,500 soldiers.

ARMY
ALLIED

In November, the Japanese landed additional forces, but they were too weak to challenge the Americans, who launched an attack and trapped the enemy force almost as soon as it began to move off the beach. Only about half the original force escaped. Fresh Marine and Army units arrived to give the battered First Marine Division a rest. By December 1942, American troops were on the offensive. By early February 1943, the remaining Japanese troops were withdrawn from the island, and Americans were in full control of Guadalcanal.

Other clashes between U.S. and Japanese forces in the Solomons

Between October and November 1942, the American and Japanese navies clashed three more times in the waters around Guadalcanal:

>> One night, American warships clashed with the Japanese as the Japanese tried to bring reinforcements to Guadalcanal in secret. This clash involved destroyers and cruisers.

>> Two other battles involved large carrier-based fleets.

- In the first engagement, the Americans lost a carrier; the Japanese lost nearly 100 aircraft. In addition, three Japanese carriers were damaged.

- The second engagement — a battle that lasted three days — ended the Japanese threat in the Solomons. The Japanese used a large fleet to protect 12 troop transport ships headed for Guadalcanal. In the battle that ensued, 10 of the transports (and the troops they carried) were lost, along with two battleships, a destroyer, and two cruisers. The Americans lost two cruisers and seven destroyers. (This was the first time that U.S. and Japanese battleships met in direct combat.)

Looking at Guadalcanal blow by blow

As the Japanese knew, Guadalcanal was the fork in the road, the decisive battle that changed the direction of the war. The U.S. stopped the Japanese advance in the Pacific, and the Allies were now on the offensive. Having been driven from the Solomon Islands, the Japanese navy and its supply line were more vulnerable to attacks from the Allies.

Guadalcanal also marked the beginning of the dominance of the United States Navy. Although often outmatched by superior ships and weapons, the American navy fought with determination and won, and the aircraft carrier proved to be one of the most valuable assets in naval warfare.

The Americans and Japanese threw just about everything they had at each other for control of Guadalcanal. Neither side wanted to give up, but the American naval power was decisive, and so were the fighting skills of American Marines and soldiers defending Henderson Field. When the Japanese finally called it quits, their chances of victory in Guadalcanal became very slim.

The costs to the Japanese and the Americans were heavy: Both navies lost many ships and thousands of sailors and navy pilots. In fact, the waters north of

Guadalcanal came to be known as "Iron Bottom Bay" because of all the ships that were sunk.

Even today, when you see a Marine from the First Division, the shoulder patch on his uniform has a blue number 1, with the word "Guadalcanal" in white stitched vertically over the number. This is a way of remembering and honoring those rain-soaked, fever-ridden, and exhausted men who changed the course of the war and embodied the fighting spirit of the United States Marines.

Nimitz Takes the Offensive

American Admiral Nimitz, commanding military operations in the Pacific, was given the mission to strike Japanese defensive outposts in the Central Pacific. Specifically, he was to target the clusters of islands named the Marshalls, the Carolines, and the Marianas. These islands formed a barrier to Allied naval and air operations in the Pacific and had to be neutralized. Once in Allied hands, the Allies could use the islands as supply and air bases to support fleet operations.

These islands also marked a sort of stepping stone path toward the Japanese islands and the Philippines. Here's why this is important:

>> General Douglas MacArthur was already intent on using New Guinea as a base to begin the invasion of the Philippines in 1944.

>> Nimitz's offensive against the Central Pacific islands would force the Japanese to fight in two places at once while bringing American land, air, and sea power together to deal with the Japanese homeland.

The first stepping-stone in this campaign was the Gilbert Islands, located about halfway between Australia and Hawaii. The attack would be directed against two Japanese-held islands: Makin and Tarawa.

Japan's suicide defenders at Tarawa

The Japanese garrisons defending these islands were small. On Tarawa, there were about 4,600 men; on Makin, only about 800 men. But the Japanese defenders had orders from Tokyo that they were part of the "zone of absolute defense" and were to defend their positions to the last man. They were to sacrifice themselves without support from the Japanese navy so Japan could buy time to rebuild its naval air power and build more ships for a future strategic counterattack against the Americans. The Japanese dutifully swore to die rather than surrender the islands. On Tarawa, they constructed camouflaged concrete defenses connected by trenches, digging tanks into the sand so that only their turrets stood out. They dug in four heavy coastal defense guns captured from the British at Singapore and 25 lighter artillery pieces and placed machine guns to hit attackers from nearly every angle of approach.

Running aground: A bitter surprise

Prior to the landing on November 21, 1943, American aircraft and naval gunfire from three battleships and 21 destroyers bombarded the islands of Makin and Tarawa. At Makin, Army units quickly overcame the Japanese defenders. At Tarawa, however, the Second Marine Division encountered determined resistance. Although the two-mile-long island had been saturated with bombs and shells, little had been destroyed.

As the Marines approached the island in small boats, the Japanese hit them with artillery fire. Worse than this, though, was the discovery that the water was not deep enough to bring the landing craft ashore. Most of boats ran aground on a coral reef more than 700 yards off the beach. The Marines had no choice but to hop over the side and wade through the water carrying weapons, ammunition, and equipment. The Japanese machine guns took a terrible toll. The units that did land on the beach found themselves under heavy fire. Unable to move forward, they hugged the small strip of sand and waited for help.

The Marines take the island

It took near point-blank fire from destroyers and pinpoint air bombing to destroy the Japanese defensive positions. Meanwhile, reinforcements landed, giving the Marines enough force to begin crawling forward to engage the well-hidden defenders. Small squads of men took out the Japanese positions one by one with grenades, flamethrowers, and machine guns. After four days, the island belonged to the Marines.

Only one Japanese officer and 16 soldiers survived the battle. The Marines had lost 3,000 men, one third of them killed. The U.S. experience on these islands helped them prepare for later battles. But with the Japanese prepared to fight literally to the last man and fully alerted for an attack, there would be no easy way to take the next islands. The Marines faced a daunting task in 1944.

The battles in the Pacific were all-or-nothing campaigns for the Japanese and the Americans. None of the battles between 1942 and 1943 were brilliant, clean, or elegant the way that they were planned or fought. They were born out of the simple requirement to stop the enemy, even if it meant fighting to the last man and to the last ship. Whoever could hold on longer would win and gain the strategic momentum.

Chapter **16**

Planning for the Rest of the War, 1943

The year 1943 marked major progress for the Allies, as well as a fatal turning point for the Axis. Italy was out of the war; the Americans and British pushed the Germans out of North Africa and were in Italy. The Soviets stopped the great German attack at Kursk, Russia, and they were preparing to mount their own great offensive. The Japanese lost their ability to project power at the Battles of the Coral Sea, Midway, and Guadalcanal. Also, by 1943, American industrial power was becoming colossally strong, building enough ships, planes, combat vehicles, rifles, and bullets to equip not only the military needs of the rapidly expanding American armed forces but the needs of all the other Allied forces as well.

For the Allies, the first offensives brought success. But a skillful enemy showed how unready American forces were to conduct large-scale operations. A mixture of luck and overwhelming force glossed over some big errors in planning and execution that the Allies made. Decisions on what to do next were going to be difficult.

The Big Three: Conference at Teheran

The conference at Teheran, Iran began on November 28 and ended on December 1, 1943. It was the first time Churchill, Roosevelt, and Stalin — the three leaders of the Allied coalition — met personally to map out future strategy. It wasn't going to be easy. Each country had different ideas about what should happen next in the war:

>> The Soviets wanted a second front in Europe to relieve the pressure on the Soviet Union.

>> The British wanted to continue the Mediterranean strategic approach.

>> The Americans still wanted to launch an invasion across the English Channel as soon as possible.

American President Roosevelt looked forward to his meeting with the Soviet dictator Josef Stalin, whom he persisted in calling "Uncle Joe." Roosevelt believed that his charm and savoir-faire would pull Stalin to the American point of view. He even told one of his advisors that he would have no trouble handling Stalin, whom he referred to as the "old buzzard."

In the ensuing struggle over what to do next, the three leaders came to the following agreements:

>> The Allies would perform a cross-channel invasion (codenamed OVERLORD) in May 1944. The Allies would also invade southern France at the same time, an idea that Stalin pressed hard for.

A GLIMPSE OF THINGS TO COME

The most important parts of strategic direction for 1944 were worked out in Teheran. But looming in the background were troubling political questions about the future of Europe. On what Europe would look like after the war, Stalin had these ideas:

- He believed that Germany needed to be cut into pieces and that tens of thousands of Germans should be executed.

- He wanted the current Polish-Soviet boundary to be left as is, but he believed that the western boundary of Poland should expand at Germany's expense.

- He refused to discuss the future freedom of the Baltic States of Latvia, Lithuania, and Latvia, which the USSR had seized in 1940.

>> Stalin committed the Soviet Union to participate in the war against Japan after Germany was defeated. (This was the only commitment Stalin made.)

>> The Italian campaign would continue but would be limited in scope.

While each leader did not get all he wanted at this conference, each did get something. Such is the importance of compromise in alliances fighting wars.

Winds of Change in 1943: From the Axis Perspective

For the Axis powers, 1943 demonstrated the growing power of the Allies, especially in the air and on the sea. Although strategic bombing efforts were causing pain, the Axis was most hurt by Allied fighter superiority over the battlefields of Europe and Asia. Allied fighters and bombers working closely with ground forces were nearly unbeatable. In the Atlantic and the Pacific, the sheer number of Allied ships was staggering. The Americans were producing more (and better) ships than the Axis could sink — a bad omen for both the German U-boats and the Japanese Imperial Fleet.

Playing both sides of the fence: The Japanese

For the Japanese, things looked grim but not hopeless. The war against China had bogged down, with no clear winner in sight. Much of the Japanese ground force in China would have to be deployed against the Americans. Japan still controlled Burma, Singapore, the Philippines, and the Dutch East Indies, even though they had abandoned the Aleutians and had lost Tarawa. The key to Japan's survival was twofold:

>> They had to hold the Americans and British at bay, essentially to fight for a stalemate. To do this, they had to hold Rabaul (the Japanese naval and air bases in the East Indies) and protect the approaches to Japan from the Central Pacific.

>> They had to keep the Soviet Union out of the war. To accomplish this, the Japanese had to accommodate the Soviet Union, even at the expense of Germany.

Japan was uneasy with the fall of Italy and the beating the Germans were taking in the Soviet Union. Although they had a non-aggression pact with the USSR, the Japanese feared that as the Soviets grew stronger, they would turn against Japan, which seemed to be growing weaker and more vulnerable to attack. Thus, the Japanese made no effort to limit the Soviets from taking units from the Chinese border and sending them to fight against the Germans.

Holding out for now: The Germans

For the Germans, the good news was only less bad than the really bad news.

» The Germans were holding the lines against the Soviets, but only temporarily: They had to endure yet another terrible Russian winter while they waited for what promised to be a big Soviet offensive in the spring.

» The German line was holding in Italy, but it was a drain on resources that were badly needed to fight the Soviets.

The bad news was even gloomier:

» The submarine war was going badly, and the bombing of German cities continued day and night.

» Although German factories were producing new and better weapons and equipment, the demands for manpower and materials were rising.

» Above all, they had to watch for an Allied invasion of France, which was an ever-increasing possibility.

If the Germans could stop this invasion, they would at least be able to maintain the status quo for another year.

The Panorama of 1943: From the Allied Perspective

The Allies spent most of 1943 fighting each other almost as much as they fought the Axis. The British and Americans especially had a great deal of difficulty coming to terms on strategic issues, and neither side was ever fully satisfied. What the Allies learned, though, is that when they cooperated, things went well.

Although they had still not opened the real second front against Germany, the British were making limited progress in Burma and the Americans and Australians seemed to have found the formula for operations against Japanese strongholds in the Solomons and New Guinea.

Stepping up production: The Americans

For the Americans, the war was going okay, but not fast enough:

>> The cross-channel invasion had to start soon so that America could defeat Germany and turn all efforts to Japan.

>> The strategic bombing of Germany would continue, not only to weaken German resolve, but also to cripple the formidable arms industry and stop Germany from developing advanced weapons (such as the V-1 and V-2 rockets) that could threaten Britain.

The main question for the Americans was how to coordinate the dual Nimitz-MacArthur thrusts against the Japanese in the Pacific (see Chapter 15 to find out more about their joint command of the Pacific forces). Should they meet in the Philippines or should they meet in Formosa (today's Taiwan)? Everyone agreed that the Japanese mainland islands were the next target.

Although an allied victory was still uncertain in 1943, the Allies had already won the production battle against the Axis powers. In that year, the Allies together produced 100,000 aircraft and 58,000 tanks; in comparison, the Axis produced 26,000 aircraft and 11,000 tanks. This success was due in large part to the Americans.

MILITARY STRATEGY

American industrial production took off, with nearly three quarters of everything being produced going toward the war. American factories produced 125,000 planes, 75,000 tanks, and 10 million tons of merchant shipping. American shipyards were producing three 10,500-ton merchant ships a week. In 1942, the Navy planned to build 17 battleships, 12 aircraft carriers, 54 cruisers, 201 destroyers, and 150 other ships by 1945; by the end of 1943, most of these had already been built, many of them at a rate of one every three days. No nation on earth could match such an effort.

Preserving and restoring the British Empire

For the British, the cross-channel invasion preparations would take place on their home island. Their strategic focus on keeping the Atlantic secure from U-boats (German submarines) continued, as did their interest in the strategic bombing of Germany.

In Europe, however, the British still preferred a Mediterranean approach, even at the expense of the cross-channel invasion. Such an approach would advance the Allied forces up the Italian peninsula to attack Germany from the south through Austria.

Much of Britain's strategic concern in the Pacific centered on mounting an offensive in Southeast Asia to preserve and ultimately restore the British Empire. Churchill was keenly concerned with Japanese strength in Burma, for example, and its potential threat to India, another British colony.

Creating a new role for itself: The Soviet Union

For the Soviets, the goal was to drive the Germans out of the Soviet Union and crush the Nazi menace. If Stalin had been cruel to the Soviet people, the German barbarities conducted in the occupied parts of the Soviet Union seemed far worse. The Soviet Army had held, and with the help of lend-lease, Russia was now poised to launch a great offensive.

Soviet industry was producing mass amounts of remarkably good military equipment in quantities that the Germans could not match. The entire nation had been mobilized to fight the war, and the Soviet people took a great deal of pride in being the only nation to fight the Germans to a standstill.

As Soviet military power grew in size and quality, opportunities for a new role of the Soviet Union in Europe began to emerge. Victory would again bring changes to the map of Europe. Germany would pay heavily for starting the war, and the Soviet Army would help to assure that the Soviet Union would never be threatened again.

Riding the storm out: China

Chinese leader Chiang Kai-shek's Nationalist forces were crippled by inefficiency and corruption within the government. Most were military forces in name only, more interested in looting and exploiting the peasants than fighting the Japanese. Nationalist control was limited to a relatively small part of China's interior. The rest belonged to the Japanese or to Chinese Communist leader Mao Tse-tung's Communist guerrillas.

The great concern shared by Chiang Kai-shek and the other Allies was that the Communists didn't take out the Nationalists after the war was over. Given Chiang Kai-shek's limited control over the war effort and his own troops, as well as a lack of any strong Japanese pressure, Chiang was content to ride out 1943, taking whatever supplies came from over land or by air, until the Americans defeated the Japanese.

5

The Long Haul, 1944

IN THIS PART . . .

Find an overview of the brutal and bitter campaigns conducted to recapture territory occupied by the Axis.

Uncover jungle fighting and amphibious assaults on heavily fortified islands in the Pacific.

Take a look at the cross-channel invasion of Europe.

Realize the climax of the Russo-German war.

See the Allies knock Italy out of the war.

Examine the more famous battles of the Pacific and European campaigns.

Chapter **17**

The Italian Campaign and Soviet Victories in the East

When Italy surrendered to the Allies in 1943 (see Chapter 13), the Germans invaded and captured Rome. The Allies, working their way up the Italian peninsula, found themselves battling war-hardened German troops. The Germans kept the Allied troops at bay, ably parrying every thrust until little else could be done. For the Allies, Italy was a frustrating mess that strained American–British cooperation. In the meantime, the bulk of Allied combat power was headed to Britain to prepare for the invasion of Europe (called Operation OVERLORD).

While the Allies and Germans fought in Italy and the Allies prepared for OVERLORD, the Soviet Army made impressive advances against the Germans, pushing them out of the USSR and opening the way to the nations of Eastern Europe. The Germans fought desperately to hold back the Red tide.

Changing Plans: End Run on the Winter Line

Allied frustrations over its lack of progress in Italy led to a change in plans for 1944. They decided to make an amphibious assault on the west coast of the Italian peninsula as a way to get around the *German Winter Line*, the formidable mountain defensive line about 125 miles south of Rome. The amphibious assault had two advantages:

>> It put Allied forces behind the Germans, which would force them to retreat or fight in two directions (something no commander wants to do).

>> It would put the Allies on the road to Rome, the capital of Italy and an important symbol of victory.

The site chosen for the assault was Anzio, a beach town about 50 miles south of Rome.

The strategy and potential problems

A combined American and British force made up of two divisions, supported by tanks and commandos, would make the landing on Anzio. Simultaneously, Allied forces would attack the Winter Line to hold the Germans in place. The landing force was to drive the enemy's rear and capture Rome.

Of course, nothing in war is simple. The Allies had to first deal with two problems:

>> **How to get the troops onshore.** The main problem was lack of landing craft (small boats to ferry the soldiers to the shore). The Allies had the existing landing craft in Britain for Operation OVERLORD and for training the invasion troops there. Without sufficient landing craft, the Allies could only bring their troops in a bit at a time. By not having a single massive landing, their combat power would build up slowly, leaving them vulnerable to a strong German attack. (For more information on the D-Day invasion, see Chapter 18.)

>> **How to ensure that the Germans were distracted.** The second problem was making sure that the Germans committed their reserve forces to defend the Winter Line, leaving them nothing to use to react to the Anzio landings.

In order for the Anzio landing to work, the Allies had to get their troops in place, and they needed the Germans to use their reserves to protect the Winter Line. What actually happened, though, was not what the Allies expected, and they ended up in a stalemate with the Germans at Anzio and Cassino.

The fight at Cassino

The first part of the Allied plan involved attacking the Winter Line. The goal of this attack was to tie up German reinforcements and distract them from the Anzio beaches. To accomplish this, the attack against the Winter Line had to be strong enough to attract the Germans' attention, but not so intense to tie the Allies up in battle. This attack, after all, was intended to be a diversion from the main Allied attack at Anzio.

Just a few days before the Anzio landings, American and French troops attacked over the Rapido River toward Cassino — unfortunately the place of the most formidable German defense (called the *Gustav Line*). To make matters worse, the German response wasn't what the Allies wanted: First, the Germans had no trouble breaking up the attack, and second, the Germans didn't call for their reserves.

The Cassino battle drew the Allies deeper into an attack they only wanted to use as a diversion. So the Allies didn't get the two things they wanted. What they did get was a lengthy casualty list.

Landing at Anzio: Surprises for everyone

When the Allied landings at Anzio began on January 22, 1944, it was hard to tell who was more surprised, the Allies or the Germans: Anzio was abandoned.

The Allied commander, Major General John P. Lucas, focused on landing quickly and establishing a strong beachhead on the hostile shore so that his remaining troops and supplies could land safely. All went well, but Lucas believed that the Germans had purposely allowed him to land unopposed, thinking to give him a false sense of security and thus catch him unprepared. Lucas's superior, General Mark Clark, agreed and allowed Lucas the time he needed to build his strength and amass his supplies before advancing. This was a bad decision for a couple of reasons:

>> **The Germans really *didn't* know that the Allies were landing in Anzio.**
Actually, they were expecting a landing north of Rome. The time Lucas took to get himself ready was time the surprised Germans used to get themselves organized for a strong counterattack. At the end of two days, Lucas had plenty of troops and supplies. But so did the Germans.

>> **Hitler decided to use the battle at Anzio to send a message to the Allies.**
With the soon-to-be-launched invasion of France on his mind, Hitler decided to used Anzio as an example of what the Allies could expect if they invaded France. He sent German units from France, Germany, and Yugoslavia to reinforce the German defenders at Anzio. With these added units, the Germans established strong points along the routes from the beach.

The battle on the Anzio beach

During the battle along the beach, the Germans threw back every Allied attack. German artillery zeroed in on the beach, and a constant bombardment continued into February. On February 16, the Germans attacked with eight divisions and tried to destroy the Allied forces on the beachhead.

With their backs to the sea, the American and British troops fought desperately and stopped the German assault. The next day, the Allies counterattacked, which led to weeks of prolonged intense fighting. Like the Germans, the Allies could only advance a few miles before being stopped. The beachhead had been saved, but the Germans had the Allies bottled up.

The fight at the Gustav Line

The Italian town of Cassino lies in a valley surrounded by rugged mountains. This town was the key to the German defensive position, known as the *Gustav Line*, in central Italy. Above the town, on a high mountaintop called Monte Cassino, was an ancient Benedictine monastery, which possessed a library of priceless manuscripts.

The destruction of the town of Cassino and its monastery

The Allies came to suspect that the Germans occupied the monastery as an observation post and were convinced that the building should become a military target. In fact, the Germans had actually dug in on the front slopes of Monte Cassino. They weren't even in the monastery; they considered it too obvious a place to hide and believed it would become a target before too long. They were right.

The Indians, British, and New Zealanders were scheduled to attack the Gustav Line in March, but the commander refused to attack until the monastery on Monte Cassino was destroyed. General Harold Alexander, the Commander in Chief of Allied forces in Italy, authorized the bombing of the cultural treasure, and both it and the town of Cassino were leveled.

The bitter fruit of miscalculation

To the surprise of the Allies, the massive bombardment did not touch the German defensive positions. The Germans easily stopped the attack, and the Allied high command looked foolish, as well as savage, with a bloody mess on their hands.

The Germans moved into the rubble of the town and the monastery, and built even better defensive positions. The Allied commander, General Mark Clark, was eager for a victory, and he continued pounding against Cassino to get it. But Cassino was the absolutely worst place to attempt a major offensive.

When they attacked again, they faced an enemy largely unaffected by the intense artillery bombardment, well hidden in the rubble. As a result, the Allies had heavy casualties and little to show for it in terms of ground gained.

The Allied break through at the Gustav Line

In May, after heavy reinforcements (more than 14 divisions with 3,000 aircraft and tanks) and nearly a week of fighting, the Allies finally broke through the Gustav Line at Cassino. The honor of finally conquering Cassino came to the Polish Corps, made up of soldiers who escaped from the German invasion of Poland in 1939 and who were eager to get back at the Germans.

In many ways, the victory was a hollow one. The Allied army had broken the Gustav Line, but the cost had been high.

Rome: The First Capital to Fall — So What?

The capture of Cassino on May 18, 1944, opened the road to Rome and the broad, open terrain behind the mountains. On May 23, the Allies broke out of the Anzio defensive lines and moved forward, in conjunction with the victorious forces commanded by General Mark Clark. These troops poured through the Cassino mountain passes. They finally achieved what they had tried to do in January: force the Germans to fight in two directions.

German Field Marshal Albert Kesselring withdrew north, leaving American General Clark with an interesting decision: Give orders to capture Rome, or give orders for the pursuit and destruction of the enemy? Clark chose Rome.

When in Rome . . .

On June 4, 1944, American soldiers entered Rome. But it was another hollow victory. The world celebrated for exactly 48 hours. To General Clark's intense frustration, the spotlight of attention moved to the greatest amphibious invasion in the history of the world: the D-Day landings in Normandy (see Chapter 18).

Clark made another major mistake. Although he had Rome, the Germans were still in Italy, using the time Clark unwittingly gave them to construct another mountain defensive line about 160 miles north of Rome. The process of attacking fortified mountain ridges would have to start all over again.

Stalemate again

The Allies advanced north slowly, hampered by the destruction of key bridges and roads. Through skillful fighting, they were able to push the German defenders back but at the cost of heavy casualties. By October 1944, the Allies had had enough. Faced with high, rugged mountains and the onset of winter, they decided to hold the line rather than waste strength in fruitless attacks. This decision was also influenced by the fact that many of the veteran division had been moved to France, leaving a collection of units of different nationalities and varying quality that had not worked together before.

Steamrolling the German Army in Russia

ARMY
ALLIED

The German army was hard pressed in the first half of 1944. By that time, the advantage had clearly shifted to the Soviets: They outnumbered the Germans 2 to 1 in manpower, 4 to 1 in aircraft, and nearly 3 to 1 in tanks. The German situation in Russia looked bleak, indeed:

>> The fall of Kiev in November 1943 had ruptured the German line.

>> By spring 1944, the Soviets had relieved the siege of Leningrad in the north and pushed the Germans back toward the border of Estonia.

>> In the south, German forces had abandoned Ukraine and were standing at the Romanian border. This retreat stranded nearly 250,000 Axis troops on the Crimean peninsula. Hitler gave another of his bizarre orders to die in place.

>> The Soviets, with complete control of the skies, 600 tanks, and 500,000 troops, captured or destroyed most of the German Army in the Crimea in early May.

By mid-summer 1944, the only major German force that had not been moved very far since 1941 was Army Group Center, the last major cohesive German army left standing. It occupied Belorussia in strong defensive positions that formed a large bulge stretching 300 miles deep and 650 miles wide into the USSR.

Blitzkrieg, Soviet style

The anniversary of the German invasion of the Soviet Union was a bad day for German Army Group Center. Blitzkrieg, Soviet style, had finally arrived (see Figure 17-1). This operation was codenamed BAGRATION after the Russian general who had opposed Napoleon's invasion of Russia. This offensive was to be the showcase demonstration of Soviet military power and operational skill. The three-month preparations included an elaborate deception plan that completely fooled the Germans, causing them to move their tank forces in exactly the wrong place, away from the real point of attack.

MILITARY
STRATEGY

The Soviets launched a devastating attack, with a massed artillery bom-bardment concentrated on a 250-mile front, followed by 5,000 tanks and a 1.2 million infan-trymen assault accompanied by 6,000 fighter aircraft and bombers.

The sheer numbers involved in the Soviet attack essentially guaranteed that the German defenders wouldn't be able to stop the attack. Hitler, of course, gave his customary no retreat orders, but within two weeks, the German armies were reeling back to Poland or fighting for their lives. Nearly half a million German soldiers surrendered.

By August, Soviet troops had advanced into German-occupied Poland, just a few miles from Warsaw, and were finally halted by lack of supplies and a hastily organized defense. BAGRATION, intended to complement the D-Day invasion, had succeeded brilliantly and had inflicted a crushing defeat on Germany.

THROUGH THE GATES OF HELL

In their advance into Poland, the Soviet troops came across an abandoned camp at Majdenek, about 100 miles southeast of Warsaw. What they found there horrified them. Within the wireenclosed barracks area, they found gas chambers, ovens, and piles of bodies — men, women, children — some partially cremated, others not. It was the first clear evidence of Adolf Hitler's Final Solution: the destruction of the European Jews. See Chapter 11 for more information about the war Hitler waged against the Jews in Europe.

Driving into the Balkans: The Soviets take over

For Hitler, the news from the eastern front continued to grow worse in August 1944. The Soviets sent nearly 1 million soldiers and 1,400 tanks crashing into Romania. German forces, stripped of all but a few hundred tanks for the Bagration offensive (see the preceding section), were overwhelmed.

>> 400,000 German soldiers became prisoners, and Bucharest fell to the victorious Soviet Army.

>> Romania surrendered, and Stalin promptly set up a pro-Soviet government and placed the Romanian army under Soviet control.

Bulgaria, seeing the writing on the wall, desperately tried to convince the British and Americans that it really didn't mean its declaration of war in 1941. Although Bulgaria had never declared war on the Soviet Union, Stalin, not one much interested in legal hairsplitting, declared war on Bulgaria and invaded. The Bulgarian government, in a hopeless attempt to win favor, declared war on Germany. Undeterred, Stalin established a pro-Soviet Communist government in Bulgaria. In the newly "liberated" Bulgaria or Romania, anyone suspected of pro-German sympathies (or democratic tendencies) was imprisoned or killed.

Stalin's view, as he once explained it, was that whoever occupies territory imposes his own social system on it as far as his armies can reach. He had no intention of giving up anything the Soviet Army conquered. By fall 1944, the military might of the Soviet Union was poised to drive into Germany through Poland, Yugoslavia, and Hungary.

Courageous uprising in Warsaw

With the disaster befalling German forces in Russia, the Polish Home Army (a group of nearly 40,000 resistance fighters) opened a battle with the Germans for control of Warsaw. Armed with a few captured weapons and hope, the Polish Home Army seized most of the city in August 1944, in anticipation of assistance from the Soviet Army, which was closing in on the city.

The Germans reacted with extreme brutality. To crush the uprising, Heinrich Himmler, the dreaded leader of the Reich's internal security, used anti-partisan forces (essentially German soldiers given orders to kill indiscriminately). These units were known for committing atrocities against the civilian population of occupied Europe. Himmler also sent in captured Russian soldiers who worked more or less as mercenaries (soldiers-for-hire), doing whatever the Germans told them to do.

The citizens of Warsaw fought courageously against increasingly desperate odds. Their bitter hatred of the Germans kept them fighting street by street and building by building. Boys as young as 10 years old fought in the streets, while young girls carried messages through the sewer system. The Soviet army never arrived. In October, lacking food, water, and ammunition, the epic resistance of the citizens of Warsaw ended. More than 215,000 Poles had been killed, along with 26,000 German soldiers. As 15,000 members of the Polish Home Army (including 2,500 women and children) were taken away to prison camps to an uncertain fate, they sang the Polish national anthem.

Chapter **18**

Liberating Europe: From Normandy to Paris, and Beyond

The invasion of Europe was the most anticipated event of World War II. From the moment British and French troops escaped from Dunkirk in 1940, it was clear that the Allies would have to return to the continent of Europe. The Germans knew the invasion was coming, they just didn't know when or where. The Allies wanted to keep it that way. Regardless of when and where the invasion occurred, it would lead to a battle that determined who won the war in Europe.

From the beaches of Normandy, the Allies fought some of the best German units and liberated France, advancing nearly to Germany's borders. The war might have ended then and there if the pipeline that supplied the beans, bullets, and fuel for over 1 million men and several million vehicles had been able to keep things moving. It didn't. Supreme Allied Commander, General Dwight Eisenhower, had to make very hard choices in the fall of 1944. One choice ended in disaster for the British airborne; another led to Hitler launching his last offensive in a desperate gamble to turn back time and save Germany from invasion.

Deciding on Strategy: OVERLORD

General Eisenhower, as Supreme Allied Commander, was appointed overall commander for the invasion of Europe, codenamed OVERLORD. Under him were the following men:

>> **General Bernard Montgomery,** who commanded the five British, American, and Canadian divisions that would make the initial landing in France

>> **British Admiral Bertram Ramsay,** who commanded the naval forces

>> **British Air Chief Marshal Trafford Leigh-Mallory,** who commanded the air forces.

The planning staff faced many obstacles preparing for the invasion of Europe. They decided on Normandy as a landing site quickly because the beaches were within range of fighter aircraft, which would provide overhead cover for the troops, and the area was near major ports.

REMEMBER

OVERLORD was not about an invasion as much as it was about grabbing a foothold so that the Allies could pour supplies into suitable facilities. To make this plan work, the Allies needed to do three things:

>> **Shut down the German counterattack that inevitably would come sometime after the initial landings.**

>> **Coordinate the invasion at a time when the weather, tide, and moon cooperated.** Thus, they needed the following conditions from Mother Nature:

   • High tide to get landing craft on the beaches

   • A new moon (no illumination) so that aircraft, paratroopers, and gliders could land in protective darkness

   • Clearing skies so that combat aircraft could fly in support of the invasion

   • Generally calm seas to support the rapid movement of troops and equipment ashore

   To complicate matters, this combination of tides and moon happened only on three days in every month.

>> **Trick the Germans into believing that the attack was coming at Pas de Calais on the northern coast of France.** Pas de Calais was a key port city situated only a few miles across the Channel from England and a seemingly obvious choice of location to launch a massive invasion from England. By keeping the Germans focused on Pas de Calais, they would forget about quiet, isolated Normandy.

Need a plan, a real big Allied plan

The Allied plan itself was relatively simple:

>> Take the limited landing craft available and land five divisions at five Normandy beaches (codenamed Sword, Juno, and Gold for the British and Canadians; Omaha and Utah for the Americans) and then shuttle in four more divisions across the beaches that day.

>> Each day after the initial landing, another division would land, along with tons of supplies, to keep the forces moving.

>> Three divisions of paratroopers — two American, one British — would precede the landings. The paratroopers would land behind the main beaches to disrupt enemy defenses and reinforcements.

>> Naval gunfire and aerial fire would also precede the actual landings and then support the assault once the troops were on the beaches.

The following sections explain how the planners of the Normandy invasion met the three critical tasks: shutting down the German response, coordinating the time of the landing with the right weather and tide conditions, and fooling the Germans that the invasion was coming from somewhere else.

Shutting down the German counterattack

The British and Americans had plenty of fighter aircraft to keep the German fighter aircraft at bay as the troops hit the beaches. The problem came when the Allied troops moved inland. The farther they went, the harder it was for the Allied fighters, with their limited fuel capacity, to cover them. So instead of relying only on the fighter pilots to prevent or slow down the German counterattack, Allied bombers attacked the road and railroads that the Germans used to get to Normandy. The bombers also hit strategic factories and oil refineries to slow supplies of new equipment or fuel to the German defenders.

Getting the troops ashore

The whole plan depended upon the humble landing craft. The simple fact was that the Allies didn't have enough of them. As a result, OVERLORD planners had to delay the planned May landing until June, when more landing craft could be shipped from the U.S. In June, the only three days available to launch the invasion (that is, days when the tides, moon, and weather were cooperating simultaneously) were June 5, 6, and 7. If, for whatever reason, the invasion couldn't be launched on those days, everyone would have to wait another month.

Fooling the Germans

The Germans were so sure that Pas de Calais was the spot for the invasion that they fortified the area heavily. The Allies decided to convince them that they were right and came up with following plan: The Allies created two fake Allied armies — one headed for Norway, the other headed for Pas de Calais. Dummy radio traffic poured out of fake headquarters. Real commanders, such as General Patton, were assigned to command some of these fake units.

The Germans bought the deception completely. In fact, when the real invasion at Normandy began, the Germans were convinced that it was the deception, meant to turn them away from the *real* invasion.

A PAINFUL LESSON

On August 19, 1942, over 6,000 Canadian and British commandos attempted an amphibious raid on several German coastal fortifications at the town of Dieppe on the French coast. The idea of the raid was to capture prisoners and to test how well German defenses' capabilities could stop an invasion across the English Channel. Supporting attacks by British units above and below Dieppe were to eliminate gun positions that could threaten the main landing. The Canadian infantry would make the main attack and secure the beach for landing craft to bring in tanks. Unfortunately, the predawn raid was discovered before the troops even debarked; one supporting unit arrived late, the other had only moderate success.

The main attack shouldn't ever have happened. The beach, made up of smooth rounded rocks that inhibited movement, wasn't good for landing either troops or vehicles. In addition, it was dominated by high cliffs where the Germans, fully alerted to the attack, poured machine gun and artillery fire on the Canadians. Additional troops landing on the main beach and in the vicinity took heavy losses. The tanks arrived, but they had trouble moving on the rocky beach and couldn't get over the anti-tank defenses. The trapped Canadians held out, all hope of victory long gone. The commander of the raid, on board a British destroyer, never knew the extent of the disaster and even sent in his reserve units to take advantage of what he thought was a breakthrough. Most of these men were killed as soon as they landed. The withdrawal order was given six long hours after the initial landing. About 1,600 Canadians made it back; over 3,300 men had been killed, wounded, or captured.

Germans step up their defenses

MILITARY STRATEGY

Hitler had every intention of stopping the invasion at the beaches. With time to prepare, he sent thousands of laborers to France to establish defenses. They created a complex of concrete emplacements, walls, trenches, barbed wire, minefields (containing a total of 2.5 million mines!), water obstacles, anti-tank ditches, and heavy artillery that stretched across the north coast of France. This immense defensive fortification was known as Hitler's *Atlantic Wall*. Field Marshal Erwin Rommel, one of the genuine heroes of the German army, supervised the effort. Hitler also sent 58 divisions, 5 of them tank divisions, to France with 1,800 tanks. These tank units, so badly needed in the war against the Soviets, were among the best in the German army, with years of combat experience.

In creating their defense plan, the Germans had to take into account two factors:

» They had a limited number of aircraft that they could use against the Allies during an invasion.

» They also had (besides their more experienced soldiers) a number of poorly trained and equipped ground units.

So they came up with the following plan:

» The poorly trained and equipped ground units would defend the beaches, even though this would mean that the Germans couldn't put up much of a fight against the initial landings.

» The best equipped, trained, and most experienced German tank and infantry divisions would hold the rear. These units would engage in counterattacks to drive the invading forces into the sea.

Actually, this plan was a pretty good one because the Allies would have mostly infantry on the beaches. Without tanks or artillery to support them as they moved off the beaches, the lightly armed Allied ground troops would be easy targets for the powerful mechanized German divisions.

The only problem with the plan was that Hitler had personal control of most of the divisions. No one could move anything until the Führer himself gave the order. He, of course, was nearly half a continent away directing the military disaster that he created in the USSR, and he had little appreciation for the situation in the West — both things that would leave the defenders of Normandy helpless for several critical days.

The toughest job: Eisenhower makes the call

The original day for the Normandy invasion (*D-Day* in military planner's jargon) was set for June 5, 1944. But bad weather forced Eisenhower to postpone the operation for 24 hours. Facing the proposition of having his vast armada discovered and having to wait nearly another month before attempting another start, Eisenhower made the fateful decision. After a long and deliberate pause, knowing how much was riding on this, he looked up and gave the word: "O.K., we'll go," he said. June 6 would be D-Day (see Figure 18-1).

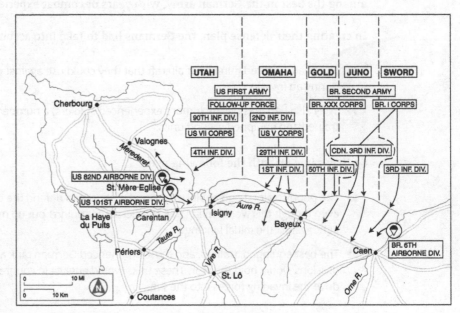

FIGURE 18-1: The D-Day landings, June 6, 1944.

D-Day: Invasion and Breakout

At 2 a.m. on June 6, American and British paratroopers were the first Allied forces to land on German occupied Europe. British paratroopers captured key bridges that would enable the British and Canadian forces to move inland; the American paratroopers landed in the rear of the section of Normandy beach (codenamed UTAH) to seal off main roads that the Germans would use to launch their counter-attack. Hitler's defenses had been pierced! Soon afterward, Allied ships began a heavy bombardment of the coast fortifications. At 6:30 a.m., the landing craft began hitting the beach.

Surprised and shocked by the intensity of the bombardment, the German defenders, mostly poor quality troops good only for non-combat duties, reacted slowly to the danger.

Some success for the Canadians and British at Gold, Juno, and Sword beaches

By the end of D-Day, the Allies had landed about 156,000 men on the beaches of Normandy.

At Sword beach

On Sword beach, British and French *commandos* (elite raiding forces composed of 10 to 20 men) helped clear landing sites and eliminate German strong points for the infantry and tanks coming ashore.

The British linked up with the paratroopers who were holding the key bridges that allowed access off the beaches, but their advance to the key objective of Caen, a large town a few miles from the beach, was halted by the arrival of German tanks. The tank units had been on an exercise in the area by pure chance and were able to react quickly enough to hold the town.

That evening, over 500 aircraft dropped supplies and gliders filled with reinforcements around Caen in a display of Allied might that stunned the German defenders. The advance soon bogged down before Caen, as German reinforcements blocked any further advance.

At Gold beach

At Gold beach, most of the Allied units met light to moderate resistance and began a rapid advance inland. By the end of the day, 25,000 British soldiers had landed and were firmly established eight miles inland. They were close to capturing the town of Bayeux (home of the famous tapestry commemorating another invasion, the Norman invasion of England in 1066), which soon became a major supply center.

The British on Gold beach could thank the paratroopers for their good fortune. The paratroopers landing in the early morning of the invasion had drawn German reinforcements to the outer areas, leaving the Gold beach sector only lightly defended. In the days to come, however, the Germans would rush reinforcements to defend the area, making the best use of the terrain and bringing the British advance to a halt.

At Juno Beach

At Juno beach, the Canadians found themselves hampered by obstacles and mines that made the landings very hazardous. Beach defenses were strong there, and the Canadians ran into trouble right away. They had to fight forward in small groups, attacking beach defenses one by one. Casualties were heavy; nearly 1,000 men were lost in the landings. But the Canadians broke through and made the deepest penetration off the beach by nightfall. Once inland, the Canadians faced German counterattacks and defeated them but could not make any further progress forward. A stalemate quickly developed.

Success for the Americans at Utah beach

At Utah beach, the first wave of Americans landed in the wrong place. Although it seems that having landed on the wrong beach would present a problem, it actually ended up being a good thing.

Realizing that they had landed in the wrong place and seeing that the second wave was landing close by, General Theodore Roosevelt Jr. (son of U.S. president Theodore Roosevelt and cousin to FDR) had to make a decision. Should the American troops move north a mile to the proper site, or should they fight where they were? "We'll start the war from right here," he told his officers. He made the right decision. This beach was a good place to land because it was lightly defended. With tank support, the Americans were soon across the beach and into the interior of France. By 11:00 a.m., they had linked up with American paratroopers. By afternoon, Utah beach was filled with thousands of vehicles and men moving steadily off the beach, building a three-mile-wide beachhead.

A near disaster at Omaha

The troops at Omaha beach did not have the same good fortune as the Allied soldiers who landed at the other beaches (see the preceding sections). Unlike the other beaches, a high quality German division defended Omaha beach and its defenses were elaborate and solidly built. The heavily burdened American infantrymen had little chance to cross the nearly 300 yards of open sand in the face of brutally accurate enemy fire.

The battle was difficult in another way. It was beyond the control of generals. It would be up to the small groups of American fighting men to either win or die. Many did both. Colonel Charles Canham of the 116th Infantry Regiment made up of National Guardsmen from Virginia, put it best: "They're murdering us here! Let's move inland and get murdered!" But at the end of the day, the Americans moved off the beach and up the bluffs into open ground. It was only about 1,500 yards, purchased at the cost of 2,000 casualties, but it was enough.

THE BUZZ BOMB AND THE ROCKET BOMB

Just a few days after D-Day, Germany launched its first strategic weapons against England with the intention of winning the war. Hitler called them *vengeance weapons*. The Allies called them *buzz bombs*. The V-1s were pilotless flying bombs, powered by a pulsejet engine that made a loud sputtering or rattling sound as it flew through the air. Moving at a 400 miles per hour and carrying nearly 1,900 pounds of explosives, the buzz bombs packed a punch. Hitler believed that launching these weapons by the hundreds every day for weeks would eventually weaken British morale, forcing Britain out of the war. Between June 1944 and March 1945, the Germans launched 6,000 buzz bombs from the coast of France and Holland. Nearly two-thirds were shot down by antiaircraft guns, guided by radar or by fighter aircraft. Buzz bombs were aimed at not only London and southern England, but at Antwerp as well. In England, 24,000 people were killed or injured by the bombings. More dangerous were the V-2 rocket bombs, the world's first short-range ballistic missile. With a one-ton warhead, these rockets traveled at a high trajectory and made no noise. Over 1,000 fell on England, causing extensive damage from September 1944 to March 1945. Despite the fear they inspired, the British population's morale was not seriously affected.

A day late and a dollar short: Another Hitler blunder

The reason that the Allies succeeded at Normandy was that once the German units defending the beaches were overwhelmed, they had no reinforcements. The large, crushing counterattacks that the Allies expected never came. Here's why:

>> In the German command headquarters, folks were confused over whether the attack at Normandy was the real attack (see the earlier section "Fooling the Germans" to find out why). Because of the confusion, the German generals decided to wait before launching any heavy counterattacks. In fact, they waited nearly six weeks before finally sending the majority of the tank units south to Normandy.

>> Hitler, who had heard early reports about American troops struggling to survive on Omaha, became overconfident and refused to release the powerful divisions he controlled.

Of course, by the time the real situation became known, the release order came too late to do any good for the Germans. The Allies actually reinforced the beaches faster than the Germans could stop them. In ten days, the Allies had more than a half million troops on the ground and controlled the air. With continuous bombing, the Allies successfully sealed off the road and rail networks that the Germans needed to move forward, and they attacked any German units that moved toward the beaches.

Expanding the Beachhead

The Allies had chosen Normandy as the landing site primarily because of its weak defenses. One drawback to the location, however, was the lack of a major port to bring in the tons of supplies needed to sustain the growing number of divisions pouring onto the beachhead. The Allies floated prefabricated harbors (codenamed Mulberry) across the English Channel to the Gold and Omaha beach sites to accommodate the flow of men and material, but these harbors were only temporary fixes. To solve this problem, the Allies set out to capture the major port of Cherbourg after they secured the beachhead.

The Allies captured the city of Cherbourg on June 27, but before it was won, four U.S. divisions had to be committed to the fight. American casualties were very heavy, and to complicate things, the port had been so badly damaged in the assault that it wouldn't be functional again until late fall of 1944.

The Germans understood that the longer they could delay the Allies from using the ports, the better the chance they could keep the Allies tied to the Normandy beachhead. Nevertheless, an average of 30,000 tons of supplies and 30,000 troops a day came across the beaches. By July 1944, the Americans had several divisions in Normandy organized under the leadership of some of the best generals the Allies had: U.S. General Omar Bradley, U.S. General George Patton, U.S. General Courtney Hodges, and British General Field Marshal Bernard Montgomery.

The battle for Caen

The city of Caen was meant to be taken on D-Day. Without Caen, the British and Canadians could not move any farther off the beach. Unfortunately, German tanks arrived in strength ahead of the Allies. So General Montgomery and his troops spent most of July fighting to capture the city.

A massive air attack had turned the ancient city of William the Conqueror (originator of the first Normandy invasion in reverse: to England in 1066) into rubble and accomplished very little. Like they did at the town of Cassino in Italy a year earlier (see Chapter 17 for details), the Germans used the destroyed city to their advantage, building defensive positions in the wrecked buildings. When German armored divisions arrived at Caen, the British began to suffer heavy casualties.

An Allied attack (codenamed Goodwood) began on July 18, 1944; the goal was to blast past the German defenders of Caen with firepower alone. The Germans holding the area were veterans of the war with the Soviets, and despite devastating air and artillery bombardments, they stopped the British and Canadians in their tracks, destroying 200 tanks in one day and killing several thousand in the Allied infantry. By July 20, the Allies realized that a breakout would have to come from somewhere else.

The Allied breakout into the open

While German tanks held the British and Canadians before the town of Caen, more than 50 miles to the west, the Germans tried to hold the ever increasing American forces that inched their way around the German defenses to get into the open countryside behind the enemy. The Germans knew that if either the British and Canadians or the Americans broke into the open, nothing would stand between the Allies and the German border. If the German troops couldn't hold the Allies, the entire front would collapse.

Despite the odds against success, the Germans conducted a skillful defense, holding the Americans behind marshes and rivers and guarding the fields. Poor weather limited Allied air power, giving the Germans another advantage. Still, the Americans captured the key town of St. Lô on July 18, but the cost was heavy: During the first two weeks of July, the Americans had suffered over 40,000 casualties.

As American ground combat strength grew, along with the tons of supplies needed to sustain it, preparations began for a breakout called Operation COBRA. In Cobra, the Allies used a combination of massed air and ground attacks to blast their way out of the constricting terrain and into the open where they could use their tank units effectively. Fifteen hundred aircraft dropping 3,400 tons of bombs on the narrow front preceded the breakout, literally blasting the Germans away. American armor drove through the gap and into open country. General Patton, commanding the 3rd Army, got into the open in early August 1944 and began to surround the German defensive line.

Forcing the German retreat:
The disaster at Falaise

Although the situation in Normandy was bad for the Germans, it wasn't hopeless. With their mobility and the advantages of the difficult terrain, the Germans could shift forces and blunt the American attacks. They had already halted the British.

Now they needed Hitler's approval to shift reserves in order to keep the Allies blocked in the vicinity of Caen and St Lô.

Hitler finally gave his permission. But he couldn't stop there. He also gave orders on exactly which reserve units were to be used and how. He ordered the reserve tank divisions to counterattack into what he perceived as a gap between the Americans and British. It wasn't really a gap though; it was the expanding jaws of a deadly enveloping movement as the Allies slowly but steadily pushed forward. Charging into the gap was like sticking one's head into the lion's mouth — not too smart and not too prudent. Yet the Führer's orders had to be obeyed. The finest soldiers and tanks of the German army headed to destruction.

Pressed on one side by the British at Caen, the Canadians at Falaise, and the Americans at Argentan (where they had advanced after capturing St. Lô), the German attack quickly turned into a desperate retreat as they found themselves in a rapidly closing trap. Thousands of men and vehicles were packed into a 42-mile long corridor with an opening at one end, trying to escape before the jaws closed at the top of it. Allied aircraft bombed the columns constantly, creating complete disorder.

American General Omar Bradley had orchestrated the operation, taking advantage of a golden opportunity given to a military commander only once in a hundred years. He ultimately failed to accomplish the complete destruction of the enemy, however. He halted General Patton to avoid possible friendly fire exchanges with the British and Canadians and left a 15-mile gap at the top of the 42-mile long corridor that proved to be the salvation for more than 40,000 Germans.

MILITARY STRATEGY

The Allies captured 100,000 enemy soldiers and had killed 10,000 more. Of the 50 German divisions that faced the Allies in Normandy in June, only 10 survived. All in all, the Germans lost 500,000 troops (including 200,000 prisoners) since D-Day.

Liberating Paris

As the Germans raced for their lives eastward, the Allied armies, led by General Patton, were close on their heels. By August 25, the Allies had liberated Paris. French General Charles de Gaulle and the French 2nd Armored Division entered the city, fortunately untouched (the German commander in Paris disobeyed Hitler's orders to destroy the city and surrendered it to the Allies). General de Gaulle, ignoring the bullets singing all about him, walked among the ecstatic Parisians and took the first steps toward restoring the prestige of France.

Too Far, Too Fast: More Decisions

As the Allies moved further inland (which was a good thing), they moved further away from their supply source: the beaches in Normandy (which was a bad thing). So General Eisenhower found himself in a good news/bad news situation. The good news was that the Germans were in full retreat and the Allied advance into France was way ahead of schedule. The bad news was that the Allies were running out of everything. No fuel, no ammunition, no food. To ship supplies forward to the front lines, the Allies needed to rebuild all those road and rail lines that their planes had so thoroughly and efficiently destroyed in June.

As the roads were rebuilt, the front line of the Allied combat units had to stop because of a lack of fuel. This delay gave the Germans time to regroup and organize a defense. Prior to the war, Germany had built a series of fortifications and defensive obstacles along its border with France to deter an attack. It was called the *Siegfried Line* or the *West Wall*. These defenses now served as a rallying point for the German divisions and a major barrier to any further Allied advance.

Tough choices for Eisenhower

American General Eisenhower faced a dilemma: The Allies had only enough supplies to support one offensive movement. Who would make the offensive — the Americans or the British? Here are the things he had to consider:

>> The Allies were in control of most of France, Belgium, and Luxembourg. They also occupied Antwerp.

THE RED BALL EXPRESS

With the French transportation system in a shambles from Allied bombers and no ports near the Allied line of advance, supplies could only come by road. To supply the fast moving divisions, American logisticians came up with a truck convoy system. Starting at St. Lô, 6,000 trucks loaded up to the limit and moved along a narrow one-lane, one-way road headed for General Patton's 3rd Army. After the truck drivers delivered their cargoes, they headed back on a different one-way road. This continuous stream of traffic moved day and night for two weeks. The troops called it the "Red Ball Express," which was railroad slang for a train that moved passengers or cargo straight through without stopping. The Red Ball Express went into Army lore as an example of the cando spirit of the Army logistician, who provides everything the combat forces need.

>> The German border was within spitting distance of the American 1rst and 3rd Armies, with the Rhine River 60 or so miles beyond. On the other side of that major barrier was the heart of Germany — its industrial base in the Ruhr — and victory.

General Eisenhower needed to solve his supply problems, so Antwerp, a key port for supplies, was the answer. Going after Antwerp wouldn't be easy, though, because German troops controlled all the approaches to the city, making it useless to the Allies. By combining an offensive to push the Germans out of the Netherlands with the opening of Antwerp for supplies and sustainment, General Eisenhower would keep the momentum of the Allied offensive going and meet the needs of his armies.

Eisenhower couldn't accomplish this goal *and* keep all his armies fighting at the same level of intensity all across the front lines, however. Europe at the time just didn't have enough stockpiles of ammunition and fuel. So Eisenhower faced another tough decision: Who would stay put while the others got the supplies necessary for a major attack?

Eisenhower made his decision, based on both sound strategy and the need to keep the Alliance together and not shortchange the British. In the end, Eisenhower decided the following:

>> He gave the priority of all supplies to General Bernard Montgomery and the British army. The British would launch an offensive to cross the river obstacles in Holland and throw the Germans off balance by threatening a vulnerable sector to the north.

>> The American forces were told to hold in place.

The British offensive: Monty miscalculates

General Montgomery (known to everyone as "Monty") decided to take General Eisenhower's gifts and make an even bigger splash, one that he hoped would end the war in a single stroke. Why just push the enemy away from Antwerp when they could jump the Rhine in Holland and outflank the entire German western defenses? Montgomery put together a plan, codenamed MARKET GARDEN.

The plan: Operation MARKET GARDEN

In his plan, General Montgomery would use the Airborne Army, which consisted of two American airborne divisions, one British airborne division, and one Polish airborne brigade in England to seize several key bridges along a 60-mile stretch of highway that his ground forces would use to drive across Holland, over the Rhine River, and into Germany. It was a bold plan — one that relied on perfect timing, a weak and disorganized enemy, good weather, and luck:

>> The paratroopers needed good weather for jumping onto their drop zones and for aerial resupply.

>> The paratroopers, who were lightly armed, depended on a quick link-up with rapidly moving mechanized forces.

>> The enemy had to be caught by surprise, and they had to be too weak to put up much of a fight.

>> Finally, everything had to go exactly according to plan. Any delays anywhere would throw the whole plan off.

Despite the fact that so many separate things had to come together in perfect harmony, General Eisenhower gave Monty the go ahead to launch MARKET GARDEN. Unfortunately, Montgomery ended up facing bad timing, bad luck, bad weather, and a battle-hardened enemy.

The bridge too far

On September 17 and 18, 1944, the Airborne Army, carried by 2,800 planes and 1,600 gliders, dropped near their targets. The American paratroopers seized one objective, but encountered tough resistance at another key bridge. This resistance delayed the advance of the British ground forces. About 60 miles away, at the town of Arnhem, the British First Airborne Division discovered what General Montgomery had overlooked — two German tank divisions were resting and refitting.

Tanks and lightly armed paratroopers don't mix. The British found themselves fighting for survival as they held the bridge with little more than hand grenades and rifle bullets. With the Allied relief units held up, the British paratroopers had little chance. Surrounded and outnumbered, the paratroopers surrendered on September 21. The next day, the British tanks reached the bridge, but they could advance no further.

MARKET GARDEN, for all its heroism and sacrifice, did little:

>> Allied forces had advanced, but the Germans were still in control of all the territory that mattered.

>> Antwerp was still unusable and would be until the last days of November 1944.

>> The Germans controlled Holland and the approaches to the Rhine River.

In the end, supplies still came through in a trickle, leaving the frustrated Allied forces to make limited and costly offensives against well-prepared defenders who fought with great skill and determination.

Americans bloody Germany's nose on the border

As Operation MARKET GARDEN went on (see the preceding section), American forces fought exhausting battles at the German cities of Aachen and Metz through October. Aachen, the first German city captured by the Allies, fell on October 21. But the Americans went from the fire to the frying pan, entering the Hümuertgen Forest east of the city:

Four American divisions took nearly a month to clear 31 miles of trees at the cost of over 20,000 casualties. To make matters worse, the weather turned bad. As a result, the Americans began to suffer non-battle casualties, such as trench foot, which weakened the divisions further. The weather also prevented Allied aircraft from flying missions to support the ground forces.

The Americans finally captured Metz in November, but the battle had worn out Patton's men, and the Germans were holding fast on the Siegfried Line, the pre-war defenses built to protect Germany from an attack from France.

Combat fatigue all along the line

The U.S. 6th Army Group, made up of American and French army units, continued to advance until they met with Bradley's 12th Army Group advancing from northern France. The 6th Army Group had been fighting south of General Patton's 3rd Army and reached Strasburg in November. But the Allied units in the area had extended their forces dangerously thin, leaving a large number of German troops in the area of Colmar, France.

By December, many U.S. divisions all along the front lines had lost a great deal of their combat effectiveness. Most of their experienced soldiers and leaders had become casualties. Replacements with no or little combat experience filled the ranks. In addition, the advance from October to December had opened a gap between the 1st and 3rd Armies. In between that gap was the Ardennes Forest, a quiet sector that was covered by understrength units. The whole front had bogged down from a combination of bad weather, determined enemy resistance, and a lack of combat experience within the front line divisions.

The Air War: Wearing Germany Down

Without the support of fighters and bombers, the Allies wouldn't have gotten very far from Normandy. The breakout from Normandy was just that — a breakout, largely due to overwhelming use of bombers that blasted gaps in the German defenses wide enough for Allied tank units to drive through. As the Allied forces moved out into the open countryside, fighters and bombers again harassed the Germans without end.

HISTORICAL TRIVIA

With total control of the air, nothing moved during daylight without being subject to Allied attack. General Rommel, riding in a staff car on a French road, was attacked and wounded by an American fighter. The most able German commander was taken out of battle at a crucial point in the campaign.

Allied attacks on war production factories

The Allied strategic bombing campaign against Germany slowed in early 1944 to concentrate on targets in France, specifically transportation networks that would be used to reinforce the front at Normandy. The success of this campaign stopped the Germans from moving quickly and limited the Germans' ability to properly sustain and supply their units in the crucial weeks after the invasion.

In the first three months of 1944, the Allies continued their deep strikes into the heart of Germany, attacking Berlin (they destroyed 2,000 acres of the city) and hitting key war production factories.

The offensive intensifies

By 1944, the 15th Air Force, flying from bases in Italy, flew throughout southern Germany and parts of Eastern Europe. Although the Germans had dispersed production facilities to prevent damage from these bomber raids in 1943, American B-17s could now hit targets virtually anywhere they wanted.

REMEMBER

Previously, American fighters did not have the fuel capacity to escort the bombers deep into Germany. But with airfields in France and new aircraft that carried drop tanks, limited range (because of fuel) stopped being a problem for the fighter escorts. They could take on the *Luftwaffe* (see Chapter 3) throughout the bombing missions. They no longer had to leave the slow-moving bombers to continue their way into Germany alone.

THE AIRPLANE THAT COULD HAVE WON THE WAR

The Germans had experimented with a new design of aircraft since the late 1930s. This aircraft used jet propulsion rather than a piston driven engine. By 1943, a prototype jet fighter aircraft had been developed. Hitler observed its flight test and immediately appreciated what such an aircraft could do to the mass of Allied bomber formations. With a top speed of 540 miles per hour, no other combat aircraft on earth could match it. Squadrons of these aircraft would give Germany control of the skies over Europe in a matter of weeks. Der Führer ordered the aircraft to be put into full production immediately, which was an excellent idea. Unfortunately, he followed it with a really *bad* idea: He ordered that the plane be both a fighter *and* a bomber.

This boneheaded requirement led to redesigns and consequent delays in manufacturing. All the while, the Allied bombing campaign was growing more effective. By the time the Me 262 (as the new aircraft was known) was actually deployed to combat in late 1944, the numbers were too small to have a decisive effect, and airbases were often vulnerable to capture. Fuel shortages and inexperienced pilots who did not master the capabilities of such a weapon compounded the problem. The Me 262 did mark the end of an era, ushering in the age of the jet airplane.

Feeling the effects

MILITARY STRATEGY

In 1944, Allied bombers dropped 750,000 tons of bombs on Germany. Allied bombing raids numbering 1,000 planes nearly cut off German fuel production and closed down urban transportation networks critical for the movement and support of combat units. Germany was bombed day and night to disrupt and ultimately halt war production. Nearly 1.4 million German citizens were killed or injured in these raids. Between February and March of 1944, the Germans lost nearly 1,000 fighters in air combat. These losses, along with limits on fuel and poorly trained pilots and crews, caused the decline of the *Luftwaffe* as a serious threat.

The Allies lost nearly 500 bombers a month in 1944, and about 100,000 British and American air crewmen perished. The cost was high. But by the end of 1944, Germany's military forces were starving from a lack of fuel and supplies because of the bombing. The *Luftwaffe* was defeated.

Hitler's Gamble: The Battle of the Bulge

Even as MARKET GARDEN was collapsing in failure in September 1944 (see the earlier section "The British offensive: Monty miscalculates"), Hitler was making big plans. As if time stood still, he decided that the way to victory was a surprise offensive against the Allied forces in the West. The advance, as it had in 1940, would come through the Ardennes Forest. Instead of the English Channel being the target, it would be Antwerp (to cut off the Allies from their potential supply base).

But the days of German victory had passed. The men and machines of 1940 were gone, buried in the mud and snow of Russia or in the fields of Normandy. Hitler's generals were skeptical, viewing this plan as little more than an exercise in nostalgia. At the very least, they argued, the Allied armies should be the goal of the offensive. But Hitler fixated on Antwerp as the key to victory. Despite their reservations, the German commanders assembled a fairly credible and capable force of 24 divisions (ten of them tank divisions) from bits and pieces of units and awaited the opportunity to strike.

Through the Ardennes Forest again

Just as the French had overlooked the Ardennes Forest as a credible route of attack in 1940, the Americans did the same to a certain extent in 1944. Their line of troops was stretched nearly 1,000 miles across the border between France and Germany. General Eisenhower, with the supply situation improved, was looking to the north and south of the rugged woodlands of the Ardennes as points of attack. Although he still needed the Ardennes defended, he didn't want to use his best fighting divisions to do it. So Eisenhower gave the 75-mile-wide area to just four divisions that were either recovering and refitting from earlier battles or were brand new to the war and had no combat experience.

NOW, LET ME GET THIS STRAIGHT . . .

General Sepp Dietrich had been a close associate of Hitler since the early days of the Nazi party; he also founded Hitler's bodyguard. Dietrich had been a noncommissioned officer in the Great War (World War I), but he showed sufficient skills to become the commander of an army in World War II. When told of Hitler's plan for the Ardennes offensive, Dietrich had some choice words. "All Hitler wants me to do is cross a river (the Meuse), capture Brussels, and then go on to take Antwerp. And all this in the worst time of year, through the Ardennes, when the snow is waist deep . . . when it doesn't get light until eight, and it's dark again at four, and with reformed divisions made up chiefly of kids and sick old men — and at Christmas."

In December 1944, the weather turned bad, eliminating any Allied air cover. On December 16, with a crushing artillery barrage at dawn, the German divisions advanced, catching the Americans completely off guard. To succeed, the Germans needed three things:

>> The bad weather had to hold to keep Allied aircraft grounded. Without the Allies controlling the air, the Germans had an even chance against the Allied ground forces.

>> German units had to move fast. The Ardennes had few roads, and thousands of combat vehicles had to travel on them. The Germans had to control of a number of key crossroads so that they could move their divisions out into open terrain. Fuel was limited, so getting into the Allied rear areas quickly meant capturing fuel supplies to continue the offensive.

>> The breakthrough had to be wide enough to rupture the enemy line sufficiently so that Allied forces could not close the gap behind them and trap the German divisions.

As it turned out, the Germans failed to meet these critical requirements. Because they failed to do so, the Battle of the Bulge, as it became known, was doomed to failure (see Figure 18-2).

Narrowing the gap: The Allies just keep fighting

It's called the Battle of the Bulge for a good reason: between December 16 and 26, the German divisions punched a hole in the American lines that on the battle maps (and in the newspapers), looked like a bulge. The Bulge, though 50 miles wide, narrowed rather quickly to only ten miles at its deepest point of penetration. There were several reasons for this:

>> First, the Americans, although outnumbered and outfought, still held the German advance up. In fact, several key crossroads, such as St. Vith and Bastogne, became American strongpoints that the Germans couldn't bypass, even though they spent precious time and fuel trying to take them. Eventually, the Germans captured St. Vith, but Bastogne held.

>> The Germans didn't widen the breakthrough. Fifty miles seems large, but with the number of vehicles and troops involved, it got crowded quickly, especially because of the heavy snows that fell before and during the battle. The Allies were able to keep the size of the gap limited, squeezing the Bulge to only 35 miles wide. This forced German army commanders to dispatch units to keep it open.

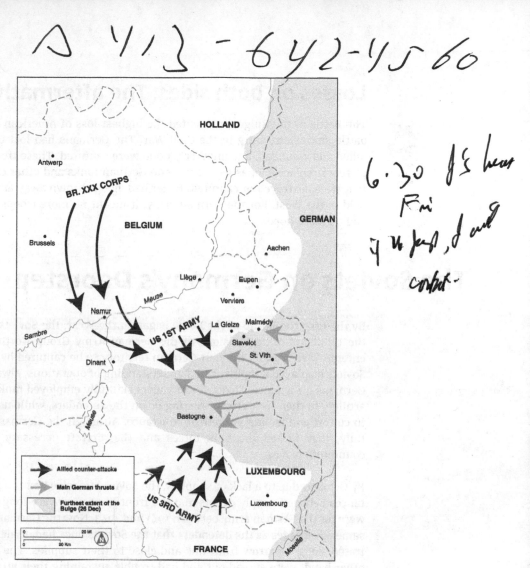

FIGURE 18-2: The Battle of the Bulge, December 1944 through January 1945.

>> The Allies reacted quickly and effectively — far faster than the Germans expected. As German combat power dwindled, Allied combat power grew stronger, with divisions shifting rapidly from one sector of the front to the Bulge.

>> By December 23, the weather cleared enough to allow the Allied air forces to wreak havoc on the German tanks and supply vehicles, including the horse-drawn wagons that were the predominant means of supply for the German army.

By January 16, the Allies closed the Bulge. The Americans suffered 75,000 casualties (including the massacre of 85 American prisoners at Malmédy).

Losses on both sides: The aftermath

HISTORICAL TRIVIA

The Battle of the Bulge represented the highest loss of American soldiers in one battle since Gettysburg in the Civil War. The Germans had lost 69,000 soldiers killed and wounded, and another 50,000 were captured. These troops were completely irreplaceable, as were the 1,400 German tanks and other combat vehicles that were destroyed or captured. Hitler had again thrown away any advantage he held in the West. For the German army, it meant no more troops, no more fuel, and no more hope.

The Soviets on Germany's Doorstep

By the time the Battle of the Bulge began in the West, the Soviets had sealed off the remnants of 26 divisions of the German Army Group North in Latvia and entered East Prussia, the first German territory to be captured by the Allies. The Soviets displayed a sophisticated understanding of operations, always keeping the Germans off balance. Soviet commanders skillfully employed tanks, aircraft, and artillery to their best effect, wearing down the defenders, while using maneuvers to cut off and isolate pockets of resistance. Although the Germans fought skillfully, they lacked the tank forces and the aircraft necessary to mount any counteroffensives.

By October, due to a lack of supplies, the Soviet offensive had run its course. Distances between supply depots and the front lines were very long — just as they were for the German army between 1941 and 1943. Now the German forces had the same advantages as the defenders that the Soviets once had, their forces concentrated along a narrow front line and close to their supplies. The Soviets, on the other hand, were spread out and had trouble sustaining their attack. By October 1944, the general Soviet advance slowed to a halt.

Advancing into Yugoslavia and Hungary

While the central Soviet armies held in place on the Vistula River, another Soviet front pushed into eastern Yugoslavia, where they linked up with the Yugoslav guerrillas. With support from Britain and America, the guerrillas, numbering more than 150,000, had been fighting the Germans since the summer of 1941. They had been successful largely due to their charismatic leader, Jossip Broz, whose nickname was "Tito."

Tito's mixture of Communist ideology and patriotism held the movement together and allowed him to take control of large sections of the country. With the Soviet's assistance, Tito formed a provisional government that even had the approval of the exiled Yugoslav government in London. (The British and the Yugoslav governments would later regret their enthusiastic endorsement after Tito took power and excluded all other participants in the new government.)

The Germans and Soviets also battled for control of Hungary. In October 1944, the Germans tried to protect the Hungarian oil fields; Budapest also became a major objective. As a result, Hitler diverted valuable tank divisions from both Poland and the West, leaving both areas open to Allied attack. The Germans held the Soviets and defended Budapest until February, but not until the Soviets had established another pro-Communist provisional government (as they had in Yugoslavia with Tito) that would eventually determine Hungary's postwar destiny.

On April 13, 1945, Soviet forces moved into Vienna. The real show took place with Soviet armies driving through Poland into eastern Germany and the British and Americans driving across the Rhine River into central Germany. The Balkans were forgotten.

IN THIS CHAPTER

» Winning the Pacific island by island

» Returning to the Philippines

» Slugging it out with the fleets

» Fighting in Burma, India, and China

» Keeping China in the war

Chapter **19**

Japan Begins to Crack

By 1944, the Japanese knew that they had to hold the Americans as far away from the home islands of Japan as possible. Wherever the Americans chose to attack, they would have to face Japanese soldiers, who were willing to die rather than surrender or retreat and who were supported by land-based Japanese fighters and bombers. At the same time, the Japanese fleet would actively seek out the American fleet in open battle for the seas. The goal of the Japanese was to make the battles for territory in the Pacific so costly that the Americans would give up and seek negotiations to end the war.

For the Americans, the goal was to find the best and quickest route to the Japanese home islands. To do this, the Allies needed island bases they could use to launch strategic bombing raids against Japanese cities in an effort to cripple morale and industry.

The stage was set for a gigantic struggle that would encompass vast numbers of land, air, and sea forces across thousands of miles of land and water.

The Island Assault Plan: The Marshalls and Then the Marianas

To secure a route to the Japanese home islands, the Allies decided that American General Douglas MacArthur would move from the Solomon Islands through New Guinea, East Indies, to establish a base to attack the Philippines. At the same time, American Admiral Chester Nimitz would penetrate the Japanese defenses in the Marshall and Mariana Islands in the Central Pacific on his way to the Philippines.

To defeat Japan, the Allies had to cut off and isolate its home islands. They could do this in two ways:

>> Submarines would sink Japanese merchant vessels carrying supplies to and from Japan.

>> Strategic bombers would conduct air attacks on cities and military targets in Japan.

To get the bombers close enough to attack Japan, the Mariana Islands in the Central Pacific were essential air bases. With these islands, American air power could completely dominate the sea lanes from Japan, leaving the Japanese vulnerable to having their supplies lines to the Philippines and Southeast Asia disrupted. But to get to the Marianas, the Marshall Islands had to be captured first. Nimitz set out in January 1944 to initiate his first step in the defeat of Japan (see Figure 19-1).

Marshall Islands: Learned Lessons Well Applied

The United States Navy and Marine Corps had learned a number of important lessons from the battle of Tarawa (see Chapter 15). Tarawa, an American target because of its strategic location, was heavily fortified by the Japanese. The ill-prepared Allied landing and the fierce Japanese resistance resulted in a high number of casualties that, when broadcast by the news media, shocked the American public, as well as the American planners of the invasion. To avoid another debacle like that on Tarawa, the attack on the two main islands of the Marshalls (Eniwetok and Kwajalein) was shaped by what Allied planners had overlooked or had failed to do at Tarawa. The following planning issues were a result of these lessons:

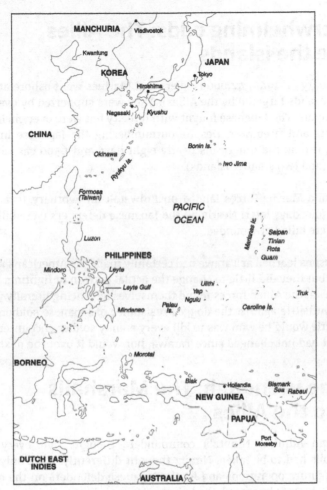

FIGURE 19-1:
Operations in
the Pacific,
1944–1945.

» The landing force on the Marshalls would have overwhelming strength against the Japanese (it was nearly 6 to 1).

» The American soldiers and Marines going in would have lots of firepower, including flamethrowers, automatic weapons, tanks, and artillery.

» Before American troops would even land, the islands would take a terrible pounding from naval and air bombardment for nearly a month to destroy Japanese defenses.

Overwhelming odds: The Allies take the islands

On January 31, 1944, 42,000 soldiers and Marines went ashore at Kwajalein (one of the islands targeted by the Allies). They were supported by over 200 ships and 700 aircraft. The Japanese fought with ferocity but were overwhelmed by superior numbers and firepower. Despite outnumbering the Japanese in men and firepower, it took the Americans nearly eight days and 1,500 casualties to clear the island (and two smaller islands).

ARMY ALLIED

Army and Marine forces landed on Eniwetok on February 19 and captured the island four days later. Nearly all the Japanese defenders were killed; 700 Americans were killed or wounded.

The lessons learned at Tarawa had certainly made the Americans more effective in battle, but they did little to change the actual pattern of fighting. Just as they had at Tarawa, the Allied forces found themselves advancing literally yard-by-yard in constant battle against the dogged resistance of Japanese soldiers. The only way the battle would be won was to kill every enemy soldier encountered. That sobering fact had not changed since Tarawa, nor would it over the next year.

Some is enough: The Marshalls go to the Allies

American Admiral Nimitz's commanders thought that every island in the Marshalls had to be taken. Nimitz thought differently: Take only what's important to future operations and let the Japanese defenders on the other islands sit and watch. Once bypassed, the Japanese were no longer dangerous, so why expend time and manpower to capture them? Nimitz was right.

The Japanese commander also believed that the Americans would take every island. So, hoping to wear down the American attackers before they reached the main islands of Kwajalein and Eniwetok, the Japanese moved most of their forces to the smaller forward islands. Kwajalein and Eniwetok were left lightly defended.

Nimitz made sure that Japanese airplanes could not threaten the American carriers: By the time the ground forces landed, every Japanese plane had been destroyed. Nimitz also attacked the Japanese support base at Truk, about 700 miles southwest of Eniwetok. American bombers and fighters devastated the area, sinking merchant ships and blasting 120 aircraft on the ground.

With Truk neutralized and the two big islands of the Marshalls serving as air and support bases, Nimitz could now concentrate on the Marianas.

Mauling the Marianas

The Mariana Islands were 1,000 miles from Eniwetok, only 1,500 miles from the Japanese main islands, and 1,200 miles from the Philippines. The Americans targeted two main islands: Saipan (including the smaller island of Tinian) and Guam.

The Japanese expected Nimitz's next move and heavily reinforced the islands, sending troops and aircraft and preparing a naval force with carriers to attack the American fleet as soon as it came within range.

The American attack began as it had in the Marshalls, with intense air and naval bombardment. Japanese aircraft from Saipan and Tinian attacked the fleet, but they were nearly totally destroyed and caused minimal damage. Thus began the island-by-island Allied assault.

Saipan

On June 15, 1944, two Marine divisions landed on Saipan. After one day of heavy fighting, an Army division landed to continue the attack. The airfield was captured, and with tanks and support from artillery and naval gunfire, the ground troops made progress.

The fight for Mount Tapotcheu was exceptionally difficult because Japanese defenders hid in caves and ravines, which were very hard to destroy with bombs or artillery fire. Often the only way to attack these positions was to use rifle and machine gun fire, hand grenades, explosives, and flame throwers. It took the Allies ten days of yard-by-yard fighting to capture Tapotcheu.

GOING DOWN FIGHTING: THE BANZAI CHARGE

In the Pacific war, American infantrymen and Marines often encountered an unusual Japanese tactic — the *banzai charge*. The term comes from the words that the Japanese soldiers shouted as they attacked: *"Tenno heika banzai!"* which means "Long live the Emperor!" It was a mass-infantry assault directed against American defensive positions without regard to casualties. The Japanese would attack when it was clear that defeat was imminent. Reminiscent of the days of Napoleon, the Japanese chose to die by making a charge rather than face the possibility of capture. The banzai charge usually marked the last phase of combat operations. Such attacks during the battles for Saipan and Guam, although having no effect on the outcome of events, nevertheless caused heavy American casualties.

By July 9, the Japanese had ceased organized resistance (although Army troops would be fighting small groups of Japanese soldiers for nearly two months afterward). Of the 29,000 Japanese men defending the island, 27,000 were killed. The other 2,000 were taken prisoner. Japanese civilians on the island preferred to kill themselves by leaping off cliffs into the sea rather than face the shame of defeat and conquest. The Americans suffered over 16,000 casualties.

Guam

Guam was the first American possession to be recaptured in the Pacific. It was a hard-fought 20-day battle against heavily armed Japanese soldiers defending steep ravines and high ridges. Faced with defeat, the Japanese military tried to drive the Marines and Army defenders off the beach with a suicide attack, most of them screaming, "Wake up Americans, and die!" (*Suicide attacks* were mass-infantry Japanese assaults directed against American defensive positions without regard to casualties.)

Tinian

The Allies also captured the small island of Tinian. The Marines, with support from battleships and other warships, were able to drive the Japanese defenders into a corner of the island, where they were annihilated. The Marines faced the expected suicide attacks as well, but they held and secured the island after nine days of heavy fighting.

HISTORICAL TRIVIA

Tinian has the dubious distinction of being the first place where *napalm* (a mixture containing a thickening agent and gasoline) was used in combat. Napalm was used in fuel bombs that when detonated, exploded in fireballs, and then burned slowly and stuck to their targets, resulting in mass destruction or fatalities.

The Japanese Navy Weighs In: The Battle of the Philippine Sea

The Japanese plan called for a do-or-die defense by the army on the islands, while the navy attacked the American warships. Therefore, while the Saipan landings were going on in the Marianas Islands, the Japanese navy prepared to ambush the American fleet that supported the island landings.

**MILITARY
STRATEGY**

The Japanese fleet of 9 carriers — with nearly 500 aircraft, 5 battleships, 13 cruisers, and 28 destroyers — moved against the huge American fleet off Saipan, which had 15 carriers with over 950 aircraft, 7 battleships, 21 cruisers, and 69 destroyers. A major battle loomed. The winner would determine whether the Japanese or the Americans would dictate the tempo of operations in the Pacific for the rest of 1944. In fact, the commander of the Japanese fleet sent the following message to his ships: "This operation has immense bearing on the fate of the Empire."

The Marianas "Turkey Shoot"

On June 19, 1944, the Japanese had the Americans where they wanted them — focused on the Saipan landings, within range of the Japanese land-based aircraft, and vulnerable to strikes from carrier aircraft. In 1942, with the superbly trained naval aviators of the Imperial Japanese Navy, the Marianas would not have been a contest. But this was 1944; the experienced pilots were gone; the Japanese pilots who now flew against the American fleet were rookies, inexperienced and poorly trained. These pilots faced battle-hardened and experienced American pilots.

Almost as soon as the Japanese land-based aircraft took off, they were attacked and destroyed by clouds of American fighters protecting the fleet. Moreover, by the time the Japanese carrier planes arrived to make their attacks on the fleet, the Americans were ready and waiting. Because of their limited training, the brave Japanese pilots made basic errors in their attacks that left them easy targets. Those not shot right out of the air by American pilots fell to the massive antiaircraft fire sent up by the American battleships and carriers.

At the same time, American bombers hit the airfield on Guam to prevent the Japanese from using it as a base of operations. In eight hours, over 400 Japanese aircraft were shot down. The American fleet had no serious damage, and only 13 American pilots were lost. Because of the ease with which their targets had been hit, the Americans referred to it as a "Turkey Shoot." The name stuck.

Bad news for the Japanese fleet

While the Japanese air attacks met disaster, the Japanese fleet also faced ruin. First, American submarines, which had been shadowing the fleet and had given the Americans early warning, torpedoed two Japanese carriers. The Japanese commander didn't realize the extent of the disaster until late that night. Nevertheless, he readied his fleet for action the following day. The Americans located the fleet late in the afternoon and launched 240 carrier planes for a strike before it turned dark. The Japanese tried to outrun the attackers, but the American bombers and torpedo planes were able to sink one carrier and damage four others before breaking off the attack to return to the American carriers.

MacArthur's island hopping

While Nimitz pursued the eastern approach to the Philippines, General MacArthur pursued his own path for the southwest. Instead of open ocean, he faced a mass of large and small islands defended by large numbers of Japanese troops and supported by ships and aircraft from the major naval base at Rabaul (on New Britain Island). MacArthur had two choices:

>> Fight long, drawn-out, exhausting battles for territory, such as the New Guinea campaign to take Buna in 1942 (see Chapter 15 for details on this battle). This, of course, is what the Japanese hoped he would do. The Japanese were prepared to use naval and air power to support the land forces defending key areas and make the Americans pay for every foot of ground.

>> Use the leverage that he had with his own naval and air power to strike where he chose and put ground forces where the Japanese didn't expect them to be.

The objective of MacArthur's campaign was not to capture the heavily defended and well protected Japanese positions; his mission was to control those areas of land and water that would let the Americans establish bases for further operations against Japanese forces in New Guinea, the Solomons, and the Bismarck Sea. Achieving his goal often meant that MacArthur had to avoid direct battles and bypass large numbers of Japanese forces. This pursuit of decisive points over enemy forces came to be known as *island hopping*.

Kicking Off the New Guinea Campaign

After their defeat at Buna in 1942, the Japanese were hardly willing to give up on New Guinea, which had excellent harbors and good locations for airfields and supply bases. New Guinea also served to protect the main air and naval base at Rabaul on the island of New Britain. Thus, in early 1944, the Japanese sent a large number of reinforcements to New Guinea to establish strong defensible positions to hold off any possible attacks. This strategy was sound, but it was based on two assumptions:

>> The Japanese aircraft and navy from the base at Rabaul would support their defense of New Guinea.

>> The range of American aircraft would be limited.

MacArthur's strategy made a mess of these two assumptions. Between January and February, American forces pushed in two directions:

>> The Marines moved up the Solomon Islands and secured island bases, including a base less than 200 miles from Rabaul.

>> American aircraft were being equipped with external fuel tanks, which allowed them to support MacArthur's long-range attacks.

>> The Army began to make attacks up the coast of New Guinea with the intention of putting American forces between the Japanese defenders in New Guinea and their support base in Rabaul.

With every base captured, American planes flew strikes against Japanese garrisons throughout the area, and American carrier aircraft ranged freely, attacking Japanese ships and shooting down large numbers of Japanese aircraft.

Rabaul is encircled

While the Japanese looked to the south for an attack, General MacArthur struck from an unexpected direction and captured a key airfield on the Admiralty Islands north of Rabaul in late February. The Japanese, taken by surprise, couldn't do anything. Besides, the Japanese faced another problem. At the beginning of March, U.S. forces landed on the far tip of New Britain, the island where Rabaul was located (refer to Figure 19-1).

Outmaneuvered, the Japanese ground troops retreated toward Rabaul, but they quickly found themselves trapped on the narrow neck of land near the Japanese base. At this point, Australian troops moved in and served as the cork in the bottle, trapping nearly 100,000 troops on the island. Now without air or naval support, the Japanese lingered on ineffectively until they surrendered in 1945.

Dominating the air: Hollandia

MacArthur now turned to New Guinea, a place where nobody wanted to fight. Heavy jungles, high mountains, and terrible weather made it miserable for both attacker and defender. As defenders, however, the Japanese had the advantage:

>> They could select the best places to dig in and await an attack.

>> In defending the coast, they presented the Americans and Australians with the prospect of taking heavy losses if they attempted an amphibious landing.

Anticipating a major land assault, the Japanese commander reinforced his defenses further down the coast by moving most of the ground troops from the airbase and supply field at Hollandia (located about halfway up the northern coast of New Guinea) to the beach. As a result, the Japanese supply base and airfield were left largely undefended. The Japanese were not overly concerned about this, though: They believed that the base was secure from attack because of the limited range of American aircraft. The Japanese, however, had miscalculated.

With the Australians pushing up the New Guinea coast to fool the Japanese into believing that this was the expected main attack, MacArthur struck Hollandia in April 1944. The Japanese defenders there were shocked to see American bombers escorted by fighters, which supposedly couldn't carry enough fuel to get them this far (the fighters had been equipped with extra gas tanks). Following the fighters came hundreds of carrier aircraft that hit Japanese planes parked on the ground. In a few short hours, 500 Japanese aircraft were destroyed.

With American dominance of the air, American troops landed at Hollandia and moved to capture the supply base and the five airfields in the area. More U.S. troops pressed south along the coast, trapping 50,000 Japanese soldiers between them and the Australians advancing up the coast. The Japanese had nowhere to go: The mountains and jungles and Allied troops hemmed them in.

ARMY ALLIED

With the United States Navy in full control of the sea and the U.S. 15th Air Force in control of the skies, the Japanese were essentially beaten. Like the defenders at Rabaul, the Japanese defenders of New Guinea would languish in the terrible jungle for months, facing starvation or surrender. For them, the war was over.

Controlling the sea: Biak

With the air bases at Hollandia in his hands, MacArthur turned toward the far tip of New Guinea to the airbase on the island of Biak, 225 miles northeast of Hollandia. Biak was important for two reasons:

>> It had three airfields big enough to support the heavy bombers of the Fifteenth Air Force. With these airfields, the Allies could extend their range to strike the Dutch East Indies, the Philippines, and Saipan (which Nimitz was about to attack in June).

>> It was the last Japanese base that threatened MacArthur's planned advance to the Philippines.

The Battle of Biak, which began on May 27, 1944, was similar to Saipan in many ways: The troops landed unopposed but then faced intense combat against well-prepared Japanese soldiers hidden in caves and in positions dug into steep valleys.

Over 28,000 Americans landed to capture the island from 11,000 Japanese defenders. MacArthur claimed that the island had been taken on June 3, but in reality, the real battle for the island had just begun. It took ten weeks to eliminate the defenders and prepare the island for the heavy bombers.

Biak gave MacArthur control of the air and sea around New Guinea and left more than 200,000 Japanese troops stranded. Over 1,000 Japanese aircraft had been destroyed, and 300 ships had been sunk or damaged.

Same old mistakes: Peleliu

The island of Peleliu in the Palau Islands, about 800 miles southwest of Guam, was only about six miles long. But it had an excellent airfield, one that Nimitz believed was needed to support a future attack on the Philippines. Because MacArthur and Nimitz had made far better progress than expected, the order came from Washington to initiate the attack on the Philippines in October, nearly two months earlier than planned. This change in plans meant that Peleliu's airfield wasn't needed.

The island could have been bypassed without much trouble, but the attack (supported by 800 ships with an Army division and the fabled First Marine Division from Guadalcanal; see Chapter 15) went on anyway. All the problems of Tarawa seemed to come back to haunt the Marines.

» The naval bombardment and air attacks that were to have destroyed most of the Japanese defenders failed to do any damage.

» The 10,500 Japanese defenders were prepared to hold out to the last man.

Peleliu was different from Tarawa in one respect: It was a coral island with many caves, which only served to make it harder to capture.

The Marines landed on September 15 and ran into a buzz saw that chewed up units quickly. At a coral outcropping called *"Bloody Nose Ridge,"* Marines fought the Japanese at close range day after day with no end in sight. The Army division landed and finally completed the terrible task of rooting each and every enemy soldier out of his defensive position. No suicide attacks occurred at Peleliu; the Japanese no longer wanted to be such convenient targets for the Americans.

Instead, they stayed in their positions in order to kill as many Americans as possible before they themselves died. The Japanese soldiers' willingness to die rather surrender made the island much harder to capture. It took nearly four weeks of exhausting effort to eliminate all resistance.

ARMY ALLIED

Peleliu was a costly victory, with 8,000 American casualties, equal to the losses at Tarawa. By the time that the Americans had captured the island, the spotlight had already moved to the drama on display in the Philippines. Peleliu had been forgotten.

Preparing to Take Leyte

While American Admiral "Bull" Halsey's 3rd Fleet's carrier planes attacked key locations on the Philippines, MacArthur and Nimitz began planning in early September 1944 for their joint attack in October. The news from Halsey's pilots was encouraging. A large number of Japanese planes had been destroyed, and the enemy seemed completely unprepared for an attack. Halsey was both right — and wrong — for the following reasons:

>> He was right in reporting that the Japanese were unprepared, especially in some of the smaller islands, such as Leyte (where MacArthur intended to make the initial landings).

>> He was wrong in believing that MacArthur would not need the dedicated air cover for all his carrier aircraft.

During the invasion, when MacArthur needed air cover the most, Halsey reduced the number of planes available to the Army, which was a mistake for the following reasons:

>> The 270,000 defenders under Japanese General Tomoyoku Yamashida were building airstrips to receive additional aircraft.

>> The Japanese were also building defenses on the main island of Luzon, the location of the capital city of Manila.

>> In the vicinity was the Japanese fleet, with what was left of its carrier aircraft.

The Japanese defense plan was this: While the ground forces punished the American invasion force, the fleet would attack and destroy the American ships protecting and supporting the landings. The Philippines appeared to be the perfect battleground for the Japanese strategy.

Like the Americans, the Japanese made a major mistake as well: Torpedo planes attacking Halsey's ships claimed to have sunk half his fleet, when only two cruisers had been damaged. This inaccuracy led the Japanese to believe that they could easily defeat the Americans on the beaches when they landed. Unfortunately for the Japanese, they guessed wrong.

MacArthur returns

MacArthur chose Leyte, a small narrow island sitting roughly in the center of the Philippine islands, because it would serve as a giant aircraft carrier. As he had done in New Guinea (see the earlier section "Dominating the air: Hollandia"), MacArthur captured territory to establish air bases from which he could then move infantry forward under the protection of American air cover.

On October 19, 1944, nearly 700 Allied ships and transports arrived off the coast of Leyte carrying 175,000 American soldiers. The next day, after heavy naval bombardment and massive naval airstrikes, 50,000 more American troops landed. A few hours later, General MacArthur and his staff, along with the president of the Philippines, walked through the surf 50 yards from the open ramp of a landing craft to the beach. "I have returned," MacArthur said simply.

Although the Americans made good initial progress, bad weather slowed the attack and prevented the engineers from building the airstrips for the 15th Air Force needed to provide air cover for the infantry. The Japanese took advantage of the weather and sent ground reinforcements to Leyte and conducted air attacks from their own operational bases on Luzon.

American Admiral Halsey had reduced the number of carriers supporting MacArthur because he had discovered a Japanese carrier force and was eager to get after them. Meanwhile, the Americans continued to battle a disorganized but determined enemy force in the hills of Leyte.

The Battle of Leyte Gulf

The Japanese navy committed itself to a final showdown with the Americans and divided its fleet into three groups:

>> **The decoy.** The first strike group was the decoy with all the carriers and what was left of their aircraft. It was meant to be a target so inviting that it would pull Admiral "Bull" Halsey's fleet away from its support to Leyte and give chase.

>> **The northern strike group.** As the decoy drew Halsey's fleet away, the northern strike group with over 30 ships, including two of the largest battle-ships ever built, would come from the north of Leyte.

>> **The southern strike group.** A southern strike group with seven ships supported by a group of seven additional ships would sneak in south of Leyte.

The two real strike groups would meet in the middle — in Leyte Gulf, off the island of Leyte, where hundreds of vulnerable American supply and support ships were anchored — and destroy these ships and any warships protecting them. Such a stroke would cripple the United States fleet, perhaps permanently, and isolate thousands of American troops on Leyte, where they could be destroyed by superior numbers. For the Japanese plan to work, Halsey had to take the bait.

Halsey takes the bait

The Japanese northern strike group ran into trouble early, losing several ships to American submarines on October 23, 1944, but they plowed onward. On October 24, as the group began its transit through the straits, it was hit several times by Halsey's carrier planes, which damaged several ships and sank one of the massive battleships. Planes also damaged ships from the Japanese southern strike group, giving the Americans advance warning of the fleet's approach to Leyte. Japanese planes from Luzon attacked and heavily damaged one American carrier, which later sank.

Convinced that the ships his planes hit were nothing more than an escort for the Japanese carriers and were no longer a danger, Halsey took his fastest carriers and battleships on a wild goose chase for several hundred miles to track down the Japanese decoy: the four carriers that had been spotted far to the northeast. Mean-while, the southern strike group continued toward Leyte (see Figure 19-2).

A wild night off Leyte: The Allies repel the Japanese

The Japanese southern strike group of two battleships, one cruiser, and four destroyers steamed into the straits off Leyte, just as planned, with the support-ing group of three cruisers and four destroyers following. They ran into 39 small torpedo boats that gave advanced warning to the American collection of 28 destroyers, 6 cruisers, and 6 battleships that waited for them in the Surigao Strait.

ARMY ALLIED

But the American battleships were quite special: All but one had been at Pearl Harbor on December 7, 1941, and each one had been damaged by Japanese bombs or torpedoes on that day. Two of the group of six battleships, the *West Virginia* and the *Tennessee,* had been anchored behind the *Arizona,* which sank with over 1,000 men on board. Both had taken several hits from Japanese bombs and torpedoes.

Now, here they were, nearly three years later, facing Japanese ships in a combat action for which they had been designed and built. The combined gunfire of the Peal Harbor survivors destroyed the Japanese strike force so completely that the other seven ships following in support retreated and played no part in the battle.

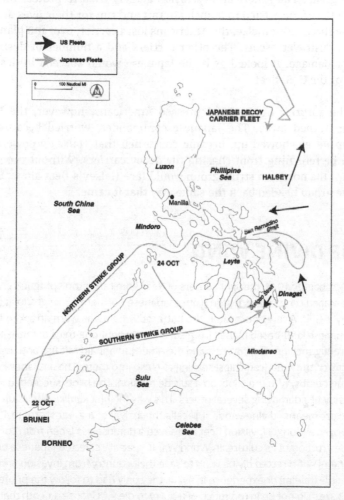

A wilder morning off Leyte: The Japanese surprise the Allies

At dawn on October 25, the Japanese northern strike group made its approach to link up with the southern strike force in Leyte Gulf. (The Japanese commander didn't know that the southern strike force had been destroyed the night before.) The northern strike group surprised a group of small American escort carriers and destroyers that supported the Leyte landing operations. The Americans, who thought that Halsey was still watching the northern approaches, were caught unawares.

A mad scramble ensued as the Japanese warships tried to catch and destroy the little group. The American destroyers gamely tried to protect the little carriers, while the carriers tried to launch aircraft and run for their lives at the same time. In the three-hour melee, the Americans lost 1 carrier, over 100 planes, 1 destroyer, and 1 destroyer escort. The other carriers and a number of destroyers suffered major damage. It looked as if the Japanese would succeed in destroying a good part of the U. S. fleet.

To the surprise of the hard-pressed Americans, however, the Japanese strike group turned away. The Japanese commander, worried because the southern group never showed up, became concerned that Halsey's powerful fleet would soon be returning from chasing the decoy carriers. Without the southern strike group, the northern strike group would face Halsey's fleet alone. So the Japanese strike group headed back the same way that it came.

THE DIVINE WIND

On October 25, 1944, the light carriers of Rear Admiral Clifton Sprague's group had just escaped certain destruction from a Japanese northern strike group at the Battle of Leyte Gulf. A few hours later, the battered Americans were attacked by about 60 Japanese land-based planes from Luzon. But about one-third of these planes acted differently, making no effort to avoid the American antiaircraft fire and bearing down directly on the American ships, seeking to crash into them. The airplanes had become human bombs, with the pilots on a suicide mission. The pilots succeeded in sinking one carrier, while damaging several others. This was the first *kamikaze* mission. In Japanese, *kamikaze* means "divine wind." It recalls the arrival of a great storm in 1281 that destroyed a Mongol invasion fleet and saved a defenseless Japan from conquest and the destruction of its culture. In World War II, specially selected Japanese pilots acted as Japan's self-directed divine wind to save their country from invasion and conquest. With little training or experience in flying, they only had to follow the prime rule of the kamikaze: "Do not be in too much of a hurry to die . . . Choose a death that creates a maximum result."

The *kamikaze* attacks severely damaged a number of ships, including three carriers from Halsey's fleet, during the battle for the Philippines. To protect U.S. carriers from kamikaze attack, many American planes were taken from ground support missions, limiting MacArthur's ability to move against the Japanese. The *kamikazes* continued to pose a major threat to naval operations for the rest of the war and highlighted the determination of the Japanese to fight for their land to the last man.

Halsey's carrier aircraft, which had arrived late in the day, harassed and harried the retreating Japanese group and continued to attack the next day. The Japanese lost three destroyers and a cruiser in their escape.

The result

HISTORICAL TRIVIA

The Battle of Leyte Gulf, as these three engagements are collectively known, was the largest naval battle in modern history. Japan lost 4 carriers, 3 battleships, 10 cruisers, 12 destroyers, and nearly 10,000 men. The Americans lost 1 fleet carrier, 3 light carriers, 4 destroyers, and 3,000 men.

The power of the Japanese navy had been broken once and for all. Crippled by losses and lack of fuel, the remainder of the once-proud fleet could only stand by helplessly as the Americans dominated the ocean. With the last of their carriers gone, the Japanese could no longer challenge American pilots to protect Japanese troops defending Pacific islands. The Battle of Leyte assured the defeat of Japan.

MacArthur: Bogged down in Leyte

American General MacArthur's army ran into severe weather that slowed operations and prevented several airfields from being used. The Japanese also decided to fight for Leyte, reinforcing the island with 20,000 additional soldiers, including some of the best units in the Japanese army. By November 1944, Leyte was drawing the last resources of the Japanese Empire. Another 1,000 combat aircraft arrived, and transport ships arrived to ferry reinforcements and supplies to the Japanese defenders. However, the Japanese suffered terrible losses as the Americans bombed airfields and attacked ships. Allied air and naval dominance allowed the Americans to land troops virtually anywhere on the island (essentially forcing the Japanese to fight in two directions) and bring reinforcements to isolated key areas so American bombers and fighters could attack Japanese defensive positions.

A hard won victory

By late December, American infantry had broken Japanese defenses in the mountains and driven them into an isolated finger of land. The Japanese were no longer a combat-effective force.

The situation had been a mess — the weather had been terrible, the Japanese had fought stubbornly and skillfully, and the trails and mountains were treacherous. American losses for the three- month campaign amounted to 12,000 killed and wounded. The Japanese lost over 56,000 men. Only 389 Japanese soldiers were captured. These losses don't include the 40,000 Japanese soldiers who drowned when their ships were sunk.

Aftermath of Leyte: Marching on Mindoro

Two weeks before Leyte was declared conquered, MacArthur was already setting the stage for the attack on the main island of Luzon. Frustrated at weather delays and Japanese resistance, he realized that Leyte was not going to be suitable as an airbase to support the invasion. MacArthur sought another island to serve that purpose and decided on Mindoro, the large island only 100 miles south of the capital city of Manila and 300 miles northwest of Leyte. Philippine guerrillas, including some American survivors of the 1942 Battle for Bataan (see Chapter 8), assisted in capturing key landing sites for the invasion force. The landing was accomplished without casualties, and construction of three airfields began right away. By December 20, aircraft were on their way to targets throughout Luzon. The Japanese continued to suffer heavy losses of aircraft and ships while MacArthur built up his forces for the decisive attack to free the Philippines.

Operations in the Pacific: An Appreciation

Air and sea power were the keys to American victory in the Pacific in 1944. By 1943, the United States Navy had not only replaced all the ships it lost in 1942, but it had added hundreds more, leaving the Japanese completely outnumbered and outgunned. In addition, American factories were producing combat aircraft at a rate of 8,000 per month in 1944, completely dwarfing Japanese production. By 1944, the Japanese could no longer match the skill of American naval aviators or the quality of their new aircraft.

REMEMBER

In addition to air and naval superiority, the American two-pronged strategy in the Pacific froze the Japanese in place. Having to defend against MacArthur and Nimitz at the same time forced Japanese ground and naval commanders to spread themselves too thin and forced them to shift their focus from one area to the next. The Japanese never knew where the next attack would come, nor did they appreciate the speed with which the Americans were able to mount large-scale offensives. Thus, they were often caught by surprise.

Dependent on merchant ships for reinforcement and supply, the Japanese were vulnerable to supply shortages simply because these ships were not able to move freely throughout the Pacific. In fact, by the end of 1944, supply became a serious problem, and Japan's ability to continue the war was crippled as American submarines sank more than half the Japanese merchant marine fleet.

In general, General MacArthur and Admiral Nimitz outflanked, outran, and outfought the Japanese by doing three things well:

>> **They neutralized Japanese air power.** Without control of the air, the Japanese defensive strategy was ineffective. Before any Allied advance took place, MacArthur and Nimitz made sure to eliminate land-based aircraft and seize key airfields.

>> **They isolated Japanese ground forces.** Although stronger in numbers than the Allies, Japanese ground troops were often in the wrong places to do any good. Rather than attack force on force, MacArthur and Nimitz first cut off large concentrations of troops from support by use of land, sea, and air forces.

>> **They employed the ground/air/navy team.** In the Pacific, no force could conduct successful combat operations alone. No ground force moved against the enemy without complete control of the air. Likewise, naval forces always backed the ground attack and could operate offshore protected by aircraft. Combining the capabilities of the team allowed the Allies to move faster and strike harder than the Japanese.

When all was said and done, though, the Japanese were still not beaten. The warrior code of the Japanese soldier, sailor, and airman remained as strong as ever. The code that looked upon surrender as the greatest dishonor and upon death in combat as eternal glory made him a formidable foe. As the Japanese commander at Saipan told his troops before the battle, "I will advance with those who remain to deliver still another blow to the American Devils and leave my bones on Saipan as a bulwark of the Pacific." American soldiers and Marines knew all too well what he meant. No battle against such men would ever be easy.

The China-Burma-India Theater

After the disaster of 1942 that drove the Allies out of Burma (see Chapter 8 for details), the plan had always been to go back, but politics played an important role in this theater: Great Britain was far less interested in keeping China in the war than it was in preventing an outright pro-Japanese rebellion in India. Chinese leader Chiang Kai-shek and the Chinese Nationalist government seemed to be doing their best to do little more than consume supplies.

Stuck between the Chinese and the British was American General Joseph Stilwell, who served as Chief of Staff of the Chinese Nationalist Army and Deputy Commander to Vice Admiral Lord Louis Mountbatten, Commander in Chief of

Southeast Asia. Stilwell spoke Chinese fluently and was one of the most capable American field soldiers in the war. He did not suffer fools gladly, had little use for the British, and was completely disgusted with Chiang Kaishek's leadership, especially his toleration of corruption. He also never hesitated to make his opinions known. "Vinegar Joe" was his nickname, for good reason.

Little happened in China and Burma because this theater always lacked sufficient resources to initiate a major campaign, and the terrain (high mountains, heavy jungle, and few roads) was exceptionally difficult to conduct large-scale operations in and supply forces in combat (see Figure 19-3).

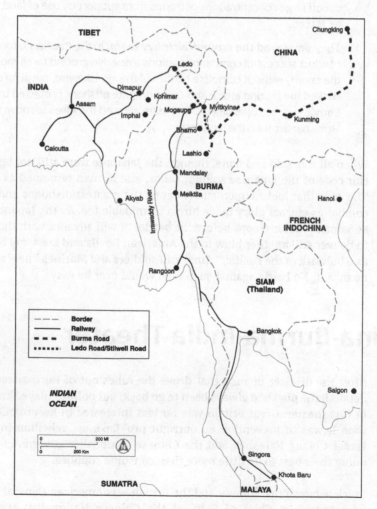

FIGURE 19-3: The campaign in Burma and India, 1944–1945.

Allied Hit and Runs in Burma

In China, Burma, and India, the Allies relied on small expeditions rather than large scale attacks to attain their objectives. Burma essentially became the testing ground for such strategies, and the success of the Chindits (see the following section) inspired other small groups to think big.

British General Wingate and the Chindits

The Allies satisfied themselves in 1943 with small unit operations, led by British General Orde Wingate, against Japanese rail lines. These small units were called *Chindits* (a corruption of the Burmese word *chinthe*, the statues of winged lions that guard Buddhist temples). Made up of British, Burmese, and Gurkha troops, the Chindits struck Japanese rear areas in Burma in February 1943. The 3,000-man force was initially successful, but the lightly armed Chindits couldn't sustain any long-term damage. Pressed hard by the Japanese, they escaped by foot over 1,000 miles back to India.

In 1944, 20,000 Chindits landed behind Japanese lines in gliders and built short landing strips in the jungle for resupply. They then began to cut rail lines behind Japanese lines. The Japanese drove the Chindits into the mountains, but disease and combat wounds had reduced the brave Chindits by 5,000 men. Killed in a plane crash, General Wingate was among those lost.

All in all, Wingate's Chindits made an important contribution to the war in Burma. They tied up large numbers of Japanese troops and inflicted significant casualties. The Japanese never knew where the Chindits were coming from or where they would go next. The Chindits proved that a small group of well-trained soldiers could accomplish strategic results against a larger enemy force.

Chinese troops and Merill's Marauders

Taking a page from Wingate's innovative Chindit concept, a 3,000-man American volunteer unit was formed to fight in Burma. Codenamed GALAHAD, the unit became better known as Merrill's Marauders, after its commander General Frank D. Merrill.

The American unit would join Stilwell's Chinese division in an offensive against the Japanese. Stilwell was eager to prove that well-trained and well-led Chinese troops could contribute to the war. Stilwell had supervised the training of a Chinese division in India, and in February 1944, he moved against the Japanese in Burma, with the support of the Marauders.

The Chinese succeeded in driving the Japanese back, and the Americans maneuvered around and behind the enemy, forcing them to retreat. In effect, the Allied soldiers were using the same tactics that the Japanese used so effectively against the British in 1941 and 1942 when they rapidly conquered Burma and Malaya (see Chapter 8).

Supplied entirely by air, the small Allied force reached the key town of Myitkyina, Burma, in May 1944, after three months of fighting over 150 miles through rugged terrain and appalling conditions. The town of Myitkyina had the best airfield in north Burma and was the last station on the main railroad from Rangoon. Capture of this town would break the Japanese stranglehold on China by allowing direct supply flights to the Nationalists.

Although they captured the airfield, the Chinese troops were too exhausted by battle and disease to do much more. Stilwell flew reinforcements and supplies by air and fought on until August, when the Japanese withdrew. Five thousand Allied soldiers had been killed and wounded; the Japanese lost about 3,000. From Myitkyina, Stilwell could send more supply flights to China and could begin building an overland supply route to Chiang's Nationalist forces.

The Japanese Tip the Balance in China

One ongoing problem was how to keep China in the war long enough for American forces to win the war in the Pacific. Chiang was content to hold where he was and wait it out, knowing that President Roosevelt was committed to supporting China. Chiang tried to keep up appearances of meaningful action against the Japanese by calling loudly and often for support for his armies. Most of the supplies never reached the Chinese soldiers, however, after corrupt officers took their cut.

Regardless of the seeming futility, the only way to supply the Chinese was by air over the Himalayas — the world's highest mountains — to a series of airfields built to accommodate combat aircraft. Looking toward the future struggle with the Chinese Communists (who had no air power), Chiang liked the idea of the airfields lined with fighters and bombers.

Unfortunately, the airfields also served as a magnet for the Japanese, who had no intention of allowing Allied air power to dominate the skies over China. In April 1944, the Japanese opened a crushing offensive against the Chinese Nationalists to capture the airfields. In the process, they inflicted 300,000 casualties and effectively ended any possibility of an Allied air threat. Morale collapsed in the Nationalist army, leaving Chiang powerless to do little else but avoid angering the Japanese again.

Stirring Up Trouble: The Japanese Offensive against India

The Japanese in Burma decided to invade India. Having little respect for the British or Indian forces, the Japanese reasoned that a breakthrough into India would lead to an all-out rebellion by the various Indian ethnic groups against British rule. Such a situation would certainly cripple the British war effort and lay a deathblow to the British Empire in Asia.

In March 1944, 100,000 Japanese troops, tanks, and artillery crossed the Chindwin River on a makeshift bridge of boats. They had no supply line; the troops carried everything they would need to sustain combat for 28 days. The message was clear — conquer or die. There was no turning back.

The Japanese targets were the cities of Imphal and Kohima. The Japanese counted on taking these important bases for two reasons:

>> With Imphal and Kohima, they could get the supplies they needed for their westward advance.

>> The capture of Imphal and Kohima also meant that the Allies would have to abandon the Assam railway, which provided supplies to the entire Allied front line and Stilwell's troops currently fighting in Burma. Assam also served as the base for the Chinese supply line over the Himalayas. Beyond the rail line was India.

By April, both towns were under attack by the Japanese.

Battle at Imphal

At Imphal, three divisions of British-Indian soldiers fought for 86 days against desperate Japanese attacks. Even as their supplies dwindled, the Japanese fought on. The British held on only because of the effort to resupply them with supplies and replacements by air. During the long drawn-out battle, 13,000 troops and nearly as many tons of food, ammunition, and fuel arrived to sustain the battle. The Japanese, weakened by losses and starvation, were forced to retreat after a major counterattack.

Battle at Kohima

At Kohima, only about 1,500 men were under British Colonel Hugh Richards, a member of the Chindits and an experienced combat leader. Richards had to defend the little town from the onslaught of 12,000 Japanese soldiers.

The hills around Kohima became British strongholds as the Japanese surrounded Kohima and tried to overwhelm the defenders. The British and Indian troops held out for several days, but the Japanese forced them onto a single hill. From this hill, the Allies threw back the Japanese in brutal hand-to-hand fighting.

Just when it appeared that Richards and his surviving soldiers couldn't withstand another attack, reinforcements from the British Second Infantry Division arrived to break the siege. Now the British had to drive the Japanese defenders from the hills that they had captured in previous fighting. In late April, the monsoons began, making the battlefield a quagmire. In the mud and rain, British and Indian soldiers fought dug-in Japanese defenders foot by foot up steep hills with artillery, flamethrowers, tanks, and air strikes.

By early May, the Japanese defenses at Kohima breached. Still, despite starvation and disease, the Japanese fought to the last man. The survivors were ordered to retreat. They joined the defeated remnants of the two divisions that fought at Imphal. When the Japanese crossed the Chindwin River again, they did not resemble an army, and 60,000 Japanese casualties had been left behind. The British and Indian units had lost 17,500 casualties.

The End of the Line in Burma: Good-bye to Stilwell and the Japanese

General Stilwell and his Allied forces were still fighting the Japanese in Myitkyina while the British and Indian forces were fighting at Imphal and Kohima (see the preceding section). The retreat of the Japanese from India set the stage for the British to begin a new offensive to retake Burma. Ironically, both the Japanese and the man who helped the Chinese repel the Japanese got booted out of China. General Stilwell came to the end of the line in late 1944; the end came for the Japanese in early 1945.

A victim of politics: Exit Vinegar Joe

Stilwell could claim the following successes:

» His victory at Myitkyina opened a shorter air route to China and gave engineers the opportunity to build an overland supply route and an oil pipeline from Ledo in Burma to Kunming in China. It would be a monumental feat of skill that would eventually bear Stilwell's name.

» He had proven the effectiveness of well-led and well-trained Chinese soldiers in Burma.

Stilwell was planning to drive the Japanese from north Burma in October, but his time was up. For years, he had been hectoring Chiang Kai-shek to reform the Chinese Nationalist Army and eliminate corrupt leaders before it was too late. Chiang did not act on Stilwell's advice and found his straightforward manner a little too discomforting.

With the unwitting help of the Japanese, Chiang found a way to remove Stilwell from China.

The Japanese attack on the American airfields in eastern China and their advance on the Chinese capital of Chungking pushed the Chinese to near collapse in the early fall of 1944. The Chinese army was totally ineffective; unless something was done quickly, Japan could finally conquer China. With the backing of his military advisors, President Roosevelt urged Chiang Kai-shek to put Stilwell in direct command of Chinese land forces, supported by the American 14th Air Force in China. Chiang agreed, but on the condition that Stilwell left. Ever mindful of political sensitivities, Roosevelt conceded and sent another General (General Albert C. Wedemeyer) to take Stilwell's place in China. The blunt but truthful Stilwell was gone.

Ironically, Wedemeyer found that he couldn't make much headway against the Japanese. To solve the problem, he brought from Burma the Chinese divisions that Stilwell trained (see the earlier section "Chinese troops and Merill's Marauders"). These troops were finally able to stabilize the Chinese front.

Breaking Japanese resistance: Clearing Burma

The hard task of ending Japanese resistance in Burma fell to the British Fourteenth Army. The British offensive, under the command of Lieutenant General Sir William Slim, began in November 1944. Slim used armored maneuver, deception, and air power to outflank and outfight the Japanese defenders and push them steadily back into the narrow peninsula where Rangoon was located. The British gained a great advantage when the Burma National Army revolted and joined Slim's forces.

ARMY ALLIED

Slim used amphibious landings to trap and isolate Japanese forces while his troops were supplied largely by air. Slim captured key airfields by bringing in infantry by aircraft. The Japanese, lacking support and adequate supplies, could only fight a delaying battle. With the fall of Meiktila in March 1945, the capture of Rangoon was assured. The surviving Japanese forces retreated into Thailand, and Rangoon fell into British hands on May 3, 1945.

6

Starting Over: The War's Aftereffects, 1945

Find out what makes World War II important today?

Understand how World War II solved some real threats to the progress of civilization.

Recognize the new challenges and dangers raised by World War II.

Appreciate how the Allied victory remains the defining event of the twentieth century.

Chapter **20**

Ending the War (Almost): The Final Offensive

After the Battle of the Bulge (see Chapter 18), the Allies had one last barrier to cross — the Rhine River. By chance and by design, Allied forces jumped the river and entered Germany. They eliminated the last pockets of resistance as they drove into central Germany and Czechoslovakia. The Allies finally broke out into the broad plains of northern Italy, and the bombing campaign reached new heights of destruction. As Supreme Allied Commander, American General Dwight Eisenhower made a crucial decision concerning the stopping point for American, British, and Canadian forces in Germany.

From the east, the Soviets were making the final approach as well, battling fierce resistance to reach Berlin. In Berlin, Hitler, finally facing the terrible truth, ended his life with a curse on the Jews, the Bolsheviks, and the German people who had failed him.

As war in Europe came to an end, the politicians took center stage. America took a heavy blow with the death of President Franklin Roosevelt. An untried political operator from Missouri became the new president — and had to craft a postwar settlement with the likes of Russian leader Joseph Stalin and British Prime Minister Winston Churchill. The pall of what would become the Cold War began to creep over the landscape of Europe.

The Allies Cross the Rhine, the Germans Turn a Corner

January 1945 opened with the Allies pushing the remaining German forces out of the Bulge, the relatively small area that the Germans claimed in their offensive through the Ardennes Forest (see Chapter 18 for more information about this battle). The Allies then began to push forward to the Rhine River and Germany just beyond (see Figure 20-1).

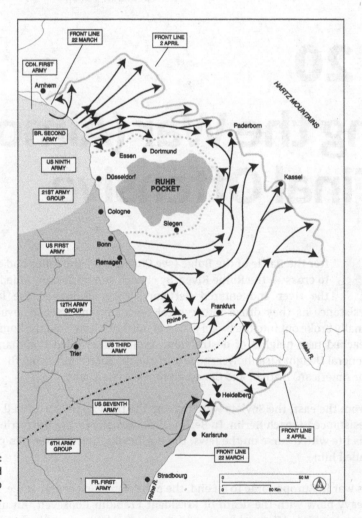

FIGURE 20-1: The Allied advance into Germany.

Can't someone shut this guy up? — Hitler tries again

Even though the Ardennes offensive was clearly lost, Hitler tried to revive it. On New Year's Eve 1944, Hitler ordered the last reserve army in the west to recapture Strasburg and link up with the German forces holding Colmar. He believed that this action would pull American forces south, allowing the German forces in the Bulge to resume the offensive. Hitler's strategy made no sense (for the German army, nothing made sense any more), and the generals protested, but to no avail. The French stopped the German attack at Strasburg. The Americans gave ground and let the German attack fizzle out before they counterattacked.

This wasted effort did the following:

>> It cost the Germans 25,000 men (the Allies lost 16,000).

>> It allowed the French 1st Army to eliminate German forces at Colmar.

>> It enabled the Allies to drive to the west bank of the Rhine, where they controlled the area from Strasburg to the Swiss border.

By the end of 1944, German losses in the West amounted to 1 million men.

Another bridge awaits: Pushing the river

General Eisenhower pushed the armies of British General Bernard Montgomery and American General Omar Bradley forward to the Rhine. Montgomery's Twenty-First Army Group — along with British, Canadian, and U.S. forces — advanced. With the help of massive Allied air attacks that cut German road and rail networks, the Army Group isolated German defenders.

The Rhine River was a formidable obstacle, both physically and psychologically:

>> Physically, the Rhine was wide and powerful and flowed past high banks and granite cliffs. No enemy had successfully crossed the Rhine to invade Germany since Napoleon.

>> Psychologically, the Rhine represented Germany's will to resist.

The Allies couldn't cross the Rhine without a major bridge. (In fact, Montgomery's ill-fated MARKET GARDEN operation had been an attempt to capture bridges along the Rhine; see Chapter 18 for details.) As Montgomery and Bradley's forces moved steadily toward the Rhine, Hitler kept his forces fighting in front of the river. At the last minute, Hitler gave the order to destroy all the bridges that ran across it. All of the bridges fell — except one.

A tale of two crossings

Upon reaching the Rhine River, Field Marshal Montgomery, as usual, developed an elaborate plan to mount a crossing. He had nearly 60,000 engineers and a quarter of a million tons of supplies assembled for the job. About 125 miles south, General Patton searched for his own crossing site after trapping thousands of Germans between his forces and the Rhine. (Hitler's no retreat orders again had played into American hands.) In the middle, between Patton and Montgomery, was the 1st Army under American General Courtney Hodges.

The crossing at Remagen

On March 7, 1945, at the little town of Remagen, one of Hodges's leading units found an intact bridge over the Rhine. General Eisenhower ordered Hodges to push everything he could across the bridge and establish a strong defensive position on the other side.

Hitler sent the Me 262 jet fighter-bombers and V-2 rockets in an unsuccessful attempt to destroy the bridge before the Americans could cross in strength (see Chapter 25 for info on these weapons). Although the old railroad bridge lasted only 10 days before it collapsed from bombing damage and the passage of thousands of tanks, trucks, and troops, it was enough time to eliminate the Rhine River as the last great barrier to the German heartland. Oddly enough, neither General Eisenhower nor General Bradley did anything with this advantage. They were content to await Field Marshal Montgomery's long-planned, big show.

Patton and then Montgomery cross

Two weeks later, General Montgomery and General Patton crossed the Rhine as well. General Eisenhower had given Montgomery's army the priority for the advance into Germany, expecting to link up with the Soviet Army somewhere near Berlin.

The Germans: Down but not out

The operations in the first three months of 1945 had been devastating for the Germans. The losses in killed, wounded, and captured soldiers mounted into the hundreds of thousands. The German army appeared to be in a state of collapse. Many soldiers simply disappeared, donning civilian clothes and heading home. Others, unwilling to fight or die for a losing cause any longer, refused to obey orders and gave up at the earliest opportunity. But often at the most unexpected times, German soldiers displayed incredible resiliency, striking just as hard and as effectively as they always had. The battle for Germany wouldn't be a cakewalk.

The Soviets Move Forward

The Soviets had held at the Vistula River in Poland since October 1944, mostly because of the need to refit, reorganize, and resupply (see Chapter 18). The Germans used this time to focus on the British and Americans in the west. The Germans also built defenses and restored divisions in preparation for the coming Soviet attack.

Regaining Hungary

The Soviets renewed their attack in Hungary to capture Budapest. Hitler directed an offensive to relieve the trapped defenders in the city, but his offensive failed, mostly because he ordered units that had just been pulled out of the Battle of the Bulge back into another fight.

As in the Battle of the Bulge, the Germans made some initial advances, but could go no further. With only the last 600 tanks available from the reserve, the Germans were crushed in the Soviet counterattack. By the end of March 1945, Hungary was largely in the hands of the Soviet Army, and Vienna was only a few miles away.

Clearing the way to Berlin

On the central front, the Soviets concentrated on preparing for the advance over the Vistula River, while they continued to seal off German forces in Latvia. The Soviet objective was Berlin and the Elbe River, about 60 miles west of the capital city.

To accomplish the task, the Soviets assembled the largest military force in European history. This force included four Soviet Fronts (Army Groups) made up of 163 Soviet divisions in addition to Bulgarian, Czechoslovakian, Romanian, and Polish divisions. They also had 6,500 tanks and 32,000 pieces of artillery.

Because Hitler had moved units that were defending the Vistula to launch the Battle of the Bulge and then sent these and other units to fight in Hungary, the German force left at Vistula was pretty sparse. It was hardly strong enough to resist *any* major offensive — let alone the biggest offensive in history.

The Soviet attack began with a massive artillery bombardment that obliterated the weak German defenses. As the armored spearheads began the advance into Germany, the Soviet air force provided cover. In two weeks, the Soviets had moved 300 miles to the Oder River, which was less than 40 miles from Berlin.

Fearing the worst: The German exodus

Millions of German citizens, enduring bitter cold and snow, fled before the Russians. Over 2 million civilians and soldiers were evacuated by ships from Baltic ports. Soviet submarines sank many of these ships.

The Soviet soldiers, aware of the destruction to their own country and the murder of hundreds of thousands of Russian civilians, had already come across the German death camp at Auschwitz. (See Chapter 11 to find out about Germany's war against the Jews in Europe.)

Filled with the knowledge of what their own countrymen and women had endured at the hands of the Germans and now aware of what unspeakable crimes the Germans had inflicted on Jewish men, women, and children, there was little remorse for the murder, torture, rape, and pillage Soviet soldiers inflicted on the German civilians they encountered in their advance. Only the most desperate fighting by the Germans, who were fully aware of what was in store for them if they lost, halted the Soviet attack. Stalled before the Oder, the Soviets turned northward, sealing off the defenders in East Prussia and capturing the port city of Danzig.

Hitler appointed Heinrich Himmler, chief of the SS (the German Protection Squad), to take command of a new army group to defend the Baltic coast. (Hitler had created this Army Group mostly on paper; in reality, there were few forces on the ground.)

Himmler, who had no more business commanding soldiers than he had flying to the moon, was a total failure. The Soviets had no trouble clearing the Baltic coastline of German forces. To hold his troops in place along the front, Hitler organized *flying court-martials*, essentially death squads with the authority to execute any German soldier found apart from his unit or any officer who had ordered a retreat. Faced with death on the front lines or death from his own army's execution squads, most German soldiers chose to stand and fight.

Fighting in the Air and at Sea: The Final Acts

MILITARY STRATEGY

By 1945, the Allies controlled the skies over Europe. During just one week in March — when Patton and Montgomery crossed the Rhine, for example — U.S. heavy bombers made 14,400 attacks, medium bombers made 7,200 attacks, and fighters made nearly 30,000 attacks. The Allies were in control of most of Europe's airbases and could fly at will.

Similarly, the Allies essentially had wrested control of the Atlantic Ocean from the Germans and eliminated the threat posed by the German U-boats (see Chapter 14). Nevertheless, the Germans continued to fight, even though everyone (with the exception of fanatic Nazis and Hitler himself understood that the German cause had already lost.

Air attacks: The bottom line

In hopes of breaking Germany's morale and its ability to wage war, the Allies increased their air attacks on Berlin, the cities in the industrial Ruhr, Cologne, and Dresden. Dresden was completely destroyed by American and British bombers, and 30,000 people died in the attack. In the Ruhr, 87,000 people were killed, and in Cologne, there were 15,000 casualties from Allied bombers. Still, these attacks did little to affect German morale or war production.

Finally (after several years of targeting industrial centers and other such locations), the Allies figured out what *would* affect Germany's ability to stay in the war: They began bombing strikes against the synthetic oil plants. These strikes reduced Germany's war machine to such an extent that neither planes nor tanks could fight.

>> Although the *Luftwaffe* (German air force) could, at times, muster sufficient aircraft for combat, the pilots were insufficiently trained to offer much of a threat to the experienced Allied pilots.

>> Any losses the Germans inflicted on the Allies were quickly made up, while German losses were not.

An end to the U-boat threat

Allied control of the air spelled the end of the German navy as well. German U-boats, once the terror of the sea, had become a negligible threat. Unable to surface without being attacked by aircraft, German U-boats adopted a snorkel system that let them charge their batteries while submerged. This method had limited success. Although the German U-boats sank some Allied ships in 1945, the U-boats were plagued by the inexperience of their own crews (the more experienced seamen were long gone) and the overwhelming capabilities of the enemy. These things resulted in high losses for the Germans without having any effect on the course of the war.

In 1944, the German surface fleet could operate only in the Baltic Sea. This fleet protected iron ore shipments from Sweden, supplied German forces trapped in East Prussia by the Soviet Army, and rescued thousands of German civilians from

Soviet control. By 1945, the Allied aircraft had sunk most of the fleets and captured key ports. By the end of the war, only a handful of German cruisers and destroyers remained to surrender.

Capturing German Territory

By April 1945, the British, Canadians, and Americans were capturing large sections of German territory:

>> The Canadians occupied Holland.

>> The British units headed to capture Hamburg.

>> The Americans of the 1st and 9th Armies were driving to encircle the Rhur, an area about the size of Massachusetts.

MILITARY STRATEGY

The Germans had first performed this kind of grand maneuver in the Soviet Union in 1941 and 1942. The Soviets had practiced it against the Germans in 1943 and 1944. Now the Americans were showing their prowess as well, surrounding and capturing 325,000 high quality German troops. Another 150,000 soldiers simply melted into the countryside.

With the multiple Allied advances, the German resistance in the West effectively disappeared:

>> General Patton's 3rd Army made a headlong rush into southern Germany and captured the town of Hof on the German-Czech border.

>> The French 1st Army and units of the U.S. 7th Army crossed the Rhine River and were headed for Nuremberg and Stuttgart.

>> By April 11, elements of the 9th Army had reached the Elbe and were establishing bridgeheads for an advance on Berlin, only 50 miles away.

As they moved eastward into Germany, American and British forces discovered what the Soviets had seen earlier at Auschwitz: evidence of Nazi atrocities against the Jews. On their way to Berlin, the Allies liberated the concentration camps at Bergen–Belsen, Buchenwald, and Dachau.

Symbolic spoils: The fate of Berlin

Everyone believed that Berlin was the next stop for the Americans: Even Churchill urged Roosevelt to move with all speed to the east to prevent the Soviets from claiming the lion's share of the victory over Germany. And Stalin himself was suspicious that the Americans and British were conspiring to cheat the Soviets out of Berlin, the symbolic high prize of the war. So he gave orders to press the advance forward as quickly as possible to capture the city.

Nevertheless, the Supreme Allied Commander, General Eisenhower, ordered no further advances beyond the Elbe.

Understanding Eisenhower's decision

Should General Eisenhower have given the order to go to Berlin? His decision is still debated today in light of the events that followed victory in Europe. Regardless of what happened since (see Chapter 23 for information about the fall of the Iron Curtain and the beginning of the Cold War), here's why he made the decision to leave Berlin to the Russians and stop the Allied troops at the Elbe River.

>> Eisenhower had only one mission to undertake and that was the destruction of German forces. Berlin to him was nothing more than a symbol and not worth fighting for.

>> Eisenhower was concerned about rumors of a Nazi *redoubt* (stronghold) in southern Germany, where the remaining fanatics had stockpiled supplies for a last stand.

>> Eisenhower understood the politics involved: The Allies had already divided Germany up into zones of occupation in anticipation of the end of the war in Europe. The Soviet Union would have the chunk of territory that contained Berlin. If the Soviets were going to have it anyway, Eisenhower seemed to ask, why take it from them?

>> Not trusting the Soviets, Eisenhower pushed forces forward to make sure the Soviet Army advanced no farther than the Elbe.

Roosevelt's Last Act and Stalin's Coup at Yalta

In February 1945, the Allied armies in the West were pushing toward the Rhine River; in the East, the Soviets were swallowing up Hungary and driving to the Oder River. With these dramatic events serving as a backdrop, the three Allied wartime leaders met in the city of Yalta on the Crimean peninsula in the Soviet Union to discuss the postwar arrangements for Europe.

The meeting at Yalta was to be Franklin Roosevelt's last meeting with Churchill and Stalin. Recently sworn in as the American president for a fourth time, Roosevelt was seriously ill with a heart ailment. He lacked the physical stamina to meet the responsibilities that this meeting imposed on him.

HISTORICAL TRIVIA

Even if Roosevelt had been well, he still was at a disadvantage at Yalta: His closest advisor, Harry Hopkins, was a Soviet agent. Other highly placed Soviet agents, such as Alger Hiss in the U.S. State Department, were passing critical information to Stalin on a number of subjects, including American progress on an atomic bomb. Thus, Stalin knew in advance all the cards that were being played. And just so he wouldn't miss anything, Stalin also had the rooms bugged during the conference.

Winning over Uncle Joe (not)

Roosevelt continued to use the gambit he had pursued at the Teheran conference (see Chapter 16). Believing he could win the Soviet dictator over to his side with personal charm, Roosevelt sought to gain Stalin's cooperation and partnership in shaping the postwar world. Several topics were discussed at the Yalta conference:

>> The formation of the United Nations (UN), an organization similar to the League of Nations (see Chapter 2), that would secure world peace.

>> The fate and structure of Eastern Europe.

>> The political structure of the liberated and vanquished nations.

>> The USSR's role in the war against the Japanese.

But Stalin had an agenda, and he pursued it with determination. Outside of military action, the British and Americans had little choice other than to accept those demands.

REMEMBER

The Americans and British were helpless to change the shape of events that had taken place since the Soviet Army overran Poland. Soviet forces controlled Bulgaria, Romania, Hungary, Poland, and half of Germany. Only a direct military confrontation between the United States and the Soviet Union would force Stalin to give up control of what he had captured from the Nazis.

On the United Nations

In discussions about a the future formation of the United Nations, Stalin wanted the Soviet Republics of Ukraine and Belorussia to be independent members of the

General Assembly (the decision making body in the UN). This would bolster the Soviet Union's power in the UN:

>> As a permanent member (along with China, the United States, Great Britain, and France) in the UN Security Council, the USSR would have veto power.

>> Having Ukraine and Belorussia as independent UN members (even though they both took their orders from Moscow) gave the Soviet Union two additional votes in the General Assembly.

Roosevelt and Churchill agreed.

On the fate of Poland

Stalin had no interest in cooperating on any postwar alignment in Eastern Europe, except the one that placed the Soviet Union in complete control. So, of course, he refused to compromise on Poland:

>> Stalin wanted to expand the Polish borders westward at the expense of Germany.

>> Stalin wanted the USSR to control the future of the postwar Polish government. (Stalin already had a pro-Soviet government in place in Poland, despite the fact that the Polish government in exile, which had been operating in London since 1939, was the only legitimate government body. See Chapter 18 for a similar arrangement in Soviet-liberated Yugoslavia.)

Roosevelt and Churchill reluctantly agreed. Roosevelt, however, did get a promise from Stalin in the form of a declaration that pledged the three nations would "arrange and conduct free elections" in the areas of Europe that they controlled. Roosevelt knew this promise was a political fig leaf (in other words, a lie), but it took the sting away temporarily from having to accept Stalin's dictate.

On the future of Germany

Stalin sought an agreement that would leave Germany permanently weakened. This included the following:

>> The permanent division of Germany.

>> The payment of reparations in the form of billions of dollars of industrial production machinery to be shipped to the USSR.

On this point, the British and Americans had the upper hand because Germany's industrial base in the Ruhr was located in the area occupied by the British and American armies. As a result:

>> Roosevelt and Churchill agreed to the Soviet request for billions in reparations in principle, knowing that they could withhold transfers to the Soviet Union at any time (since they controlled the Ruhr region).

>> They also divided Germany into zones of occupation, a situation that implied a temporary division, rather than the permanent division Stalin had wanted.

On the USSR's involvement in Japan

One of the most important agreements made during the Yalta conference was Stalin's commitment to enter the war against Japan once Germany was defeated. Roosevelt wanted the USSR in the war against Japan for a couple reasons:

>> Although the U.S. had no desire to fight a war of annihilation against the Japanese on their home islands or put American troops in China to fight Japanese forces to the death there (a process that could possibly have taken years), there was no guarantee that either of those worst case scenarios wouldn't happen. If they did, Roosevelt wanted to draw on Soviet manpower.

>> Roosevelt feared that if the Soviet Union wasn't included in the Pacific war, Stalin could wreak havoc in Europe while the United States and Great Britain focused on Asia.

Stalin agreed — but only after he got Roosevelt to promise that the Soviet Union would gain control of ports, bases, and rail lines in Manchuria, as well as the lower half of Sakhalin Island (north of the main Japanese island of Hokkaido), all of which had been lost in the treaty that ended the Russo-Japanese War in 1905.

Brokering this agreement without Churchill's knowledge, Roosevelt acceded, knowing full well that such an agreement would make Manchuria a colony of the Soviets and put Chinese leader Chiang Kai-shek in a very difficult situation.

A bitter pill

Roosevelt and Churchill left Yalta with very little to show for their efforts, except for a formal recognition of the status quo. Roosevelt had poorly prepared America for what it would confront in Europe after the war was finally over. There would be many unpleasant surprises. The greatest surprise, perhaps, was the rapid disappearance of Roosevelt's beaming and non-threatening Uncle Joe.

EXIT STAGE LEFT: ROOSEVELT WORKS TO THE END

On April 12, 1945, although quite weak and visibly tired, Roosevelt was having his portrait painted while he worked on official papers. During the session, he said quietly, "I have a terrific headache." He slumped over in his chair and, in a little over two hours, was dead from a cerebral hemorrhage.

Roosevelt's name was placed at the top of the casualty list published in the newspapers the next day. He was listed as Commander in Chief. In notifying her sons (who were all in the military at the time) of their father's death, Eleanor Roosevelt wrote, "He did his job to the end as he would want you to do." One of the most unique and puzzling men ever to be president, and probably the nation's greatest war leader, passed from the scene just as the war reached its climax.

With the Soviet Army moving on Berlin, the Soviet Union had the initiative in determining the future of Europe. Stalin intended to occupy as much territory in Europe as he could before the British and Americans advanced any further into Germany. The capture of the German capital city of Berlin was the keystone of Stalin's plan.

The War in Italy Ends, and Germany Succumbs

The battle lines drawn in northern Italy in the winter of 1944 remained the same in the opening months of 1945 (see Chapter 17). Little had changed except that most of the German troops had been pulled from the Italian front to plug holes on the rapidly shrinking defensive lines in Germany. The Allies also transferred troops, including a Canadian Corps transferred to General Montgomery's command in Western Europe.

REMEMBER

An earlier campaign in Italy (such as Churchill envisioned in 1944) could have succeeded and perhaps put Allied forces on the German and Austrian border by 1944. But it was poorly supported because the Allies were building their invasion force for Normandy (see Chapter 18). As a result, the multinational force in Italy faced the extremely difficult task of fighting against a skillful enemy who was defending mountainous terrain.

The battle in northern Italy

The decisive attack in Italy began on April 9, 1945, with a series of attacks to break through heavily defended strongpoints. The battle bogged down into a slugging match between infantrymen — a slow and painful contest of wills.

Hitler refused to allow the Germans to retreat. Rather than trading space for time and delaying an Allied breakthrough, the German defenders were overwhelmed by a combination of air power and determined ground attacks. The German commander finally ordered a withdrawal in defiance of Hitler's orders, but it was too late.

Defying Der Führer: The Germans surrender

On April 29, German commanders decided to negotiate a cease-fire and surrender their forces — in complete defiance of Hitler's orders. The unconditional surrender took effect on May 2, 1945, and Allied forces, after three long, bloody, and frustrating years, finally broke into the north Italian plain and occupied the mountain passes that gave them access to Austria and Germany.

Stalin Moves on Berlin

MILITARY STRATEGY

In April 1945, Stalin wasted no time in crossing the Oder River and covering the last 40 miles to Berlin (see Figure 20-2). The Soviets massed 8 armies — a total of 2.5 million men — on a 75-mile-wide front. Artillery pieces were crammed so tightly all along the front line that there were about 450 for every mile. Another Soviet front stood ready to advance northwest to the Baltic ports near the Elbe River and deny the British and Americans access.

The German defenders numbered nearly 1 million. They were a collection of experienced combat troops and raw recruits, with a heavy injection of People's Guard (*Volkssturm*) — the last able-bodied men between the ages of 16 and 60 capable of using a weapon. Boys as young as 11 or 12 also fought in the front lines. These soldiers were given minimal training and provided any weapon available. The armies (and they were armies in name only) lacked fuel for their few trucks and tanks, ammunition was scarce, and the *Luftwaffe* disappeared from the skies. But they had the advantage of well-prepared defenses intended to force the Soviets to fight long and difficult battles in order to advance.

FIGURE 20-2: Soviet Advance into Germany, 1945.

The Soviet onslaught

Despite nearly overwhelming advantages when the battle began on April 16, 1945, the Soviet advance was slowed by fierce German resistance.

Pressed by Stalin to make progress as quickly as possible, the Soviet commanders made reckless infantry attacks. Despite heavy casualties, the weight of the Soviet offensive power was too much for the Germans to hold for long. By April 19, the Soviet Army was in the Berlin suburbs, attacking the city from several directions. German front line forces were surrounded or pushed back quickly and did not contribute to the defense of the city.

Because of Nazi ineptitude (Propaganda Minister Joseph Goebbels was the military and political leader of Berlin's defense) and the symbolism of a united people in arms, the civilians were not evacuated from the capital. The last Allied bombing raid, before the advance of Soviet troops, had destroyed electrical power and water lines, leaving the population in a miserable state. Soviet air force planes took over, attacking streets and buildings throughout the city. As Soviet units approached the center of the city, where the Nazi government buildings were located, resistance grew.

For nine days, the battle for the capital raged — house-to-house and often room-to-room — in much the same way the Germans and Russians had fought over Stalingrad. There was little organized German defense, mostly small pockets of soldiers and tanks struggling to survive the Soviet onslaught. Many *Volkssturm* were simply given a one-shot anti-tank weapon and sent out into the streets to find a tank to kill.

On April 30, Soviet soldiers flew the flag of the Soviet Union (the hammer and sickle) over the Reichstag, the German parliament building in the center of Berlin.

The end of Berlin's most notorious citizen: Hitler

Hitler, a virtual prisoner within an air-raid bunker in the center of the city, clung to the belief that a miracle would save the Third Reich. He gave orders to surrounding units, ordering attacks that could not be accomplished. He demanded reports from army-level commands that existed in name only. He no longer controlled anything. Other Nazi leaders abandoned Hitler and tried to save their own skins:

» Heinrich Himmler made contact with the Western Allies, seeking a deal to end the war. He tried to negotiate as the de facto head of state (and painted himself as a humanitarian in a pathetic attempt to gloss over his leading role in the destruction of millions of innocent people).

» Hermann Goering was arrested in southern Germany for suggesting that he take control of the government.

Only Propaganda Minister Joseph Goebbels and Martin Bormann (Hitler's personal secretary) remained by Hitler's side. Hitler named Admiral Karl Doenitz as his successor, giving him the title of Reich President, the title that Hitler had eliminated when he took power in 1933. Goebbels became the new Chancellor of Germany, and Bormann became Party Minister.

SO WHATEVER HAPPENED TO *IL DUCE*?

After his rescue by German commandos in 1943 (see Chapter 13), Italian Fascist dictator Benito Mussolini headed a puppet government in Italian territory still occupied by German forces. Mussolini enjoyed the company of his mistress, while allowing the Germans to dictate policy. With total defeat approaching in April 1945, Mussolini prepared to escape with German forces across the Alps into Germany for a final stand.

Italian partisans blocked all roads out of Italy. They allowed German units to go on but arrested all Italian Fascists. Here Mussolini and his mistress were taken prisoner. Both were executed by a Communist partisan on April 28, 1945. Before killing them, the Communist partisan announced the death sentence: "By order of the High Command of the Volunteer Freedom Corps, I have been charged to render justice to the Italian people." Mussolini's body (as well as those of his mistress and 13 other Fascists) was taken to a bombed-out filling station in Milan, where the Germans had executed 15 Italians in 1944. The bodies were strung up by their heels and subjected to indignities from an angry mob. "God what an ignoble end!" General Eisenhower said when he heard the news. "You give people a little power and it seems like they can never be decent human beings again."

With these arrangements made, Hitler dictated his last testament. It was his final hateful attack on "International Jewry and its helpers" as the cause of the war. Hitler himself, of course, was blameless for the disaster that had befallen Germany. On the same day that the Reichstag fell, Hitler married his mistress, and then they both committed suicide. Their bodies were taken out of the bunker and burned.

The next day, Goebbels and his wife died by suicide as well, after killing their six children. Bormann and others fled the bunker just as Soviet troops reached the area. Those that fled the bunker tried to escape before the Soviets surrounded the city. Bormann apparently was killed before he got out.

The fall of Berlin

With the Nazi political leadership gone, the ranking German military officer in Berlin surrendered on May 2, 1945. Immediately, German Communists, who had been in exile in the Soviet Union since Hitler had taken power, were flown into the city to establish the standard pro–Soviet government that also existed in Poland, Bulgaria, and Romania.

THE STRANGE TALE OF HITLER'S BONES

As the battle for Berlin opened, Stalin feared that Hitler might escape and return one day to begin yet another war with a revitalized Nazi state. When word came from German officers during surrender negotiations that Hitler was dead, Stalin wanted to make sure. In the days immediately after the surrender, the Soviets located and identified the charred remains of Hitler and his mistress. From there, a portion of Hitler's skull and jawbone were placed in a box and taken, in Indiana Jones fashion, to Moscow, where they were hidden away until 1991, when, after the fall of the Soviet Union, many curious secrets were exposed.

Those bones are still in Moscow. The rest of Hitler's body, his mistress's body, and the Goebbels family remains were carted off secretly and buried in a Soviet military base in Germany. In 1970, at the orders of KGB Chief Yuri Andropov, they were exhumed, pulverized into dust, and scattered into a nearby river. It is interesting that the ghost of Hitler could haunt a nuclear superpower so completely that the Soviet Union went to such extraordinary lengths to prevent their greatest fear from becoming a reality: a new Nazi movement arising from the literal ashes of the dead Führer.

No Way Out: The Germans Surrender

Well aware of the disaster he inherited, Admiral Karl Doenitz, as the new Reich President, attempted to continue the war, but only to salvage some honor out of it. Interestingly enough, he had a captured map, obtained during the Battle of the Bulge that outlined the proposed zones of occupation for Germany. He wanted to move as many German troops and civilians toward the Western Allies as possible.

The German surrender to the British and Americans

Doenitz tried to make a deal with British General Montgomery on May 3 to surrender all German forces, including those facing the Soviets, to him as commander of the Twenty-First Army Group. Montgomery refused, demanding only unconditional surrender. After discussing Montgomery's response with his German officers, Doenitz returned to Montgomery's headquarters on May 4 to sign an unconditional surrender of forces facing the Twenty-First Army Group.

Hostilities would end on May 8, 1945. The following day, the German delegation traveled to Eisenhower's headquarters at Rheims, France to sign another instrument of surrender. The Germans tried again to make a separate deal with the Americans, but Eisenhower refused. He did, however, agree to keep his lines open for another 48 hours to let Germans cross into the Western sector to get a signed surrender.

Alfred Jodl, representing Admiral Doenitz, signed the unconditional surrender for all German forces to take effect one minute past midnight on May 9, 1945. Between May 8 and 9, about 2 million German soldiers entered American and British lines to surrender rather than fall into Soviet hands. When the deadline under the surrender document passed on May 9, 1.25 million Germans soldiers became Soviet POWs.

One more time! Stalin demands another surrender

Angry that the Germans had sought out Eisenhower to sign a surrender agreement (even though Eisenhower was the Supreme Allied Commander), Stalin was determined that the Soviet Army would not be robbed of its opportunity to take center stage. Thus, with Field Marshal William Keitel, Hitler's headquarters Chief of Staff, available to sign, the Soviets held their own signing ceremony in Berlin, with representatives of France, the United States, and Great Britain standing by. Marshal Gregori Zhukov, the hero of the defense of Moscow and Stalingrad, represented Stalin and the Soviet Union.

Celebrating VE Day

For the Allies, May 8 was declared Victory in Europe Day, or VE Day. May 9 was the Soviet Union's official victory day.

The happy stuff: Allies celebrate

In Moscow, 3 million people crowded into Red Square to celebrate. One observer noticed a curious blending of unrestrained joy with a sense of loss and sadness.

In London, there were no blackout restrictions for the first time in six years. People mobbed the streets, and Princess Elizabeth met the crowds outside the palace.

In New York, 500,000 people crammed Times Square chanting "It's over! It's over!" Like the Russians, Americans could celebrate and be sad at the same time. The nation was still mourning the death of President Roosevelt.

In Paris, Amsterdam, Brussels, and Oslo, celebrations were similar. British Prime Minister Winston Churchill summarized the Western Allies' emotions during his address to the nation on May 8: "The evil-doers are now prostrate before us. . . . But let us not forget for a moment the toils and efforts that lie ahead. Japan, with all her treachery and greed, remains unsubdued."

The not so happy stuff

Although the end of the war in Europe was certainly a time to celebrate, no conflict that lasts years, kills and wounds millions, and reshapes countries is ever completely over by the time the ink dries on the surrender declaration. A lot of things still have to be resolved, and for many, the first moments of jubilation eventually give way to the realization of what little is actually left. Consider the following:

>> Although the fighting officially ended at midnight on May 9, 1945, some scattered units continued to fight, not knowing that the German Reich ceased to exist.

>> For weeks after the war, millions of refugees (or *DPs — displaced persons* in military jargon) moved across the plains of Europe in great migratory masses, returning to what they remembered was home.

>> Most of European Jews who survived the Holocaust found themselves ill (having suffered the abuses of the Nazi concentration camps), homeless (their property stolen from them by Nazism or destroyed by war), and alone (their wives and husbands and children and parents and sisters and brothers murdered). Even today the debate goes on about how these people can possibly be compensated for all that they lost.

>> Hundreds of thousands of German POWs (prisoners of war) had to be dealt with. Most German POWs under Soviet control would perish in camps under harsh conditions. A few survivors would be released more than ten years after the end of the war. Russian POWs returning to the Soviet Union were considered traitors and were either sent to the Soviet GULAGs or killed outright.

Reconstructing a New Germany: The Potsdam Conference

Admiral Doenitz's government continued in existence for two weeks following his signing of the surrender documents, mostly to ensure that all German units, including U-boats still at sea, surrendered quietly. After those two weeks had passed, the entire government was arrested; some of the members would be tried for war crimes.

With the disappearance of the German government, the territory that made up Germany was divided into four zones of occupation (French, British, Soviet, and American), reflecting the priorities of the nations controlling the zones (see Figure 20-3): The Soviets set up a state-directed economy; the Western powers established freedom of the press and democratic elections. Austria was also divided into zones of occupation (it would be reunited as a neutral country ten years later).

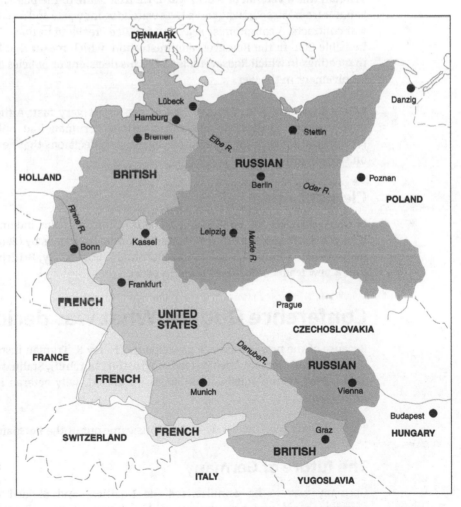

FIGURE 20-3:
Germany Divided, 1945.

Getting thrown into the pot: The newcomers

In the midst of these changes, the Allied leaders met from July 17 to August 2, 1945, in Potsdam, a city outside of Berlin, to decide the future course of events in Europe. There were a couple new faces at the table in Potsdam: new American President Harry S. Truman and new British Prime Minister Clement Atlee.

Harry Truman

Truman was a veteran of World War I. He first came to the public's attention as a Senator from Missouri who served as a watchdog for waste and fraud in government war contracts. A compromise selection for Vice President in 1944, Truman was the invisible man in the Roosevelt administration, which meant that he wasn't privy to meetings in which Roosevelt discussed his decisions or policies about America's involvement in the war.

When Roosevelt died, Truman had to get smart very fast. Although he was a quick learner, dedicated, and conscientious, Truman had only the briefest familiarization with the momentous events and decisions that he was now called on to deal with.

Clement Atlee

Midway through the conference, Winston Churchill, the indomitable wartime leader, was replaced as Prime Minister in national elections by Clement Atlee, who had served in Churchill's coalition government. Essentially, British voters decided that a new leader would lead them in peace.

Conference Outline: What was decided

Because of the new conference participants (Harry S. Truman instead of Franklin Roosevelt and Clement Atlee instead of Winston Churchill), Stalin was left standing alone, first among equals, so to speak — an old, wily veteran in the midst of newcomers.

The following sections list what decisions came out of the Potsdam conference.

The future of Germany

Germany was to be demilitarized, de-Nazified, and divided. In place of a government, it was agreed that an Allied Control Council would administer Germany. But the plan amounted to nothing because each power had absolute control over what it did in its own zone of occupation.

The war against Japan

The U.S. battle for Okinawa had just ended, with terrible American casualties (see Chapter 22), and Truman had already approved plans for an invasion of the Japanese home islands in November 1945. Fearing heavy losses, he needed Stalin's guarantee that Soviet forces would join the war and keep the Japanese forces in China and Manchuria busy. Stalin agreed to join the war by August 15.

The borders of Poland

Stalin pressed for new borders for Poland that would stretch far to the west and eliminate most of eastern prewar Germany. The other Allies agreed to this with the mandate that the existing German population would be removed from the territory now declared to be Poland.

In addition, everyone pledged to support free elections in Poland, but no timetable was set.

German war payments to the Soviets

Stalin demanded that the Germans pay for the destruction inflicted on the Soviet Union during the war. Stalin wanted people, machinery, and goods to be transferred wholesale to Soviet control. No one wanted to hand over Germans, who would, for all intents and purposes, become slave laborers for the Soviets (hence the condition that the German population be removed from Poland; see the preceding section). In the end, the following was decided:

>> The Soviets would take their reparations from their own zone of occupation. No one doubted they would have done this anyway, but the agreement gave Stalin legal authority to strip the Soviet zone of everything of any value.

>> The Western Allies agreed to provide additional reparations support in the form of the transfer of non-essential industry, in return for food and raw material transfers from the Soviet zone.

>> This agreement was largely symbolic: Both sides realized that no one was going to get much more than what they already physically possessed in their zones.

Tying up loose ends: Plans for another conference

Because there was little agreement, many decisions were to be deferred to a final peace conference that supposedly would settle all the issues. The formal peace treaties and other arrangements were to be worked out by a Council of Foreign Ministers.

TRUMAN, STALIN, AND THE BOMB

Before arriving in Potsdam, President Truman was notified of the successful testing of the first atomic bomb in New Mexico. Truman had been briefed on the project and was aware of its potential destructive power, but until the test actually occurred, the concept was still theoretical. Now that the bomb was a reality, Truman expected that the weapon would be considered for use against Japan. With Churchill's approval, Truman decided to tell Stalin about the top-secret program. Truman mentioned his information in a confidential aside to Stalin. The dictator showed only a casual reaction, which puzzled Truman. In reality, many of the key scientists working on the atomic bomb project from its very beginning were Soviet agents. At this point, Stalin may have known more about the program than Truman did. The only new information Truman provided was that the bomb actually worked. In fact, months before, Stalin had already harnessed the best scientific knowledge of the Soviet Union and put them on a crash program to develop a Soviet atomic bomb, using plans provided by the Soviet agents. Only Stalin knew that the nuclear weapons race had already begun.

By the time these meetings were held, however, the Soviets no longer needed to cooperate with the Western Allies. Stalin already had a Communist government operating in Poland, and he had little interest in fulfilling his pledge of free elections. He also possessed much of Germany and Eastern Europe and directed all activities there.

Warning Japan: The secret threat

The Potsdam Declaration to Japan was a mixture of threats and promises:

>> Unconditional surrender remained mandatory.

>> Japan's military infrastructure and the military's control of the government would be eliminated.

>> Japanese sovereignty would extend only to its home islands.

>> Korea would be free and independent.

>> Japan would be occupied and disarmed, and war criminals would face trial.

>> Japan would be guaranteed a democratic government and a return to normal relations with other nations at some time in the future.

In some ways, the offer to Japan was a far better deal than Germany got. Essentially, though, the Allies gave Japan a threatening ultimatum — they hinted that they possessed power far greater than that which destroyed Germany. If Japan didn't surrender soon, the Allies guaranteed it "prompt and utter destruction" — a veiled reference to the atomic bomb, which the U.S had already tested.

The Japanese publicly rejected the declaration, but behind the scenes, the Japanese government sought Stalin's help in serving as a mediator to negotiate a peace settlement. Stalin would have nothing of it. He wanted to get in on the war against Japan to gather in as much territory in the Far East as he could before the atomic bomb ended the war.

Loose Ends of a Bitter Victory

The war in Europe was over, but the fruits of victory were bitter for all the Allies:

>> Great Britain was a wounded lion, weakened by the exertions of war and the prospect of more fighting against Japan, as it put the British Empire back together in Asia.

>> The Soviet Union, faced with devastation at home and the ruined nations of Eastern Europe at its feet, had gained the security buffer it desired and a dismembered Germany. The Soviet Union would now turn toward establishing and expanding its dominance, while looking to the Far East for additional acquisitions.

>> The United States stood in wonderment at what had been wrought in Europe, satisfied that the blight of Hitler and Nazism had been destroyed, but also troubled by the Soviets and their ambitions. Even President Roosevelt came to the understanding that Uncle Joe was not going to cooperate as he had expected. For the Americans, VE Day was only a breather. The war was not over until Japan surrendered. And in August of 1945, that still seemed to be very far away.

Chapter **21**

The Japanese Defeat

B y 1945, the power and strength of American military might began to press heavily upon the Japanese. Since 1942, the Allies had fought the war in the Pacific with minimal support. Now, as the war in Europe came to an end, the pipeline for troops, supplies, and equipment opened for the Americans (General Douglas MacArthur and Admiral Chester Nimitz) who led the fight against the Japanese. The Americans had 1.5 million troops, nearly 1,000 combat ships, tens of thousands of landing craft and assault ships, and nearly 30,000 aircraft — a force unmatched in history.

On paper, it appeared that winning the war would be a cakewalk for the U.S. But wars aren't fought on paper: They are fought with steel and blood and spirit. Although badly weakened economically and with most of its air power and sea power destroyed, the Japanese were still formidable foes. The Japanese army fought with reckless bravery and determination that tended to negate the big numbers of the American military. The *kamikaze* pilots, unafraid of death, were capable of destroying ships with their suicide planes. The Japanese people were united in their effort to continue to resist. Loyal to the Emperor, they were willing to endure whatever hardships — and to fight themselves, even if it meant dying — to protect the home islands from an invader.

The last months of World War II were to be the most bloody and terrible of an already long and terrible war.

Returning to the Philippines

MacArthur had waged an effective campaign against Japanese forces in the Philippines up to 1945 (see Chapter 19). As he had done in his island hopping campaign between 1943 and 1944, MacArthur sought to control key areas that could be used as airbases to support amphibious or overland ground attack. Because they never knew where MacArthur would attack next, the Japanese ended up fighting in multiple directions, trying to defend everything at once.

The Philippines, however, were different. The landing at Leyte (discussed in Chapter 19) had surprised the Japanese, but everyone knew that the real battle of the Philippines would take place on the main island of Luzon:

>> Manila, the capital of the Philippines, was located on Luzon, as was most of the Filipino population.

>> Luzon was also the location of Bataan and Corregidor Island, the sites of humiliating American defeats in 1942 (see Chapter 8).

>> The Japanese held thousands of American and Filipino prisoners of war on Luzon.

The Japanese knew that the Americans were coming; they also knew that losing control of Luzon would cut off the supply lines to Japan from the Dutch East Indies and also put American air power closer to Japan (see Figure 21-1). The battle for Luzon would be an all or nothing fight for the more than 200,000 Japanese defenders under command of one of the most capable generals in the Japanese Army, General Tomoyuki Yamashita.

Luzon: The First Phase

On January 9, 1945, MacArthur sent the 68,000-man 6th Army, commanded by General Walter Kreuger, into battle first. On its way to the gulf, the invasion fleet ran a gauntlet of kamikaze attacks, which sank one escort carrier and damaged dozens of additional ships. The 6th Army landed at Lingayen Gulf, the same place the Japanese had landed to begin their invasion of the Philippines in 1941. The landing party received the following support:

>> Admiral Halsey's fleet began a campaign in the South China Sea that devastated Japanese combat power and prevented any reinforcements to the Philippines. His planes attacked Japanese airfields at Formosa (Taiwan) and Indo China (Vietnam), destroying nearly 600 aircraft and sinking over 100 Japanese ships in a little less than three weeks.

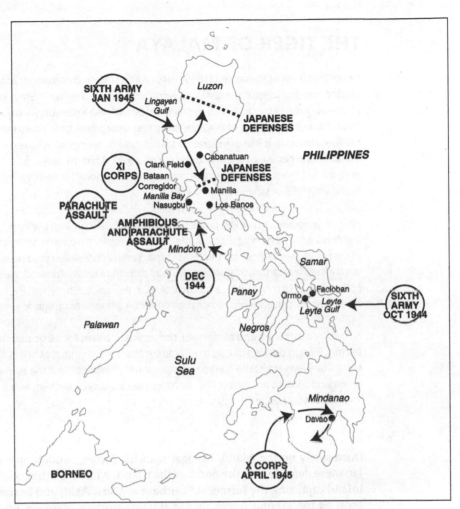

FIGURE 21-1:
Liberation of the
Philippines.

The map includes the following labels:

SIXTH ARMY JAN 1945
Lingayen Gulf
Luzon
JAPANESE DEFENSES
PHILIPPINES
XI CORPS
Clark Field
Bataan
Corregidor
Manilla Bay
Nasugbu
PARACHUTE ASSAULT
AMPHIBIOUS AND PARACHUTE ASSAULT
Mindoro
Cabanatuan
JAPANESE DEFENSES
Manila
Los Banos
Samar
DEC 1944
Panay
Ormo
Facloban
Leyte
Leyte Gulf
SIXTH ARMY OCT 1944
Palawan
Negros
Sulu Sea
Mindanao
Davao
X CORPS APRIL 1945
BORNEO

>> While a large fleet protected the landing, American aircraft from Mindoro,
Leyte, and the Palau Islands (Peleliu — captured by American Marines in
September 1944; see Chapter 19) covered the skies, harassing Japanese
defenders and preventing reinforcements from arriving to protect the
beaches.

>> Filipino guerrillas attacked garrisons, communications, and bridges to slow
and confuse the Japanese.

The landings were successful, and Kreuger was able to open a beachhead 15 miles
wide and 4 miles deep against almost no enemy opposition. MacArthur himself
waded ashore to the beach with the soldiers.

THE TIGER OF MALAYA

General Tomoyuki Yamashita (1885–1946) was a superb commander and active in political intrigue against the civilian government before the war. Always highly respected for his abilities, Yamashita rose to prominence with the Kwantung Army in China. By 1941, he took command of the 25th Army and led it against the British stronghold of Malaya. His brilliant use of infiltration tactics, his knowledge of Western habits and thinking, and his use of feints and deception allowed him to defeat a far superior enemy and capture the strategically important port of Singapore. He became a national hero and the symbol of Japan's military skill.

Political jealousies, however, pushed this most able soldier into the background just as the Allies were beginning their counteroffensive against Japanese strongholds. Although in charge of overseeing operations in China, Yamashita's skills could have been better used elsewhere at this critical time. He was summoned to command the defense of the Philippines in October 1944, a bit too late to make much difference. By September 1945, he personally surrendered rather than continue a hopeless struggle.

A military court tried and sentenced Yamashita to death for atrocities committed against Filipino civilians during the Battle for Manila, a charge that still is a thorny issue for military lawyers: Is the commander personally responsible if the soldiers under his command commit atrocities? The sentence was controversial then, and it still is today. Yamashita was hanged in 1946.

Once safely on the island, Krueger split his forces, sending one corps to seal off Japanese defenders in the north of the island, while his other corps moved rapidly inland capturing the former U.S. airbase at Clark Field, and headed for Manila. As soon as the ground forces moved inland, airbases were set up behind them to provide air support to the troops in combat.

By 31 January 1945, the Japanese had suffered 15,000 casualties, the Americans less than 6,000. By the beginning of February, American forces had split the Japanese into isolated groups. Without the means to coordinate their defense, Yamashita had lost the campaign. Yet no one was giving up.

Nothing is spared: Terror in Manila

The attack on Manila began on February 2, 1945. The 18,000 Japanese who defended the city were primarily a collection of naval forces, most of which were not under Yamashita's direct command. The naval commander positioned his troops so that they were facing the wrong direction when the attack came, and he had to change his battle plans quickly. He ordered that no one in his command be taken alive.

Unlike other cities that had been spared destruction, central Manila became a death trap for American infantry. The Japanese destroyed bridges, buildings, and water lines. They set fires that often raged out of control. Although MacArthur limited the use of artillery and air attacks to spare further destruction of the once beautiful city and limit civilian casualties, the Japanese took advantage of the situation to inflict revenge on the Filipinos. Many innocent Filipinos were killed and wounded by the Japanese and by American air and artillery attacks.

The Japanese and Americans fought house to house and street to street. By February 22, the city was in ruins, and the Japanese commander and the last remnants of his command were holed up in the old city, which had walls 40 feet thick and 16 feet high in some places. There they had 4,000 Filipino hostages as well. Appeals to surrender were ignored and U.S. artillery and tanks blasted huge gaps in the walls at point blank range. It took more than a day to destroy the enemy and an additional eight days finally to bring the city under control. Only 4,500 Japanese survived the battle. The Americans suffered 6,500 casualties. The Filipinos suffered most of all, with more than 100,000 killed in the fighting.

Death from above at Corregidor

While the battle for Manila continued, MacArthur ordered that American forces take the island of Corregidor. The island fortress was the symbol of American strength and had played a key role in the defensive plans of the Philippines. It was the place where MacArthur himself had left his men when President Roosevelt ordered him to go to Australia. And it was the site of a humiliating surrender for the U.S. Army.

On February 16, 1945, veteran paratroopers of the 503rd Parachute Infantry Regiment landed on top of the island. The paratroopers fought for two solid weeks in a nightmare of daylight destruction of tunnels and traps, followed by nighttime attacks by the Japanese.

Supported by an amphibious landing of additional reinforcements, the U.S. infantrymen were spared the horror of fighting the Japanese in the deep underground tunnels that once housed American defenders. The Japanese blew up the tunnels, killing themselves rather than face capture. Only 19 of nearly 5,000 defenders left the island alive. American losses were less than 700.

ARMY
ALLIED

On March 2, 1945, MacArthur stood by as soldiers raised the American flag once again over Corregidor, on the same flagpole that stood when the Japanese hauled down the U.S. flag in 1942.

Finishing the battle to clear Luzon

With the fall of Manila, Bataan, and Corregidor, it is often assumed that the battle in the Philippines ended. Hardly. Over 100,000 Japanese defenders put up strong resistance in the mountains in north Luzon. Japanese forces also hid in a network of tunnels and holes in the mountains east of Manila. Advances were often measured in yards. American infantry had to clear each hillside with artillery and air bombing attacks, hand grenades, and flamethrowers.

ARMY
ALLIED

The battle to clear Luzon continued until September 2 when Yamashita surrendered his mostly starved and exhausted forces. When it was all over, Luzon had cost nearly 8,000 American lives since January 1945. Another 32,000 had been wounded. The Japanese lost 192,000 men. Only 9,700 were captured at the war's end.

Mindanao: Still more fighting to do

At the big island of Mindanao, MacArthur sent several American divisions to destroy 43,000 Japanese defenders there and capture the major city of Davao. The island matched the conditions on New Guinea (see Chapter 15): mountainous, swampy, thick jungles, and terribly hot. Filipino guerrillas assisted the American amphibious assaults on the island, which faced no serious resistance. The Americans made a grueling cross-country movement to Davao, splitting the Japanese defenders in half.

MILITARY
STRATEGY

Davao was abandoned, forcing the final battles to be fought in the thick jungle, where the Japanese had all the advantages, except two:

>> **Resupply:** Without food or ammunition, the Japanese defenders could not fight for long.

>> **Air power:** Without friendly air cover, the Japanese had no one to protect them from — or at least slow down — the Allied bombs that fell on them day and night.

Still, the remnants of the Japanese army defending the island didn't give up until June 30. Nearly half of the defenders surrendered, a remarkably high number given the Japanese willingness to die rather than surrender. The loss to American forces was about 800 men.

A sometimes forgotten triumph: The Philippines

The campaign to take the Philippines is one of the forgotten triumphs of American arms. The remarkable fact is, though, that in less that two months Allied forces cleared the Japanese from the Philippines, even though the Japanese resistance in the face of hopeless odds lengthened the campaign to its bitter end.

ARMY ALLIED

Despite the conditions of the campaign, where small units fought in jungle and in cities, overall combat losses were light — a far cry from the combat losses in Europe from November 1944 to May of 1945. As a combined campaign, using air, sea and ground forces in harmony to create a single effect, the Philippine operation is unmatched in World War II.

Attack from Air and Sea: Japan Is Next

In the midst of the Philippines campaign, the strategic bombing against the home islands of Japan began in earnest. The undersea campaign against Japanese shipping reached its climax as well. The dual air and sea attack was intended to accomplish two objectives:

>> Starve the war-making capacity of Japan by cutting its supply lines in the sea.

>> Destroy Japan's ability to continue the war by destroying its industrial base.

The Allies used two tools to accomplish these objectives: the submarine and the B-29 Superfortress.

MILITARY STRATEGY

The B-29 was a high altitude precision bomber that first saw combat over Asia in June of 1944. About 4,000 B-29s were produced during the war. With a crew of ten, a pressurized cabin, remote control guns, and radar to assist with bombing, the B-29 was the most modern bomber in the world. It could carry 20,000 pounds of bombs over 3,200 miles (4,000 miles with extra fuel tanks) and could fly at an altitude of 31,000 feet. Its wingspan of 142 feet was twice as long as the B-25 Mitchell bomber (71 feet) that flew off the deck of the USS *Hornet* to attack Japan in 1942. Head to Chapter 25 to find out about other weapons that were important in World War II.

With the end of the war in Europe, the 8th Air Force was transferred to the Pacific to join with the 20th Air Force. Their task was to attack targets in Japan. After November 1944 when the Allies captured these islands (see Chapter 19), the Marianas became the base for bombing attacks. (Previously, attacks on Japan came from air bases in China.)

Targeting Tokyo, Osaka, and other cities

Beginning in March 1945, American Major General Curtis LeMay sent his bomber command, all 279 aircraft, against Japanese targets at night at low level using firebombs (incendiaries). The results were devastating for the Japanese. Over 13,000 tons of bombs fell on Tokyo, Kobe, Nagoya, Yokohama, and Osaka. Over 2,000 tons of bombs fell on Tokyo alone, killing tens of thousands of people. The Tokyo attack on March 9 and 10 was the most destructive air attack in history up to that time.

With the capture of Iwo Jima (see the later section "The Fight for Iwo Jima"), U.S. fighters could escort the bombers to their targets. With near total dominance of the skies over Japan, the bombers flew lower and dropped bombs more effectively. Between January and August of 1945, about 162,000 tons of bombs fell on Japan:

>> Groups of 50 to 100 planes crossed over Japan in a regular stream, wrecking Japan's war industries one by one.

>> Nearly 1 million civilians died, and millions more were homeless.

>> Bombers dropped mines into the coastal waters around the islands to further cripple efforts to supply the Japanese by sea.

The bombers brought the war to the Japanese people in a way none ever dreamed; Japanese industry was largely wrecked and nearly all normal functions of daily life had been disrupted.

Targeting merchant ships: Submarine operations

Japan depended on her merchant fleet to supply the needs of the Japanese people and supply the raw materials Japan needed to sustain its war production. Japan also needed to provide support to Japanese troops spread out over hundreds of islands in the Pacific. This meant a constant movement of merchant ships, oil tankers, and ammunition and troop ships traveling back and forth to Japan through the sea lanes of the Pacific. The destruction of these ships meant the end of Japan's capability to fight.

The submarine was the key weapon in fighting this essential part of Japan's war effort. Although the Japanese used convoys to protect merchant ships, they weren't well organized or sufficiently protected with warships to discourage the Allied submarines.

By 1943, American submarines were sinking Japanese merchant ships faster than Japanese shipyards could build them. In 1944, the Allies sank over 3 million tons of merchant shipping while the Japanese built less than 1 million tons. By 1945, U.S. submarines were having trouble finding targets.

With no more ships venturing out into the open sea, Japanese industry began to starve for raw materials and oil. The Japanese population also suffered, especially from the lack of sufficient food.

The crews of the U.S. submarine force accomplished with Japan what the Germans had been unable to do with Britain: Bring an island nation to its knees economically through the use of unrestricted submarine warfare. Yet, the significant contribution of these men to the defeat of Japan has been largely forgotten.

The Fight for Iwo Jima

MILITARY STRATEGY

Iwo Jima is a volcanic island about eight square miles and 760 miles from Tokyo. By 1945, Iwo had become one of the most important pieces of rock in the Pacific for the following reasons:

>> It was the only island that had air bases. These airbases would allow medium bombers to hit Japan with the B-29s; fighters based on Iwo Jima could escort bombers to their targets.

>> It was midway between Saipan and Tokyo, making it ideal for emergency landings by bomber crews.

Defenses like never before: Japanese preparations

The Japanese knew how important the island was to the defense of the home islands. So the 21,000-man force led by General Kuribayashi Tadamichi moved the civilians off the island. Then taking all the experience learned from the previous island battles with the Americans since 1943, they constructed 11 miles of underground and above ground defenses:

>> Every point of land was covered by either machine guns or artillery.

>> The beaches were blocked with obstacles and thousands of mines.

>> The Japanese constructed deep underground bombproof shelters, tunnels, and carefully camouflaged fighting positions using the natural contours of the terrain to their advantage.

>> The numerous natural caves became strongholds.

General Tadamichi intended to hold off the attackers as long as possible, while the kamikaze planes wrecked the American fleet. If that plan didn't work, then the defenders were prepared to fight to the last man, each man vowing to kill at least ten Americans before he himself was killed.

Throwing a lot of stuff: Bombing before the attack

Hard experience had shown the Americans what to expect from the Japanese. No one doubted that as American troops got closer to Japan the Japanese would fight harder. They also knew that the Japanese defense of Iwo Jima would give them a glimpse of what future battles with the Japanese would be like.

The 75,000 U.S. Marines, under the command of Lieutenant General H. M. ("Howlin' Mad") Smith, who were slated to make the attack on Iwo Jima had no desire to take on the Japanese without serious preparatory fires. So the Allies hit Iwo Jima for 72 straight days with everything American naval and air power could throw at it. Although the beach obstacles and mines were largely destroyed, the Japanese defenders were safe in their tunnels and shelters.

Hitting the beach and a flag raising at Mount Suribachi

When the Marines landed on February 19, 1945, the Japanese were waiting and fully prepared (see Figure 21-2). Once the Marines were on the beach, they found themselves sinking into deep volcanic sand that hindered movement and that was so fine and loose it was almost impossible to dig into.

The Japanese fired heavily and accurately at the advancing Marines, causing the U.S. attack to slow to a literal crawl. The Marines somehow made progress, advancing against heavy fire with flame throwing tanks, grenades, artillery, and bulldozers. One of their goals was to cut off the Japanese on the southwestern portion of the island from the rest of the defenders. In the initial landing, over 2,000 Marines had already been killed or wounded.

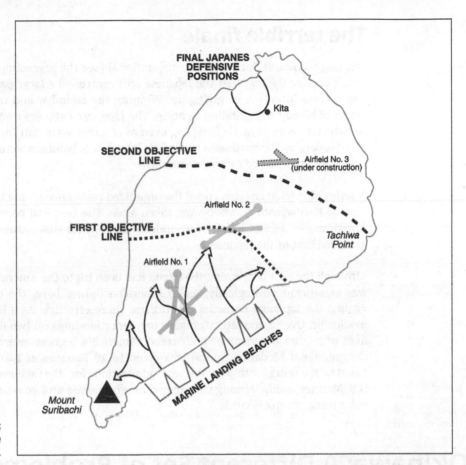

FINAL JAPANES
DEFENSIVE
POSITIONS

Kita

SECOND OBJECTIVE
LINE

Airfield No. 3
(under construction)

Airfield No. 2

FIRST OBJECTIVE
LINE

Tachiwa
Point

Airfield No. 1

MARINE LANDING BEACHES

Mount
Suribachi

FIGURE 21-2:
The Battle
of Iwo Jima.

ARMY
ALLIED

On that portion of the island was Mount Suribachi, rising 550 feet over the island. It was a natural fortress that took four days of difficult and bitter fighting to capture. As a group of Marines reached the summit on February 23 and raised the American flag on a piece of broken water pipe they had found, other Marines were still fighting Japanese attackers. The flag, seen all over the island, was greeted with American cheers.

HISTORICAL
TRIVIA

A few hours later, a larger flag came ashore and was taken up Suribachi. Here Associated Press photographer Joe Rosenthal took one of the most famous photos in history. The new flag raising appeared in the photo as perfectly composed as a classic Greek sculpture. Its beauty and symmetry gave it a serenity that contrasted with the reality of death and terror that surrounded the young Marines. The photo captured the essence of the American war effort and symbolized for the entire world the spirit of Americans in battle. Near Arlington cemetery, a giant sculpture of the Marines at Suribachi stands as a monument to all Marines who have died in battle.

The terrible finale

The flag on Mount Suribachi was inspirational (see the preceding section), but it didn't change the fact that the Japanese still controlled a large part of the island and had no intention of giving up. Winning the island would take three more weeks of bloody and grinding fighting. The Japanese defenses forced the Marines to fight for every yard. By March 4, even as Marines were battling the last group of defenders on the northwest part of the island, U.S. bombers were making emergency landings on the captured airfields.

A series of suicide charges ended the organized resistance on the island. Only 216 men of Kuribayashi's 21,000 were taken alive. The cost had been severe for the Americans — 24,800 killed or wounded. For the first time, American casualties exceeded that of the Japanese.

Although the cost of winning the island had been high, the American-held island was significant strategically. As an American fighter base, the bombing effort against the Japanese home islands became more effective. As a lifesaver, it was invaluable. Over 2,200 aircraft made emergency landings on Iwo Jima, saving the lives of 25,000 American aircraft crews. America's highest award for valor, the Congressional Medal of Honor, was given to 26 Marines at Iwo Jima. Admiral Nimitz, speaking with the deepest admiration for the achievements of the U.S. Marines, said, "Among the Americans who served on Iwo Island, uncommon valor was a common virtue."

Okinawa: A Different Set of Problems

While the battle for Iwo Jima entered its final phases, another U.S. 10th Army, under the command of General Simon B. Buckner, was making preparations for another assault to capture the island of Okinawa. Buckner's army had a strength of 225,000 men and was organized into infantry divisions and amphibious divisions, and included Marine and Army air units to provide direct support to the ground forces.

Lying about 330 miles southwest of Japan, Okinawa was a long, narrow island, with an area of about 450 square miles. Okinawa was essential as a future base of supply to support U.S. operations against the home islands of Japan. It had five airfields and space for more, with several good harbors and bays for ships and landing craft (all of which were needed to support the invasion of Japan). But capturing it presented problems for the Allies:

>> **The terrain:** In places the island was very hilly, with heavy vegetation.

>> **The civilians on the island:** Okinawa had several major towns and was heavily populated with non-Japanese, who nonetheless were hostile to the Americans. Up to this point, U.S. forces had never had to deal with large native populations, which presented a whole new set of problems: How were American forces going to protect, control, and provide for these noncombatants?

>> **The distance away from established U.S. bases:** As American troops got closer to Japan, the U.S. supply lines got longer. Everything the combat forces needed would have to travel a very long distance to get to the island. Therefore, supplying the troops would take time and, if supplies ran out during the battle, could slow down the pace of the U.S. attack.

On familiar ground: Okinawa's defenders

The Japanese were playing on their home ground. They knew Okinawa very well: They had trained their army units on the island for years and considered it part of Japan. Thus they had every intention of making the battle for Okinawa the most costly for the Americans.

The strategy was the same as it had been at Iwo Jima — defend every position to the last man while kamikaze planes destroyed the American fleet (see the section "The Fight for Iwo Jima"). To that end, nearly 2,000 kamikaze planes prepared for the arrival of the 1,500 ships that would make up the Allied invasion force. In addition, 350 suicide torpedo boats were in place to attack the fleet.

The Japanese 32nd Army under Lieutenant General Mitsura Ushijima was well trained and equipped and numbered about 100,000 men, including 20,000 members of the Okinawan home guard.

Unlike in past campaigns, the Japanese wouldn't defend the beaches. Ushijima centered his defenses around the walled town of Shuri in the southern tip of the island:

>> Around Shuri, he built concentric rings of defensive positions and then stretched bands of defensive lines across the narrow neck of the island.

>> The ridgelines that these defenses were anchored on were a maze of caves, tunnels, passageways, trenches, and underground forts, all carefully camouflaged and protected from bombardment.

>> Every foot of the defensive lines was covered by artillery or machine gun fire.

The easy landing

In early March, the Allies began the preparation for the 10th Army landings on Okinawa:

>> B-29s and carrier-based aircraft attacked airfields on the Japanese islands to limit the threat from what was left of Japan's air force.

>> U.S. battleships and naval aircraft began hitting targets on Okinawa.

>> Several smaller islands off Okinawa were captured to stave of the suicide boat threat and establish offshore depots for fuel and ammunition.

>> Minesweepers cleared channels for the fleet.

On April 1, 300 U.S. naval vessels were offshore. Meanwhile the 2nd Marine Division conducted a deception landing on the southeast end of Okinawa. A line of landing craft eight miles long streamed toward the main landing beaches.

By the end of the first day, 50,000 U.S. troops were ashore, establishing a beachhead eight miles wide and three miles deep. Japanese resistance had been minimal. The following day, the island was split in half. The Marines moved north and the Army began to move south.

The Marines had little trouble in reaching their objectives. By April 19, they occupied the northern two-thirds of the island, opposed only by 2,500 Japanese defenders on an isolated peninsula. The Army, however, ran into the first of the Japanese defensive lines and halted (see Figure 21-3).

Kamikaze attacks

In April, as the U.S. Army and Marines moved across Okinawa, hundreds of kamikaze planes swarmed about the 5th Fleet. More and more planes were needed to protect the ships (limiting air support for the lightly engaged ground forces). In the first attacks, over 380 kamikaze planes were shot down, but others found their targets, sinking 3 destroyers, 1 landing ship, 1 ammunition ship, and damaging 24 other ships.

Several days later the attacks included a new type of aircraft, a rocket powered, man-guided flying bomb, called *Okha* (cherry blossom), that was launched from a bomber. The Okha carried more than a ton and a half of explosive and traveled at speeds of over 500 miles an hour. The Americans, in reference to what they thought of the mental state of the pilots flying these bombs, called them *Baka* (fool). The attacks largely ended after April for several reasons:

FIGURE 21-3:
The Battle of
Okinawa.

>> The American attacks on the airbases in Japan had an effect.

>> American aircraft became more adept at intercepting the aircraft before they reached the fleet.

>> The Japanese high command decided to preserve what was left of its kamikaze force for the invasion of the home islands.

Before the battle for Okinawa was over, 32 U.S. ships had been sunk and another 380 damaged, causing a total of 9,800 casualties. The Japanese sacrificed over 1,800 pilots.

The end of the Japanese fleet

The last of Japan's battle fleet moved out to engage the enemy, but by this time, there wasn't enough fuel in all of Japan to move the ships very far. The eight destroyers, one cruiser, and the largest battleship ever built, *Yamato*, would make a one-way trip in a doomed attempt to take on the American fleet.

The ships had hardly started out when American carrier aircraft discovered them. Without air cover, these ships were sitting ducks. Several hundred aircraft made three separate attacks over two days. The entire fleet sank, including *Yamato*, which blew up in a giant fireball that could be seen for a hundred miles. Thus was the end of Japanese naval power.

The battle for the ridges

The main Japanese defensive lines stretched across the narrow neck of land that protected the island's main city. The defensive positions were well chosen, using the deep valley and gorges to their advantage. The 100,000 defenders had hundreds of artillery pieces they would use to break up any American attack.

The Allies had to take the first defensive line yard by yard over a period of three weeks. Once through one defensive line, the Allies faced another line two miles behind it, and the process began all over again. General Buckner brought up the Marines, who had completed their clean up of the northern portion of the island.

On May 4, the Japanese launched a massive counterattack that lasted for three days. During the counterattack, American firepower in the air and on the ground had a terrible effect: About 5,000 Japanese soldiers were killed in the open. For the haggard infantrymen, it only meant that there would be 5,000 fewer Japanese who would have to be dug out of caves. Much of the Japanese artillery was destroyed as well, leaving the Japanese to depend on individual strongpoints and fighting positions on the Shuri Line. Located in the southern part of Okinawa on a highpoint between the eastern and western beaches, the Shuri Line was the key line of defense for the Japanese. It was nearly impenetrable and had interconnected tunnels that would be almost impossible to clear.

The mud of May and the Shuri Line

Heavy rains in May made the situation on Okinawa miserable. The weather combined with complex defenses of the Shuri Line, made breaking through nearly impossible. U.S. naval gunfire, massed artillery, and airstrikes evened the odds against the American soldiers and Marines. Often the fighting took place in desperate hand-to-hand struggles.

By the end of May, the Army had broken through the Shuri Line. The Marines captured the city of Naha and linked up with the Army forces moving to surround the Japanese defenders from behind. About 63, 000 Japanese had been killed. The surviving Japanese skillfully withdrew to a final defensive position on the southern tip of the island.

Okinawa: Another costly victory

By June, the Americans were hammering against the Japanese defenders with all the power they could muster. The defensive position was strong, however, and the only way to break it was to attack with infantry, supported by tanks and aircraft. The Marines and Army infantry fought their way through the outer defenses in mid-June, breaking the remaining defenders into three pockets that the Allies finally managed to defeat on June 20, 1945. The battle for Okinawa had been terrible:

>> The Americans captured 7,400 prisoners, but the rest of the Japanese were dead. The Japanese lost nearly 8,000 aircraft and 131,000 men.

>> Okinawan civilians suffered as well; over 42,000 had been killed or wounded.

>> American ground force casualties totaled 15,500 killed (including General Buckner) and 51,000 wounded. The Navy lost nearly 10,000 men. About 1,000 American aircraft were lost.

If the battle for Okinawa was anything like what the Americans could expect when they invaded the home islands of Japan, 200,000 or more dead would not be an unrealistic estimate. Yet even before the fighting ended, Okinawa and several other smaller islands nearby were being turned into massive air and supply bases to support bombers and fighters in preparation for the final attack on Japan.

The Planned Invasion of Japan

Fairly late in the war, the U.S. reorganized the forces in the Pacific:

>> MacArthur, promoted to General of the Army (five stars) — one of only a few to ever hold the rank (the first being George Washington) — was given command of all ground forces in the Pacific and those coming from Europe to the Pacific.

>> Admiral Nimitz became a Fleet Admiral and was given command of all naval forces in the Pacific.

>> The B-29 bomber force, along with the bombers of the 8th Air Force from Europe, were consolidated into a Strategic Air Force under direction of the Joint Chiefs of Staff in Washington.

>> The Far East Air Force remained with MacArthur; the 11th Air Force in Alaska and the Aleutians were under Nimitz's command.

Such a reorganization of the forces in the Pacific at this late date in the war had one single purpose: The task given to MacArthur and Nimitz — the two most powerful military commanders in history — was nothing less than the invasion and conquest of Japan.

Planning considerations

In planning for the Allied invasion of Japan, the strategists had to consider several things: how well prepared the Japanese were for an invasion, their proven preference of death over surrender, and what the Japanese troops in China would do once Japan's home island came under attack.

Japanese morale

Indications were clear that Japan was close to collapse economically. The navy had established a blockade around the islands that would only make the economic situation even more difficult. But economic destitution did not mean the morale or will of the Japanese government and people had been affected. The devastation that the American B-29 bombers had unleashed on Japan throughout 1945 had not affected Japanese morale in any significant way.

The preparation of the Japanese

One of the primary concerns for the Allies remained the nearly 2 million Japanese soldiers — not to mention the Japanese citizens — defending the main islands of Japan.

>> Japanese troops since Guadalcanal had shown a steadfast refusal to surrender, no matter how hopeless the situation. The Japanese soldier was most dangerous when he was in a prepared defensive position and completely prepared to die.

>> Several thousand Japanese pilots were more than willing to become the kamikaze to save the homeland from invasion.

>> Japanese civilians would resist and die rather than live under the heel of a conqueror.

Fighting on the Japanese homeland would be like fighting Tarawa, Guam, Manila, Iwo Jima, and Okinawa all at once.

Japanese army in China

Above all these rather sobering realities was the question of what the Japanese army in China would do? At least 2 million veteran Japanese troops still occupied large parts of China. Would the Allies have to fight a brutal, bloody, and lengthy series of campaigns in China and Manchuria to bring about the final military defeat of Japan? It was a possibility no one wanted to contemplate.

Taking down Japan: The plan

According to the plan, the conquest of Japan would be launched in November 1945 and it would be accomplished in two parts, codename OLYMPIC and CORONET. Then, if necessary, the Allies would turn their attention to defeating the Japanese in China (see Figure 21-4).

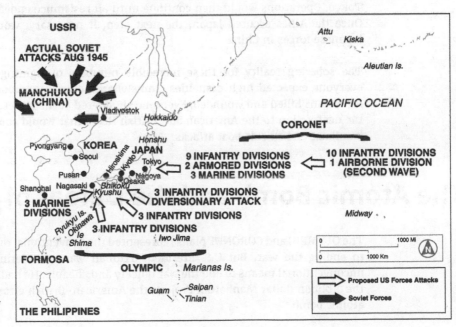

FIGURE 21-4: The Planned Attack on Japan and the Soviet Invasion of Occupied China.

OLYMPIC

The first part of the Allied invasion plan would send forces against Kyushu, the large southern island of Japan. After an air attack of nearly two thousand aircraft combined with a naval bombardment of a thousand ships, a total of about 770,000 U.S. troops would land on the island. The aim of this landing party wasn't to conquer the island. Their goal was to seize and control only a part of the island to establish air and support bases for the knockout blow, codenamed CORONET that would begin in March of 1946.

The reason for not conquering the island was that American forces would most likely face up to 680,000 defenders, essentially the entire population of the island, supported by thousands of kamikaze planes.

CORONET

After the bases had been established on Kyushu, the Allies would launch the assault against Tokyo. Nearly 4,000 aircraft would support this attack. A force of about 1 million men, most of them transferred from Europe, would land near Tokyo. Operations would then continue until all resistance ended on the islands. Once the Allies secured Japan, the next step, if necessary, would be to defeat Japanese forces in China.

The sobering reality for these incredible numbers of fighting men was that everyone expected high casualties, somewhere between 200,000 and 1 million Americans killed and wounded. Everyone shuddered at the losses, not to mention the destruction to the American and British fleets that would come as a result of kamikaze and suicide boat attacks.

The Atomic Bomb and the Defeat of Japan

The OLYMPIC and CORONET plans represented the conventional military approach to ending the war. But U.S. President Truman was considering an alternate, unconventional means to end the war quickly and cheaply. He had been briefed on the 2 billion dollar Manhattan Project, the American-British effort to produce an atomic bomb.

Truman knew that the atomic bomb had been successfully tested, and he understood its power. Despite the immense destruction that the bomb would cause, he considered it a preferable alternative to an invasion of Japan. The big question, then, wasn't "Should we or shouldn't we?" The question was "Where?"

Hiroshima: The first target

Only two bombs would be available for employment. Therefore, the targets had to be military-related and had to have a direct effect on the will of the Japanese people to carry on the war. Several cities were examined, including Tokyo (the capital and home of the Emperor), but the target list came down to Hiroshima, Kokura, Nagasaki, and Niigata. Hiroshima, which had not been hit by B-29s and was a major training center, supply depot, and transportation point, became the unlucky city.

On August 6, 1945, the B-29 named *Enola Gay* (for the pilot, Paul W. Tibbets's mother) took off from the island of Tinian carrying the bomb nicknamed Little Boy. Following him were two planes carrying instruments and observers.

FROM ATOMIC THEORY INTO MILITARY REALITY

It began as a scientific theory in the early 1930s that sketched out the concept of atomic fission, splitting atoms to produce energy. Albert Einstein in 1940 tried to enlist President Roosevelt's help to get funding to conduct experiments to test if a weapon could be made using such a concept. Although uninterested at first, by 1941, Roosevelt was willing to listen. Roosevelt committed hundreds of millions of dollars to get the best scientists and engineers in the world to turn this theory into reality. It became one of the greatest scientific and engineering achievements in history.

By 1945 the concept had become reality. Not only was the theory proven, but scientists had collected enough of a specific Uranium isotope and the byproduct of a nuclear reaction involving a Uranium isotope, called Plutonium, to be put into a bomb. By purposely creating a rapid chain reaction of sub-atomic particles, these substances could explode and release energy in unimaginable amounts (The complete details of this process are beyond this book and await the publication of *Nuclear Physics For Dummies*). The question was how to set the chain reaction to work when and where it was intended to explode on target.

By 16 July 1945, the project administrator, Brigadier General Leslie Groves and the chief scientist, J. Robert Oppenheimer, were ready to test a Plutonium bomb in the New Mexico desert. It exploded as planned with the force of 17,000 tons of TNT and a giant mushroom cloud rose 40,000 feet into the air. Truman, at the Potsdam conference with Stalin and Churchill at the time, received news of the successful test. It was then that he passed on to an already well-informed Stalin the existence of a weapon of great destructive power. The only question now was how and where to use the next bombs produced.

The people in Hiroshima, including 43,000 soldiers, heard an air raid warning and entered the shelters, only to get an all clear just before a single B-29 appeared overhead. At 8:16 a.m., 31,000 feet over Hiroshima, the first atomic bomb was used against a military target. It exploded about 1,900 feet above the ground. The explosion was estimated to be equal to 12,500 tons of TNT. The heat and blast effect of the weapon caused the highest number of casualties. A few days later, people in large numbers began to die from radiation poisoning.

Japanese government reaction

As information slowly filtered into the members of the Japanese government, it became clear that the Americans were playing an entirely new game. They heard President Truman's announcement of the Hiroshima bombing and his assertion that the United States was ready to wipe out every city in Japan. The Japanese armed forces were unmoved by the news. Many thought the Americans were bluffing and suspected that the U.S. had only one bomb. The Japanese government, meanwhile, decided to await a full report on the bombing from Hiroshima before making any decisions.

Meanwhile, B-29s continued to fly over Japan at will, dropping thousands of tons of conventional bombs on industrial targets. With no response from the Japanese, the U.S. prepared the second atomic bomb. But before it was ready, the Soviet Union played its card in the stacked deck against Japan.

The Soviets declare war on Japan

The Soviet government delivered a declaration of war to the Japanese ambassador in Moscow an hour before midnight on August 8, 1945. On August 9, the USSR launched nearly a half million men, nearly 4,000 aircraft, 3,700 tanks, and 1,800 self-propelled guns (essentially a large, armor shielded artillery piece on a tank chassis) against the Japanese army in Manchuria.

Although on paper the Japanese army outnumbered the Soviets, they were generally poor quality troops. The best had been stripped to fight against the Americans on the Pacific islands in 1944 and 1945. The Japanese had no aircraft or weapons of any sort to stop tanks. Thus, they were at the mercy of the Soviet Army. The Soviets rapidly drove into the interior of what had been undisputed Japanese territory since 1931.

Nagasaki next

While the Soviet attack was underway in China, Fat Man, the second atomic bomb, was ready for delivery to its target, Kokura. The B-29, flown by Major Charles Sweeney, was named *Bock's Car*. Sweeney flew over the target on the island of Kyushu, but cloud cover prevented an accurate drop. So Sweeney headed his plane to his secondary target, Nagasaki.

The city was home to one of the largest shipyards in Japan. Despite poor weather over the target, Sweeney let the bomb go at 29,000 feet. The bomb exploded off target, but it detonated with the equivalent of 22,000 tons of TNT. The blast and heat effects were similar to the effects in Hiroshima, although the surrounding valleys and hills shielded parts of the city from greater destruction.

The cost

The estimates of casualties vary widely, but the two atomic bombs are believed to have killed 100,000 to 200,000 people. The desire to save American lives and end the war as quickly as possible without an invasion of Japan made the use of the atomic bombs inevitable.

When considering the destructive power of the atomic bombs, remember that the Japanese mainland was being hit regularly with B-29 attacks that routinely delivered 4,000 to 5,000 tons of bombs in a single attack. Thus, to American planners, the atomic weapons delivered roughly the same tonnage that the enemy was already being hit with. The difference, of course, was the destructive effect from one massive explosion created by an atomic bomb from one aircraft versus the effect of thousands of smaller explosions from a rain of bombs from hundreds of planes.

The end of an era: The Emperor submits

The news was all bad for the Japanese leadership meeting in Tokyo after the bombing of Nagasaki. The Supreme War Council, which had run the war, was divided evenly. Three wanted to continue the war, three wanted to make peace and submit to the Allied terms, but with one exception: The Emperor of Japan, revered as a god-man for centuries, could not be affected.

The Japanese sent a message to the Allies with this proposal, but the Allies rejected it. Unconditional surrender came the reply on August 10. The Emperor would reign, but he would be subject to the Supreme Commander of Allied Forces, who would be the de facto ruler of Japan during the occupation by Allied forces.

This reply set the war council into another series of meetings that lasted four days. To help the Japanese along with their decision, over 700 Allied B-29s appeared again on 14 August and dropped almost 4,500 tons of explosives on military targets. That day, the Emperor arrived at the council meeting to make an announcement. "I have surveyed the conditions prevailing in Japan and the world at large," he told them, "and it is my belief that a continuation of the war promises nothing but additional destruction." He had decided to accept the Allied terms and would make an announcement to the people of Japan.

The announcement to the Japanese people

At noon on August 15, 1945, the Emperor of Japan addressed his people by radio. He had never spoken to the people before, and using an obscure court dialect (that no doubt sounded to many listening like the voice of God), Emperor Hirohito told them that "the war situation has developed not necessarily to Japan's advantage." Following the Emperor's address was an announcement stating that the two atomic bombs were the reason for Japan's surrender.

Despite the words of the Emperor, some in the Japanese military were willing to disobey orders and continue resistance. The War Minister committed suicide, and a group of officers attempted to break into the palace to convince the Emperor to continue the war. When ordered to surrender, the soldiers committed suicide. In fact, the Japanese army in Manchuria fought on until August 22, despite announcements of a cease-fire. Japanese units fought the Soviets on Sakhalin Island until September 3. The Soviets eventually took 2.7 million Japanese soldiers into captivity, using many of them as forced labor.

The Japanese surrender

Once the Japanese government had submitted, Allied forces (except the Soviets, who had been desperately trying to get an invasion of the Japanese islands underway before the surrender) began to move into Japan. In Manchuria, the Soviets began carting away factories and raw materials as they had in Germany, claiming it was their fair share of reparations for entering the war.

**ARMY
ALLIED**

On September 2, with the most powerful fleet in the history of the world in Tokyo Bay, the Japanese delegation arrived on the battleship *Missouri* to sign the formal surrender document, while 2,000 aircraft flew over in formation as a reminder of Allied power. MacArthur and Nimitz signed the document, along with representatives of the Allied nations (including the USSR). MacArthur signed as the Supreme Allied Commander and asked Generals Wainwright and Percival, two officers who had just been released from prison camp, to accompany him. (Wainwright had surrendered the Philippines to the Japanese in 1942 and Percival had surrendered

Singapore in 1942. MacArthur wanted them to share in the triumph that had been denied them as commanders.) MacArthur concluded the brief ceremony with these words: "It is . . . the hope of all mankind that from this solemn occasion a better world shall emerge from the blood and carnage of the past."

Posted conspicuously where the Japanese could see it was an American flag with 31 stars. It was the flag that Commodore Matthew C. Perry flew when the first American warship first entered Tokyo Bay in 1853.

The Allied Occupation of Japan

MacArthur, as Supreme Allied Commander, had personal responsibility for running the occupation of Japan. He worked out of the Dai Ichi building in Tokyo (in Japanese, *Dai Ichi* means Number One). MacArthur was the *Dai Ichi*, supervising the day-to-day activities of the Japanese government and respecting the Emperor's unique role in Japanese life. He helped to rebuild Japanese life after the war by doing the following:

>> Abolishing the armed forces.

>> Instituting democratic reforms.

>> Giving women the right to vote.

>> Reorganizing business practices to resemble American corporations.

MacArthur also oversaw land reform programs and in a short time became something of a demigod in his own right among the Japanese people. He would remain in Japan until relieved of command and recalled by President Truman in 1951 during another war; this one in Korea.

Chapter **22**

The Uneasy Peace

The plain fact is that 60 million people died in World War II. Of those 60 million dead, more had been civilians than soldiers. The destruction — physical, psychological, and spiritual — was unimaginable. Entire cities lay in ruin; some of the world's greatest architectural and cultural treasures had been destroyed. Factories, public buildings, canals, dams, dykes, and bridges were destroyed. Every nation involved in the war — except the United States — had been financially exhausted.

The world at the end of 1945 was a very different place than the world of 1938. In some ways, it was better, and in some ways it was worse. Today, we're still dealing with the aftermath — and the memories — of those years.

The Costs: A Global Assessment

Every country that engaged in World War II paid a price for its participation. Some countries — particularly the European countries and Japan — where battles were fought within the country's borders paid a higher price. Here's a quick — and very grim — rundown of the human cost of World War II:

» The Soviet Union lost the most, with a staggering 25 million deaths; only about a third of them were combat related.

- China's death toll is incomplete, but estimates are between 15 and 22 million.

- Poland suffered 6 million deaths, including 3 million Jews, roughly 20 percent of its prewar population.

- Germany lost 4 million soldiers, listed as dead or missing, and over 2 million civilians — many of them women.

- The Japanese had 1.2 million battle deaths and another 1.4 million soldiers listed as missing. Almost 1 million Japanese civilians were killed in the bombing raids between 1944 and 1945.

- Over 1.7 million Yugoslavs and half a million Greeks died in the war.

- France lost 200,000 soldiers and 400,000 civilians.

- Italy lost 330,000 people.

- Hungary lost 147,000 men in combat; Bulgaria lost 19,000 in combat, and Romania lost 73,000.

- Great Britain lost 264,000 soldiers to combat deaths and 60,000 civilians to bombing raids.

- The United States lost 292,000 soldiers.

- The Dutch suffered 10,000 military casualties and almost 190,000 civilian casualties.

- Australia lost 23,000 men in combat, and Canada lost 37,000.

- India lost 24,000 men in battle, New Zealand lost 10,000, and South Africa lost 6,000.

These totals don't include the 6 million Jews who perished in the Final Solution of Nazi Germany or the 17 million dead as a result of Japan's policies in Asia from 1931 to 1945.

Remaking the World: War and Technology

The nations at war developed rockets, jet planes, plastics, synthetics, and hundreds of other things that changed the world. Technological advancements began to rapidly change the lives of people around the world, a process that continues today.

When the mystery of the atom was unlocked, the world had to deal with the consequences, both good and bad. Knowledge of the atom's power, and advancing technology, created many benefits to humankind in energy and medicine, but it also led to vast arsenals of nuclear weapons that contained the power to destroy the world. Today, we still debate the role of atomic power, and we are still threatened by those who would use it to threaten the peace of the world.

Giving Peace a Chance: The United Nations

Organized in April 1945, the United Nations was intended to be a successor to the ineffective League of Nations from World War I (see Chapter 2). The signatories of the charter, which included the United States this time, dedicated themselves to maintaining peace and resolving potential conflicts without war. The United States would play a key role in supporting the United Nations.

Despite its lofty goals, the UN faced obstacles almost immediately. Initially intended as an international police force, the United Nations was hard pressed in the realities of the postwar world to actually enforce peace. The Security Council — the primary decision-making body within the UN — came into deadlock almost immediately. Responsible for declaring a nation an aggressor and authorizing sanctions or military force to ensure compliance, the Security Council members (Great Britain, France, the United States, the Soviet Union, and China) couldn't agree. And without unanimous agreement in the Security Council, the UN couldn't act.

In the unsettled postwar world, the Security Council was nearly impotent. The Soviet Union regularly vetoed resolutions. This often left Britain — and then more and more frequently, the United States — to act outside of the United Nations in dealing with world crises.

A New World Emerges

World War II was fought in Europe to save Western Civilization from the scourge of Nazism. It was fought in Asia to prevent a militaristic Japan from dominating the Pacific and imposing its own brand of tyranny on the people who lived there. In this narrow context, the Allies accomplished their objectives. But the war created new situations that led to further wars and conflicts that continue to trouble us today.

>> In Asia and the Middle East, Great Britain and France attempted to step back into their roles as colonial rulers as if WWII never happened. The Dutch quickly found that folks in the East Indies were no longer interested in remaining a colony. In Burma, Singapore, and India, the British were less than welcome. The French found Communist guerrillas, armed largely with Japanese weapons, waiting for them. In just a few years, the great empires of France and Britain — in existence for hundreds of years — would dissolve with remarkable swiftness.

>> Nationalist Chinese leader Chiang Kai-shek and Communist Chinese leader Mao Tse-tung resumed their civil war in earnest, each hoping to gain and keep the battlefield initiative.

>> In the Middle East, Jews wanting to return to their ancestral homeland, combined with the British-American sponsorship of a permanent Jewish homeland in Palestine, led to a direct confrontation with Palestinian Arabs.

>> In Europe, the continent became starkly divided. At Yalta and Potsdam, Stalin had cemented politically what he had won on the battlefield.

>> Eastern Europe became a reflection of the totalitarian Stalinist state. Czechoslovakia fell in a Soviet-engineered coup shortly after the war, and Tito, the erstwhile Yugoslav Communist guerrilla chieftain turned head of state (see Chapter 18), while nominally following Stalin's dictates, tried to mold an independent nation out of the numerous ethnic identities that formed Yugoslavia.

>> Old Germany had been replaced completely. Over 10 million Germans had been deported from the Soviet-controlled east and moved into the western occupation zones. Millions more were refugees who had fled west in the last months of the war.

>> The Soviets pushed Poles into the vacated German territories and moved Russians into old Poland, now part of sovereign Soviet territory. It was ethnic cleansing, and it allowed Stalin to redefine the map of Europe between a communist east, led by the Soviet Union, and a democratic west, led by the United States.

In short, Europe was quite different after the war (see Figure 22-1).

FIGURE 22-1:
Europe, 1945.

The Beginnings of the Cold War

By 1946, the alliance that had defeated Germany consolidated its gains (in the case of the Soviet Union) or protected what it had left (in the case of Western Europe and the United States). There would be no cooperation between the two. Casting a shadow over all of this was the power of nuclear weapons, held solely by the United States at first, and then by the Soviets as well.

As the ideological and political differences between the USSR and the U.S. turned into open animosity, and as both nations felt the threat of the other's growing nuclear arsenal, the rancor and distrust solidified into what eventually became known as the *Cold War*.

THE IRON CURTAIN

British Prime Minister Winston Churchill, who had no equal when it came to using the English language to summon people to a higher calling, put his finger on what was occurring in postwar Europe. In 1946, at Westminster College in Fulton, Missouri, Churchill defined the new world for everyone: "A shadow has fallen upon the scenes so lately lighted by the Allied victory . . . . From Stettin in the Baltic to Trieste in the Adriatic, an iron curtain has descended across the Continent . . . . [T]his is certainly not the Liberated Europe we fought to build up. Nor is it one which contains the essentials of permanent peace."

It was a Cold War because it couldn't be resolved by direct confrontation. A direct confrontation with nuclear weapons was unthinkable. So this war had to be fought by other means and would last as long as it took for one side or the other to give up.

The Cold War was a war of beliefs, fought both in public forums (like the United Nations) and through clandestine activity and covert actions (think spies and espionage). It was fought by proxy states or by the U.S. and Soviet combat forces in outlying areas of the world, such as Korea, Vietnam, Angola, and Afghanistan.

Some Final Thoughts

World War II began with an uneasy peace and ended with an uneasy peace. Many of the troubles that plague the world today have their roots in the aftermath of the greatest and most terrible war in human history. But many of the economic and political benefits that have given many of the nations of the world a chance to develop and flourish in the modern world stem from the victories won and the lives sacrificed at those obscure places listed in the beginning of this book. Without such victories, the world would be a place of unendurable misery and oppression, of barbaric law, and organized mass murder. Perhaps now those obscure places will have more meaning.

7

The Part of Tens

Chapter **23**

Ten Formidable Military Leaders of World War II

When putting together such a list, you're always going to exclude someone who deserves recognition. Anyone can make an equally strong argument for or against someone on (or not on) this list. I base these selections on personal leadership, overall ability to apply the art of war, the ability to lead and inspire men in combat, and the application of personal will to achieve national objectives. To avoid too much controversy, I list these names alphabetically.

Winston S. Churchill: Timeless Excellence

**ARMY
ALLIED**

Churchill was Prime Minister of Britain in its darkest days and led a great nation to victory with little other than a righteous cause, the power of the English language, and the strong right arm of the United States (which he was not afraid to twist every now and then to get what he needed). Winston Churchill was a giant among other great men: He was a man of insight, intelligence, wit, and, above all, will. He personified the wartime spirit of Great Britain and the British Empire, unwilling to concede anything to Hitler, even in the darkest days of the war, and always pointing to the inevitable victory.

As a strategist, Churchill had flaws — he often looked so broadly at strategic objectives that he ignored real obstacles and limits to success — but he excelled at the political art. Churchill understood better than any other wartime leader the connection between politics and war. His friendship with Roosevelt helped win the war, but Roosevelt's wooing of Stalin caused Churchill agony. He saw Stalin's objectives clearly and attempted to block the tide that was turning against him.

**HISTORICAL
TRIVIA**

A nineteenth century man in many ways, Churchill remains the greatest man of the twentieth century.

Dwight D. Eisenhower: Don't Worry, Be Happy

**ARMY
ALLIED**

Unlike MacArthur (see the following section), Eisenhower never commanded troops in combat, nor did people find him abrasive. As Supreme Allied Commander in Europe, Eisenhower got along with people and could subdue his own ego to accomplish the primary goal: Allied victory in Europe. In the difficult world of alliances and coalitions, Eisenhower kept everyone pulling together.

Eisenhower directed strategy and oversaw the coordination of British, Canadian, American, and French forces into a (mostly) harmonious whole. Eisenhower also had to make very difficult decisions, not as an American but as an ally. His decision to launch D-Day on June 6 is universally praised, but his decisions to give British General Montgomery the priority for fuel and ammunition in 1944 to execute the botched MARKET GARDEN offensive and his decision to stop U.S. and British forces at the Elbe are often second guessed, even today. (See Chapters 18 and 21 for discussions of these events.) Still, Eisenhower made necessary decisions at necessary times, which is what a commander does.

Douglas MacArthur: Damn the Torpedoes!

**ARMY
ALLIED**

American General Douglas MacArthur was one of the most visible leaders in World War II, outstaging the master showman himself, Franklin Roosevelt, at times. Sometimes hard to deal with, MacArthur acted as if he knew he was going to win the war and that all he needed were the proper resources.

MacArthur's campaigns in the Pacific were often successful because he quickly mastered using bombers and fighters to support the troops maneuvering on the ground. By effectively combining the strengths of his air, ground, and naval forces, MacArthur kept the Japanese off-balance. He led an exceptional fighting force to victory with minimal losses against a determined foe.

HISTORICAL TRIVIA

In peace, MacArthur led the reform of Japan, thereby helping to cement a friendship and partnership between the Americans and the Japanese that lasted two generations — something unthinkable in 1945.

George C. Marshall: Sterling Dedication

ARMY ALLIED

American George C. Marshall was Chief of Staff of the Army and architect of victory during World War II, Secretary of State after the war, and author of the Marshall Plan that saved Europe from economic ruin, famine, and Communism. Saying which George C. Marshall did better is hard.

As Chief of Staff of the United States Army, Marshall remained in Washington to direct the strategic direction of the war. He was Roosevelt's right-hand man and trusted advisor. As such, Marshall helped shape the most important strategic decision of the war: Attack Germany first.

Marshall monitored the atomic bomb project and made the decisions concerning who got what resources when. Each year of the war, Marshall gave directives to Eisenhower and MacArthur listing priorities and objectives. Without Marshall's firm and steady guidance, it's hard to say what direction the war may have taken or whether it would've gone on longer. Marshall was a man with great strategic insight and enormous moral stature who translated political goals into clear military objectives.

Chester W. Nimitz: Master of the Sea

ARMY ALLIED

A friendly man with a relaxed approach to his duties, American Admiral Chester W. Nimitz often hid an iron will and a strategic brilliance that justifiably made him one of the greatest naval commanders in history.

As commander of the Pacific Fleet, Nimitz displayed exceptional skills in picking subordinates, fleet commanders, and Marine generals who weren't afraid to get into a fight. His strategy employed attacking the Japanese at key points and challenging the Japanese naval dominance of the Pacific while conserving American combat power. Nimitz understood the role of the aircraft carrier in naval warfare and put it to use better than anyone else. The Doolittle raid (see Chapter 19) launched from the deck of a carrier was a quick answer to Pearl Harbor. He was willing to fight the Japanese on their own terms using carriers at Midway (explained in Chapter 15).

Nimitz, a submariner by trade, understood the role submarines should play in the eventual defeat of Japan. While his ever-growing fleets of ships and aircraft hit Japanese defensive points and his Marines assaulted the islands, Nimitz's submarines slowly destroyed the Japanese merchant fleet. Nimitz nearly single-handedly turned the naval war in the Pacific around in a matter of months against one of the best and most experienced navies in the world. His skill in executing his strategy resulted in a remarkable fact: By 1944, after the Battle of Leyte Gulf (see Chapter 19), the Japanese fleet ceased to exist for all intents and purposes.

George S. Patton: A Warrior for All Seasons

**ARMY
ALLIED**

American General George S. Patton was a remarkable combat leader in war and a terrible soldier in peacetime. No other American was as dedicated to his craft as Patton. Patton embraced the new concept of armored warfare and helped perfect it just before World War II started. He was ruthless in carrying out his plans and sought to move rapidly against the enemy. He was at his best in exploiting enemy weaknesses and maneuvering rapidly. Patton was so emotionally tied to soldierly ideals that he sometimes lashed out at those he believed did not live up to those ideals.

Although not good at *static warfare* (holding positions rather than advancing), Patton excelled at leading an army on the move. When he had the chance to crush the Bulge (in the Battle of the Bulge) in December 1944 or drive into Czechoslovakia in the spring of 1945, Patton was at his best. (See Chapter 18 for info on these events.)

Patton chafed at restrictions placed on him due to political decisions and didn't hesitate to share his opinion with his superiors, specifically Allied Supreme Commander Dwight Eisenhower and American General Omar Bradley. Before dying in a car accident, Patton requested to be buried with his troops in the 3rd Army cemetery in Luxembourg.

Irwin Rommel: The Desert Fox

ARMY AXIS

Irwin Rommel is one of the best and most respected German generals in World War II. Rommel is remembered for his use of tanks, his aggressive approach to warfare, and his willingness to take risks, as well as his tactical brilliance. He helped give the German Army its image of invincibility in the desert campaign of 1942. The image of Rommel — dust goggles, trench coat, and leading from the front — also gave the Germans a much-needed boost in morale as the attack against the USSR ground to a halt.

Rommel was the first German Commander that the British and Americans had to deal with in their African offensive (see Chapter 13). Always a dangerous opponent, Rommel won respect from his enemies. He directed the West Wall Defenses in France (Chapter 20) and commanded the army group that resisted Allied landings in Normandy, waiting in vain for the tanks that would eventually turn the battle around (Chapter 18).

Fighting skillfully but in a doomed effort, Rommel was wounded before experiencing Germany's inevitable defeat. He gained far greater respect for his support of the plot to kill Hitler in 1944 (see Chapter 9). Choosing suicide, Rommel spared his family and associates from a public trial and death.

Franklin D. Roosevelt: Artful Dodger

ARMY ALLIED

Without proper political direction, no war can be successful. President Franklin D. Roosevelt provided that political direction for the United States. A brilliant politician (certainly one of the most effective in American history), Roosevelt brought America to the edge of war, skillfully ducking and dodging the legal restrictions of the Neutrality Acts. He kept Britain alive in 1940 and 1941 with the legal sleight of hand he called Lend-Lease. (See Chapter 7 for more about the Neutrality Acts and America's lend-lease policy.)

Roosevelt risked open war with Germany by escorting merchant ships with U.S. warships and then arming neutral merchantmen. He challenged the Japanese by using the only lever he had to direct them away from aggression: He cut them off from American oil, scrap metal, and steel, and then finally froze Japanese assets in America. Some people view these acts as waving the red flag in front of a bull. Perhaps Roosevelt saw it as an attempt to warn potential enemies not to threaten the U.S.

As a war leader, President Roosevelt allowed the military to direct strategy, but he contributed the concept of unconditional surrender, something that the military didn't like but carried out. Roosevelt led and inspired the American people during the war. His death in April 1945 marked a turning point in American political and diplomatic history.

Isoroku Yamamoto: Samurai Warrior

Opposed to the idea of Japan going to war against the U.S., Japanese Admiral Isoroku Yamamoto was still considered one of the great military leaders of the war. American educated (he attended Harvard in the 1920s), Yamamoto believed that the Japanese would be victorious during the first year of a Japanese-American conflict but that after that, Japan was destined to lose due to the U.S.'s industrial and military might.

Still, when called to serve his country, Yamamoto served well and courageously. Believing that a conventional war against the United States was futile, he planned the Japanese attack on Pearl Harbor. After Pearl Harbor, Yamamoto turned his attention to destroying the U.S. fleet in the Pacific, near the island of Midway. With the advantage of surprise, Yamamoto's plan would have likely inflicted grave damage on the U.S. fleet. As it happened, the U.S. had broken the Japanese fleet code and thus knew of the attack and were prepared when they arrived at Midway. Yamamoto also fought to hold Guadalcanal in what ended up being a drawn-out, brutal battle between Allied and Japanese soldiers. (See Chapter 15 for a discussion of these battles.)

Understanding the danger posed by Yamamoto's strategic skill and grim determination to fight to the end, the Allies, upon intercepting a radio message indicating Yamamoto's position, sent Allied fighters to shoot down his plane on April 18, 1943. Yamamoto, regarded as a special hero by the Japanese, was killed in the attack.

Georgi Zhukov: Leading the Masses

ARMY
ALLIED

Soviet General Georgi Zhukov was responsible for the defense of Moscow in 1941, the event that prevented the collapse of Stalin's regime. As Deputy Supreme Commander in Chief, Zhukov skillfully directed the war against Germany, winning the decisive battle of Stalingrad with a mixture of desperation and hardheaded stubbornness. He did the same in directing operations to relieve the siege of

Leningrad. (See Chapter 6 for a discussion of these battles.) After the front stabilized, Zhukov directed the massive counterblows that ruptured the German front and led to the great Soviet victories of 1943 and 1944. He personally directed the assault on Berlin in April 1945 and received the formal surrender of the Germans on May 8 (see Chapter 21).

During the early battles with the Germans, the Soviets lacked (or didn't make effective use of) military weapons at their disposal. The one weapon they had that Germany couldn't match — and that Zhukov was more than willing to use — was sheer numbers of troops. Zhukov used massed attacks, in which the Soviet soldiers didn't necessarily outfight the Germans but overwhelmed them with numbers. This strategy usually guaranteed victory but at the cost of heavy losses to the Soviet Army. Despite the brutality of such warfare, the Soviet people dutifully and willingly made the sacrifice to save their country. In fact, the war is known to the Soviets as the Great Patriotic War and represents a shining moment in their history.

Chapter **24**

Ten Weapons That Made a Difference

From the rifleman to the atomic bomb, the issues of World War II were decided in the end by superior weapons. Whoever had the most of the best came out on top. Although the Germans produced superior weaponry, for example, they didn't produce sufficient quantities to make a difference. This chapter presents a list of World War II weapons that represent the best in quality and innovation at the time.

The German MG-42 Machine Gun

ARMY AXIS

Germany was unmatched in light weapons design. In World War II, the finest light machine gun in the world was the MG-42. It was capable of firing 1,200 rounds per minute at a range of about 4,000 yards, which amounted to significant fire-power for a squad or platoon. The MG-42 was lightweight (a big plus for the soldiers carrying it day after day) and, best of all, was easily mass-produced.

HISTORICAL TRIVIA

The MG-42 machine gun was so good that the United States later copied the design for its own machine gun, the M-60. In fact, the MG-42 design was copied by arms manufacturers around the world. These variations of the MG-42 basic design continue to serve modern armies today.

The German Tiger Tank

ARMY AXIS

The Tiger tanks had no equal on the battlefield of World War II. Originally designed for use in Russia, this 60-ton monster tank fought throughout Europe. The Tiger tank had the best combination of protection and firepower of any tank in World War II:

>> Massive armor on the hull and on the turret

>> An 88-millimeter main gun

>> Wide treads for cross-country travel

>> The capability to cross through water up to 16 feet deep

Unfortunately, the Tiger's engine was underpowered, and it was not as effective as expected in moving over muddy or snow-covered ground (in Russia, the ground is either one or the other most of the time). Likewise, the tank was not successful in Italy because of the hilly terrain and lack of bridges strong enough to hold it. In Normandy, however, and in the battlefields in France and Germany, the Tiger performed at its best.

The Americans, Canadians, and British found that virtually none of their weapons was powerful enough to stop a Tiger Tank. The best hope the Allies had was either to knock off a tread and immobilize it or to literally mass the firepower of several tanks at once and try to hit it in the rear, where the Tiger's armor protection was lightest.

As effective as the Tiger was, production numbers were low because they were produced late in the war. The last version of the Tiger was the 80-ton King Tiger, which Americans met in the Battle of the Bulge. The Tiger influenced tank design around the world for many years after the war.

The M-1 Garand Rifle

ARMY ALLIED

American General George Patton called the M-1 Garand rifle "the greatest battle implement ever devised." The M-1 rifle was the basic American infantryman's weapon in World War II. Its accuracy, volume of fire, and reliability were exceptional.

MILITARY STRATEGY

The Germans and Japanese used *bolt action rifles*, which meant that soldiers had to load a new round of ammunition manually before they could fire the weapon again. The M-1 was *semi-automatic*, meaning that soldiers could fire round after round by simply squeezing the trigger. Trained soldiers could deliver eight aimed rounds in 20 seconds. (Anybody can shoot bullets out of a weapon in a few seconds; what matters is being able to take aim and hit what you intend to hit.) Aimed fire from the M-1 meant that American soldiers were able to send more bullets in the enemy's direction than the enemy could return. With the enemy ducking for cover, American troops maneuvered against enemy positions and destroyed them. The M-1 weighed 9½ pounds and was ruggedly built to withstand abuse and rough handling. The M-1's combat range was 50 yards, but it was capable of firing out to 3,500 yards.

HISTORICAL TRIVIA

No war has ever been won (and it's safe to say that no war will ever be won) until infantrymen are standing on the ground that the enemy wants to defend. American infantrymen won the ground (and therefore World War II) with the M-1 rifle.

The V-2 Rocket

ARMY AXIS

The first V-2 rocket hit England in September 1944, moving at a speed of 3,500 miles per hour. It was the world's first medium-range ballistic missile, the grand-daddy of the infamous SCUD missiles of the Gulf War and the intercontinental ballistic missiles (ICBM) that make up the strategic arsenals of the United States and Russia.

The V-2 was one of Hitler's "wonder weapons," intended to turn the tide of the war. Launched from the coast of Europe, the missile with a one-ton warhead could travel a maximum range of 225 miles. It was undetectable until it hit. The V-2 didn't change the course of the war, mostly because it wasn't very accurate, but its effect on the future of military technology and warfare, as well as the space program, was far reaching.

The basic design of the V-2, although highly modified by modern technology, is essentially the starting point for all rocket and ballistic missile technology. You can see a real V-2 at the Smithsonian Air and Space museum in Washington, D.C.

The P-51 Mustang

ARMY ALLIED

The P-51 Mustang was one of the miracles of American military production. Developing from a British suggestion for a new fighter in 1940 to full-scale production in 1942, the Mustang first appeared over German skies with American pilots in 1943.

With its speed and maneuverability, the P-51 Mustang had no equal in air combat. Most importantly, the Mustang's extended range and fuel tanks enabled the Allies to provide protection for the B-17s from their bases in Britain to their targets in Germany and then back to Britain again. The Mustang was also able to fly at the same high altitudes that the B-17 bombers flew. When Mustangs began escorting the B-17 bombers to targets in Germany, the *Luftwaffe* (see Chapter 2) got a nasty surprise: They found that the big bombers were no longer easy targets. The Mustang kept the enemy at bay and therefore contributed significantly to the success of the Allied strategic bombing campaign.

With the Mustang flying alongside the B-17s, the effectiveness of the Allied strategic bombing offensive improved, and bomber losses declined. The P-51 Mustang also effectively supported ground troops by firing rockets mounted on the wings or dropping 1,000-pound bombs with devastating effect on German tanks and infantry.

The Mustang dominated the skies, assuring the success of Eisenhower's ground campaign and giving the strategic bombing campaign the capability to inflict increasing damage on German war industries.

The Me-262 Jet Aircraft

ARMY AXIS

The Me-262 (Me is the abbreviation for *Messerschmidt*, the German manufacturer) is one of the most beautiful aircraft ever built (in my opinion anyway). It was also the first military jet aircraft whose advanced capabilities were not matched by any nation until 1949. The design was actually on paper as early as 1938, and an experimental model was built and flown in 1941, but the Nazi bureaucracy had no interest. Overconfident after a series of too-easy victories, no one believed such an aircraft was necessary. It wasn't until Allies began regular bombing raids on German cities that Hitler decided to take an interest.

The Me-262 was intended for use as a fighter, and in that role, no Allied aircraft could've matched it. However, Hitler ordered it built as a fighter-bomber — a request akin to asking that all-terrain tires be put on a sports car! Hitler's change in design slowed this Me-262 down to speeds where the Allies' agile P-51 Mustang (see the preceding section) could challenge it. Although the Germans eventually redesigned it as a fighter, this change came too late to turn the tide of the war back in Germany's favor.

Although the Me-262 had no effect on the outcome of the war, it did have an extraordinary effect on the future of combat aircraft design for nearly a generation.

The B-17 Bomber: The Flying Fortress

ARMY ALLIED

The B-17 was the workhorse and symbol of the United States strategic bombing offensive in Europe. It represented the raw power of high explosive bombs delivered by aircraft and it became the centerpiece of United States Air Force doctrine.

First built in 1935, the B-17 was one of the few advanced weapon designs that the U.S. produced prior to the war. The bomber's greatest asset was its capability to fly long distances — nearly 2,000 miles. The B-17 was heavily modified in the first years of the war with additional machine gun mounts and became known as the *Flying Fortress*.

The Americans put the B-17 to use in the daylight raids against Germany, relying on the B-17's armament and toughness to overcome *Luftwaffe* (see Chapter 2) air attack and antiaircraft fire from the ground. By 1944, the B-17 was the dominant bomber used in Europe, with as many as 1,000 planes at a time hitting targets. The B-17 proved its worth many times over in contributing to the defeat of Germany.

The 88 mm Gun

ARMY AXIS

The most famous artillery piece of the war was the German 88 mm (millimeter) gun, known as the 88. Originally designed as an antiaircraft gun, the 88 was quite effective in that role. However, German General (later Field Marshal) Irwin Rommel, a bright student of war, pointed it at a tank rather than an airplane. The results were extraordinary! In 1941, the British lost more than 40 tanks to Rommel's 88s used as anti-tank guns.

HISTORICAL TRIVIA

The 88 forced the Allies to change their tank designs after 1941. The American Sherman tank was designed with the capabilities of the 88 in mind. The Germans incorporated the 88 into the main armament of its Tiger Tanks, and the 88 was mounted on tank destroyers as well. Although British, Soviet, and American weapon designs tried to match the capabilities of the 88, they never could.

The German 88, as a separate anti-tank gun or incorporated into a tank or tank destroyer, ruled the armored battlefield of World War II.

The Yorktown and Essex Class Carriers

ARMY ALLIED

The future of America in 1941 and 1942 rested on the flat tops of six aircraft carriers in the Pacific (*Wasp, Hornet, Yorktown, Enterprise, Saratoga,* and *Lexington*). By 1942, only the *Enterprise* and *Saratoga* hadn't been sunk in combat with the Imperial Japanese Navy. Without its carriers, the United States was powerless. As these original carriers succumbed to the Japanese fleet, America's industrial might produced replacements, called the *Essex* class aircraft carriers. Larger and faster than the carriers they replaced, this class of carrier could carry more aircraft. Altogether, the U.S. produced 11 of these carriers, some of which took the names of the original six aircraft carriers.

By 1943, the *Essex* class carriers turned the tide of battle, controlling the air and sea in the Pacific, isolating Japanese defenders, and allowing American ground forces to engage and destroy the enemy. If naval power won victory in the Pacific, the *Yorktown* and *Essex* class carriers were the source of that power. The Japanese couldn't match these carriers in quality or quantity, which guaranteed Japan's military defeat.

The Atomic Bomb

ARMY ALLIED

A weapon of enormous power, the atomic bomb ended World War II in a way that no other weapon could have. The destructive power of the two bombs that blasted Hiroshima and Nagasaki convinced the Emperor and the leadership in Japan to accept Allied conditions for surrender. As such, the bombs may have saved hundreds of thousands of American lives, and they may have spared the Japanese people the larger agony of a war of annihilation. No one will ever know for sure. What is known is that the atomic bomb ushered in a new age, one with the frightening potential of seeing a general war fought with atomic weapons. And it became the main weapon in the U.S. and Soviet arsenals of the Cold War, reminding each country of the other's ability to destroy it (see Chapter 22).

The United States developed the atomic bomb technology first. Who knows what would have happened if Stalin or Hitler had developed the bomb first? One thing is certain, the atomic bomb used in World War II ushered in the atomic age, and the world has not been the same since.

Chapter **25**

Ten "What Ifs?" of World War II

E xploring "what ifs" when discussing World War II is a pleasant game that most historians play. Even the casual reader of history is hard pressed not to occasionally wonder "what if."

Victory in war is never a sure thing. And, like every other human endeavor, it's affected by chance, luck (both good and bad), and circumstance. The world today would probably be quite different place if one or any of the "what ifs" I include in this chapter had actually happened.

What If Hitler Conquered Great Britain Instead of Attacking the Soviet Union?

This scenario is one of the more basic questions of World War II. If Great Britain had been conquered or starved into submission, or isolated and sufficiently weakened as a military power, what would've happened? Here are some guesses:

» The British fleet, those ships captured or recovered in the aftermath of the collapse of Britain, would have come under the control of the German navy.

>> With the captured ships from the British Fleet, Germany would have dominated the Atlantic and the northern route to the Soviet seaport of Murmansk, thus cutting off U.S. supplies or lend-lease aid to the Soviet Union and isolating the United States from Europe.

>> Faced with such a situation, Stalin may have accommodated Hitler to stave off the inevitable war that Hitler desired. As a result, establishing an alliance with Stalin would've been hard for the U.S. — especially if the Soviet dictator didn't see an immediate threat to the Soviet Union.

>> When Germany would turn on the Soviets, without Britain to keep Hitler occupied, the Soviet Union would've been in trouble. The full power of the *Luftwaffe* (the German Air Force), not wasted in the Battle of Britain, would've been available to attack Soviet target, as would the powerful British ships in the Nazi's hands.

>> Without Britain to resist them in Europe, the Nazis quite possibly would've dominated Europe, perhaps permanently. The next target would have been the United States.

What If U.S. Carriers Had Been at Pearl Harbor?

If United States aircraft carriers had been at Pearl Harbor on December 7, 1941, the war in the Pacific would've been over rather quickly.

>> Without the carriers, the U.S. wouldn't have been able to launch any counter-attacks against the Japanese until at least 1943, when a sufficient number of new carriers could be built.

>> While the United States built a new fleet of aircraft carriers to fight Japan, the Japanese would have consolidated their territorial gains, stockpiled strategic raw materials, fortified their island strongholds, and built a large air force.

>> The war in the Pacific would've gone on for several more years, with the Americans battling a powerfully armed and fully prepared enemy (which, come to think about it, is exactly what the Japanese had in mind).

What If Hitler Pursued Proper Strategic Programs?

Hitler made all the decisions about what kinds and how many tanks and aircraft to produce. Unfortunately for the Nazi cause, he was a poor judge of what the Germans needed, both strategically and operationally, to fight the war effectively. For example, he ignored the jet fighter until it was too late, and he didn't take advantage of the capabilities of the V-1 and V-2 rockets. So, what if Hitler had been a little smarter or had allowed people who knew about this stuff to make the decisions?

>> If Hitler allowed the production of the jet fighter as soon as he was made aware of it (in the early 1940s), he would have had his best pilots flying the most advanced airplanes in the world over German skies from the very beginning. Piloted by the skilled men the *Luftwaffe*, these planes could have stopped the United States' strategic bombing offensive. Without the bombing offensive, there probably wouldn't have been an Allied invasion of Normandy.

>> If Hitler had allowed the V-1 and V-2 rocket program to expand, he could've perfected a ballistic missile with a one ton warhead and an accurate delivery system. Such a weapon could very possibly have eliminated the threat of a cross-channel invasion by hitting Allied assembly areas, airports, and harbors. In large numbers, the missiles also could've devastated the large Soviet formations spread over the plains of Russia. In time, the missiles could have been improved to strike the mainland of the United States.

What If There Had Been No Attack on Pearl Harbor Until 1942?

If the Japanese had been willing to make some concessions to the United States for a year to ease the growing crisis, what would have happened? By making concessions, the flow of oil, steel, and scrap metal would've continued to Japan from American ports. By waiting, they also could have lured the United States into a false sense of security that would have caused the Americans to delay a major buildup of forces.

With a stockpile of strategic material at home and a complacent United States, the Japanese could've struck the blow at Pearl Harbor a year later and perhaps have accomplished their objectives in Asia without much of a fight. The United States, not wanting a two-front war, may have ignored Japan while being occupied with the crisis in Europe.

REMEMBER

Hitler is one who declared war on the United States after the Japanese bombed Pearl harbor. With the United States reluctant to get into the war in Europe, a year's delay may have given Hitler the time he needed to conquer Europe. Thus the United States would've been in a very difficult situation, faced with a war in the Pacific and no reliable allies.

What If Hitler Liberated the Russians?

Hitler liberating the Russians is hard to fathom given his single-minded mania of destroying the Jews and Slavs to open *Lebensraum* (see Chapter 3) for Germans moving east. But if Hitler had been persuaded to hold back his eradication programs for just a few years, the Germans would've reaped enormous short-term strategic benefits. The fact is that the citizens of the Soviet Union, especially in Ukraine and the Baltic States, welcomed the Germans as liberators from Stalin's tyranny.

If the Germans had accommodated the people in the western Soviet Union, they would've had a solid base of support, supplies, and recruits. This base could've been significant enough to topple Stalin and end the war in 1942. Instead, the Germans treated these people with barbaric brutality, including wholesale destruction of farms, livestock, and wells, which gave the Soviet Army and the Soviet people a reason to seek revenge.

What If France Held Out in 1940?

France in 1940 was not as weak as history often portrays. The country was actually a formidable military power, on paper quite stronger and more capable than the German Army. France collapsed from a lack of will to fight as well as surprise when the Germans drove through the Ardennes Forest to the coast. If French forces had resisted as General Charles de Gaulle wanted, even by putting up a minimal fight, the Germans would've been hard pressed to conclude the war on their terms.

Even fighting for a stalemate would've worked to France's advantage. The Germans simply didn't have the tanks and equipment they needed to eliminate a determined enemy. The longer the war with France went on, the weaker Germany would become. Hitler's promise of victory against the ancient enemy would've gone sour and perhaps ended his ambitions altogether.

What If the Bulge Had Worked?

The attack on the Allied armies in December 1944 was Hitler's attempt to replay the German victory of its attack on France in June 1940. Even though everything was different by 1944, Hitler visualized German tank columns across the Meuse River, battling into the seaport of Antwerp. Despite all the factors that made a German victory here in 1944 nearly impossible, what would've happened if the Germans had succeeded in the Battle of the Bulge?

Most likely, a German success would've delayed the Allied entry into Germany by six to eight months:

» A success would've disrupted the Allied supply lines and given the Germans a significant advantage in using captured supplies and sustaining the advance.

» The Allies would've shifted their attack from south to northeast, leading to a fight on a narrow front and eliminating the advantage the Allies enjoyed in manpower and equipment.

» The Allies would still have enjoyed full dominance with air power, and eventually the Bulge would've been closed, but only after tremendous cost and delay.

» The Siegfried Line, another German defensive position, still awaited the Allies, while the Soviets were still advancing from the East. The British and Americans may have met the Soviets at the Rhine River instead of the Elbe River.

What If Hitler Had Been Assassinated?

If the assassination plot against Hitler in 1944 had worked, along with the coup against the Nazi government, the war would have ended. The Allies declared unconditional surrender for the Nazis, but most likely, the Allies would've negotiated with a moderate anti-Nazi government. Germany would've been spared many agonies, although the seeds of another war between the Soviet Union and Germany would've been sown. (Stalin wouldn't have been able to gain control over the large sections of Eastern Europe that he did, which may have led to further tensions that may have culminated in a war.)

Nevertheless, a peaceful united Germany and a number of independent states in Eastern Europe would've served as a significant counterweight to Soviet power in the years after 1945. Having a counterweight to Soviet power, in turn, would've eliminated NATO, preserved Great Britain's status as the leader of Europe, and would have lessened America's role in postwar Europe.

What If Hitler Let His Generals Plan Strategy?

Hitler took over personal control of the war after 1942, even though he had little military training or skills (he was a corporal in WW I) and had never attended any type of military schooling, let alone a senior staff college like his generals had. In making decisions, Hitler was rash and hasty; he made unrealistic assumptions and gave ridiculous "no retreat" orders or full-scale attack orders with little understanding of the realities that his commanders faced. He was consumed with the destruction of Jews and Bolsheviks to the point that little else mattered. Hitler's ignorance of strategy and operations and his refusal to listen or trust his military advisors led him to make terrible mistakes that certainly helped the Allies.

Yet if Hitler would've stepped back and let the generals run the war, the war would've been less disastrous and less costly. Would the Germans have won if the generals had run the war? Probably not. But, they would've made it far more difficult for the Allies to win.

What If the Japanese Navy Had Survived?

What would've happened if the Imperial Japanese Navy had not been defeated at the Battle of Midway (see Chapter 15)? What if the Japanese aircraft carrier fleet continued to be a major threat until 1943 or 1944?

>> The Japanese would've been able to threaten Midway and Pearl Harbor, limiting the free flow of supplies and reinforcements to Australia. This in turn would've made MacArthur's job more difficult (see Chapter 15).

>> Japanese carrier and land-based aircraft could've challenged American aircraft for possession of the skies over the Bismarck Sea, at Guadalcanal, or at Leyte (see Chapter 15).

>> American Admiral Nimitz at some point would've had to risk a major battle with the American fleet to beat the Japanese Navy once and for all before beginning his own campaign to capture Tarawa, Saipan, Guam, and Peleliu (see Chapter 19).

>> The war in the Pacific certainly would've gone on longer. In fact, the entire Allied plan for the war in the Pacific would've changed dramatically, leaving the United States to make far more cautious advances.

Index

Numbers & Symbols

A

USS *Panay,* sinking by
Japanese, 125
USS *Reuben James,* sinking by
Germany, 130
USSR (Union of Soviet Socialist
Republics). *See* Soviet Union
Utah beach, 270

V

V-2 rocket, 385
VE Day, 333–334
Versailles, Treaty of. *See* Treaty
of Versailles
vertical envelopment, 106
Vichy France, government
removed by Hitler, 198
Vichy French, defeat in Iraq by
British, 190
violence, Fascist ideas about, 34
Volkssturm, Bormann's
command of, 44

W

Waffen SS, 46
Wainwright, Jonathan, 144
Wake Island, Japanese attack on,
142–143
war
blitzkrieg, 82
Fascist ideas about, 34
Hitler's desire for with France
and Britain, 57
Hitler's determination to
wage, 52
Mussolini's attitude toward, 55
outlawing, *Kellog-Briand
Treaty,* 26
Warsaw, Polish Home Army
uprising, 261–262
Wavell, Archibald, 190

weapons
88 mm antiaircraft gun, 387
atomic bomb, 360, 388
B-17 Bomber, 217–218, 387
B-24 Liberator, 220
B-29 bomber, 350
Essex class aircraft
carriers, 388
M-1 Garand rifle, 384–385
Me-262 jet fighter, 280,
386–387
MG-42 machine gun, 383
Molotov Cocktail, 87
P-51 Mustang fighter, 386
Soviet, quality of, 166
Soviet T-34 tank, 117, 215
technological
advancements, 368
Tiger tank, 384
V-2 rocket, 385
Yorktown class aircraft
carriers, 388
*Wehrmacht, Oberkommando der
Wehrmacht,* 60
West Wall fortifications, 55
Western Task Force (North
Africa), 196
Weygand, Maxime, efforts
during German invasion of
France, 96
Wilson, Woodrow, fourteen
points, 25–26
Wingate, Orde, 307
Winter Line
Allied plan to circumvent, 254
fighting at Cassino, 255
wolf-pack tactics (U-boats),
19, 130
women, contribution to U.S. war
effort, 162

World War I
aftermath, 22
end, date of, 22
global economy after, 12–13
peace agreement ending, 12
political allegiances in, 22
Treaty of Versailles, 23
trench warfare, 22

Y

Yalta conference, 324
aftermath of, 326
discussions about United
Nations, 324–325
fate of Germany, 325–326
fate of Poland, 325
Roosevelt's attempt to woo
Stalin, 324
Soviet assistance with war
against Japan, 326
Yamamoto, Isoroku, 135, 380
tactics at Midway, 232–236
Yamashita, Tomoyuki, 342
brief biography, 344
Yorktown class aircraft
carriers, 388
Yugoslavia
creation of, 12, 30
death toll, 368
German defeat of, 105
resistance to German pressure
to join Axis, 104
Soviet troops enter, 284

Z

Zhukov, Georgi, 119, 380–381
drives Germans from
Moscow, 120

About the Author

Keith D. Dickson, Ph.D, is a Professor of Military Studies at the Joint Forces Staff College, National Defense University and teaches classes on U.S. military operations in World War II. He has also given public lectures and presented papers at academic conferences on various aspects of World War II. A graduate of the Virginia Military Institute, he has a Master's degree from the University of Richmond and a Ph.D. from the University of Virginia. His career has included government service in both U.S. Army Special Operations and intelligence, as well as teaching duties as an Assistant Professor of History at the Virginia Military Institute. There, he was the first officer since the Civil War to serve simultaneously as both a professor and as Commandant of Cadets. He is the author of a number of books, including *Civil War For Dummies, World War II Almanac, Sustaining Southern Identity* (winner of the Slatten Award for best Virginia biography in 2011), and *No Surrender: Asymmetric Warfare in the Reconstruction South.*

Dedication

This book is dedicated to two men who have had a great effect on my life:

The first is my uncle, Robert W. Dickson, who served as a forward torpedo man on the submarine USS *Blackfin* in the Pacific.

The second is my Father-in-Law, J. David Crute, who served as a merchant mariner transporting supplies to Europe.

Both of these men displayed a special brand of personal courage and fortitude that few can ever appreciate, and their efforts contributed significantly to the Allied victory. They returned from the war, raised families, and shaped the lives of many people.

I was fortunate to have grown up and matured among World War II veterans. They were my heroes and they taught me many things. I would like to recognize some of them: Mr. Donald Crews, a military policeman who helped liberate the concentration camps in Germany; Mr. R. Sams Smith, a tank crewman who fought against the best the German army had in 1944; Colonel Tyson Wilson, who fought with the First Marine Division on Guadalcanal; and a number of men from my hometown, Farmville, Virginia — the citizen-soldiers: farmers, bankers, lawyers, merchants, schoolboys — who landed on Omaha Beach at Normandy and faced even greater challenges with unshakeable courage after moving inland. Our debt to all of these men can never be repaid.

Author's Acknowledgments

The ones who must stand and wait also serve: my wife, Karen, and my children, Kathryn and Colleen. Their sometimes not-so-disguised impatience kept this project on track.

About the Technical Editor

G. Kurt Piehler is author of *Remembering War the American Way* (1995) and is co-editor of *Major Problems in American Military History* (1998). As founding director (1994-1998) of the Rutgers Oral History Archives of World War II, he has conducted over 200 interviews with veterans of this conflict. He is director of the Center for the Study of War and Society at the University of Tennessee and co-producer of "Celebrate Freedom!: Pigeon Forge Salutes America's Veterans."

Publisher's Acknowledgments

Contributing Writer: Tracy Barr

Acquisitions Editors: Roxane Cerda, Susan Decker, Lindsay Lefevere

Project Editors: Sherri Fugit, Blair Pottenger

Copy Editors: Mary Fales, Greg Pearson

Technical Editor: G. Kurt Piehler, The University of Tennessee Knoxville

Editorial Assistant: Jennifer Young, Elizabeth Stilwell

Production Editor: Siddique Shaik

Cover Image: © Matt_Gibson / Getty Images